Building a Dream

Fourth Edition

A Comprehensive Guide to Starting a Business of Your Own

Walter S. Good

Professor, Department of Marketing
University of Manitoba

McGraw-Hill
Ryerson

Toronto Montréal New York Burr Ridge Bangkok Bogotá Caracas Lisbon London Madrid
Mexico City Milan New Delhi Seoul Singapore Sydney Taipei

McGraw-Hill Ryerson Limited

A Subsidiary of The McGraw·Hill Companies

Building A Dream
A Comprehensive Guide to Starting a Business of Your Own
Fourth Edition

ISBN: 0-07-560769-7

2 3 4 5 6 7 8 9 0 TRI 0 9 8 7 6 5 4 3 2 1 0

Printed and bound in Canada

EDITORIAL DIRECTOR AND PUBLISHER: Evelyn Veitch
SPONSORING EDITOR: Susan Calvert
DEVELOPMENTAL EDITOR: Denise McGuinness
SUPERVISING EDITOR: Julie van Veen
COPY EDITOR: Rachel Mansfield
SENIOR MARKETING MANAGER: Jeff MacLean
MARKETING MANAGER: Bill Todd
PRODUCTION CO-ORDINATOR: Brad Madill
COVER DESIGN: Greg Devitt
COVER ILLUSTRATION: Curtis Parker/SIS©
INSIDE DESIGN AND PAGE COMPOSITION: Lynda Powell
PRINTER: Trigraphic Printing Ottawa Limited

Canadian Cataloguing in Publication Data

Good, Walter S.
    Building a dream: a comprehensive guide to starting a business of your own

4th ed.
ISBN 0-07-560769-7

1. New business enterprises. 2. Entrepreneurship. I. Title.

HD62.5.G66 1999   658.1'1   C99-932546-9

Contents

Preface

This self-help guide and workbook is intended to provide a vehicle to lead prospective small-business people and potential entrepreneurs in a logical and sequential way through the conceptual stages involved in setting up a business of their own.

Many people fantasize about being self-employed and having a business of their own at some stage in their lives. For most, this dream never becomes a reality. They don't really know the risks involved and feel very uncomfortable with the uncertainty associated with taking the initial step. In addition, they don't entirely understand the tasks required to get a new business venture off the ground successfully.

For the past decade or two the number of people who have started their own business has increased dramatically across North America. People's level of interest in and awareness of the entrepreneurial option has virtually exploded. This has been fostered and reinforced by governments at all levels, who have come to recognize the positive impact small-business start-ups have on job creation and regional economic development. Business magazines, the popular press and radio and television have also fuelled this interest with numerous items on the emotional and financial rewards of having a business of your own. They have glamourized the role of entrepreneurs in our society, and established many of them, such as Ted Rogers of Cantel Inc. and Rogers Cablesystems Inc., Terry Matthews of Newbridge Networks Corp., Izzy Asper of CanWest Global Communications Corp., Peter Nygard of Nygard International Ltd., and Frank Stronach of Magna International Inc. as attractive role models. This has been accentuated over the past year or so with the phenomenal success of internet-based companies such as Yahoo and eBay that has made young entrepreneurs like Jerry Yang, Dave Filo and Pierre Omidyar as well as a number of their employees paper billionaires virtually overnight.

Building a Dream has been written for individuals who wish to start a business of their own or want to assess their own potential for such an option. This includes all men and women who dream of some type of self-employment, on either a full-time or a part-time basis. This book contains descriptive information, practical outlines, checklists, screening questionnaires, and various other tools that will enable you to evaluate your own potential for this type of career and guide you through the early stages of launching a successful business of your own.

This book covers a range of topics that will increase your understanding of what it takes to succeed in an entrepreneurial career. From an overview of entrepreneurship and the entrepreneurial process, the book spreads outward to consider the skills, personality and character traits possessed by most successful entrepreneurs, how to find and evaluate a possible idea for a business, buy an existing firm, acquire a franchise, carry on your business, and protect your product or service concept or idea. It concludes with a comprehensive outline for conducting a feasibility study to evaluate the potential of your concept and a framework for a detailed and professional business plan.

Building a Dream is divided into "Stages," each of which provides a descriptive overview of a topic, some conceptual material indicating the principal areas to be considered or evaluated, and a series of outlines, worksheets, and other forms that can be completed in conducting a comprehensive assessment of that stage in the new venture development process. This provides a practical opportunity for you to realistically assess the potential of your idea and develop a detailed program or plan for your own small business.

STAGE ONE: What Is Entrepreneurship?

This Stage introduces you to the concept of entrepreneurship and provides an overview of the other elements that are required to launch a successful new business venture. In addition to the entrepreneur, these include a viable business idea or opportunity, an organization, resources, a strategy, and a business plan. It also discusses some of the myths and stereotypes that have evolved over time about entrepreneurs and entrepreneurship.

STAGE TWO: Assessing Your Potential for an Entrepreneurial Career

This Stage provides you with an opportunity to assess your personal attitudes and attributes and to see how they compare with those of "practising" entrepreneurs. It will also enable you to evaluate your managerial and administrative skills and experience and determine your financial capacity for starting a business.

STAGE THREE: Exploring New Business Ideas and Opportunities

This stage describes a number of sources from which you might obtain ideas for your prospective new venture and identifies a number of areas of opportunity for the new century on the basis of dynamic changes now taking place within Canadian society. It also outlines a six-step opportunity selection process, describes the characteristics of an "ideal" or "model" business, and presents a framework for assessing the attributes of your product or service idea in comparison to this ideal. A number of entry strategies are outlined as well that can help you decide on the best way of proceeding.

STAGE FOUR: Starting a New Business or Buying an Existing One

The obvious route to self-employment is to start a business of your own based on a new or distinctive idea. Another route to explore is the possibility of buying an existing firm. This Stage deals with such areas as finding a business to buy and the factors to consider in making the acquisition. It also discusses a number of ways to determine an appropriate price to pay for a business and the pros and cons of buying versus starting one. A comprehensive checklist is provided for considering a number of potential business acquisitions.

STAGE FIVE: Considering a Franchise

For the last few years franchising has been one of the fastest-growing sectors of North American business. More and more people are considering the franchise alternative as a means of getting into business for themselves. This Stage explores the concept of franchising in some detail. It defines franchising so that you know exactly what the concept means. The broad range of types of franchises available is presented, along with an overview of the legal requirements associated with franchising and the terms and conditions contained in a typical franchise agreement. This Stage also discusses how to find and apply for a franchise, and presents an extensive checklist for evaluating potential franchise opportunities.

STAGES SIX AND SEVEN: Conducting a Feasibility Study — Parts 1 and 2

Stages Six and Seven provide a step-by-step process for transforming your chosen new venture concept from the idea stage to the marketplace. This is accomplished by means of a feasibility study. A typical feasibility study considers the following areas:

- The concept of your proposed venture
- The technical feasibility of your idea
- An assessment of your market potential and preparation of your marketing plan
- Managing the supply situation
- Conducting a cost and profitability assessment
- Indicating your plans for future action

Comprehensive outlines are provided to enable you to assess each of these areas in a preliminary way and put your thoughts and ideas down on paper. Much of this material can be incorporated into your subsequent business plan.

STAGE EIGHT: Organizing Your Business

One of the principal issues to be resolved when starting a new business is the legal form of organization the business should adopt. The most prevalent forms a business might assume include individual or sole proprietorship, general or limited partnership, and incorporation. This Stage reviews each of these forms and discusses the advantages and disadvantages of each from the standpoint of the prospective entrepreneur. It discusses how to select and register a name for your business and presents an overview of such issues as the types of licences and permits your business might require, your responsibilities for collecting and remitting a variety of employee contributions and taxes, and the impact of provincial employment standards on your business.

STAGE NINE: Protecting Your Idea

Many entrepreneurs are also innovators and inventors, and are faced with the problem of how to protect the idea, invention, concept, system, name, or design that they feel will be the key to their business success. This Stage discusses the various forms of intellectual property such as patents, copyrights, and trademarks, and what is required to protect your interest in their development.

STAGE TEN: Arranging Financing

The principal question relating to any new venture is where the money is going to come from to get the new business off the ground. This Stage examines the major sources of funds for new business start-ups—personal funds, "love money," bank loans, government agencies and programs, and venture capital. It also provides a framework for you to determine just how much money you think you will need to launch your business and where you think that financing might possibly come from.

STAGE ELEVEN: Preparing Your Business Plan

This Stage, which serves as a capstone for the book, provides a framework for the development of a comprehensive business plan for your proposed new business venture, whether it is a retail or service business or a manufacturing company. It lays out the necessary steps in the business planning process such as:

- Developing a vision statement
- Formulating a mission statement
- Defining the fundamental values by which you will run your business
- Setting clear and specific objectives
- Developing a realistic business plan

It also explains what a business plan is, how long it should be, and why it is important that you develop such a plan for your proposed venture and actually write it yourself. It lays out the contents of a typical business plan and provides an outline to follow for developing a plan for a retail or service type business and a manufacturing company. This Stage also contains an example of a completed plan for a concept known as the "Darting Lamp." These will serve as comprehensive and useful guides for you to follow in developing your business plan.

Further Information contains:

- a list of further useful reading material you can obtain for little or no cost from banks, accounting firms, government departments and other sources,
- a number of useful contacts that can provide you with additional information on many of the topics discussed in the book,
- a comprehensive selection of Web sites that have a wealth of additional information you can use to help your business get off the ground successfully, and
- a Glossary of financial terms.

The College Edition of *Building a Dream* also includes a diskette, "Spreadsheet-Based Financial Schedules" and instructions for its use (See *Step-by-Step Guide* in the table of contents to this book). This diskette is a EXCEL-based tool to help you analyze the financial aspects of your new business idea. It will also facilitate preparation of the financial statements contained in Stage Seven to assess the feasibility of your idea, or those in Stage Eleven that you will require for your comprehensive business plan.

Following the framework outlined in *Building a Dream* will give you hands-on, practical experience with the entire new venture development process and enable you to come up with a comprehensive plan for a proposed venture of your own selection. This plan will not only give you a better understanding of the potential opportunity and success requirements of your new venture idea but also put you in a much stronger position to attract the necessary external resources and support to get your proposed business off the ground. Good luck in successfully building your dream.

Acknowledgements

Developing a workbook of this type can only be accomplished with the co-operation and support of a great many people. Much of the material would not have been developed without the dedicated effort of Steve Tax of the University of Victoria, who was largely responsible for many of the ideas that were incorporated into the first edition and have been carried forward to the current one. I am also indebted to David Milstein of David Milstein & Associates of Brisbane, Australia for contributing the material on the "Big Picture" of strategic planning and to Vance Gough of the University of Calgary for the exercise on creating thinking. My appreciation also goes to Carole Babiak who's organizational and word processing skills enabled me to keep the material moving during the revision process.

Thoughtful suggestions on improvements to the Third Edition were received from Robert Blunden of Dalhousie University, Jim Alsop of Seneca College, Neil Wolff of Ryerson Technological University, Walter Isenor of Acadia University and Lydia Dragunas of Champlain Regional College. Helpful comments on some of the early changes were received from Danielle Burke of St. Lawrence College, Vance Gough of the University of Calgary, Jim Mason of the University of Regina and Neil Beattie of Sheridan College. Their remarks were very helpful in organizing and polishing the material and refining the concept for the book. My appreciation must also go to Susan Calvert and Denise McGuinness, my editors at McGraw-Hill Ryerson, for expediting the review and production of the material and providing numerous useful comments and suggestions throughout the revision process.

I would also like to thank Moe Levy of the Asper Foundation and Shannon Coughlan of the Canada/Manitoba Business Services Centre for their comments on several components of the book and their encouragement during the early stages of the development of the concept behind the workbook. Special thanks goes to Chris Spafford for his assistance in putting together the financial templates that accompany the supplement to the college edition of the book. The belief of these individuals in entrepreneurship as a vehicle for successful economic development in Canada and faith in the premise of the self-help concept may finally pay off.

Finally, I would like to thank the college and university students and others who have used the earlier editions of the book over the years and have gone on to start new business ventures of their own. Their insatiable desire to assess their personal capacity for a career in this area and their drive to explore the mysteries of franchising, venture capital, and similar topics associated with the formation of a successful new business have enabled many of them to build their dream. I hope all of us have been able to play a small part in the process.

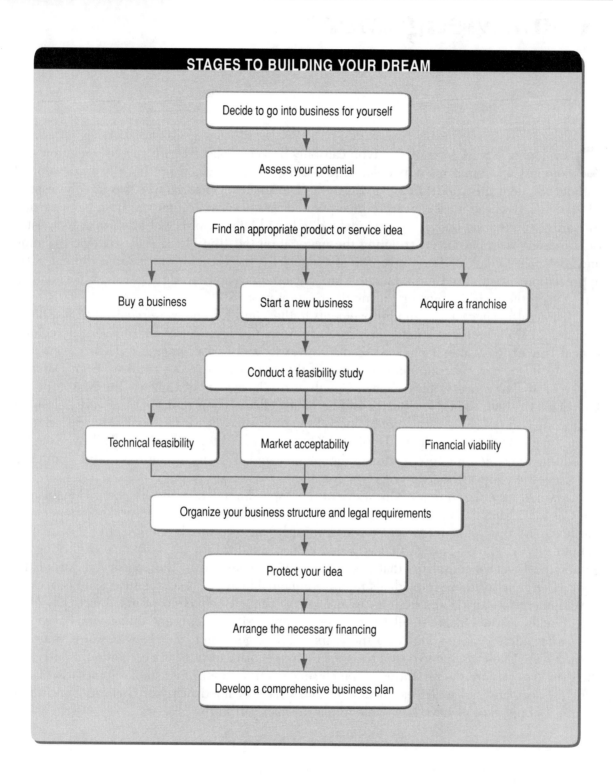

STAGES TO BUILDING YOUR DREAM

Decide to go into business for yourself

Assess your potential

Find an appropriate product or service idea

| Buy a business | Start a new business | Acquire a franchise |

Conduct a feasibility study

| Technical feasibility | Market acceptability | Financial viability |

Organize your business structure and legal requirements

Protect your idea

Arrange the necessary financing

Develop a comprehensive business plan

What Is Entrepreneurship?

Bruce Poon Tip was 22 years old and thought he could conquer the world when he started Great Adventure People (G.A.P.) in the early 1990s. Since then the company, which arranges and operates eco-tours for clients in 21 different countries, has seen its revenues grow to over $10.3 million and G.A.P. was listed as one of the 100 fastest-growing businesses in Canada during 1998 by PROFIT magazine.

Bruce Poon Tip and other Canadians like him are starting businesses of their own more frequently than ever before. Of the more than 2.1 million businesses in Canada, over 99% are small- and medium-sized. Every year more than 150,000 other Canadians join this number by initiating new start-ups. This has led to a major entrepreneurial revolution and caused the small business sector of Canadian society to become more widely acknowledged by secondary and post-secondary educational institutions, the chartered banks and other financial institutions and all levels of government.

The overall economic impact of this revolution on the country is difficult to determine precisely but it is substantial. It is being fuelled by such factors as structural changes, like organizational downsizing or "rightsizing," the loss of middle-management positions in many larger companies and government departments, younger people wanting more independence, and the increasing number of immigrants who would have difficulty with conventional employment because of their limited skills and/or language issues. It is clear, however, that the proportion of total employment in the country accounted for by these smaller firms has increased dramatically. They have created the lion's share of new jobs while employment levels in large businesses have remained constant or decreased.

This book has been developed for people who may be aspiring entrepreneurs and are giving some thought to the possibility of joining the many others who have started some kind of business of their own. Most of us have given some thought to owning and managing our own business at some point in our lives. And provided you know what it takes to be successful, it can be a very rewarding way of life. These rewards may be financial in terms of providing you with a return for the time and money you and others may invest in the business and the risks you take in operating your own firm. Having an independent business also gives you the freedom to act independently, make your own decisions and be your own boss. This can be a very important motivating factor for many people. It can also be a very satisfying way of life full of the "fun" and personal satisfaction derived from doing something that you genuinely love to do.

Table 1.1 illustrates the principal reasons that Canadians have decided to go into business for themselves. The primary considerations were to achieve a strong sense of personal accomplishment and to be their own boss.

TABLE 1.1   WHY PEOPLE START BUSINESSES

To achieve a sense of accomplishment	82%
To be their own boss	73%
To have an element of variety and adventure	66%
To make better use of their training and skills	63%
To be able to adapt their own approach to their work	62%
To be challenged by new opportunities	61%

Source: *Royal Bank Reporter*, Fall, 1988

Starting a new business, however, can be very risky at the best of times. It typically demands long hours, hard work, a high level of emotional involvement and commitment, as well as significant financial risk and the possibility of failure. Your chances of succeeding, however, will be better if you spend some time carefully evaluating your personal situation and circumstances and trying to anticipate and work out as many potential problems as you can, before you invest any money.

Stage One will introduce you to the concept of entrepreneurship and give you some idea of what is required to be successful. It will also discuss some of the folklore and stereotypes that exist around entrepreneurship and, hopefully, dispel some of the myths that have come to surround entrepreneurs.

What is Entrepreneurship?

Entrepreneurship is difficult to define precisely. Entrepreneurs tend to be identified, not by formal rank or title, but in retrospect—after the successful implementation of an innovation or an idea. The example of Bruce Poon Tip in Entrepreneurs in Action #1 may help to illustrate the definition problem for you.

It is difficult to say the precise moment at which Bruce became an entrepreneur. Early on he felt that he couldn't work for other people. At the age of 12 he lasted less than a month at his job with a real estate company before he was fired. At 16 he was fired by McDonald's on his first day of work because he wouldn't wear a hairnet. He realized he had very strong interests related to travel and the music industry and would likely end up working in one of those two fields. While he studied travel and tourism at college, he knew he wanted freedom and independence in his life and would not end up working as a travel agent. Soon afterward he started G.A.P. to share travel adventures with clients who wanted to experience exotic cultures around the world. With only a vision and little capital, he went ahead and built the business to its present level of success.

For some people like Poon Tip, entrepreneurship is a conscious and deliberate career choice. For others, there may be some kind of significant *triggering* event. Perhaps, the individual had no better career prospects than starting a business of their own. Sometimes the individual has received an inheritance or otherwise come into some money, moved to a new geographic location, been passed over for a promotion, taken an early retirement, or been laid off or fired from their regular job. Any of these factors can give birth to a new business.

There are many formal definitions of entrepreneurship. Perhaps one of the most straight forward and simplest is that an entrepreneur is "someone who perceives an opportunity and creates an organization to pursue it".[1]

Many people have said that entrepreneurship is really a "state of mind." Though you may be extremely innovative and creative, prepared to work hard, and willing to rely on a great deal of luck, these qualities may still be insufficient to guarantee business success. The missing element may be a necessary entrepreneurial mind-set: a single-mindedness and dedication to the achievement of a set of personal goals and objectives; confidence in your intuitive and rational capabilities; a capacity to think and plan in both tactical and strategic terms; and an attitude which reflects a penchant for action, frequently in situations in which information is inadequate. Poon Tip, for example, doesn't feel that his work is finished because G.A.P. has been successful up to this point in time and achieved an impressive level of sales growth. He wants to continue this success and plans to grow G.A.P. to $50 million in sales by 2004. "I don't personally consider that I'm even half way up the mountain," he says. "I've just reached base camp and I'm starting to climb."[2]

[1] William D. Bygrave, "The Entrepreneurial Process," in William D. Bygrave, Ed. *The Portable MBA in Entrepreneurship,* Second Edition, John Wiley & Sons, Inc., 1997, pp. 2.

[2] Aaron Lam, "Bruce Poon Tip," *Business $ense,* March, 1999, pp. 23-25.

1   ENTREPRENEURS IN ACTION

No More Hanging Out in Tibet

LAURA ARSIE

Bruce Poon Tip first knew he wanted to be an entrepreneur 15 years ago — at the tender age of 16. "I was fired by McDonald's on my first day of work because I wouldn't wear a hairnet," he confesses. "So I knew early on I wasn't going to do well working for someone else." Instead, the Trinidad-born, Calgary-raised Poon Tip moved to Toronto in 1991 to try his hand in the travel business. "I have two passions, music and travel," he says with customary rapid-fire delivery. "I knew I would build my company on one or the other—and travel won out." Today, Poon Tip's adventure travel agency, G.A.P. Adventures Inc., operates in more than 21 countries and 1998 sales topped $10.3 million, a five-year gain of 3,702%.

Poon Tip's own views on travel were shaken up by two trips he took to Thailand a decade ago. "I took a five-star coach tour through the country, and I came away with a certain image of Thailand," he says. "then I went back with a backpack and a $10-a-day budget, and I really saw the country. I realized I'd gone to another country before, but I hadn't seen it. I had been trapped in a Western environment." Convinced that others would share his vision, he designed tours to far-flung locales such as Borneo and Tibet. The idea: visitors would get a close-up of the country's authentic culture and its people, while interfering as little as possible with its local environment. That meant small-group tours, staying in local guesthouses, and using local transportation.

"If you want the comforts of home, then stay home," says Poon Tip. Increasing numbers of travellers are choosing otherwise. Today, G.A.P.'s 700 travel packages on four continents have set a standard for sustainable eco-tourism. "Our future growth is in conservation," says

Poon Tip. It's a business as well as a personal philosophy, reflected in Poon Tip's work with Conservation International in Washington and the World Bank, where he consults on issues of sustainable development and tourism. "We're involved with projects to teach communities to sustain themselves through tourism," says Poon Tip, "giving them alternatives to logging or being in the drug trade." To share that vision, he also helped a Toronto community college develop a post-diploma program in eco-tourism and adventure travel. "Part of my job, I believe, is to educate," he says. "And we want to get travel agents while they're young."

Now Poon Tip has set a new goal: growing G.A.P. to $50 million by 2004. He'll do that by conquering new territory — such as TV. Poon Tip is currently working with a producer to develop an adventure travel show that focusses on people, not just the destination. "I wanted to do a show that's different from anything on TV now," he says.

Ironically, business has forced Poon Tip to curtail his own travels of late. G.A.P. is constructing new "swanky swish" digs in Toronto and Poon Tip is also in demand as a dinner speaker. "In the last year we've been embraced by the business community," he says, somewhat amused. But that embrace works both ways. As the firm matures, Poon Tip's to-do list includes building an infrastructure that will serve G.A.P. as it makes the leap to corporate enterprise. While he still travels, he says wistfully, "There's no more hanging out in Tibet."

Source: Hilary Davidson, "5 Entrepreneurs You Need to Know," *PROFIT: The Magazine for Canadian Entrepreneurs*, June, 1999, pp. 91-92. Reprinted with permission.

Entrepreneurship is not the same as management. The principal job of professional managers is to make a business perform well. They take a *given* set of resources — such as money, employees, machines and materials — and orchestrate and organize them into an efficient and effective production operation. Managers tend to delegate much of their authority and rely on the use of formal control systems and are usually measured on the basis of organizationally determined objectives. In contrast, entrepreneurs typically rely more on an informal, hands-on management style and are driven by their personal goals. Their principal job is to bring about purposeful change within an organizational context. They break new ground and, in many cases, each step is guided by some larger plan.

As agents of change entrepreneurs play, or can play, a number of roles in the economy or perform a variety of different functions. They can, for example:

1. Create new product and/or service businesses

2. Bring creative and innovative methods to developing or producing new products or services

3. Provide employment opportunities and create new jobs as a result of growing their business consistently and rapidly

4. Help contribute to regional and national economic growth

5. Encourage greater industrial efficiency/productivity to enhance our international competitiveness

You should keep in mind, however, that other people also play a significant role in determining who will suceed or who will fail in our society. For example, entrepreneurs will succeed only when there are customers for the goods and services they provide. But, in many circumstances, it is the entrepreneurs themselves who play the principal role in determining their success or failure. Many still manage to succeed in spite of poor timing, inferior marketing, or low-quality production by combining a variety of talents, skills, and energies with imagination, good planning, and common sense. The entrepreneurial or self-employed option has many attractions, but along with these come risks and challenges and the chance of failure.

The Entrepreneurial Process

The launch of successful new business ventures requires a number of other components in addition to an entrepreneur. For example, while there may be any number of specific parts, virtually every new start-up also requires:

- a viable business idea or opportunity for which there is a receptive market
- an organizational structure for the business
- access to financial and other resources, and
- a distinctive strategy which will set the business apart from its competitors and enable it to become established if effectively implemented

As illustrated in Figure 1.1, all of these elements are outlined and captured in the business plan.

Figure 1.2 illustrates how these components interrelate, the action required at each phase of the implementation of the process, and where these issues are addressed in the book. It all begins with the entrepreneur who has conducted some assessment of his or her own resources and capabilities and made a conscious decision to launch a business. The entrepreneur must then find a concept or idea that they feel has the potential to develop into a successful enterprise. The concept behind the business must be carefully evaluated to determine whether there is likely to be a market, and if it might represent a viable opportunity. The object is to determine the magnitude of the returns that might be expected with successful implementation. An organization structure must then be established with a manager or management team and a form of ownership. Some essential financial and other resources must be obtained and, once a start-up appears likely, then a specific strategy must be developed and a business plan prepared. This plan can then be used to assist in obtaining the further resources necessary to actually launch the business and guide the implementation of the strategy.

This process proceeds in one manner or another, step-by-step in a logical fashion to a conclusion resulting in the implementation of the business. While the model gives the appearance this is a linear process and that the flow is sequential from one Stage to another, this has been done to provide a logical structure for the book and is not necessarily the case. For example, the entrepreneur may pursue two or three different elements at the same time, such as finalizing an organizational structure while also trying to compile the resources necessary to get the business initially off the ground.

FIGURE 1.1   **THE COMPONENTS OF SUCCESSFUL ENTREPRENEURIAL VENTURES**

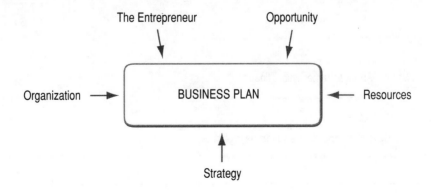

FIGURE 1.2   OUTLINE OF THE ENTREPRENEURIAL PROCESS

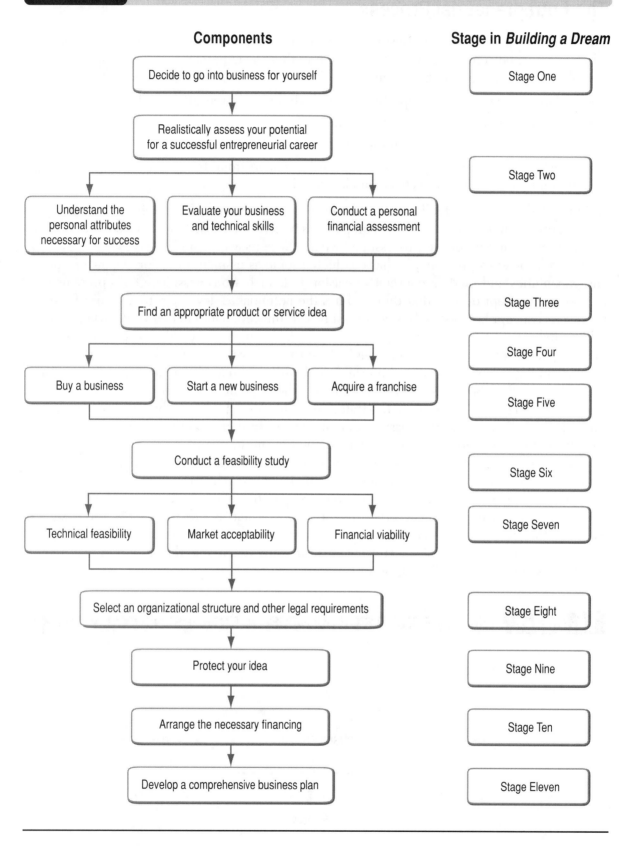

Myths and Realities Concerning Entrepreneurship

According to noted author-lecturer-consultant Peter Drucker, entrepreneurs defy stereotyping. He states, "I have seen people of the most diverse personalities and temperaments perform well in entrepreneurial challenges."[3] This suggests that some entrepreneurs may be true eccentrics while others are rigid conformists; some are short and fat while others are tall and thin; some are real worriers while others are very laid-back and relaxed; some drink and smoke very heavily while others abstain completely; some are people of great wit and charm while others have no more personality than a frozen fish.

Despite all that is known about entrepreneurs and entrepreneurship, a good deal of folklore and many stereotypes remain. Part of the problem is that while some generalities may apply to certain types of entrepreneurs and certain situations, most entrepreneurial types tend to defy generalization. The following are some examples of long-standing myths about entrepreneurs and entrepreneurship.[4]

- **Myth 1**   Entrepreneurs are born, not made.

  Reality   While entrepreneurs may be born with a certain native intelligence, a flair for innovation, a high level of energy and a core of other inborn attributes that you either have or you don't, it is apparent that merely possessing these characteristics does not necessarily make you an entrepreneur. The making of an entrepreneur occurs through a combination of work experience, know-how, personal contacts and the development of business skills acquired over time. Other attributes of equal importance can, in fact, also be acquired through understanding, hard work, and patience.

- **Myth 2**   Anyone can start a business. It's just a matter of luck and guts.

  Reality   Entrepreneurs need to recognize the difference between an idea and a real opportunity to significantly improve their chances of success. If you want to launch and grow a high-potential new venture you must understand the many things that you have to do to get

By permission of Johnny Hart and Creators Syndicate, Inc.

---

[3]   Peter Drucker, *Innovation and Entrepreneurship: Practice and Principles* (New York: Harper and Row, 1985), p. 25.

[4]   Adapted from Jeffrey A. Timmons, *New Venture Creation: Entrepreneurship for the 21st Century*, 4th Edition, (Homewood, IL: Richard D. Irwin, 1994), p. 23.

the odds in your favour. You cannot think and act like a typical bureaucrat, or even a manager; you must think and act like an entrepreneur.

- **Myth 3   Entrepreneurs are gamblers.**

  Reality   Successful entrepreneurs only take what they perceive to be very carefully calculated risks. They often try to influence the odds by getting others to share the risk with them, or by avoiding or minimizing the risk if they have the choice. They do not deliberately seek to take more risk or to take unnecessary risks, but they will not shy away from taking the risks that may be necessary to succeed.

- **Myth 4   Entrepreneurs want to run the whole show themselves**

  Reality   Owning and running the whole show effectively limits the potential for the business to grow. Single entrepreneurs can make a living, perhaps even a good one, but it is extremely difficult to grow a business by working single-handed. More successful ventures typically evolve to require a formal organization, a management team, and a corporate structure.

- **Myth 5   Entrepreneurs are their own bosses and completely independent.**

  Reality   Most entrepreneurs are far from independent and have to serve a number of constituencies and a variety of masters including partners, investors, customers, employees, suppliers, creditors, their families and pressures from social and community obligations. They do have the choice, however, to decide whether and when to respond to these pressures.

- **Myth 6   Entrepreneurs work longer and harder than corporate managers.**

  Reality   There is no evidence at all that entrepreneurs work harder than their corporate counterparts. Some do, some don't. Both are demanding situations that require long hours and hard work.

- **Myth 7   Entrepreneurs face greater stress and more pressures, and thus pay a higher personal price in their jobs than do other managers.**

  Reality   Being an entrepreneur is undoubtedly stressful and demanding. But there is no evidence it is any more stressful than numerous other highly demanding professional roles, such as being the principal partner in a legal or accounting practice or the head of a division of a major corporation or government agency. Most entrepreneurs enjoy what they do. They have a high sense of accomplishment. For them it is fun rather than drudgery. They thrive on the flexibility and innovative aspects of their job and are much less likely to retire than those who work for someone else.

- **Myth 8   Starting a business is risky and often ends in failure.**

  Reality   This statement is undoubtedly true in many instances. Some studies have indicated that upwards of 80 percent of new business start-ups fail within their first five years. However, success tends to be more common than failure for higher-potential ventures because they tend to be directed by talented and experienced people able to attract the right personnel and the necessary financial and other resources.

  Vince Lombardi, the well-known ex-coach of the Green Bay Packers, is famous for the quotation, "Winning isn't everything — It's the *only* thing." But a lessor known quote of his is closer to the true entrepreneur's personal philosophy. Looking back on a season, Lombardi was once heard to remark, "We didn't lose any games last season, we just ran out of time twice." The entrepreneur learns from the experience and is inclined to believe they have failed if they quit.

Owning your own business is a competitive game and entrepreneurs have to be prepared to run out of time occasionally. Businesses fail but entrepreneurs do not. Many well-known entrepreneurs experience failure, sometimes several times, before achieving success.

- **Myth 9   Money is the most important ingredient for success.**

  Reality   If the other important elements and the people are there, the money tends to follow. But it is not true that entrepreneurs are assured of success if they have enough money. Money is one of the least important ingredients of new venture success.

- **Myth 10   New business start-ups are for the young and energetic.**

  Reality   While youth and energy may help, age is absolutely no barrier to starting a business of your own. However, many people feel there is some threshold for an individual's perceived capacity for starting a new venture. Over time you gain experience, competence, and self-confidence: these factors increase your capacity and readiness to embark on an entrepreneurial career. At the same time, constraints such as increases in your financial and other obligations grow and negatively affect your freedom to choose. The tradeoffs between individual readiness and these restraints typically result in most high potential new businesses being started by entrepreneurs between the ages of 25 and 40.

- **Myth 11   Entrepreneurs are motivated solely by their quest for the almighty dollar.**

  Reality   Growth-minded entrepreneurs are more driven by the challenge of building their enterprise and long-term capital appreciation than by the instant gratification of a high salary and other rewards. Having a sense of personal accomplishment and achievement, feeling in control of their own destiny, and realizing their vision and dreams are also powerful motivators. Money is viewed principally as a tool and a way of "keeping score."

- **Myth 12   Entrepreneurs seek power and control over other people so that they can feel "in charge."**

  Reality   Successful entrepreneurs are driven by the quest for responsibility, achievement, and results rather than for power for its own sake. They thrive on a sense of accomplishment and of outperforming the competition, rather than a personal need for power expressed by dominating and controlling other people. They gain control by the results they achieve.

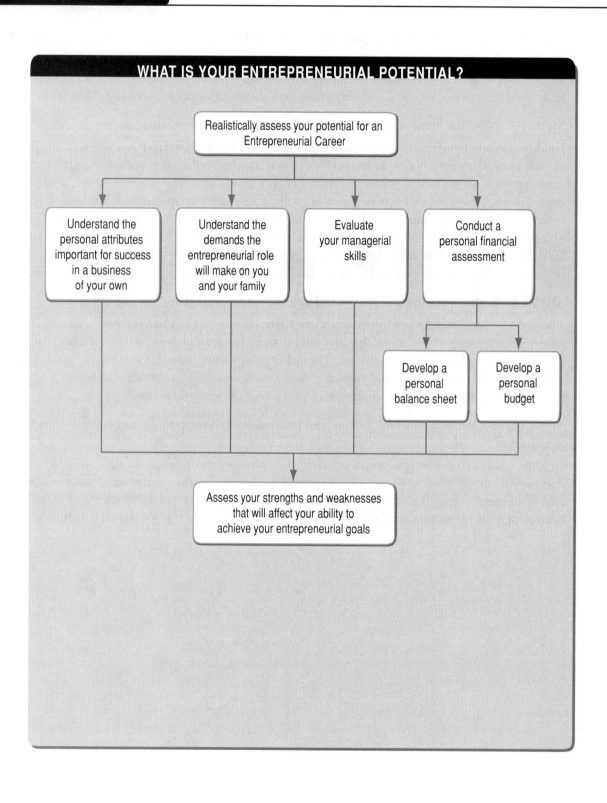

WHAT IS YOUR ENTREPRENEURIAL POTENTIAL?

Realistically assess your potential for an
Entrepreneurial Career

Understand the
personal attributes
important for success
in a business
of your own

Understand the
demands the
entrepreneurial role
will make on you
and your family

Evaluate
your managerial
skills

Conduct a
personal financial
assessment

Develop a
personal
balance sheet

Develop a
personal
budget

Assess your strengths and weaknesses
that will affect your ability to
achieve your entrepreneurial goals

Assessing Your Potential for an Entrepreneurial Career

The discussion in Stage 1 should have served to dispel many of the popular myths concerning entrepreneurship. This section will expand upon the theme of entrepreneurial characteristics by proposing and discussing two important questions which are vital to you if you are interested in an entrepreneurial career:

1. Are there certain common attributes, attitudes, and experiences among entrepreneurs which appear to lead to success?

2. If such attributes, attitudes, and experiences exist, can they be learned or are they inborn and thus available only to those with a "fortunate" heritage?

Research into these questions suggests that the answer to question 1 is yes while the answer to question 2 is both yes and no. These answers, of course, are of little value to you on their own without some further explanation.

Entrepreneurs Are Born and Made Better

In 1980, Tom Wolfe wrote a perceptive bestseller that examined the lives of America's leading test pilots and astronauts. According to Wolfe, becoming a member of this select club meant possessing "The Right Stuff" — i.e., the proper mix of courage, coolness under stressful conditions, a strong need for achievement, technical expertise, creativity, etc. While Wolfe was not talking about entrepreneurs, his viewpoint is similar to the basic thesis held by many members of the "people school" of entrepreneurship: a position which states that a person has to have the "right stuff" to become a successful entrepreneur.

There is considerable evidence, however, that a great deal of the ability and "right stuff" needed to become a successful entrepreneur can be learned (though probably not by everyone).

Entrepreneurial Quiz

While most writers in the field of entrepreneurship agree that there is no single profile, no specific set of characteristics, that defines a successful entrepreneur, there do appear to be some common attributes, abilities, and attitudes. Prior to our discussion of these entrepreneurial characteristics, it is suggested that you take the Entrepreneurial Quiz that appears as Figure 2.1. This will enable you to compare your personal attitudes and attributes with those of "practising" entrepreneurs.

What Attributes are Desirable and Acquirable?

In a study of the 21 inductees into the Babson University Academy of Distinguished Entrepreneurs, only three attributes and behaviours were mentioned by all 21 as the principal reasons for their success, and they were all learnable:

1. Responding positively to all challenges and learning from mistakes
2. Taking personal initiative
3. Having great perseverance

Other research has uncovered different lists of common learnable attributes. These qualities are very desirable, also, in the people with whom entrepreneurs want to surround themselves in building a high-potential business.

Following is a summary of the attitudes and behaviours that can be valuable in turning a business dream into reality. The proposed characteristics represent the conclusions of over 50 separate research studies into the essential nature of the entrepreneur.

Commitment, Determination, and Perseverance

More than any other single factor, a combination of perseverance and total dedication is critical. In many cases these qualities have won out against odds considered impossible to overcome.

Determination and commitment can compensate for other weaknesses you may have. It requires substantial commitment to give up a well-paying job, with its regular paycheques, medical insurance, and pension and profit-sharing plans, and start out on your own.

Success Orientation

Entrepreneurs are driven by an immense desire to achieve the goals they initially set for themselves and then to aim for even more challenging standards. The competitive needs of growth-minded entrepreneurs are to outperform their own previous best results rather than to just outperform another person. Unlike most people, entrepreneurs do not allow themselves to be concerned with failure. What they think about is not what they are going to do if they don't make it, but what they have to do in order to succeed.

Opportunity and Goal Orientation

Growth-minded entrepreneurs are more focussed on the nature and extent of their opportunity rather than resources, structure, or strategy. They start with the opportunity and let their understanding of it guide these other important issues. Entrepreneurs are able to sense areas of unmet needs and their potential for filling these gaps. Effective entrepreneurs set goals consistent with their interests, values, and talents. These goals are generally challenging but still attainable. Their belief in the "reality" of their goals is a primary factor in their fulfilment of them. Having goals and a clear sense of direction also helps these persons to define priorities and provides them with a measure of how well they are performing.

Action Orientation and Personal Responsibility

Successful entrepreneurs are action-oriented people; they want to start producing results immediately. They like to take the initiative and get on with doing it, today. The true entrepreneur is a doer, not a dreamer.

Persistent Problem-solving, Need to Achieve

Entrepreneurs are not intimidated by the number or severity of the problems they encounter. In fact, their self-confidence and general optimism seem to translate into a view that the

Avg.

impossible just takes a little longer. They will work with a stubborn tenacity to solve a difficult problem. This is based on their desire to achieve the goals they have established for themselves. However, they are neither aimless nor foolhardy in their relentless attack on a problem or obstacle that can impede their business, but tend to get right to the heart of the issue.

Reality Orientation

good

The best entrepreneurs have a keen sense of their own strengths and weaknesses and of the competitive environment in which they operate. In addition, they know when they are in trouble and have the strength to admit when they are wrong. This reality orientation allows them to avoid continuing on an ill-advised course of action.

Seeking and Using Feedback

good

Entrepreneurs have a burning desire to know how they are performing. They understand that to keep score and improve their performance they must get feedback, digest the results, and use the information they receive to do a better job. In that way they can learn from their mistakes and setbacks and respond quickly to unexpected events. For the same reason, most entrepreneurs are found to be good listeners and quick learners.

Self-reliance

Avg.

Successful entrepreneurs trust the fate of their ventures to their own abilities. They do not believe that external forces or plain luck determine their success or failure. This attribute is consistent with their achievement and motivational drive and desire to achieve established goals.

In a similar vein, entrepreneurs are not joiners. Studies have shown that the need for affiliation, or a high need for friendship, often acts as a deterrent to entrepreneurial behaviour.

Self-confidence

good *Avg*

The self-confidence displayed by entrepreneurs is based on their feeling that they can overcome all the necessary challenges and attain their desired goal. They almost never consider failure a real possibility. While this self-confidence implies a strong ego, it is a different kind of ego — an "I know I'm going to do well" type of attitude.

"You don't have to be a loser, Todd. With hard work, determination, and a solid set of goals, you could become mediocre!"

© Randy Glasbergen. Reprinted with permission from www.glasbergen.com.

2 Tolerance of Ambiguity and Uncertainty

Avg.

Entrepreneurs tolerate ambiguous situations well and make effective decisions under conditions of uncertainty. They are able to work well despite constant changes in their business that produce considerable ambiguity in every part of their operation.

Entrepreneurs take change and challenge in stride and actually seem to thrive on the fluidity and excitement of such undefined situations. Job security and retirement are generally not of great concern to them.

Moderate Risk-taking and Risk-sharing

good *Avg*

Despite the myth that suggests entrepreneurs are gamblers, quite the opposite is true. Effective entrepreneurs have been found, in general, to prefer taking moderate, calculated risks, where the chances of losing are neither so small as to be a sure thing nor so large as to be a considerable gamble. Like a parachutist, they are willing to take some measurable and predetermined risk.

The strategy of most entrepreneurs also includes involving other parties in their venture to share the burden of risk: partners put money and reputations on the line; investors do likewise;

and creditors and customers who advance payments and suppliers who advance credit all share in the financial risk of the business.

3 Response to Failure ✗

Avg

Another important attribute of high-performance entrepreneurs is their ability to treat mistakes and failures as temporary setbacks on the way to accomplishing their goals. Unlike most people, the bruises of their defeats heal quickly. This allows them to return to the business world again soon after their failure.

Rather than hide from or dismiss their mistakes entrepreneurs concede their errors and analyze the causes. They have the ability to come to terms with their mistakes, learn from them, correct them, and use them to prevent their recurrence. Successful entrepreneurs know that they have to take personal responsibility for either the success or the failure of their venture and not look for scapegoats when things do not work out. They know how to build on their successes and learn from their failures.

Low Need for Status and Power

good

Entrepreneurs derive great personal satisfaction from the challenge and excitement of creating and building their own business. They are driven by a high need for achievement rather than a desire for status and power. It is important, therefore, to recognize that power and status are a result of their activities and not the need that propels them.

In addition, when a strong need to control, influence, and gain power over other people characterizes the lead entrepreneur, more often than not the venture gets into trouble. A dictatorial and domineering management style makes it very difficult to attract and keep people in the business who are oriented toward achievement, responsibility, and results. Conflicts often erupt over who has the final say, and whose prerogatives are being infringed upon. Reserved parking spaces, the big corner office, and fancy automobiles become symbols of power and status that foster a value system and an organizational culture not usually conducive to growth. In such cases, the business' orientation toward their customers, their market, or their competitors is typically lost.

Successful entrepreneurs appear to have a capacity to exert influence among other people without formal power. They are skilled at "conflict resolution." They know when to use logic and when to persuade, when to make a concession and when to win one. In order to run a successful venture, entrepreneurs must learn to get along with many different constituencies, who often have conflicting aims — customers, suppliers, financial backers, and creditors, as well as partners and others inside the company.

Integrity and Reliability

good

Long-term personal and business relationships are built on honesty and reliability. To survive in the long run, an approach of "Do what you say you are going to do!" is essential. With it the possibilities are unlimited. Investors, partners, customers, suppliers, and creditors all place a high value on these attributes. "Success" resulting from dishonest practices is really long-term failure. After all, anyone can lie, cheat, or steal and maybe get away with it once, but that is no way to build a successful entrepreneurial career.

Team Builder

good

Entrepreneurs who create and build successful businesses are not isolated, super-independent types of individuals. They do not feel they have to receive all of the credit for their success, nor do they feel they have to prove they did it all by themselves. Just the opposite situation actually tends to be true. Not only do they recognize that it is virtually impossible to build a substantial business by working alone, but they also actively build a team. They have an ability to inspire the people they attract to their venture by giving them responsibility and by sharing the credit for their accomplishments. This hero-making ability has been identified as a key attribute of many successful corporate managers as well.

In addition to these characteristics, other attributes that have been associated with successful entrepreneurs are the following:

1. They are determined to finish a project once it has been undertaken, even under difficult conditions.
2. They are dynamic individuals who do not accept the status quo and refuse to be restricted by habit and environment.
3. They are able to examine themselves and their ideas impartially.
4. They are not self-satisfied or complacent.
5. They are independent in making decisions while willing to listen to suggestions and advice from others.
6. They do not blame others or make excuses for their own errors or failures.
7. They have a rising level of aspirations and expectations.
8. They have a good grasp of general economic concepts.
9. They are mature, self-assured individuals who are able to interact well with people of varying personalities and values.
10. They are able to exercise control over their impulses and feelings.
11. They have the ability to make the very best of the resources at hand.

The consensus among most experts is that all of these personal characteristics can be worked on and improved through concerted practice and refinement. Some require greater effort than others, and much depends on an individual's strength of motivation and conviction to grow. Developing these attributes should not be very different from personal growth and learning in many other areas of your life.

The Not-So-Learnable Characteristics

The attributes listed next are those that many experts consider to be innate, and thus not acquirable to any great degree. Fortunately the list is quite short. It is from these not-so-learnable characteristics that the conclusion that entrepreneurs are "born, not made" is principally derived. However, while possessing all these attributes would be beneficial, there are many examples of successful business pioneers who lacked some of these characteristics or who possessed them to only a modest degree:

1. High energy, good health, and emotional stability
2. Creativity and an innovative nature
3. High intelligence and conceptual ability
4. The ability to see a better future and a capacity to inspire others to see it

It is apparent from this discussion that entrepreneurs work from a different set of assumptions than most "ordinary" people. They also tend to rely more on mental attitudes and philosophies based on these entrepreneurial attributes than on specific skills or organizational concepts.

The following are some of the points that, perhaps, sum up the general philosophy of the entrepreneurial approach to business — an "Entrepreneur's Creed," if you will:

1. Do what gives you energy — have fun.
2. Figure out how to make it work.
3. Anything is possible if you believe you can do it.

4. If you don't know it can't be done, then you'll go ahead and do it.
5. Be dissatisfied with the way things are — and look for ways to improve them.
6. Do things differently.
7. Businesses can fail. Successful entrepreneurs learn from failure — but keep the tuition low.
8. It's easier to beg for forgiveness than to ask for permission in the first place.
9. Make opportunity and results your obsession — not money.
10. Making money is even more fun than spending it.
11. Take pride in your accomplishments — it's contagious.
12. Sweat the details that are critical to success.
13. Make the pie bigger — don't waste time trying to cut smaller pieces.
14. Play for the long haul. It is rarely possible to get rich quickly.
15. Remember: only the lead dog gets a change in view.

Answers to the Entrepreneurial Quiz

The answers provided in Table 2.1 for the Entrepreneurial Quiz represent the responses that best exemplify the spirit, attitudes, and personal views of proven, successful entrepreneurs. Here they are *not* arranged in numerical order (1–74) but by the characteristic that they are measuring (personal background, behaviour patterns, and lifestyle factors).

What Does Your Score Mean?

The Entrepreneurial Quiz is *not* intended to predict or determine your likely success or failure. However, if you have answered and scored the questionnaire honestly, it does provide considerable insight into whether you have the attitudes, lifestyle, and behavioural patterns consistent with successful entrepreneurship.

Indicate the total number of questions for which you gave the most desirable response on the following scale:

NUMBER OF MOST DESIRABLE RESPONSES

0	10	20	30	40	50	60	70

TABLE 2.1 ANSWERS TO ENTREPRENEURIAL QUIZ

PERSONAL BACKGROUND

Most Desirable Response	Question Number
Rarely or No	30, 36, 37, 43
Mostly or Yes	17, 18, 23, 28, 32, 35, 28, 42, 44, 74

BEHAVIOUR PATTERNS

Most Desirable Response	Question Number
Rarely or No	8, 9, 10, 11, 12, 14, 24, 39, 40, 48, 54, 57, 64, 65
Mostly or Yes	2, 4, 5, 6, 7, 13, 16, 20, 21, 22, 26, 27, 29, 31, 33, 41, 45, 46, 47, 49, 50, 52, 53, 55, 56, 58, 60, 61, 62, 66, 68, 69

LIFESTYLE FACTORS

Most Desirable Response	Question Number
Rarely or No	25, 34, 51, 67, 71
Mostly or Yes	1, 3, 15, 19, 59, 63, 70, 72, 73

The higher your number of most desirable responses — the closer you are to the right-hand side of this continuum — the more your responses agree with those of successful entrepreneurs. High levels of agreement indicate that you *may* have the "right stuff" to succeed in an entrepreneurial career. You should make certain, however, that your responses reflect your real opinions and attitudes.

The word *may* is highlighted above because of the overwhelming importance of one particular set of attributes/characteristics: commitment, determination, and perseverance. Scoring well on the test is not necessarily a guarantee of entrepreneurial success. Anything less than total commitment to your venture, and considerable determination and perseverance, will likely result in failure, regardless of the degree to which you may possess other important attributes. Your total commitment and determination to succeed helps convince others to "come along for the ride." If you are not totally committed, both financially and philosophically, to the venture, it is unlikely that potential partners, your employees, bankers, suppliers, and other creditors will have the confidence in you to provide the level of support your business will require.

Personal Self-Assessment

The purpose of this discussion is to have you evaluate your personal attitudes, behaviour tendencies, and views to determine whether you fit the typical entrepreneurial profile. Figure 2.2, a Self-Assessment Questionnaire, should help you summarize your feelings regarding your potential for self-employment.

Evaluating Your Business Skills

There is a lot more to succeeding as an entrepreneur than just having the proper background, attitudes, and lifestyle. This next section discusses another factor you should consider in assessing your potential for becoming a successful entrepreneur: Do you have the requisite managerial and administrative skills needed to manage and operate a business?

Possessing the necessary managerial skills is an essential ingredient to succeeding in any small venture. It is estimated the principal reason for the failure of small firms is poor management. Witness the experience of restaurateurs Richard Jaffray and Scott Morison (Entrepreneurs in Action #2). They thought they had learned a lot in building up their chain of Cactus Club Cafes in the lower mainland of British Columbia. They figured they "could do no "wrong," decided to branch out, open four additional Clubs, two each in Calgary and Edmonton. Within six months, they knew they had a problem and six months later it all fell apart.

What could have gone wrong for these relatively seasoned entrepreneurs? "Everything," says Jaffray. Restaurant locations were selected by price rather than by location as they had been in B.C. They changed the original concept of the restaurants and abandoned their long-time practice of grooming existing employees to take over the management of new restaurants. They neglected to take local culture into account and charged B.C. prices, which were 10% to 20% higher than comparable price levels in Alberta. In the end, three of the four Alberta locations were closed and the whole experience ended up costing them about $3 million.

Having learned their lesson and rebuilt the business in B.C., the pair are now looking to take their concept back into Alberta and also to the United States. This time they are not too worried. They feel they have been through it before and can be successful now. "Had we not gone right to the very bottom, I don't think we'd be as successful as we are today," says Jaffray.

2

Rock Bottom and Back

It's 4:00 p.m. on a Monday, and business is booming in the newest uptown Vancouver location of Cactus Club Cafe. Hip young 20-somethings lounge in leather armchairs at tables surrounding a massive centrepiece mahogany bar, drinking Cactus Bellinis, a peach/rum/champagne/sangria slurpie billed as "better than sex." Others relax in plush leather booths next to massive windows framed with crushed velvet drapes. Still others gather around glowing-eyed gargoyle fountains, kibitzing with service staff as they sample diverse cuisine, ranging from jerk chicken and sea-salted fries to the Millionaire's Cut filet mignon.

It's an opulent yet informal, eclectic atmosphere that's become the tongue-in-cheek trademark of restaurateurs Richard Jaffray and Scott Morison. From the bawdy paintings in heavy gilt frames to the glass-enclosed courtyard, river-rock fireplaces and signature moose heads, the new $1.8-million restaurant is fanciful and fun. And that's a key component in Cactus Club's recipe for success, says Jaffray. The other ingredients? Innovative, high-quality food at a reasonable price, he says, and a service culture bent on entertaining customers. It's a formula that's proving popular with West Coast consumers, fuelling Cactus Club's growth into a 10-chain restaurant with 1998 sales of $20 million — up from $17 million in 1997.

But that success hasn't come without challenges. In 1996 an overzealous expansion into Alberta brought the company to the brink of ruin. Opening four restaurants in less than 15 months without adequate research and preparation proved nearly fatal, says Jaffray. Undaunted by the near-disaster, the ambitious partners rolled up their sleeves to retrench and reorganize. The firm's 1999 sales are expected to climb to $24 million, says Jaffray, and the partners have set Cactus Club on a new course for steady yet cautious growth. Their long-term goal? No less than 200 restaurants across Western Canada and the U.S. in the next 20 years. "Our objective," says Jaffray, "is to be the best upscale, casual, fun restaurant in North

America." A lofty ambition, perhaps, but one the partners are confident they can meet by learning from their past mistakes and adhering to the first rule of business: know thy customers.

In fact, that axiom was instrumental in Jaffray's decision to abandon his initial idea of launching a company that would offer party cruises upon arriving in Vancouver from Calgary in 1984. After living in his '74 Dodge Dart at a local beach for a month, he discovered that Vancouver's often inclement weather isn't well suited to cruising.

Instead Jaffray began waiting tables for Earl's Restaurants Ltd., a popular family-restaurant chain. It was there he met Morison, a fellow waiter and would-be entrepreneur. Eager to strike out on their own, two years later the then 21-year-olds hatched a plan to capitalize on the

PERRY ZAVITZ

popularity of Expo 86, launching an ice cream and cappuccino bar called Café Cucamongas.

Revenues reached $250,000 in the first year, enough to attract the attention of the pair's former boss at Earl's, Stan Fuller. Impressed with the duo's enthusiasm and commitment, Fuller approached them in 1987 about a potential partnership in a new restaurant geared to a younger clientele. His timing was perfect, since Jaffray and Morison were already looking beyond Cucamongas. It was win-win, explains Jaffray. The partnership provided them with the capital they needed to develop a full-scale restaurant chain, plus access to Fuller's expertise and experience. In return, Earl's got an investment in a new market without having to manage it. The pair were even given access to Earl's budgets and financial statements. "It allowed us to see some of the inner workings of another organization," says Jaffray, "and the struggles they were going through."

Morison and Jaffray sold Cucamongas and wrangled a $225,000 bank loan, giving them enough cash to finance their half-share in the new venture. In March 1988, the first Cactus Club Café opened in club-starved North Vancouver. The concept was simple: to combine the best attributes of a pub, restaurant and nightclub in a single nightspot. The vision, says Jaffray, was to establish a restaurant that would become a local neighborhood handout, with its own character and vitality. A place where the food and atmosphere would entice customers into making a full night of it — not merely stop in for a drink or dinner.

Cactus Club seemed to fit the bill. Its quirky decor, music, party atmosphere and progressive menu proved popular with hip consumers. The menu featured Vancouver firsts such as tortilla wraps and microbrewed beer on tap. Staff, hired as much for their outgoing personalities as their waiting skills, were encouraged to engage and entertain customers. One waiter proved especially adept, for instance, at organizing an impromptu limbo contest. By 1995 Cactus Club had grown to include five restaurants in the lower mainland. "We could do no wrong," says Jaffray.

Emboldened, in 1996 Jaffray and Morison decided to branch out, opening four Cactus Clubs, two each in Calgary and Edmonton. "Within six months, we knew we were headed for trouble big time," says Jaffray. "Six months later, it all fell apart."

What went wrong? "Everything," says Jaffray. For starters, restaurant locations were chosen not by market research as they were in B.C., says Jaffray, but by price. They tweaked their original concept and ended up with more of a bar than a fun eatery. A longtime practice of grooming existing staff to take over the management of new restaurants was abandoned; they neglected to take into account local cultures such as Edmonton's tradition of "happy hour" discount drinks. Plus, they charged B.C. prices — 10% to 20% above local price points — despite the fact that Alberta costs were lower. Unimpressed by the West Coast whiz kids, customers stayed away.

Staunching mounting losses in Alberta consumed the pair's attention. The inevitable result — sales flatlined and even dropped for their B.C. locations. "We were trying to put out a fire in the corner," says Jaffray, "but in the meantime the whole house was burning down." Within a year of opening in Alberta, they realized they would have to cut their losses or lose everything.

In the end, three of the four Alberta locations were closed. "The whole exercise cost about $3 million." says Jaffray. "We've been paying it off for four years."

Fuller is impressed with the pair's courage. "To their credit, they rolled up their sleeves and changed direction," he says. "They went back to what they knew and then made it better, and worked themselves out of the hole." Indeed, getting back on track meant building change into the company's overall management philosophy. The menu for example, which had remained the same for two years, is now changed twice a year. Menu covers are updated every six weeks. To foster a team spirit and keep their 800 employees informed on the company's progress, Jaffray and Morison now practice open-book management. Staff are encouraged to use their own creativity when it comes to service, and managers are responsible for establishing and regularly updating goals. These initiatives seem to be working. Today Cactus Club's nine restaurants are all profitable, and posting annual sales increases of 5% to 22% for the past three years.

While Jaffray and Morison remain cautious about again expanding into a new market, they aren't overly worried. They've been through this before. "Had we not gone right to the very bottom, I don't think we'd be as successful as we are today," says Jaffray. "We now know all the things that can go wrong."

Source: Diane Luckow, "Rockbottomandback," *PROFIT: The Magazine for Canadian Entrepreneurs,* April, 1999, pp. 53-55. Reprinted with permission.

What Skills Are Needed by Small-Business Owners?

Businesses, whether large or small, have to perform a number of diverse functions to operate successfully. An entrepreneur, because of the limited amount of resources (human and financial) at his or her disposal, faces a particularly difficult time.

The business skills required by an entrepreneur (or some other member of the organization) can be broken down by function, as shown in Table 2.2.

TABLE 2.2   BREAKDOWN OF ENTREPRENEURIAL BUSINESS SKILLS

1. **Managing Money**
   a. Borrowing money and arranging financing
   b. Keeping financial records
   c. Managing cash flow
   d. Handling credit
   e. Buying insurance
   f. Reporting and paying taxes
   g. Budgeting

2. **Managing people**
   a. Hiring employees
   b. Supervising employees
   c. Training employees
   d. Evaluating employees
   e. Motivating people
   f. Scheduling workers

3. **Directing business operations**
   a. Purchasing supplies and raw materials
   b. Purchasing machinery and equipment
   c. Managing inventory
   d. Filling orders
   e. Managing facilities

4. **Directing sales and marketing operations**
   a. Identifying different customer needs
   b. Developing new product and service ideas
   c. Deciding appropriate prices
   d. Developing promotional strategies
   e. Contacting customers and making sales
   f. Developing promotional material and media programs

5. **Setting up a business**
   a. Choosing a location
   b. Obtaining licences and permits
   c. Choosing a form of organization and type of ownership
   d. Arranging initial financing
   e. Determining initial inventory requirements

Where Can You Acquire the Necessary Skills?

It should be apparent from this lengthy list that few people can expect to have a strong grasp of all of these skills prior to considering an entrepreneurial career. The key question then becomes where and how you can acquire these skills. The available means for developing these business skills are outlined below.

Job Experience

Every job you have had should have contributed to the development of some business skills. For example, working as an accountant might teach you:

1. How to prepare financial statements
2. How to make financial projections and manage money
3. How to determine the business's cash requirements, among other things

Working as a sales clerk might teach you:

1. How to sell
2. How to deal with the public
3. How to operate a cash register

Perhaps the best experience, however, is working for another entrepreneur. In that case you will learn to understand the overall process and skills required to operate your own business.

Club Activities

Many of the functions that service clubs and similar organizations perform in planning and developing programs are similar to those performed by small businesses. Some examples of what can be learned from volunteer activities are:

1. How to organize and conduct fundraising activities
2. How to promote the organization through public service announcements and free advertising
3. How to manage and coordinate the activities of other members of the organization

Education

Universities, community colleges, and high schools, and government agencies such as local business development organizations and the Business Development Bank of Canada, provide many programs and individual courses in which essential business-related skills can be acquired. Some examples of applicable skills which can be learned from these programs include:

1. Business skills (from particular business classes)
2. Socialization and communication skills (from all school activities)
3. Bookkeeping and record-keeping skills (from accounting classes)

Your Friends

Most of us have friends who through their job experience and education can teach us valuable business skills. Some examples of useful information we may acquire from this source are:

1. Possible sources of financing
2. Assistance in selecting an appropriate distribution channel for your products
3. Information on the availability of appropriate sites or locations for your business
4. Sources for finding suitable employees

Your Family

Growing up with an entrepreneur in the family is perhaps the best learning experience of all, even though you may not be aware of the value of this experience at the time. Some examples of what you might learn from other members of your family are:

1. How to deal with challenges and problems
2. How to make personal sacrifices and why
3. How to keep your personal life and business life separate
4. How to be responsible with money

Home Experiences

Our everyday home experiences help us develop many business skills. Some examples of such skills are:

1. Budgeting income
2. Planning finances
3. Organizing activities and events
4. Buying wisely
5. Managing and dealing with people
6. Selling an idea

It can be hard for a single individual to wear all these "hats" at once. Partnerships or the use of outside technical or general business assistance can be an excellent supplement for any deficiencies in characteristics and skills a small business owner may have. Thus, it often becomes essential to identify an individual, or individuals, who can help you when needed. This outside assistance might come from one of the following sources:

1. A spouse or family member
2. A formal partnership arrangement
3. Hired staff and employees
4. External professional consultants
5. A formal course or training program
6. Regular idea exchange meetings or networking with other entrepreneurs

Inventory of Your Managerial and Administrative Skills

Now that you understand the range of skills necessary to enable your new business to succeed, the Managerial Skills Inventory in Figure 2.4 can be used to develop an inventory of your skills and capabilities in several aspects of management. Your present level of expertise may be anything from minimal to having a great deal of skill. The goal of the inventory is to assess your present skills, with the purpose of identifying areas, which may need improvement. Since each of these management skills is not required at an equivalent level in all new business situations, completing this inventory might also provide you with some insight into the type of business opportunities for which you are best suited.

Assessing Your Personal Financial Situation

In addition to your managerial capabilities, your financial capacity will be a very important consideration in your decision as to whether an entrepreneurial career is right for you. It will certainly be a critical factor to those you may approach for a loan to provide investment capital for your venture.

Your Personal Balance Sheet

Your personal balance sheet provides potential lenders with a view of your overall financial situation so they can assess the risk they will be assuming. Generally, if you are in a strong financial position, as indicated by a considerable net worth, you will be considered a desirable prospect. On the other hand, an entrepreneur with a weak financial position and a large number of outstanding debts may not meet the standards of most lenders.

From a personal standpoint you might also want to reconsider becoming a small-business owner if you cannot afford a temporary or perhaps even a prolonged reduction in your personal income.

Your personal balance sheet includes a summary of all your assets — what you own that has some cash value — and your liabilities or debts. Preparing a personal balance sheet is a relatively simple process:

- **Step 1** Estimate the current market value of all your "assets" — the items you own that have cash value — and list them.
- **Step 2** Add up the value of these assets.
- **Step 3** List all your debts, also known as "liabilities."
- **Step 4** Add up your liabilities.
- **Step 5** Deduct your total liabilities from your total assets to find your "net worth."

Figure 2.3 shows a Sample Balance Sheet Form that you can use to help organize your assets and liabilities. The items listed are not exhaustive; the form is provided only as a guide for thinking about your present position. Since every business opportunity has its own unique capital (money) requirements there is no specific dollar value for the personal net worth necessary to start a business. However, you should keep in mind that most private lenders or lending institutions typically expect a new small-business owner to provide at least 40 to 50 percent of the capital required for start-up. In addition, lenders consider the net worth position of a prospective borrower, in order to determine their ability to repay the loan should the new business fail.

In Entrepreneurs in Action #3 for example, consider the "Financial Snapshot" provided for Carlyle Jansen. Carlyle is a young person who has recently gone into a business of her own. The Snapshot illustrates a typical financial position for someone in that situation with relatively few other assets. Most of the assets she does have are the residual from an inheritance she received from a number of great-aunts. These have been kept in a variety of mutual fund investments and used as collateral for a line of credit to provide the working capital to run her business. Her only liability is a $10,000 loan she obtained from her family to acquire the equity interest in her business. Her Balance Sheet shows a nominal net worth of just over $27,000, which leaves her a long way from her long-term goal of being able to retire and not be poor.

Developing a Personal Budget

As well as determining your present net worth, you must also consider your personal living expenses when assessing your ability to provide the total financing needed to start a new business. In fact, you should evaluate your personal financial needs while in the process of determining whether an entrepreneurial career is right for you.

In some situations you will need to take money from the business each month to pay part or all of your personal living expenses. If such is the case, it is crucial that this amount be known and that at least that much be set aside to be paid out to you each month as a salary.

If your new business is starting off on a limited scale, you might wish to continue holding a regular job to cover your basic living expenses and provide some additional capital to your fledgling operation. In some cases, your spouse's income may be sufficient to cover the family's basic living expenses and it may not be necessary to consider your personal financial needs in making a go/no go decision.

Carlyle Jansen's Financial Snapshot also illustrates her annual expenses in relation to her annual income of $15,600. She only takes a modest salary of $1,200 a month from the business since her living expenses are very low and she figures she can live "cheaply" and doesn't mind doing it. Her largest expenses are for rent ($400/month), food ($200/month) and income tax ($150/month). Her other expenses are very small and probably much lower than a typical middle-class person living in Toronto. She has recently sold her car but has not made any financial provision for transportation. This may create a real problem for her should she decide to replace it. It is estimated that it costs roughly $4,000 a year to maintain a car in the city and she hadn't made any provision for this level of expense in her budget.

3   ENTREPRENEURS IN ACTION

A Business for Her

Visit Toronto's Harbord Street between Spadina and Bathurst and you'll find one of the city's most intriguing retail strips. Among the shops are the venerable Toronto Women's Book Store, which opened nearly a quarter-century ago, along with Parentbooks, WonderWorks (which focuses on nature and spirituality), Drum Travel Co-operative, responsible-tourism experts, and, since May 1997, Good For Her, a store devoted to "Celebrating Women's Sexuality."

Discreetly tucked into a house-turned-retail-outlet, Good For Her offers "women and their admirers a cozy, comfortable place" to buy educational and erotic books, videos and magazines, condoms, lubricants and the like. The store also hosts workshops and seminars (sample titles: "Women's Sex Toys 101," "Herbal Aphrodisiacs and Sensual Oils," "Midlife, Menopause and Sexuality").

Good For Her is the dream child of 32-year-old Carlyle Jansen, and it's a business that's very much an outgrowth of its founder's story. Born in Toronto to two doctors, Jansen grew up in middle-class comfort. Inheritances from five great-aunts financed her arrival in 1984 at the University of British Columbia. She recalls, "I didn't know what I wanted to do, but I knew I didn't want to go into business." She embarked on an arts degree, then laughs heartily as she explains, "I really don't remember applying, but in second year, I found myself in the Faculty of Commerce."

Here, Jansen discovered her interest in small business. She graduated in 1990 with a Bachelor of Commerce and a specialization in organizational behavior. By then, she'd also spent time with the Canada World Youth Program in Prince Edward Island and on a cultural exchange in Sri Lanka. In addition, she had lived at L'Arche Daybreak in Richmond Hill, Ont., a community for adults with developmental disabilities and those who wish to live and learn with them.

Jansen went on to complete the Canadian Securities Course. Her first job on graduation was in Old Crow, a Yukon community north of the Arctic Circle, where she worked for the local First Nations government, helping to establish sound accounting practices and later with land-claims negotiations. In Old Crow, Jansen met a number of people dealing with alcoholism and other social challenges, and inspired by their work, she went to Edmonton in 1992 to take the training required to become a life-skills coach. However, work in the field did not materialize, and after stints as a bicycle courier and waitress, she moved to Seattle in January 1993. Financed by an RESP held by her parents, Jansen took a master's degree at Antioch University in whole-systems design, focusing on how more effective interaction can be encouraged in educational settings.

In May 1995, Jansen attended a bridal shower in Toronto for her sister. Her gift was a selection of sex toys—definitely an unconventional choice—but far from being shocked, her sister's friends wanted to know all about them. In fact, they were so impressed by Jansen's knowledge and ease, they told her she should start giving seminars on the topic.

At the same time, her studies at Antioch were helping her hone the communication and education skills she'd been developing ever since taking up her specialty in organizational behavior at UBC.

When she realized her chosen field was overcrowded, she decided to take her sister's friends' advice. That group of women became the first to attend one of what Jansen called "Playshops in Sensuality for Women." Although the playshops never brought in a proper income, Jansen still had inheritance money from her UBC days, and an inexpensive living arrangement with her mother.

Meanwhile, the playshop participants repeatedly told Jansen they wanted to be able to buy the products she was showing them in an environment they found comfortable. Jansen's life changed yet again. In May 1996, she began doing the research that culminated in the opening of Good For Her. She designed a two-year business plan that accurately predicted her sales and expenses to date, and she has recently updated the plan.

Good For Her was launched with family money — Jansen holds personal liability for $10,000 she borrowed to buy her own common shares (and thus all voting rights) in the business. In addition, preferred shares were sold to family members. Jansen plans to buy them back at some point; she realizes she'll need a consultation with her accountant to determine whether the buyback should be done by herself or the corporation. The preferred shares will eventually be repaid with dividends — in a relaxed kind of way. "that's the great thing about family," says Jansen. "I'll pay dividends when I can afford it."

While the store isn't turning much of a profit yet, Jansen is able to support herself on its proceeds and has hired some part-time help as well. The salary she draws is modest — $1,200 per month — but her current low rent of $400 per month in the apartment she shares with a roommate helps her make do.

The inheritance money she's husbanded so carefully over the years also comes in handy now that Jansen's in business. Invested in mutual funds with a current value of $25,000, Jansen uses it as collateral against a line of credit. The corporation, she explains, pays prime plus 1%, but her fund earns money at a higher rate. In addition, Jansen has $11,000 in RRSPs: 80% held in the Ethical Growth fund, the remainder in foreign vehicles. She admits she's "not really able to save money right now." But she doesn't have grand plans for old age: "I just want to be able to retire and not be poor."

Jansen isn't driven by money, but she does want also eventually to garner enough spare money and time to raise a family. Currently she puts in a 60-hour week handling sales, managing relations with over 100 suppliers and organizing workshops and seminars hosted by the store. She hopes that as

FINANCIAL SNAPSHOT

INCOME

14,000	Income from business
1,200	Income from investments
$15,600	**Total income**

EXPENSES

4,800	Rent
240	Deductions
1,369	Income tax
1,200	RRSP contributions
2,400	Food
1,800	Entertainment
635	Household expenses
600	Clothing
900	Investments
240	Gifts
600	Vacation
240	Educational expenses
576	Club memberships
$15,600	**Total expenditure**

ASSETS

1,200	Furnishings
11,000	RRSPs
25,000	Investments
$37,200	**Total**

LIABILITIES

10,000	Family loan
$10,000	**Total**
$27,200	**Net worth**

Good For Her becomes established, she'll be able to whittle that commitment down to 30 hours per week. She wants her future children to have "access to what I had access to." That means, at the very least, a university education. Her plan doesn't involve a family homestead, though. She has no desire for home ownership, considering herself better off with extra cash and no repair bills. "Houses sometimes appreciate and sometimes don't," she explains. "That's true for mutual funds, too, but I think the batting average there is better."

As is obvious by now, Jansen isn't driven by money. In fact, she asserts, "I can live cheaply,"

and she doesn't mind doing it. What's really important is having enough to allow her to fulfil her dreams of raising a family and continuing the work that Good For Her represents: "I see women's sexuality as always being important to me. So many women want resources and information to feel comfortable about their sexuality."

Source: Sibylle Preuschat, "A Business for Her," *The Financial Post Magazine*, February, 1999, pp. 63-65. Reprinted with permission.

The Personal Living Expenses Worksheet shown in Figure 2.5 is an effective means of estimating your present cost of living. From the totals on the worksheet, you can calculate the minimum amount of money you and your family will require on a regular monthly basis and determine from what sources this regular income will be obtained.

Are You Ready for an Entrepreneurial Career?

External Role Demands

It is not enough simply to possess a large number and high level of the characteristics previously discussed as prerequisites for a successful entrepreneurial career. There are also certain external conditions, pressures, and demands inherent in the small-business ownership role itself.

While successful entrepreneurs may share several characteristics with successful people in other careers, entrepreneurs' preference for and tolerance of the combination of requirements unique to their role is a major distinguishing feature.

Many of these requirements have been alluded to earlier. What follows is a discussion of a few of the most relevant issues you should consider concerning your degree of readiness and preparedness for such a career.

Need for Total Commitment

As an entrepreneur you must live with the challenge of trying first to survive in the business world, then to stay alive, and always to grow and withstand the competitive pressures of the marketplace. Almost any venture worth considering requires top priority on your time, emotions, and loyalty. As an entrepreneur you must be prepared to give "all you've got" to the building of your business, particularly during the initial stages of its development. Anything less than total commitment will likely result in failure.

Management of Stress

Stress, the emotional and physiological reaction to external events or circumstances, is an inevitable result of pursuing an entrepreneurial career option. Depending on how it is handled, stress can be either good or bad for an entrepreneur. The better you understand how you react to stressful situations, the better you will be able to maximize the positive aspects of these situations and minimize the negative aspects, such as exhaustion and frustration, before they lead to a serious problem.

Stress, in the short term, can produce excellent results, because of its relationship to the type of behaviour associated with entrepreneurial activities, especially during the start-up stage of a new business. There is some evidence that once individuals become accustomed to producing under stressful conditions, they seem to continue to respond in a positive manner; entrepreneurs tend to create new challenges to replace the ones they have already met, and to continue to respond to those challenges with a high level of effectiveness.

Economic and Personal Values

Entrepreneurs engaged in "for-profit" as opposed to social or "not-for-profit" organizations must share the basic values of the free enterprise system: private ownership, profits, capital gains, and growth. These dominant economic values need not exclude social or other values. However, the nature of the competitive market economy requires belief in, or at least respect for, these values.

A Final Analysis

The Entrepreneurial Assessment Questionnaire in Figure 2.6 is designed to help you recap your thinking concerning what you need to become a successful entrepreneur. The questions involve considerations at various stages of a business' development, and some may not be applicable to the stage you have currently reached in your business planning. However, you should answer all applicable questions.

If you have answered all the questions carefully, you've done some hard work and serious thinking. That's a positive step. If your answer to most of the questions was yes, you are on the right track. If you answered no to some questions you have more work to do; these questions indicate areas where you need to know more or that you need to do something about. Do what you can for yourself, but don't hesitate to ask for help from other sources.

This assessment of your entrepreneurial potential is based on a series of self-evaluations, and for it to reveal anything meaningful an absolute requirement is for you to be completely honest with yourself. This, however, is only the first step. The road to entrepreneurship is strewn with hazards and pitfalls and many who start on it fall by the wayside for one reason or another. However, those who persevere and reach the end by building a successful venture may realize considerable financial and psychological rewards as well as a lot of personal satisfaction.

The remainder of this book can help you evaluate other important parts of this process and improve your chances for success. It will help you decide what else you need to consider and enable you to go after it. Good luck!

FIGURE 2.1   ENTREPRENEURIAL QUIZ

Below are a number of questions dealing with your personal background, behavioural characteristics, and lifestyle patterns. Psychologists, venture capitalists, and others believe these to be related to entrepreneurial success. Answer each question by placing an X in the space that best reflects your personal views and attitudes. The most important result of this exercise will be an honest, accurate self-assessment of how you relate to each of these dimensions.

	Rarely or no	Mostly or yes
1. Are you prepared to make sacrifices in your family life and take a cut in pay to succeed in business?	_____	_____
2. Are you the kind of individual that once you decide to do something you'll do it and nothing can stop you?	_____	_____
3. When you begin a task, do you set clear goals and objectives for yourself?	_____	_____
4. When faced with a stalemated situation in a group setting, are you usually the one who breaks the logjam and gets the ball rolling again?	_____	_____
5. Do you commonly seek the advice of people who are older and more experienced than you are?	_____	_____
6. Even though people tell you "It can't be done" do you still have to find out for yourself?	_____	_____
7. When you do a good job, are you satisfied in knowing personally that the job has been well done?	_____	_____
8. Do you often feel, "That's just the way things are and there's nothing I can do about it"?	_____	_____
9. Do you need to know that something has been done successfully before, prior to trying it yourself?	_____	_____
10. Do you intentionally try to avoid situations where you have to converse with strangers?	_____	_____
11. Do you need a clear explanation of a task before proceeding with it?	_____	_____
12. Are you a good loser in competitive activities?	_____	_____
13. After a severe setback in a project, are you able to pick up the pieces and start over again?	_____	_____
14. Do you like the feeling of being in charge of other people?		
15. Do you enjoy working on projects which you know will take a long time to complete successfully?	_____	_____
16. Do you consider ethics and honesty to be important ingredients for a successful career in business?	_____	_____
17. Have you previously been involved in starting things like service clubs, community organizations, charitable fund-raising projects, etc.?	_____	_____
18. Did your parents or grandparents ever own their own business?	_____	_____

	Rarely or no	Mostly or yes
19. When you think of your future do you ever envision yourself running your own business?	_____	_____
20. Do you try to do a job better than is expected of you?	_____	_____
21. Do you make suggestions about how things might be improved on your job?	_____	_____
22. Are you usually able to come up with more than one way to solve a problem?	_____	_____
23. Are you between 25 and 40 years of age?	_____	_____
24. Do you worry about what others think of you?	_____	_____
25. Do you read a lot of books, particularly fiction?	_____	_____
26. Do you take risks for the thrill of it?	_____	_____
27. Do you find it easy to get others to do something for you?	_____	_____
28. Has someone in your family shared his or her experience in starting a business with you?	_____	_____
29. Do you believe in organizing your tasks before getting started?	_____	_____
30. Do you get sick often?	_____	_____
31. Do you enjoy doing something just to prove you can?	_____	_____
32. Have you ever been fired from a job?	_____	_____
33. Do you find yourself constantly thinking up new ideas?	_____	_____
34. Do you prefer to let a friend decide on your social activities?	_____	_____
35. Did you like school?	_____	_____
36. Were you a very good student?	_____	_____
37. Did you "hang out" with a group in high school?	_____	_____
38. Did you actively participate in school activities or sports?	_____	_____
39. Do you like to take care of details?	_____	_____
40. Do you believe there should be security in a job?	_____	_____
41. Will you deliberately seek a direct confrontation to get needed results?	_____	_____
42. Were you the firstborn child?	_____	_____
43. Was your father or another older male generally present during your early life at home?	_____	_____
44. Were you expected to do odd jobs at home before 10 years of age?	_____	_____
45. Do you get bored easily?	_____	_____
46. Are you sometimes boastful about your accomplishments?	_____	_____
47. Can you concentrate on one subject for extended periods of time?	_____	_____

continued

Entrepreneurial Quiz — continued

	Rarely or no	Mostly or yes
48. Do you, on occasion, need pep talks from others to keep you going?	_____	_____
49. Do you find unexpected energy resources as you tackle things you like?	_____	_____
50. Does personal satisfaction mean more to you than having money to spend on yourself?	_____	_____
51. Do you enjoy socializing regularly?	_____	_____
52. Have you ever deliberately exceeded your authority at work?	_____	_____
53. Do you try to find the benefits in a bad situation?	_____	_____
54. Do you blame others when something goes wrong?	_____	_____
55. Do you enjoy tackling a task without knowing all the potential problems?	_____	_____
56. Do you persist when others tell you it can't be done?	_____	_____
57. Do you take rejection personally?	_____	_____
58. Do you believe you generally have a lot of good luck that explains your successes?	_____	_____
59. Are you likely to work long hours to accomplish a goal?	_____	_____
60. Do you enjoy being able to make your own decisions on the job?	_____	_____
61. Do you wake up happy most of the time?	_____	_____
62. Can you accept failure without admitting defeat?	_____	_____
63. Do you have a savings account and other personal investments?	_____	_____
64. Do you believe that entrepreneurs take a huge risk?	_____	_____
65. Do you feel that successful entrepreneurs must have advanced college degrees?	_____	_____
66. Do you strive to use past mistakes as a learning process?	_____	_____
67. Are you more people-oriented than goal-oriented?	_____	_____
68. Do you find that answers to problems come to you out of nowhere?	_____	_____
69. Do you enjoy finding an answer to a frustrating problem?	_____	_____
70. Do you prefer to be a loner when making a final decision?	_____	_____
71. Do your conversations discuss people more than events or ideas?	_____	_____
72. Do you feel good about yourself in spite of criticism by others?	_____	_____
73. Do you sleep as little as possible?	_____	_____
74. Did you ever have a small business of your own while in school?	_____	_____

Adapted from Judy Balogh et al., *Beyond a Dream: An Instructor's Guide for Small Business Explorations* (Columbus: Ohio State University, 1985), pp. 26–28.

FIGURE 2.2 SELF-ASSESSMENT QUESTIONNAIRE

1. What personal weaknesses did you discover from analyzing your responses to the questionnaire?

_____

_____

_____

_____

2. Do you feel you can be an entrepreneur in spite of these weaknesses?

_____

_____

_____

_____

_____

3. What can you do to improve your areas of weakness?

_____

_____

_____

_____

4. What did the questionnaire indicate as your strengths?

_____

_____

_____

_____

_____

5. Do your strengths compensate for your weaknesses?

_____

_____

_____

_____

_____

6. Does your lifestyle appear to be compatible with the demands of an entrepreneurial career?

_____

_____

_____

_____

FIGURE 2.3   MANAGERIAL SKILLS INVENTORY

The following questionnaire can be used to develop an inventory of your skills and capabilities in each of the five areas of management outlined in the Courseware. For each management area, the questionnaire lists some corresponding skills. Rate your present level of expertise for each skill listed by placing an "X" under the appropriate number in the charts below (1 indicates minimal skill, while 5 indicates a great deal of skill). Beneath each section, in the space provided, briefly describe where and when you obtained this experience.

The goal of this inventory is to assess the level of your present skills, with the purpose of identifying areas which may need improvement.

MONEY MANAGEMENT

	1	2	3	4	5
Borrowing money and arranging financing				☑	
Keeping financial records		☑			☑
Cash flow management					
Handling credit					
Buying insurance		☑	☑		
Reporting and paying taxes		☑			☑
Budgeting				☑	☑

important

Describe where and when you obtained this expertise.

_____

_____

_____

MANAGING PEOPLE

	1	2	3	4	5
Hiring employees			☒	☑	
Supervising employees		☒	☒		
Training employees		☒	☒		
Evaluating employees		☒	☑		
Motivating people				☑	☒
Scheduling workers			☑	☒	

Describe where and when you obtained this expertise.

_____

_____

_____

DIRECTING BUSINESS OPERATIONS

	1	2	3	4	5
3 Purchasing supplies and raw materials	☐	☐	☐	☒	☐
3 Purchasing machinery and equipment	☐	☐	☐	☒	☐
2 Managing inventory	☐	☐	☐	☒	☐
2 Filling orders	☐	☐	☒	☐	☐
4 Managing facilities	☐	☒	☐	☐	☐

Describe where and when you obtained this expertise.

_____

_____

_____

DIRECTING SALES AND MARKETING OPERATIONS

	1	2	3	4	5
4 Identifying different customer needs	☐	☐	☐	☒	☐
4 Developing new product and service ideas	☐	☐	☐	☒	☐
4 Deciding appropriate prices	☐	☒	☐	☐	☐
5 Developing promotional strategies	☐	☐	☐	☒	☐
4 Contacting customers and making sales	☐	☒	☐	☐	☐
Developing promotional material and a media program	☐	☐	☐	☒	☐

Describe where and when you obtained this expertise.

_____

_____

_____

SETTING UP A BUSINESS

	1	2	3	4	5
5 Choosing a location	☐	☐	☐	☒	☐
3 Obtaining licences and permits	☐	☐	☐	☐	☒
3 Choosing a form of organization and type of ownership	☐	☐	☒	☐	☐
3 Arranging initial financing	☐	☐	☐	☒	☐
5 Determining initial inventory requirements	☐	☐	☐	☒	☐

Describe where and when you obtained this expertise.

_____

_____

_____

FIGURE 2.4   SAMPLE BALANCE SHEET FORM

Name: _____

BALANCE SHEET
as of

_____ _____ _____
      (Month)   *(Day)*   *(Year)*

ASSETS

Cash & cash equivalents

Cash	_____
Chequing/savings	_____
Canada Savings Bonds	_____
Treasury bills	_____
Short-term deposits	_____
Money market funds	_____
Other	_____
Subtotal	_____

Business/property

Investment property	_____
Business Interests	_____
Subtotal	_____

Registered assets

RRSPs	_____
Employer's pension plan (RPP)	_____
RRIFs	_____
DPSPs	_____
Other	_____
Subtotal	_____

Personal Property

Home	_____
Seasonal home	_____
Cars and/or other vehicles	_____
Equipment	_____
Collectibles (art)	_____
Jewelry	_____
Household furnishings	_____
Subtotal	_____

Investments

GICs and term deposits	_____
Mutual funds	_____
Stocks	_____
Bonds	_____
Life insurance (cash surrender value)	_____
Provincial stock savings plan	_____
Subtotal	_____
TOTAL	_____

LIABILITIES
Short-term
Credit card debt _____

Personal line of credit, margin account _____

Instalment loans (e.g., car, furniture,
    personal loans) _____

Demand loans _____

Loans for investment purposes _____

Tax owing (income and property) _____

Other _____

    Subtotal _____

Long-term
Mortgage — home _____

Mortgage — seasonal home _____

Mortgage — investment property _____

Other _____

    Subtotal _____

      TOTAL _____

NET WORTH ANALYSIS
Liquid assets vs. short-term debt
Total assets _____

Total liabilities _____

Assets exceed debt by + _____

(Debt exceeds assets by) −(_____)

Debt-equity ratio (liabilities/net worth) _____

    Net worth (assets less total liabilities) _____

FIGURE 2.5 PERSONAL LIVING EXPENSES WORKSHEET — DETAILED BUDGET*

1. REGULAR MONTHLY PAYMENTS

Rent or house payments (including taxes) $ _____
Car payments (including insurance)   _____
Appliances/TV payments   _____
Home improvement loan payments   _____
Personal loan payments   _____
Health plan payments   _____
Life insurance premiums   _____
Other insurance premiums   _____
Miscellaneous payments   _____
    Total $ _____

2. FOOD EXPENSE

Food at home $ _____
Food away from home   _____
    Total $ _____

3. PERSONAL EXPENSES

Clothing, cleaning, laundry, shoe repair $ _____
Drugs   _____
Doctors and dentists   _____
Education   _____
Union or professional dues   _____
Gifts and charitable contributions   _____
Travel   _____
Newspapers, magazines, books   _____
Auto upkeep, gas, and parking   _____
Spending money, allowances   _____

4. HOUSEHOLD OPERATING EXPENSES

Telephone $ _____
Gas and electricity   _____
Water   _____
Other household expenses, repairs, maintenance   _____
    Total $ _____

GRAND TOTAL

1. Regular monthly payments $ _____
2. Food expense   _____
3. Personal expenses   _____
4. Household operating expenses   _____
    Total Monthly Expenses $ _____

* This budget should be based on an estimate of your financial requirements for an *average* month based on a recent 3- to 6-month period, and should not include purchases of any new items except emergency replacements.

FIGURE 2.6   ENTREPRENEURIAL ASSESSMENT QUESTIONNAIRE

WHAT ABOUT YOU?   Yes   No

1. Are you the kind of person who can get a business started and run it successfully?   ____ ____

2. Think about why you want to own your own business. Do you want it enough to work long hours without knowing how much money you'll end up with?   ____ ____

3. Does your family go along with your plan to start a business of your own?   ____ ____

4. Have you ever worked in a business similar to the one you want to start?   ____ ____

5. Have you ever worked for someone else as a supervisor or manager?   ____ ____

6. Have you had any business training in school?   ____ ____

WHAT ABOUT THE MONEY?

7. Have you saved any money?   ____ ____

8. Do you know how much money you will need to get your business started?   ____ ____

9. Have you figured out whether you could make more money working for someone else?   ____ ____

10. Have you determined how much of your own money you can put into the business?   ____ ____

11. Do you know how much credit you can get from your suppliers — the people from whom you will buy?   ____ ____

12. Do you know where you can borrow the rest of the money needed to start your business?   ____ ____

13. Have you figured out your expected net income per year from the business? (Include your salary and a return on the money you have invested.)   ____ ____

14. Can you live on less than this so that you can use some of it to help your business grow?   ____ ____

15. Have you talked to a banker about your plans?   ____ ____

YOUR BUSINESS AND THE LAW

16. Do you know what licences and permits you need?   ____ ____

17. Do you know what business laws you have to obey?   ____ ____

18. Have you talked to a lawyer about your proposed business?   ____ ____

HOW ABOUT A PARTNER?

19. If you need a partner who has money or know-how, do you know someone who will fit — someone with whom you can get along?   ____ ____

20. Do you know the good and bad points about going it alone, having a partner, and incorporating your business?   ____ ____

WHAT ABOUT YOUR CUSTOMERS?

21. Do most businesses in your community seem to be doing well?   ____ ____

22. Have you tried to find out how well businesses similar to the one you want to open are doing in your community and in the rest of the country?   ____ ____

23. Do you know what kind of people will want to buy what you plan to sell?   ____ ____

24. Do such people live in the area where you want to open your business?   ____ ____

25. Do you feel they need a business like yours?   ____ ____

26. If not, have you thought about opening a different kind of business or going to another neighbourhood?   ____ ____

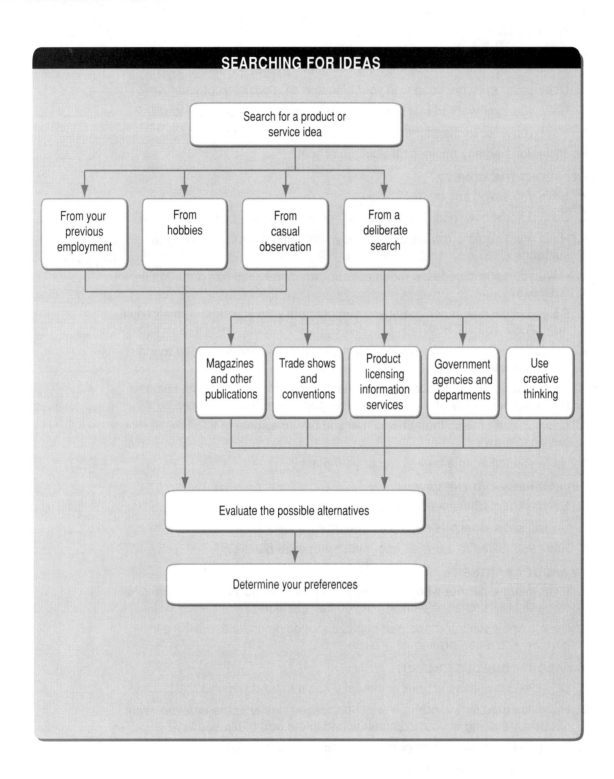

SEARCHING FOR IDEAS

Search for a product or service idea

From your previous employment

From hobbies

From casual observation

From a deliberate search

Magazines and other publications

Trade shows and conventions

Product licensing information services

Government agencies and departments

Use creative thinking

Evaluate the possible alternatives

Determine your preferences

Exploring New Business Ideas and Opportunities

In Stage Two you had an opportunity to evaluate your own potential for an entrepreneurial career from the standpoint of your personal fit with the requirements for success, the business skills required to start and run a business of your own, and the adequacy of your financial resources. Assuming that you feel you have the "right stuff" to continue to explore this career option, you will need an idea — the seed that will germinate and, hopefully, grow and develop into a profitable enterprise. This is the topic of Stage Three. Ideas that succeed are difficult to find and evaluate, but they are critical to the entire process. It is rare for extraordinary amounts of money or effort to overcome the problems associated with what is fundamentally a bad idea.

In some instances what was felt to be a good idea was the key element stimulating an individual to think of going into business. In others it was the lack of an acceptable concept that was the principal factor holding back an aspiring entrepreneur. Perhaps you fall into this category. If so, it is important not to be impatient. It may take several years to fully develop and evaluate an idea which is suited to your particular circumstances and which you feel represents a real opportunity. Don't try to force the issue. Actively pursue a range of possible options, but wait until the right situation presents itself before investing your time and money.

There is no shortage of good ideas. For example, the winners of the 1998 Canadian Woman Entrepreneur of the Year Awards were involved in a wide range of activities including a training school to teach 3D animation and computer graphics, the manufacture and distribution of medical instrumentation, the provision of equipment services, people and training to the film industry, operating a private elementary school and a national computer supply company for corporate clients:

- **Andrée Beaulieu-Green, Montreal, Québec,** left her professorship at the Université du Québec à Montréal in 1993 to create a professional training school to teach computer graphics. Today the school teaches both day and night school courses on a variety of subjects such as 2- and 3D animation, desktop publishing, cartoon animation and interactive media.

- **Marguerite Hale, Ottawa, Ontario,** is the chairperson of a family-owned firm that is a Canadian market leader in the frozen-food industry. Her company, Morrison Lamothe, was recently named by *The Financial Post* newspaper as one of Canada's 50 Best-Managed Private Companies.

- **Betty Thomas, Vancouver, British Columbia,** has gone from being a paralegal and real estate agent to Canada's first female stunt co-ordinator, to the head of her own company that provides equipment, services, facilities, personnel and training to the film industry.

- **Wendy Derrick and Joanne McLean, Toronto, Ontario,** operate a private primary school for students from kindergarten to Grade 8. Their school, Fern Hill, was developed as a centre where children's individual talents would be recognized and stretched. Their program emphasizes strong academics, music, physical education and art as fundamental components.

- **Molly Mak, Calgary, Alberta,** runs a national business as a full-service, information technology provider for major corporations. Her business evolved from a small retail store selling personal computers started by her brother in Mississauga, Ontario.

- **Julia Levy, Vancouver, British Columbia,** is one of the founders of a firm that is a world leader in developing and marketing photodynamic therapy, an emerging field in medicine that uses light-activated drugs to treat disease.[1]

In Stage Three we will describe a number of sources from which you might obtain ideas for a prospective new venture, and present a variety of techniques you can use to evaluate the conceptual, technical and financial aspects of your idea.

Long-Term Expectations for Your Business

Whether your plans are to own and operate a business for a number of years or sell it shortly after it becomes operational, you will want to consider the long-term prospects of your venture. If you plan to keep the business, you are bound to have an interest in how it is expected to prosper; if you plan to sell the business, the prospective buyer will consider the long-term viability of the business in his or her purchase offer. So, either way, the long-term performance — the kind of firm your business may become — is important in evaluating alternatives. Opportunities with higher growth potential generally offer greater economic payoffs. However, those are not the only kind of payoffs that are important. Some small but stable ventures provide very enjoyable situations and lucrative benefits to their owners.

For purposes of assessing the expected long-term prospects of your venture, three types of possibilities should be considered:

1. Lifestyle ventures
2. Small, profitable ventures
3. High-growth ventures

Lifestyle Ventures

These include most "one-man shows," mom-and-pop stores, and other lifestyle businesses such as gas stations, restaurants, drycleaning shops, and small independent retail stores. Typically, their owners make modest investments in fixed assets and inventory, put in long hours, and earn considerably less income than the average unskilled auto worker or union craftsperson. The profit in reselling these businesses tends to be quite low.

The operator of a lifestyle business often risks his or her savings to capitalize the enterprise, and works longer hours with less job security than the average employee. Most lifestyle businesses have a high risk of failure. Unless you are willing to put up with these inherent conditions, such types of businesses should probably be avoided in favour of staying with your job until a more attractive opportunity can be identified.

---

[1] From Anna Kohn, "The 1998 Canadian Woman Entrepreneur of the Year Awards," *The Financial Post Magazine,* December, 1998, pp. 37-54.

Small, Profitable Ventures

Small manufacturing firms, larger restaurants and retail firms, small chains of gas stations, and other multi-establishment enterprises commonly fall into this category. Usually they involve a substantial capital investment — $100,000 or more. Some owners put in long hours, others do not. Once established, many owners enjoy a comfortable living. The profit in reselling the business can be high to a buyer who sees both an attractive job and a profitable investment.

You might be surprised at how many small, virtually unnoticed businesses around your city or town have managed to provide a very comfortable living for their founders. Almost always there is a very particular reason that they are able to do so: a contract the entrepreneur was able to land at favourable terms, or a market that was unknown to others or too small to attract competitors which therefore permitted a high profit margin, or special skills or knowledge on the part of the proprietor which enabled him or her to charge high rates for his or her time. The business' advantage may be its location, perhaps purchased for a low price many years earlier, or a patented process others are not able to copy. It may even be simply a brand that is protected by trademark and which has become well known by the passage of time or through successful advertising.

High-Growth Ventures

Much rarer than lifestyle ventures or small, profitable ventures, but typically more highly publicized, are small firms that have the capability of becoming large ones. They include many high-technology companies formed around new products with large potential markets, and also some of the small, profitable firms which, due to such factors as having amassed substantial capital or having hit upon a successful formula for operating, can be expanded many times. Ventures of this type are often bought up and absorbed by larger companies. The potential for significant capital gain on resale of the business can be substantial.

A key factor in starting a high-growth venture is choosing the right industry to enter. The rate of growth of the industry as a whole often plays a large role in determining the growth patterns of start-ups within it. In addition, however, there has to be some property of the business that can readily be multiplied by that company but cannot easily be duplicated by others for there to be significant growth potential. In franchising, for example, it can be a format for doing business which has proven exceptionally effective and can be taught. In high-technology firms, it is specialized know-how in creating something at a hard-to-reach frontier of engineering for which there is a demand. If a technology is common knowledge and not too capital-intensive, then companies providing it generally do not grow very rapidly.

Sources of Ideas for a New Business

In Stage Two it was suggested that your previous jobs, hobbies, personal experiences, and the like could provide you with some of the requisite business and technical skills needed to operate your own business. Similarly, your past work experience, hobbies, and acquaintances can provide a starting point for developing a list of business ventures you might wish to consider for further investigation. The following is a brief description of some of the sources most often used by entrepreneurs in search of new business opportunities.

Your Job

Prior work experience is the most common source of new business ideas. It has been estimated that as many as 85 percent of the new businesses started are based on product ideas similar to those of prior employers of the founders. When you think about it the attractions of starting a business in a field in which you have experience and expertise are obvious. You are already familiar with the products and services you will provide, you understand the competitive environment, you have some knowledge and understanding of customer requirements, you may already know several prospective clients, and so on.

Ideas from your previous employment can take several forms. For example, you might set yourself up as a consultant in some technical area using the background and experience you acquired in a previous job. You might develop a product or service for which your prior employer might be a prospective customer. You might even be interested in providing a product or service similar or related to that provided by your previous employer. In this last case you should check with a lawyer to ensure your plans do not violate the legal rights of that employer. You must be certain your actions do not infringe on any patent, trademark, or other proprietary rights, break any non-competition clause of other agreements you may have signed, involve the direct solicitation of your former employer's customers, or raise similar legal or ethical problems. You might even set yourself up as a distributor of your employer's products, as illustrated by the case of Janine DeFreitas who quit her position as a Rubbermaid Canada's sales and merchandising manager to open The Rubbery, North America's first, independent, full-line Rubbermaid store (Entrepreneurs in Action #4).

4   ENTREPRENEURS IN *ACTION*

When the Rubber Hits the Road

While Rubbermaid Inc. is recognized as one of the world's most innovative companies, its employees show similar flair. When Janine DeFreitas, Rubbermaid Canada's sales and merchandising manager, saw Rubbermaid's first-ever complete housewares display sell out at Kmart in four weeks, she decided to do what no one had tried before. In September 1996, with a 100-page business plan and a $180,000 loan (from the third bank she approached), DeFreitas opened The Rubbery, North America's first independent, full-line Rubbermaid store.

Almost instantly, her Mississauga, Ont. outlet proved too small. "It was just crazy," she says. "Every week we were backlogged." Eight months after opening, the 34-year-old DeFreitas doubled her floor space to 20,000 square feet. After 11 months, The Rubbery had done more than $3 million in sales — twice DeFreitas's initial projections. And she says she hasn't even begun to grow.

Strategically situated in a "power centre" near Price Club and Home Depot, the colorful store offers products from all seven Rubbermaid divisions: housewares, Little Tykes toys, office products, Graco infant products, home health-care supplies, commercial products for industry, and specialty products such as sheds and lawn carts. "I'm doing what no other retailer can do," says DeFreitas. "I'm showing the breadth of the product."

The only threat DeFreitas sees is the big discounters who price Rubbermaid products to lure customers. "Rubbermaid is typically used as a loss leader. We try to price ourselves about 10% lower than the average retailer, but my strength is the selection."

Now DeFreitas plans to roll out her concept across Canada. "You've got to admit the retail industry is kind of stale," she says. "This is a great new concept that's proven to work." First step: a store next spring in Toronto's east end, and a tad more emphasis on the bottom line. So far the Rubbery's profit margin is running about 6%, but for next year she's targeting 8% to 10% — enough, she hopes, to begin attracting equally innovative franchisees.

Source: Donna Green, "When the Rubber Hits the Road," *PROFIT: The Magazine for Canadian Entrepreneurs,* September 1997, p. 38. Reprinted with permission. Donna Green specializes in small business and personal finance.

Your Hobbies

Some people are deeply involved with their hobbies, often devoting more time to them than to their regular job. There are many instances of such secondary interests leading to new business ventures. For example, serious athletes may open sporting goods stores, amateur photographers open portrait studios, hunters offer guiding services and run hunting lodges and game farms, pilots start fly-in fishing camps, philatelists open coin and stamp stores, and so forth.

Witness the case of Chris Griffiths in Entrepreneurs in Action #5. Chris got his first guitar at age 2 and was fascinated to see how it worked. By age 20 he had opened his first custom guitar-making and repair shop in St. John's. Now he is trying to raise $3 million to establish a plant to make mass-market guitars.

5

ENTREPRENEURS IN *ACTION*

Sharing the Vision

Chris Griffiths of St. John's, Nfld. got his first electric guitar for Christmas at the age of 12. On Boxing Day he pulled it apart to see how it worked.

Griffiths' little experiment cost $200 to fix, but that investment paid off. Griffiths' interest in instruments landed him a job in a music store at age 16. But it was packing up damaged or broken guitars for shipment to Ontario that changed his life. "The bell went off," he says. "I wondered, if there's this much work going around, why isn't anyone here doing it?" In a vivid illustration of the entrepreneurial proverb, "Do what you love and the money will follow," Griffiths apprenticed at a "guitar hospital" in Michigan before opening his own custom guitar-making and repair shop four years ago at the age of 20.

Of course, it wasn't easy. Told he needed a business plan, Griffiths wrote a five-page essay. ("People kind of giggled at it," he says now.) With the help of St. John's Y Enterprise Centre, he spent five months working on a 75-page plan that spelled out the full opportunity—and his need for $40,000 in capital. A Youth Ventures Loan provided $30,000, but the Atlantic Canada Opportunities Agency turned him down twice for the rest. Finally Griffiths wrote his MP and Newfoundland power broker John Crosbie, outlining his experiences with ACOA. He never heard from either politician, but the federal agency soon called to say it had reviewed his application and would cough up $10,000.

When Griffiths opened his shop in a strip mall in May 1993, he quickly proved his instincts right. Newfoundlanders flocked to buy his $2,000 to $3,000 custom guitars, or to have their own models repaired on-site. Griffiths hired his first employee after just three weeks

—about 11 months earlier than forecast.

At first Griffiths worked 90-hour weeks without pay, but today Griffiths Guitar Works is a clear winner. It boasts 2,000 square feet, seven employees and sales of about $250,000. Griffiths, who stopped making guitars himself two years ago, is now investing his newfound profits into his own real-estate management company. Plus, he's just opened a rock-and-roll music camp for Atlantic Canada youth which he hopes will become a year-round venture—and of course groom new customers.

But now Griffiths is looking at his biggest deal yet: establishing a new plant to make mass-market guitars. He has visited trade shows and factories to study new processes for revolutionizing the low-tech industry. "We will be building guitars like nobody else in the world," he says. Using robotics and CAD/CAM technology, "we'll be able to do it faster, we'll offer higher standards of raw materials, and we'll cost less than imported models." This time his business plan is 800 pages long. Griffiths has circulated it among venture capitalists "from here to Toronto" to try to obtain $3 million in backing. With the new teens of the baby-boomer "echo" generation boosting demand for guitars again, he's confident the money will come, even if it means giving up sole ownership of the venture. As Griffiths concludes, with the flair of a songwriter and the maturity of a veteran entrepreneur: "The more you share your vision, the better chance you have of seeing it come true."

Source: Rick Spence, "Sharing the Vision," *PROFIT: The Magazine for Canadian Entrepreneurs,* September, 1997, pp 48-49. Reprinted with permission.

Many such ventures do very well, but there can be considerable conflict. Hobbies are typically activities that you and others are prepared to do at your own expense. This can exert downward pressure on the likely profitability of your business. As a result, margins are quite low in such areas as the production of arts and crafts, small-scale farming, trading in stamps, coins, and other collectibles, antique automobile restorations, and similar hobby-based operations.

Personal Observation

For many people personal observation is the most practical way of identifying a business idea. Personal observations may arise from either casual observation or deliberate search.

Casual Observation

Often, ideas for a new product or service result from chance observation of daily living situations. This commonly occurs when people travel and observe product or service concepts being provided that are not yet available in the United States, Canada, or, perhaps, the person's local market area.

Restaurant themes and concepts, such as Thai, Mexican, health food, and salads, typically are only established in most cities after they have proven to be successful somewhere else. Sporting trends, such as sailboarding and rollerblading, and fashion colours and styles are also usually imported from outside the country.

For this type of observation to yield results, you have to recognize the need for a new type of product or service offering and then work out some kind of solution. Myles Kraut, for example, recognized that animals were reacting negatively to preservatives in dog food (Entrepreneurs in Action #6). He also recognized that the treats used as rewards in the training of dogs were moist products that stained the clothes of the dog owners and were high in fat content. His Dr. Dean's line of dog treats and snacks have no moisture, so they overcome this problem and are healthier for animals as well.

6

ENTREPRENEURS IN ACTION

He's a Dog's Best Friend

After years of struggling to start a business, a young Winnipeg entrepreneur is seeing his company go to the dogs — and he's loving it.

Myles Kraut, 24, is the sole proprietor of Dr. Dean's, a line of dog snacks and treats made in Manitoba and sold across Canada. Kraut says that after a long start-up process, he's finally seeing results.

"We can't make them fast enough," Kraut says of the dog treats.

Dr. Dean's (Dean is Kraut's middle name) are available in 475 pet stores nationwide, including Best West stores and Petland.

More to the point, Kraut is doing something he enjoys. He's his own boss, works hours he wants to work and is in control of his own destiny. It's a dog-eat-dog world, and he's loving it.

He's not the only one. A recent Angus Reid poll for the Royal Bank shows that one-third of

young Canadians want to be entrepreneurs. The Royal Bank report shows that the top career choice of Canadians between the ages of 18 and 35 is entrepreneur.

Kraut says he wasn't sure what he wanted. He drifted a bit in school, never completing his science degree at the University of Winnipeg. He jokes that he's the only one in his family, including in-laws, who hasn't finished university.

But the business world is no stranger to him. His dad owns the Charleswood Department Store, his older brother co-owns the auto store Canadian Super Shop, and his mom owns a children's clothing store in Corydon Village mall.

Kraut didn't know what he wanted, but he knew what he didn't want — he didn't want to work in retail.

He says that three years ago, he spent a horrible six months struggling with what he was going to do. Sleeping in until noon and going to bed at 4 a.m. were commonplace.

Then it came to him.

"I don't want this to sound cheesy, but I truly love animals," Kraut says.

He's always had a dog and loved them. The family had two terriers, and one had to be put down because of a seemingly incurable skin condition. It was only after that dog was gone that they discovered the animals were reacting to preservatives in dog food.

That episode launched Kraut into an eight-month investigation of the world of pet food and accessories marketing. He quickly discovered that making food was too capital intensive. So he did his own market research — on foot.

"I went in store after store and found out what products were made that had the biggest margins on them," he recalls. "I never thought anything would come of it."

But he quickly discovered that the market didn't have an all-natural dog treat in a dry formula.

Specifically, Kraut went after the rewards market — the treats used to train dogs. He says the only things out there were moist products that stained the pockets of dog owners and were high in fat content.

When he knew he had an idea that worked, Kraut sold his car for his initial capital. He then took some chicken liver he bought at Safeway and other ingredients up to the Swiss Alex Bakery in Gimli.

Kraut says that after trial and error, they came up with a dried dog treat. Because there's no moisture, the treats have a long shelf life and dogs also crave them. He says garlic is the key — dogs love the smell and taste, and Kraut says it kills germs that cause doggy breath. Honest.

He sold his house on Borebank Street to move into his parents' basement when the business became a reality.

Today, he has the packaging made in Vancouver, a national distributor in Toronto and his manufacturer is still the Swiss Alex Bakery. The Dr. Dean's web site is (www.drdean.com).

Kraut is rarely home. He says he's in Winnipeg five days a month. The rest of the time he's on the road with sales reps in pet stores across Canada. He also jets down to the United States frequently. Next week he's at a trade show in Chicago.

And he's making money. He's repaid his family the money they lent him to get the business going, and now sales are picking up in pet stores.

"Our next step is the U.S. Canada has 1,500 stores. Chicago alone has 1,500 stores," he says.

As for picking his hours, well, Kraut just laughs. He's working hard to get his business established, but he's not too concerned now.

"This is the time you work — when you're 24 or 25."

Source: Paul McKie, "He's A Dog's Best Friend," *Winnipeg Free Press,* October 3, 1997, pp. B8-B9. © Winnipeg Free Press. Reprinted with permission.

Similarly, Brian Scudamore was astute enough to recognize that trash collection could be a growth industry (Entrepreneurs in Action #7). While still a teenager he printed up cards and flyers and set up his own garbage disposal firm with a beat-up pickup truck. Since 1993 his business has grown to nearly $1.3 million in sales and he is looking to franchise his idea to other major centres across North America.

While Doug Palmer and Bryce Kumka have yet to commercially produce and sell a single unit of the Darting Lamp, they feel they are onto something special because of the tremendous increase in the number of people outfitting their homes with indoor recreation equipment (Entrepreneurs in Action #8). With his experience in the lighting industry, Palmer came up with the idea for a two-metre tall halogen floor lamp, complete with a professional quality dart board attached at regulation height. He felt the Darting Lamp could be the first indoor activity purchase for apartment dwellers or people looking to start a games room in their home without damaging the walls.

The observation may emerge from your own experience in the marketplace, be expressed by someone else who has recognized some opportunity or problem, or be the result of observing the behaviour of other people. Regardless of its source, this type of simple observation can be the source of numerous excellent new business ideas.

7

ENTREPRENEURS IN ACTION

Dial 1-800-GOT-JUNK

One person's trash is another one's treasure. That adage proved true for Brian Scudamore. The Vancouver native has developed a Midas touch when it comes to junk, turning a summer job into a million-dollar business.

Scudamore was just 18 when he was struck by the sight of a truck hauling away rubbish. "I've always been entrepreneurial," says Scudamore. "It just struck me that [trash collection] could be a growth industry." He quickly printed up cards and flyers and with a beat-up $700 pickup truck launched his own garbage-disposal firm, The Rubbish Boys. Despite the name, it was actually a one-man show that Scudamore ran during his summers off from university. It wasn't until 1993 that Scudamore went at it full-time. Since then, it's been full speed ahead. With 1998 sales of nearly $1.3 million, revenues have grown 1,169% from 1993.

The move into garbage disposal proved prescient, as Vancouver, like many other North American cities, has passed regulations that allow residents to turf just two bags of trash per week — forcing them to look for other alternatives when tackling big jobs such as renovations or yard work. From the get-go, Scudamore's plan was to differentiate himself from competitors by being more, well, professional. "Service standards were

FERRY ZAVITZ

missing," he says, "and the industry is notorious for people charging whatever they like. If you've got a Jag in the driveway, you'll pay more." Instead Scudamore — who changed the company name in 1998 to 1-800-GOT-JUNK? — puts a premium on service: he offers shiny trucks, uniformed drivers and a printed, up-front price list. Appointments are scheduled by a central office, and staff telephone customers for comments on their service. "Our approach really is different," he says, "and we get a lot of positive feedback about it."

Now Scudamore is taking that good will further afield. "We're planning to grow faster than we've grown," he says. He recently sold franchises in Seattle, Portland and Toronto. "We're expanding with other people and with other people's money," says Scudamore. "I believe that franchise owners have more of a drive to succeed than a corporate office does." Franchising is also a quick route to rapid growth, he says. "There are 30 major centres in North America that we want to be in by 2003 — and they are all markets that are larger than Vancouver." And that's not trash talk.

Source: Hilary Davidson, "5 Entrepreneurs You Need to Know," *PROFIT: The Magazine for Canadian Entrepreneurs,* June, 1999, pp. 91-92. Reprinted with permission.

Deliberate Search

While deliberate search may seem to be the most rational way of finding viable business ideas, in fact most new ventures do not start in this manner. The majority of business start-ups arise almost incidentally from events relating to work or everyday life. However, this approach should not be completely ignored, as it can be fruitful if you are committed to investigating the possibilities of starting a new business but lack the seed of any real, likely idea. A deliberate search process can be initiated by consulting the following sources:

8

ENTREPRENEURS IN *ACTION*

Scoring a Bull's Eye

Two local student entrepreneurs are hoping they've hit a bull's-eye with their award-winning invention — a darting lamp.

No, it doesn't zip around the room while you're trying to read. Instead, the two-metre tall halogen floor lamp — complete with a dart board attached at regulation playing height — could be the first indoor activity purchase for apartment dwellers or people looking to start a games room in their house.

KEN GIGLIOTTI/WINNIPEG FREE PRESS

"People living in apartments can't have a pool table, but our lamp gives them an opportunity to have a piece of indoor activity equipment," said Doug Palmer, a 23-year-old commerce student at the University of Manitoba and the product's inventor.

Palmer and his partner, Bryce Kumka, returned earlier this week from the Enterprise Creation Competition at Miami University in Oxford, Ohio, where they beat out 27 students from some of the finest entrepreneurial business schools in North America, including Loyola Marymount and Purdue.

Looked upon by many as a game played in a basement or as pub recreation over a few pints, the darts industry is surprisingly large. In 1996, there were more than 21 million dart players in North America, including two million in Canada, who spent $223 million on darts, boards, cabinets, and the most common items, replacement flights and shafts.

Joel Cutts, manager of Dufferin Game Room Store in St. James, said darts is one of their core products that has continued to grow in popularity.

"Darts, like pool, has a good following. It's something that once you start playing, you usually play it for a long time." Cutts said.

Many darters also play in leagues organized by local pubs and legions. Jay Khanuja, owner of the King's Head Pub Club, said there are 24 eight-member teams in town. And if you drop by any number of pubs on a Wednesday night, you'll find the area around the dart boards dominated by dozens of players — many wearing team uniforms — and curious onlookers.

But even on other nights, open boards are a rarity. Khanuja said 40 regulars come out to darts night each Thursday, and many weekend pub crawlers play a game or two, still looking for their first "treble 20" (three darts in the triple 20 area scoring the board maximum of 180).

"One of the biggest reasons darts is so popular is it's free," Khanuja said.

Palmer came up with the darting lamp idea last summer when brainstorming for his upcoming New Venture Analysis course. He said that after six years of working for Robinson Lighting, he noticed an increase in the number of people outfitting their homes with indoor recreation equipment.

"I thought, 'Could I put a dart board on a lamp?' No, I couldn't. Then I thought maybe I could and I called Bryce. It was 4 a.m. and he said I was crazy," Palmer said.

Their inspiration certainly didn't come from their own darting prowess, Kumka said.

"We're both very casual dart players. We like to play but neither of us is very good," he said.

Like many other crazy ideas, the darting lamp has the potential for success. The pair split a $7,500 U.S. cash prize and took home a computer each for winning the competition and they've also laid down the groundwork for the darting lamp's future. Kumka said Robinson Lighting has agreed to buy 25 and the daring duo hope to add a few more retailers this summer. The 90-pound lamps will retail for $349 and if all goes according to their business plan, stores across North America will be stocked by the fall in time for the Christmas rush. Palmer said they hope to have annual sales of 12,000 units within a few years.

Source: Geoff Kirbyson, "Students Score A Bull's-Eye," *Winnipeg Free Press*, March 24, 1999. © Winnipeg Free Press. Reprinted with permission.

Publications

Reading business publications and other printed sources such as newspapers, specialty magazines, newsletters, and trade publications can provide ideas that might stimulate your entrepreneurial thinking. Some of the more important of these sources are listed below.

Newspapers and Magazines   The *Wall Street Journal* (www.wsj.com), *The Globe and Mail* (www.theglobeandmail.com) and *The National Post* (www.nationalpost.com) offer business and classified sections which provide a listing or make other reference to available small-business opportunities. A number of Canadian magazines such as Canadian Business (*www.canadianbusiness.com*), *PROFIT: The Magazine for Canadian Entrepreneurs* (www.profitguide.com/main.asp), and *The Financial Post Magazine* (www.canoe.ca/FP/home.html), and U.S. publications such as *Inc.* (www.inc.com), *Success* (www.SuccessMagazine.com), *Entrepreneur* (www.entrepreneurmag.com), and *Fortune* (www.pathfinder.com/fortune) provide further descriptions of a range of business possibilities.

Newsletters   Thousands of newsletters are available covering almost every conceivable subject. The information they contain is current and specialized, and can provide invaluable access to opportunities in any field. For further information, contact the reference librarian at your public library, and ask for the *National Directory of Newsletters and Reporting Services* (Gale Research Company, www.gale.com). It lists every major publication.

Trade Publications   A list of available trade publications can be obtained from *Standard Rate and Data Service* (www.srds.com), *Canadian Advertising Rates and Data* (www.cardmedia.com), or similar publications available in most libraries. Trade magazines are usually the first to publicize a new product. In many cases the manufacturer is looking for help in distributing a new line. The ads will also provide information about potential competitors and their products. These trade publications are some of the best sources of data about a specific industry, and frequently print market surveys, forecasts, and articles on needs the industry may have. All this information can serve as a stimulating source of ideas.

Inventors' Shows, Trade Shows, and Conventions

Inventors' Shows   These shows provide inventors and manufacturers with a place to meet to discuss potential products for the marketplace. There are major inventors' shows held annually in the larger cities throughout Canada and the U.S. Information on upcoming shows may be available from the Chamber of Commerce in these cities or from the Office of Inventions and Innovations, National Bureau of Standards, Washington, D.C. 20234, who can provide a list of the major shows held in the U.S.

Trade Shows   Shows covering the industry you want to enter can also be an excellent way to examine the products and services of many of your potential competitors. It can also be a way for you to meet distributors and sales representatives, learn of product and market trends, and identify potential products or services for your venture. Trade shows usually take place several times a year, in various locations. You will find trade show information in the trade magazines servicing your particular field or industry, or you may refer to the following sources:

- *Trade Shows & Exhibits Schedule, Successful Meetings Magazine*, Bill Communications, Inc., 633 Third Avenue, New York, NY 10017, (www.billcom.com). This annual directory with a mid-year supplement lists national and local trade show events taking place throughout the U.S. and Canada.
- *Trade Shows Worldwide*, Gale Research Company, (www.gale.com).

Conventions   Fairs or conventions are also an excellent place to stimulate your creative thinking. At a convention you are exposed to panels, speakers, films, and exhibitions. You also have an opportunity to exchange ideas with other people attending. Information on conventions and meetings scheduled to take place around the world can be obtained from:

- *Directory of Conventions, Successful Meetings Magazine*, Bill Communications, Inc., 633 Third Avenue, New York, NY 10017 (www.billcom.com)

Patent Brokers and Product Licensing Information Services

An excellent way to obtain information about the vast number of new product ideas available from inventors, corporations, or universities is to subscribe to a service that periodically publishes data on products offered for licensing. Licensing means renting the right to manufacture or distribute a product within agreed rules or guidelines. For example, you might purchase the right to manufacture T-shirts and sweaters with the logo of Batman, Dilbert, or other popular fictional characters, or use the trademark of a popular product such as Labatt's or Coca-Cola on similar apparel. The owner of the licence retains ownership and receives a royalty or fixed fee from you as the licensee. Here are some of the information services you can contact to locate product or service licensing opportunities:

National Technology Index
Industry Canada
Innovation and Policy Branch
C.D. Howe Building
235 Queen Street
Ottawa,Ontario K1A 0H5
(strategis.ic.gc.ca/sc.inov/nti/endoc/search.html)

Government Inventions Available for Licensing
National Technical Information Service (NTIS)
U.S. Department of Commerce
Springfield, VA 22161
(www.ntis.gov)

Also:
The World Bank of Licensable Technology available through
The Canadian Innovation Network
Waterloo, Ontario
(www.innovationcentre.cal)

The Canadian Intellectual Property Office administers the Canadian Patent Database (patents1.ic.gc.ca) as one vehicle for inventors and entrepreneurs to get together. This database includes the full content of all patent files including an indication of which patent holders wish to make their patents available for sale or licensing. For more information, contact:

Canadian Intellectual Property Office
Place du Portage I
50 Victoria Street
Hull, Quebec K1A 0C9
(cipo.gc.ca)

Friends, Acquaintances, and Other Social Contacts

Discussions with those you know should not be overlooked as a source of insight into needs that might be fulfilled by a new venture. Comments such "wouldn't it be nice if someone came up with something to do away with …" or "what this place needs is …" and other complaints and observations can provide a number of potential ideas.

Federal and Provincial Government Agencies and Departments

Industry Canada, the provincial departments of economic development; the Business Development Bank (BDC); university entrepreneurship centres; small-business development centres; community colleges and various other federal and provincial government agencies are all in the business of helping entrepreneurs by means of business management seminars and courses, advice, information, and other assistance. See the listing of Some Useful Contacts in the back of the book. You can also get feedback on the viability of your business idea, or even suggestions. The cost in most cases is nominal.

Numerous other government agencies, such as the Canada Business Services Centres of Industry Canada (www.cbsc.org) also have publications and resources available to stimulate ideas for new business opportunities. Your public library can provide you with further information on all the government departments relevant to your area of interest. It is possible to get your name on mailing lists for free material, or even a government source list so that others can find out about goods or services that you may want to provide.

Use Creative Thinking

Tremendous opportunities can materialize from the simple exchange of ideas among a number of people. There are a variety of analytical techniques and creative thinking concepts that can be used to facilitate this exchange. They help to generate and subjectively evaluate a number of prospective new business opportunities. These include such approaches as the use of decision trees, force field analysis, PMI — Plus/Minus/Interesting assessment — and similar concepts (see www.mindtools.com/page2.html). Perhaps the most popular approach used for this purpose is "brainstorming."

Brainstorming is a method for developing creative solutions to problems. It works by having a group of people focus on a single problem and coming up with as many deliberately unusual solutions as possible. The idea is to push the ideas as far as possible in order to come up with distinctly creative solutions. During a brainstorming session there is no criticism of the ideas that are being put forward—the concept is to open up as many ideas as possible, and break down any previously held preconceptions about the limits of the problem. Once this has been done the results of the brainstorming session can be explored and evaluated using further brainstorming or other analytical techniques.

Group brainstorming requires a leader to take control of the session, encourage participation by all members and keep the dialogue focussed on the problem to be resolved. It is helpful if participants come from a diverse range of backgrounds and experiences, as this tends to stimulate many more creative ideas. A brainstorming session should be fun as the group comes up with as many ideas as possible from the very practical to the wildly impossible, without criticism or evaluation during the actual session.

Here is an example of a modified brainstorming exercise that you could use to help identify opportunities you might choose to develop for a new business.

A Four-Step Process:

1. Meet with someone you trust (a close friend, relation, or other person) for one hour. With this individual discuss your strengths, weaknesses, personal beliefs, values and similar topics.

In other words, focus on what you enjoy doing because you do it well (jobs, hobbies, sports, pastimes, etc.) and where your limits are in terms of interests, ethics, capabilities.

2. After considering your strengths and weaknesses, pick the activity (job, hobby, etc.) which you enjoy the most. Think of a number of problem areas that affect you when you engage in that activity. Then meet with a group of personal acquaintances (3-5) and actively brainstorm a number of potential products or services that could solve those problems (no criticism or negative comments). In an hour you should be able to come up with 80-100 potential product/service ideas.

3. Take this list of potential ideas back to the same person you met with in (1). Reflect back on what you previously identified as your strengths and weaknesses and use that information to develop a framework to narrow the 80-100 ideas down to what you think are the *five* best new business ideas for you.

4. By yourself, take the five ideas and refine them down to the *one* that you feel relates most closely to your individual interests. Answer the following questions about that top idea:

    - Why did you select it?
    - Where did the idea come from?
    - What are the principal characteristics or attributes of the idea?
    - In what context did it come up during the brainstorming session?
    - What is your ability to carry out the idea?
    - What resources would you need to capitalize on the idea?
    - How profitable is a business venture based on the idea likely to be?
    - Who else might you need to involve?
    - What do you feel is the success potential of the idea you have proposed on a scale of 1 to 5 (with 5 being a very profitable venture)?[2]

The range of sources discussed here is certainly not exhaustive. Through careful observation, enthusiastic inquiry, and systematic searching, it is possible to uncover a number of areas of opportunity.

As you go about this kind of search it is important to write down your ideas as they come to mind. If you don't, a thought that might have changed your life may be lost forever.

Areas of Future Opportunity

In searching for a unique business idea the best thing to keep in mind is the dynamic changes taking place within our society, our economy, and our everyday way of doing things. These changes are usually difficult to get a handle on, and it is hard to understand their implications for new business possibilities, but they represent the principal areas of opportunity available today. If you think about it for a minute, most of the major growth areas in business today — such as computers and information technology; cable television systems; fast food; a wide range of personal services; and direct selling by mail, telephone, and television — did not even exist just a few short years ago. But now they are so commonplace we take them for granted. Getting information on emerging trends and assessing their implications for various business situations can be a major road to significant business success.

What can we expect in the future? No one has a crystal ball that can predict these changes with 100 percent accuracy, but many books and business publications provide projections of future trends and changes that could be useful to the insightful observer. For instance, Faith

---

[2] I would like to thank Vance Gough of the University of Calgary for permission to include this exercise.

Popcorn, the consumer trend diva who first labelled the 'cocooning' trend back in the early 1980s, predicted the following up-and-coming phenomena at a "The Power of Women" conference in Toronto:

- **Clanning.** The aftermath of "cocooning" where consumers may start coming out of their homes and start interacting again but they will still be more comfortable with people and groups most like themselves.

- **AtmosFEAR.** Consumers will be increasingly wary of the possibility of polluted water, contaminated air and tainted food. Fear of tap water alone, says Popcorn, has made bottled water a billion-dollar industry in North America.

- **Egonomics.** Consumers crave to be recognized as individuals. The depersonalization of society will create opportunities not only for improved customer service, but also for new industries that offer "ultra-customization" of products and services to the specific needs of individual customers.

- **Be Alive.** People don't just want to live longer, says Popcorn. They want to live better. The quest for wellness will fuel a boom in "foodaceuticals" (food as medicine), as well as genetic engineering and even better pet care.

- **Anchoring.** Popcorn sees a return to ethics and spirituality as people wonder what they're living longer for. In particular, she says, they will increasingly want to know more about the ethics and motives of the companies they do business with.

- **EVEolution.** The increasing clout of woman as consumers and business people means there will be more and more recognition of the need to market directly to them.[3]

The kind of social changes mentioned by Popcorn help define the future orientation of our society and can all spell potential opportunity for an aggressive entrepreneur.

In a similar vein, Canadian Shirley Roberts, the author of *Harness the Future: The Nine Keys to Emerging Consumer Behaviour*, says that the future will be bright for those entrepreneurial companies that move first out of the gate just as demand starts to rise for products and services to meet consumer's changing needs. That, she says, means figuring out tomorrow's buyers today.

Predicting consumer demand, Roberts feels lies in understanding the nine drivers of consumer behaviour:

Demographics
The economy
Technology
Globalization
Government
Environmental issues
Wellness
The retail environment
The consumer psyche[4]

For example, rising personal health concerns as reflected in the "Be Alive" trend mentioned by Popcorn means future consumers will take a more proactive approach to maintaining their personal wellness. In addition, trends like increasing globalization are exposing more people to products and cultures, and changing their tastes as a result.

---

[3] Based on "Faith Popcorn's Top Trends", *PROFITeer, The Online Newsletter for Canadian Entrepreneurs,* January 25, 1999, (www.profitguidc.com/profiteer)

[4] As reported in "Know Thy Next Customer," *PROFIT*, December-January, 1999, pp. 40.

Any one of these trends could represent an area of significant opportunity for an observant individual. Keeping on top of these shifts can provide the inspiration for many significant new business opportunities. As the futurist John Naisbitt has said, "trends, like horses, are easier to ride in the direction they are going."

Some Specific Ideas and Concepts for the New Millennium

In view of all these evident trends a number of specific business ideas are expected to do well in the marketplace of the future. Roberts, for example, provides a list of her best businesses for beyond the year 2000:

1. Self-diagnostic medical tools
2. Affordable organic foods
3. Educational books, videos and CD-ROMs
4. Technology-training centres
5. Customized information services
6. Anti-aging cosmetics
7. Pet-related products and services
8. Financial services tailored to women
9. Activewear for aging adults
10. Home-safety devices[5]

The list that follows will expand upon some of the possible implications of these trends and give you some idea of specific businesses they indicate should be potential opportunities. The list is by no means complete, but it will give you a few things to think about.

Biotechnology will become a significant growth area as we expand our knowledge of genetic engineering. The world population is exploding and feeding these additional people with our existing land base will require biotechnological intervention. There will be many business opportunities in agriculture, landscaping and other food-related industries. Biotechnology will also come into play in products to extend and improve the quality of human life. Possible new venture opportunities include:

- Blood tests to screen for genetic diseases
- Genetic engineering and the development of alternative medicines
- Bionic parts and artificial replacement organs
- DNA modifications to improve disease resistance or increase plant and animal yields
- Implantable microchips in animals

The Internet is growing explosively and interest is likely to continue to be strong with the success of AMAZON.COM, eBAY.com, bid.com, Onsale.com, Yahoo, Excite, and other Internet based companies. More and more entrepreneurs are using the "Net" as an interactive communication tool to sell products and services worldwide. Online shopping is expected to reach $6.6 billion in 2000. New venture opportunities using the Net could include:

- Designing and maintaining web sites
- Internet marketing services
- Using the Net to sell small business equipment, health-related equipment and supplements, cosmetics and anti-aging products, home-delivered meals and specialty foods, gaming services

---

[5] As reported in "Know Thy Next Customer," *PROFIT*, December-January, 1999, pp. 40.

and related products, travel and leisure products and services, video games and multimedia programs, music, books and magazines and a wide range of specialty products that serve narrow markets.

Training and Professional Development is also an important growth area particularly in regards to corporate, consumer and computer training. The explosion in Internet usage, new technology and operating systems, and modified software programs will continue to fuel the need for training to keep computer skills current. In addition, more and more small businesses are becoming computerized and need the support. Consumers are also looking to renew and improve themselves, and seminars and other educational programs designed to facilitate this personal growth are likely to do well. Some specific training and development opportunities include:

- Customized on-site computer training and centralized computer training centres
- Image consultants
- Professional organizers
- Video conferencing specialists
- Programming consultants
- Personal financial planning programs
- Internet-based training and educational programs

Maintaining "Wellness" is an emerging theme that will create a growing demand for a variety of fitness and health-related products. People are focussing on experiencing a better quality of life by shaping up and healing their minds and bodies. New venture opportunities exist in the following areas:

- Healthier and organically-grown food products
- Alternative medicine and homeopathic remedies
- Spas and cosmetic surgery centres
- Holistic health clubs and fitness centres
- Holistic healing and the use of ancient remedies
- Stress relief programs
- Restaurants emphasizing low-fat and other types of "healthy" foods

Personal Indulgence is almost the opposite of the "wellness" trend with people wanting to reward themselves periodically with small, affordable luxuries. New venture opportunities here could include:

- Individual portions of gourmet foods
- Specialty ice cream and other exotic desserts
- Specialty coffee, tea, and wine shops
- Imported cigars, smoking rooms, or a cigar-of-the-month type of club
- Outlets for specialty breads, bagels, and other baked goods
- Exotic meats such as elk, wild boar, bison, ostrich, and venison
- Bed-and-breakfast places or small hotels with specialty services
- Designer clothes for children
- Aromatherapy

Children's products and services will increase in demand with an increasing birth rate due to the "echo" from the baby boom, two-income families and single-parent households trying to balance work and home. Young people, including teens and pre-teens, have also become a significant market in their own right, with considerable exposure to conventional media and billions of dollars of discretionary income of their own. In addition, parents and grandparents increasingly want their children and grandchildren to have "everything" and are prepared to pay for the "best." New business opportunities in this area include:

- Child-care centres and camps
- Juvenile safety products
- Fitness centres and play zones for kids
- Healthy food products for infants and children
- Home health care for newborns
- Designer clothing for children
- Educational toys, games, and puzzles
- Programs for children with learning disabilities
- Children's bookstores

Home health service and elder care will continue to be a rapidly growing market with the aging of the baby boom and the ever-increasing costs and declining quality of health care. Opportunities for businesses in this area include:

- Home health care providers such as physiotherapists, occupational therapists, and nursing assistants
- Door-to-door transportation services for the elderly
- Homemaking services
- Day-care centres for the elderly
- Seniors' travel clubs
- Independent, residential, and assisted-living centres
- Products and services for the physically challenged

Work-at-home products and services will grow in popularity as the stay-at-home-and-work trend continues to sweep the country. Increasing numbers of telecommuters from the corporate world and home-based entrepreneurs want to provide a comfortable, secure environment for themselves to work effectively from home. Opportunities for new business ventures include:

- Decorating and furnishing of home offices
- Home safety and protection devices
- Home-office furniture and technical equipment
- On-site equipment repair services
- Home delivery services for office equipment, furniture, and supplies

Pet care and pampering represents a significant market opportunity as well for specialized care products and services. Some opportunities for businesses here include:

- Pet day-care centres and hotels
- Pet snacks and treats
- Home grooming services for pets
- 24-hour veterinary care
- Entertainment products and videos for pets

- Baked products for dogs
- Pet furniture and clothing stores
- Restraining systems for pets

Retail boutiques with narrow sales niches will increase in number as the category killer, box stores, and discount department stores expand across the country and come to dominate most conventional retail markets like building materials, lawn and garden supplies, books, computers and office supplies, consumer electronics, food products, music, video rentals, and other categories. Opportunities for one-of-a-kind stores include:

- Second-hand goods
- Optometry
- Bakery cafés
- Specialty shoe stores
- Personal financial services
- Home decorating
- Birding
- Gardening centres
- Stress relief
- Paint-your-own pottery and similar craft stores
- Travel-related products and services
- Homeopathic remedies
- Micro-breweries

Personal services of all types will grow in popularity as people spend more time at work and have fewer leisure hours. As a result they will be willing to pay others to run their errands and handle many time-consuming home and family-related matters. These personal errand services could perform a variety of tasks such as grocery shopping, picking up laundry, theatre tickets, shoe repairs, and other items. They could also arrange for the repair and servicing of cars, taking care of pets, choosing gifts, consulting on the selection of clothes, and similar personal matters. Other opportunities in this area include:

- Personal concierge service
- Gift services
- Pick up and delivery service for guests and clients
- Rent-a-driver
- Rent-a-chef
- Personal escort service

DILBERT reprinted by permission of United Feature Syndicate, Inc.

These are just a few of the possibilities that are available to you for starting a business of your own. Becoming a successful entrepreneur means becoming a trend spotter so that you are aware of potential sources of opportunity. To this end you must be observant, listen to other people, and ask lots of questions. Keeping abreast of these changes will help you identify any number of prospective business opportunities.

Evaluating Your Ideas

Discovering ideas is only part of the process involved in starting a business. The ideas must be screened and evaluated, and a selection made of those that warrant further investigation. It is essential that you subject your ideas to this analysis to find the "fatal flaws" if any exist (and they often do). Otherwise, the marketplace will find them when it is too late and you have spent a great deal of time and money.

But how can you determine which ideas you should evaluate. Of the multitude of possible alternatives, which are likely to be best for you? Knowles and Bilyea suggest that you think of the process of selecting the right opportunity for you as a huge funnel equipped with a series of filters. You pour everything into this funnel — your vision, values, long-term goals, short-term objectives, personality, problems, etc. — and a valuable business idea drains out the bottom.[6] This opportunity selection process contains six steps:

1. Identify your business and personal objectives.
2. Learn more about your favourite industries.
3. Identify promising industry segments.
4. Identify problem areas and brainstorm solutions.
5. Compare possible solutions with your objectives and opportunities in the marketplace.
6. Focus on the most promising opportunities.

Step 1: Identify Your Business and Personal Goals

List your personal and business goals. What do you want from your business? Money? Personal fulfillment? Independence? To be your own boss? Freedom? Control over your own destiny? Think back to what stimulated your interest in thinking about going into a business of your own in the first place. List everything you would like to accomplish and what you expect your business to be able to provide.

At this stage it might help to meet with someone whom you trust — a close friend, relation, or other person — for an hour or so. With this individual you can discuss your strengths and weaknesses, goals, values, ethical standards and similar personal issues. They can help you focus your goals and refine your thinking in relation to what you enjoy doing, what you are good at, and where your limits are in terms of interests and capabilities.

Step 2: Research Your Favourite Industries

As you considered the variety of trends we discussed earlier in this Stage, there were undoubtedly a number of possibilities that captured your interest. Now you should explore a couple of these situations in more detail. These industries should be ones that interest you and about which you have some first-hand knowledge. They could be food service, travel, manufacturing, retailing, construction, or whatever.

---

[6] Ronald, A. Knowles and Cliff G. Bilyea, *Small Business: An Entrepreneur's Plan.* Third Canadian Edition, Harcourt Brace & Company, Canada, 1999, pp. 55.

After you have picked your industries, investigate all the information you can find about them from business publications, government agencies and departments, trade magazines, the Internet, and similar sources. The Industry Canada web site (strategis.ic.gc.ca) and online databases such as ABI/Inform and Canadian Business and Current Affairs (CBCA) available at your local university library can point you to hundreds of articles related to almost any field. Focus on such areas as the history of the business, the nature and degree of competition, recent industry trends and breakthroughs, number and distribution of customers, and similar topics. It will help to write a brief industry overview of each situation after you have completed your investigation.

Step 3: Identify Promising Industry Segments

With a thorough understanding of one or more industry situations you are now in a position to identify possible market segments where you think you could survive and prosper. Profile your typical target customer; a person or business who needs a particular product or service you could provide.

If you are looking at the consumer market, identify what this prospect will look like in terms of demographic factors such as age, sex, location, income, family size, education and so on, and in terms of psychographic and other factors such as interests, values, life-style, leisure activities, and buying patterns. If you are looking at a commercial/industrial market, use company size, industry, geographic location, number of employees, and so on.

Step 4: Identify Problem Areas and Brainstorm Solutions

Identify the problem areas for some of these groups of customers that you feel are currently being met effectively. What "gaps" are there in terms of the needs of these customers that you feel you can address. Get together with a group of people who know something about business and the industry. Try to actively brainstorm up a list of products and services that could represent potential ways to solve these problems. Keep your discussion positive. Let your imaginations roam. Don't be concerned with the merits or demerits of an idea at this stage. Just try to make note of as many potential ideas as you can. You should be able to come up with 80-100 or more prospective ideas in an hour.

Refine your list. Try to narrow it down to the five or ten best ideas for you based on your interests, goals and objectives, strengths and weaknesses, and available resources.

Step 5: Compare Possible Solutions With Your Objectives and Opportunities in the Marketplace

Richard Buskirk of the University of Southern California has designed a framework you can use to evaluate the pros and cons of your potential business ideas.[7] It is built around what he calls the "Ideal" or "Model" business. The framework contains 19 distinct factors that affect the chances of success for any new business. Very few ideas will conform precisely to the specifications of the model, but the more a business idea deviates from the "ideal," the more difficulties and greater risks you will encounter with that venture. Testing your concepts against the model will also help identify the areas in which you might expect to have difficulties with your business.

The model is presented in Table 3.1. Let us briefly discuss each of the factors listed.

Requires No Investment   If you don't have to put any money into your business, then you can't lose any if it fails. You only lose the time you have invested. The more money that must be committed to the venture, the larger the risk and the less attractive the business becomes. Some new businesses, such as fancy theme restaurants, may require so much initial capital there is really no way they can be financially profitable. Smart business people tend to avoid businesses that require a large investment of their own money.

---

[7] Richard Buskirk, *The Entrepreneur's Handbook* (Los Angeles: Robert Brian, Inc., 1985), pp. 41–45.

TABLE 3.1 CHARACTERISTICS OF THE "IDEAL" BUSINESS

- Requires no investment
- Has a recognized, measurable market
- A perceived need for the product or service
- A dependable source of supply for required inputs
- No government regulation
- Requires no labour force
- Provides 100 percent gross margin
- Buyers purchase frequently
- Receives favourable tax treatment
- Has a receptive, established distribution system
- Has great publicity value
- Customers pay in advance
- No risk of product liability
- No technical obsolescence
- No competition
- No fashion obsolescence
- No physical perishability
- Impervious to weather conditions
- Possesses some proprietary rights

Has a Recognized, Measurable Market   The ideal situation is to sell a product or service to a clearly recognized market that can be relied on to buy it. This may require doing a preliminary investigation of the market acceptance of your idea or concept. Look for some market confirmation of what you propose to offer before proceeding any further.

A Perceived Need for the Product or Service   Ideally, your intended customers should already perceive a need for what you intend to sell them. They should know they need your product or service now, thus simplifying your marketing efforts. If they don't recognize their need, you have to first persuade them they need the product and then convince them to buy it from you. Try to avoid products or services that require you to educate the market before you can make a sale.

A Dependable Source of Supply for Required Inputs   Make certain you can make or provide what it is you plan to sell. Many businesses have failed because they were unable to obtain essential raw materials or components under the terms they had originally planned. Sudden changes in price or availability of these key inputs can threaten the viability of your entire venture. Large corporations commonly try to directly control or negotiate long-term contracts to assure reliable and consistent supplies. You have to be just as concerned if there are only one or two sources for the materials you require.

No Government Regulation   The ideal business would not be impacted at all by government regulation. This is impossible in today's world but some industries are more subject to government involvement than others. Food, drugs, financial services, transportation, communications, etc. are all examples of businesses that require extensive government approval. If your business falls into this category, make sure you understand how government regulations will affect you in terms of time and money.

Requires No Labour Force   The ideal business would require no labour force. This is possible in one-person operations — the "one-man show." Once you hire an employee you have a lot of government paperwork to deal with relating to employment insurance, Canada Pension, and other legal requirements. You are also subject to a broad range of regulations concerning such things as occupational health and safety, human rights, and pay equity. Few small-business people enjoy dealing with these requirements, and they can be quite time-consuming. If your business demands the hiring of additional employees you must be prepared to take on the responsibility for managing these people effectively.

Provides 100 Percent Gross Margin While virtually no businesses provide a 100 percent gross margin, the idea is that the larger the gross margin, the better the business. Gross margin is what you have left after paying the *direct* material and labour costs for whatever it is you are selling. For example, say you are running an appliance repair business. A typical service call takes one hour, for which you charge the customer $50. However, this call costs you $15 in direct labour and $5 in parts and materials; therefore, your gross margin is $30, or 60 percent. Service industries like this generally have larger gross margins than manufacturing businesses.

In businesses with low gross margins, small errors in estimating costs or sales can quickly lead to losses. These businesses also tend to have a high breakeven point, making it very difficult to make a lot of money. High-margin businesses, on the other hand, can break even with very small sales volumes and generate profits very quickly once this volume of business is exceeded.

Buyers Purchase Frequently The ideal business would provide a product or service that customers purchase very frequently. This gives you more opportunities to sell to them. Frequent purchasing also reduces their risk in case your offering doesn't live up to their expectations. You are much more likely to try a new fast food restaurant that has opened in town than you are to purchase a new brand or type of washing machine, fax machine, stereo system, or other such item.

Receives Favourable Tax Treatment Firms in certain industries may receive tax incentives such as accelerated depreciation on capital assets, differential capital cost allowances, investment tax credits, or various other tax breaks. The ideal business will receive some sort of favourable or differential tax treatment. This sort of advantage can make your business more profitable and attractive to other investors should you require outside capital.

Has a Receptive, Established Distribution System Ideally, your business would sell to established middlemen and distributors who are eager to handle it. If you have to develop a new method of distribution or are unable to obtain access to the existing one, getting your product to market can be a long and costly process. If traditional wholesalers and retailers are not prepared to carry your line, achieving any reasonable level of market coverage can be extremely difficult.

Has Great Publicity Value Publicity in magazines, in newspapers, and on television has great promotional value, and what's more, it's free. If your offering is sufficiently exciting and news-worthy to grab people's attention, the resulting publicity may be sufficient to ensure a successful launch for your business. The publicity given to fashion concepts like Chip and Pepper Wetwear, the radio and television coverage of a business to clean up the "doggie doo" in one's backyard, and favourable reviews of local restaurants by newspaper food critics are all examples of tremendously helpful public notice of new products.

Customers Pay in Advance A major problem facing most new businesses is that of maintaining an adequate cash flow. Typically, small firms are chronically short of cash, the lifeblood they require to pay their employees, their suppliers, and the government on an ongoing basis. The ideal business would have customers who pay in advance. This is in fact the case for many small retail service firms, the direct mail industry, and manufacturers of some custom-made products. Businesses where customers pay in advance are usually easier to start, have smaller start-up capital requirements, and don't suffer the losses due to bad debts incurred on credit sales.

No Risk of Product Liability   Some products and services are automatically subject to high risk from product liability. Anything ingested by the customer, amusement facilities such as go-cart tracks and water slides, and many manufactured products which possibly could cause injury to the user — all are loaded with potential liability. Liability can occur in unexpected situations, such as the serious injury recently sustained by a golfer whose golf club shattered and impaled him in the chest.

Try to avoid such high-risk businesses, or take every precaution to reduce risk, and carry lots of insurance.

No Technical Obsolescence   The ideal product or service would not suffer from technical obsolescence. The shorter the product's expected technical life expectancy, the less desirable it is as an investment. Products like popcorn, shampoo, garden tools, and electric drills seem to have been with us for as long as most of us can remember. On the other hand, the CD player, videocassette recorder, and personal computer are of recent origin and are undergoing rapid technological transformation. Businesses built around these products are extremely risky for smaller firms with a very high probability of failure.

No Competition   Too much competition can be a problem, since aggressive price competitors can make it very difficult for you to turn a profit. Not having any competition can certainly make life much easier for a new small business. But if you should ever find yourself in this happy situation, you should ask yourself why. True, your offering may be so new to the marketplace that no other firms have had a chance to get established. But maybe it is just that other firms have already determined there really is no market for what you are planning to provide.

No Fashion Obsolescence   Fashion products usually have extremely short life cycles. You must be sure you can make your money before the cycle ends, or be prepared to offer an ongoing series of acceptable products season after season, if you hope to build your business into a sizeable enterprise. Fashion cycles exist not only for clothing and similar products but also for items like toys — witness what happened with the hula hoop, Wacky Wall Walker, Rubik's Cube, and Cabbage Patch dolls.

No Physical Perishability   Products with a short physical life have only a limited window available for their disposition. This applies not only to most food items but also to a wide variety of other goods such as photographic film. If your product is perishable, your business concept must include some method of selling your inventory quickly or a contingency plan to dispose of aged merchandise before it spoils.

Impervious to Weather Conditions   Some businesses are, by their very nature, at the mercy of the weather. If the weather is right for them, they prosper; if not, they may go broke. Pity the ski resort owner without any snow, the water slide operator with a year of unseasonably cold weather, the beach concession during a summer of constant rain, the market gardener in the midst of an unexpected drought. The ideal business would not be impacted by these unpredictable changes in the weather.

Possesses Some Proprietary Rights   The ideal business would possess significant proprietary rights that give it some unique characteristic and protection against competition. These rights can be in the form of registered patents, trademarks, copyrighted material, even protected trade secrets, licensing agreements that provide some sort of exclusive manufacturing arrangements, or perhaps rights for exclusive distribution of certain products in particular markets. Gendis Corporation, for example, was largely built on the rights to distribute first Papermate pens and then Sony products in Canada on an exclusive basis.

To summarize the characteristics of your business in terms of how well it fits with our "Model" business you might wish to complete Figure 3.1.

FIGURE 3.1 COMPARE YOUR IDEAS TO THE "IDEAL" BUSINESS

Directions: Evaluate your concept in comparison with a model business by indicating how well each of the ideal characteristics below applies to your concept. Use a scale from 1 to 10, where 1 means the ideal trait is not at all true for your concept, and 10 means it is perfectly true.

FIT WITH MODEL BUSINESS

No investment	1	2	3	4	5	6	7	8	9	10
Recognized, established market	1	2	3	4	5	6	7	8	9	10
Perceived need for product	1	2	3	4	5	6	7	8	9	10
Dependable source of input supply	1	2	3	4	5	6	7	8	9	10
No government regulation	1	2	3	4	5	6	7	8	9	10
No labour	1	2	3	4	5	6	7	8	9	10
100 percent gross margin	1	2	3	4	5	6	7	8	9	10
Buyers purchase frequently	1	2	3	4	5	6	7	8	9	10
Favourable tax treatment	1	2	3	4	5	6	7	8	9	10
Receptive, established distribution system	1	2	3	4	5	6	7	8	9	10
Business with great publicity value	1	2	3	4	5	6	7	8	9	10
Customers pay in advance	1	2	3	4	5	6	7	8	9	10
No product- or service-liability risk	1	2	3	4	5	6	7	8	9	10
No product obsolescence	1	2	3	4	5	6	7	8	9	10
No competition	1	2	3	4	5	6	7	8	9	10
No fashion obsolescence	1	2	3	4	5	6	7	8	9	10
No physical perishability	1	2	3	4	5	6	7	8	9	10
Impervious to weather	1	2	3	4	5	6	7	8	9	10
Proprietary rights	1	2	3	4	5	6	7	8	9	10

Total points = _____

160-190 = A concept; 130-159 = B; 110-129 = C; 80-109 = D; Below 80, drop concept.

After completing this evaluation, does it make sense to proceed with the venture? Explain your answer.

For a more formal evaluation of your invention or innovation, the Canadian Industrial Innovation Centre through the Waterloo Inventor's Assistance program will conduct a comprehensive Critical Factor Assessment to assist you in the product management decisions you must make regarding your idea. The fee for this service ranges for $245 to $595 depending on whether you are a small individual inventor or a large corporation. For more information, contact Canadian Innovation Centre, 156 Columbia Street West, Waterloo, Ontario, N2L 3L3, Phone 1-800-265-4559 or (519) 885-5870.

Step 6: Focus on the Most Promising Opportunities

Which of the ideas you have evaluated seems to be the best fit with the "Ideal" business and is most consistent with your goals and values? This is probably the one you should be looking to pursue. However, no matter how exhaustive your evaluation, there is no guarantee of success. The challenge is to do the best you can in conducting an assessment of each of your principal ideas, knowing that at some point you will have to make a decision with incomplete information and less than scientific accuracy. As a good friend of mine commented during a dinner speech not long ago, "Entrepreneurship is like bungee jumping. Both require an act of faith."

Deciding How to Proceed

Once satisfied you have identified an idea that represents a significant business opportunity, you must determine the best way to proceed. There are all sorts of *entry strategies* — ways people start new enterprises.

Reflecting on these alternatives and judging how they fit with your specific idea and your particular abilities and circumstances will enable you to turn them into real opportunities. No general rules have been developed to guarantee success, or even to indicate which concepts and strategies will work best in different situations; but being aware of the possibilities will give you a clearer picture of the job you need to do in order to succeed.

Buy a Business

One possibility is to find a business presently operating in your area of interest, buy it, and take over its operations. You may want to buy the business either because it is already quite successful but the current owners want to get out for some reason, or because the business is not doing very well under the current owners and you feel you can turn it around.

This can be a good entry strategy. A good deal of time and effort are involved in the startup phase of any business. This stage can be bypassed when you buy a going concern. You also acquire a location, customers, established trade relationships, and a number of other positive elements.

These advantages don't come for free, however. Buying an existing business may cost you more than getting into a similar business on your own. The current owner may expect to receive "goodwill" for certain assets already acquired or the effort devoted to the business so far. You may also inherit some problem, such as obsolete equipment, the bad image and reputation of the previous owners, or labour difficulties.

For a more complete discussion of this entry strategy refer to Stage Four of this book.

Acquire a Franchise

Another alternative is to buy the rights to operate a business that has been designed and developed by someone else, i.e., to acquire a *franchise*. Under a franchise agreement, an established company, the *franchisor*, with one or more successful businesses operating in other locations provides assistance to a new firm in breaking into the marketplace. In return, the new owner, or *franchisee*, pays a fee for the assistance, invests money to set up and operate the business, pays a percentage of sales as a royalty to the franchisor, and agrees to operate the business within the terms and conditions laid out in the franchise agreement.

The assistance provided by the franchisor can take many forms, such as:

- The right to use the franchisor's brand names and registered trademarks
- The right to sell products and services developed by the franchisor
- The right to use operating systems and procedures developed by the franchisor
- Training in how to run the business
- Plans for the layout of the business facilities and the provision of specialized equipment
- A regional or national advertising program
- Centralized purchasing and volume discounts
- Research and development support

While the failure rate of franchised businesses is reported to be lower than that for independently established firms, there are a number of disadvantages associated with the concept.

For more detailed information refer to Stage Five of this book.

Start a Business of Your Own

The third and probably most common means of getting into business for yourself is to start a business of your own from scratch. This is the route most frequently travelled by the true entrepreneur who wants a business that is really his or her own creation. Starting your own business can take many forms and involve a variety of entry strategies. While we are unable to discuss all the possibilities here in any detail, a few alternatives will be mentioned to get you thinking about their fit with your particular situation. Some of the possibilities available for you are:

a. Develop an entirely new product or service unlike anything else available in the market.

b. Acquire the rights to manufacture or sell someone else's product or use someone else's name or logo under licence. These rights could be exclusive to a product category, a geographic area, or a specific market.

c. Find a customer who wants to buy something. Then create a business to make that sale or serve that need.

d. Take a hobby and develop it into a business.

e. Develop a product or service similar to those currently on the market but which is more convenient, less expensive, safer, cleaner, faster, easier to use, lighter, stronger, more compact or has some other important, distinguishing attribute.

f. Add incremental value to a product or service already available by putting it through another production process, combining it with other products and services, or providing it as one element in a larger package.

g. Become an agent or distributor for products or services produced by someone else. These may be domestically produced or imported from other countries.

h. Open a trading house or become a selling agent for Canadian firms who may be interested in selling their products or services abroad.

i. Develop a consulting service or provide information to other people in a subject area you know very well.

j. Become a supplier to another producer or large institutional customer. Large organizations require an extensive range of raw materials, supplies and components to run their business. A small portion of their requirements could represent a significant volume of sales for you. This type of "outsourcing" is an excellent opportunity to pursue either through a contract or a strategic alliance with a larger organization.

k. Identify a situation where another firm has dropped what may be profitable products or product lines. They may have abandoned customer groups or market segments that are uneconomic for them to serve effectively but which may still be quite lucrative for a smaller company.

l. Borrow an idea from one industry or market and transfer it to another. A product or service that has been well accepted in one situation may well represent a substantial opportunity in other circumstances as well.

m. Look for opportunities to capitalize on special events and situations or unusual occurrences. You may be able to "piggyback" your business on these situations.

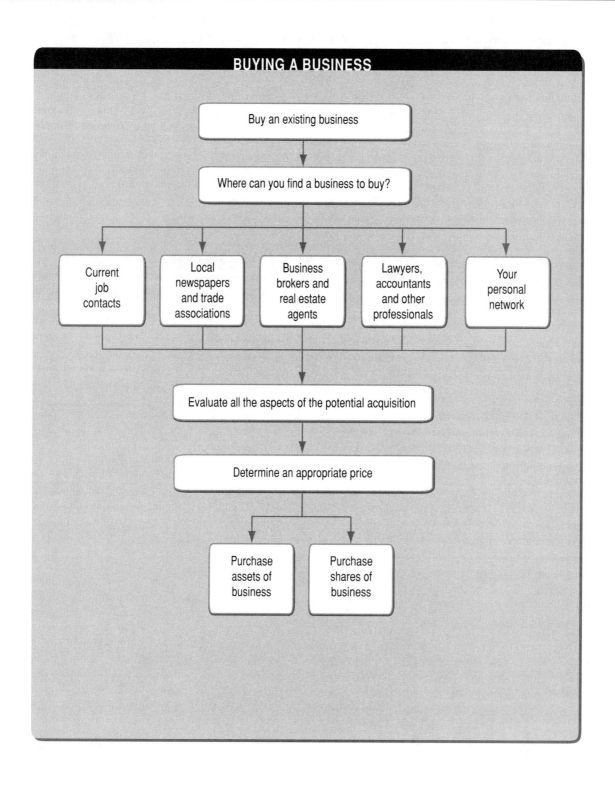

BUYING A BUSINESS

Buy an existing business

Where can you find a business to buy?

Current job contacts

Local newspapers and trade associations

Business brokers and real estate agents

Lawyers, accountants and other professionals

Your personal network

Evaluate all the aspects of the potential acquisition

Determine an appropriate price

Purchase assets of business

Purchase shares of business

Starting a New Business or Buying an Existing One

S tages Two and Three of this book have provided you with a means of evaluating your personal potential for an entrepreneurial career and a procedure for generating and evaluating the basic attractiveness of an idea upon which to base your own business. The obvious route to self-employment is to start a business of your own based on this idea. Another route which should be explored is that of buying an existing firm. For many people this may even be their preferred course of action. How do you decide which route to take?

Stage Four discusses the various aspects that should be evaluated in considering whether you should start a new business or buy an existing one.

How to Find the Right Business to Buy

Just finding a business to buy is easy. Dozens are listed every day in the "Business Opportunities" classified section of your local newspaper as well as the major business newspapers. However, what tends to be found in these classified sections are mostly hotel, motel, restaurant, and franchise propositions, which are largely high-risk, low-profit ventures generally unattractive to investors. Many of these are failing businesses that their current owners are trying to unload.

Seeking out a business acquisition to match your desires and experiences can be a very time-consuming and difficult process. Hundreds of businesses change hands every year, so it should be possible to find one that appeals to you if you are sufficiently determined and persistent. However, rather than being sold as a result of an advertisement in some newspaper, most businesses are sold to people who had some active business relationship with the company when it became available. It is usually not sufficient for an individual determined to acquire a business to sit and wait for the right opportunity to come along. One must go looking.

There are basically five different sources through which you may obtain information regarding attractive companies to buy:

1. The first is contact through your present business activity. Acquisition candidates may include present or potential competitors of your current employer; suppliers; customers; and perhaps even your present employer. These situations probably provide the best match

between your experience and strengths and the unique requirements of the business. Doug Morley, for example, was able to acquire the training arm of the company he was working for to run as an independent business (Entrepreneurs in Action #9).

2. A second source of leads results from direct independent contact. This may involve making "cold calls" on firms that look good or in which you have an interest; such firms may be identified from Chamber of Commerce directories and trade association membership lists. Another way is to place "Acquisition Wanted" advertisements in several major newspapers. In addition, despite what has been said earlier, you may wish to follow up on some advertisements in the "Business Opportunities" section of the major financial papers as mentioned previously. Every now and then an advertisement may appear in these sections which would warrant your consideration.

9 ENTREPRENEURS IN ACTION

Taking a Gamble on Education

A "company man" for almost 25 years, Doug Morley left the giant Honeywell Bull organization in 1990 when he saw middle-management jobs being squeezed by the recession.

An entrepreneur at heart, if not in practice, he bought the computer arm of Honeywell Bull, called the Institute for Computer Studies, a division he helped establish in the early 1980s to educate computer programmers and systems analysts.

In the past five years, the 53-year-old businessman has seen the institute grow from an organization that employed four trainers, taught 100 students a year and had revenue under $1 million, to one that has eight full-time instructors (plus 14 on contract), 350 students, a corporate education division, and annual revenue of about $7 million.

When he made the move, Morley remembers, some friends and colleagues questioned his decision. Under Honeywell Bull, the institute was basically a break-even operation, he says. "It did one thing: computer programming and systems analysis."

He was convinced there was room for growth in this fast-changing field. He also believed he could expand the business in a privately owned organization in ways he could not inside a large corporation.

First, Morley became the self-described chief cook and bottlewasher. "When we started I was the bookkeeper, janitor, I fixed the computers, ... I did everything." That helped chop about $100,000 off the overhead.

Hard work and quality training account for the rest of the institute's success, says Morley.

The Institute offers two courses: the career college geared at individuals who want to enhance their computer skills, and the other at corporations that want employees brought up to speed with advanced technology training.

Individuals pay about $8,800 for an intensive five-month program for which the institute is licensed by the Ontario Ministry of Education and Training to issue diplomas. Corporate education costs about $375 a day (usually for three- to five-day stints) in classes of eight people. (That compares with 30 students a class in the five-month course.)

Clients include Bell Canada, Ontario Hydro, and Bank of Montreal.

Morley says that, since opening the doors of his own business, he has not looked back. The timing, he adds, was just right.

"Large companies have changed in the past five years. When I left they were downsizing and everybody was scrambling.

"I just didn't want to be in that environment. So I decided to create an environment of my own, where I can do what I like in an organization with people I like."

Source: Excerpted from Gayle MacDonald, "Taking an Educated Gamble on Learning," *The Financial Post*, May 13, 1995, p. 34.

3. A third source of leads is middlemen such as business brokers and commercial real estate agents, professionals who work at bringing buyers and sellers together for a commission. The commission, typically payable by the seller, varies with the size of the deal but may be as high as 10 percent of the negotiated purchase price.

4. A fourth source is confidential advisors such as the loans officer at your bank, securities brokers, professional accountants, and lawyers. These advisors are often aware of what businesses are or may soon be available for sale. These sources may be difficult to use, however, because their information is shared mostly with other clients with whom they have developed some relationship over time. In many cases it may be necessary for you to have gained the confidence of the source over an extended period.

5. A fifth category includes a variety of different sources, such as venture capital firms, personal friends and acquaintances, and insurance brokers and agents. Essentially you should consider all individuals within your personal network of business contacts who may have access to information on attractive businesses for sale. This requires letting many of these people know about your search and the kind of business for which you are looking. You will need to keep reminding them about your interest, so that when the information comes along there is a good probability that it will make its way back to you. This was how Jim Iredale came to buy Ware House Hobbies (Entrepreneurs in Action #10).

Which of these lead sources you should utilize depends on many factors, such as the time you have available, whom you know within the business community, and the kind of company you are looking for. You should experiment with each of these sources and decide on the one or two that work best for you.

Important Factors to Consider

An essential requirement for the successful purchase of an existing firm is knowing how to assess and evaluate the operation. This is a complicated process, so you are well advised to have professionals such as an accountant, lawyer, or business evaluator assist you in negotiations when considering buying a business. As a potential buyer, you should also have a good understanding of the nature of the target business and the industry in which it competes to be able to assess its future performance, strengths, weaknesses, unexploited market opportunities, and other factors. Learning about a business after the fact can be a sure recipe for failure. A number of basic factors must be considered in determining the value of the business to you. Some of these are more complex and involved than others, but each one must be carefully investigated and studied. The most important of these concerns are discussed below.

Why Is the Business for Sale?

You should have this question in mind at all times during the evaluation of a possible acquisition. When the owner of a business decides to dispose of it, the reason presented to the public may be somewhat different from the facts of the situation. Owners may be quite willing to express some reasons for wanting to sell their businesses. They wish to retire, or they want to move to another city, or illness is pressuring the owner to leave the business. But there are a number of others that the current owner may not be quite so likely to volunteer. For example, they may be experiencing family pressures or marital problems, or perhaps they see a better business opportunity somewhere else. None of these reasons is cause for concern. But what if the company needs more financing than the owner can raise, or the current market for the firms' products is depressed? What if competitors are moving in with more effective products

10   ENTREPRENEURS IN *ACTION*

Model Railroader Makes Tracks

Jim Iredale is what you might call an entrepreneur by chance.

Three years ago, Iredale was holding down a regular nine-to-five job as a Winnipeg accountant/comptroller when the owner of a hobby shop he frequented — Ware House Hobbies — mentioned that he was looking for someone to buy his business.

Although he'd never harboured any entrepreneurial aspirations, the avid model railroader said he became intrigued by the notion of owning his own hobby shop.

He also realized that after 13 years as an accountant/comptroller, he was growing tired of just working with numbers. He wanted to work with people, too.

So after kicking the idea around for a couple of months, Iredale took the plunge. He quit his job, bought Ware House Hobbies, and he and his wife, Bev, became full-time small business operators.

"This was a situation that could not easily be repeated. It was the right opportunity at the right time."

Iredale said he's also surprised at how well the business has done.

"I thought I was buying a small, sleepy little business and that appealed to me," he said. "But it didn't turn out to be a slow, sleepy business at all. It's very busy."

So busy, in fact, that earlier this month he and Bev moved the store into larger quarters at 1870 Portage Ave. They've also hired a part-time helper.

The new store is twice the size of the old one, and gives them more room to display the more

than 5,000 model-railroad related items they keep in stock. It also gives them room to expand their mail-order operations and their doll houses and miniatures department.

On the mail-order front, Iredale said although the bulk of the orders come from rural Manitoba, Saskatchewan and northwestern Ontario, the shop also regularly receives orders from as far as B.C. and the Northwest Territories.

WAYNE GLOWACKI / WINNIPEG FREE PRESS

In fact, mail order sales now account for about 20 per cent of the shop's total sales, he added.

"I'm not making as much money as I used to make as an accountant," he conceded. "But there are other rewards. I like my lifestyle a lot better."

Source: Murray, McNeill, "Model Railroader Makes Tracks After Turning Hobby Into Career," *Winnipeg Free Press*, October 22, 1996, p. B1. © Winnipeg Free Press. Reprinted with permission.

or methods, or the current plant and equipment is worn out or obsolete, and the firm is no longer able to compete successfully? And what if the firm is having to contend with new government regulations that are creating some difficulties, or certain key employees are leaving the firm to set up a business of their own?

As you can see, there are many possible explanations of why a business may be up for sale. It is important that you retain a sceptical attitude, because behind each of the offered explanations may be a number of hidden ones. A sceptical attitude forces you to examine the situation from all angles and not necessarily accept everything you are told at face value. When the real reasons for selling are factors that may lead to the eventual collapse of the company, the present owner may be hard pressed to justify your purchase of the enterprise.

This is not to say that all businesses for sale are bad buys. Many companies are sold for very plausible and honest reasons. However, to keep from losing your shirt as well as your savings, a detailed evaluation should be conducted in order to determine the true character of the business.

Financial Factors

An analysis of the financial statements of the firm being sold, preferably with the help of a professional accountant, can help you assess its current health. You should not fall into the trap, however, of accepting these statements as the absolute truth. Though the statements may have been audited, many accounting techniques allow business owners to present a less than accurate picture of the financial situation of their company. You must be careful to ensure that the statements have not been biased in favour of the seller.

The most important financial factors are: (1) the trend in profits, (2) ratio analysis, (3) the value of the business' tangible assets, (4) the value of the business' intangible assets, and (5) cash flow. Let us discuss each in turn.

The Trend in Profits

A study of the records of the business will indicate whether sales volume and profits have been increasing or decreasing. If they have been going up, it is useful to know which departments within the business, or products within the firm's product line, have accounted for this increased sales and/or profitability.

If sales and profits are declining, the question may arise as to whether this is due to a failure by the firm to keep up with the competition, to its inability to adjust to changing circumstances, or perhaps to a lack of selling effort. Some experience with this type of business situation, plus a few questions directed to appropriate sources, may elicit an explanation.

Ratio Analysis

For every size and type of business there are certain financial ratios that have become generally accepted as reasonable for that kind of operation. Some information on these ratios is collected and published by trade organizations and associations such as the National Retail Hardware Association or the National Association of Retail Grocers. Ratios have been developed by various manufacturers for use by retailers that handle their product lines. Ratios for firms in a wide variety of retail, service, and manufacturing sectors are published by Dun & Bradstreet, Robert Morris and Associates, and other companies as well as Statistics Canada as part of its Small Business Data Program (SBDP). A study of the ratios of any business offered for sale, compared with standard ratios for that industry and size of company, will quickly indicate any discrepancies. These discrepancies may be due to mismanagement, neglect, carelessness, or perhaps even the lack of appropriate financing. The most frequently considered ratios are:

1. **Current ratio** The current ratio is defined as current assets divided by current liabilities. It is a measure of short-term solvency. Current assets normally include cash, marketable securities, accounts receivable, and inventories. Current liabilities consist of accounts payable, short-term notes payable, income taxes payable, and accrued expenses. A general rule of thumb is that a current ratio of 2:1 could be considered satisfactory for a typical manufacturing business. Service firms typically have a lower ratio, since they tend to have less inventory. However, as with any rule of thumb, extreme care should be exercised in evaluating this ratio. A cash-poor firm may be unable to pay its bills even though its ratio appears to be acceptable. On the other hand, many businesses with a current ratio less than the rule of thumb are quite solvent.

   Too high a ratio can indicate the business is not utilizing its cash and other liquid assets very efficiently; too low a ratio may raise questions about the firm's ability to meet its short-term obligations. In practice, however, what is more important than the absolute level of the current ratio is how the ratio is changing over time. An improving current ratio would tend to indicate improved short-term financial solvency unless the business is building up excessive or obsolete inventories.

$$\text{Current Ratio} = \frac{\text{Current Assets}}{\text{Current Liabilities}}$$

2. **Quick ratio** The quick ratio is obtained by dividing current liabilities into current assets minus inventories. The quick ratio can be used to estimate the ability of a firm to pay off its short-term obligations without having to sell its inventory. Inventories tend to lose their value faster than other assets if disposed of in a hurry. The quick ratio is probably a more valid test of the firm's ability to meet its current liabilities and pay its bills than the current ratio.

$$\text{Quick Ratio} = \frac{\text{Current Assets} - \text{Inventories}}{\text{Current Liabilities}}$$

3. **Debt to net worth** The debt-to-net-worth ratio indicates the firm's obligations to its creditors relative to the owner's level of investment in the business. Debt includes current liabilities, long-term loans, bonds, and deferred payments; the owner's net worth includes the value of common stock, preferred stock, any capital surplus, and retained earnings. Any outstanding shareholder's loans to the business should be considered part of the owner's net worth rather than as part of the business' present debt. This ratio is commonly used by creditors to assess the risk involved in lending to the firm. For example, if the debt-to-net-worth ratio is too high, say about 2:1 or 3:1, you may find it difficult to borrow additional funds for the business. Too low a ratio, on the other hand, may indicate the business is not being operated very efficiently and some profits are being sacrificed.

$$\text{Debt-to-Net-Worth Ratio} = \frac{\text{Total Outstanding Current and Long-Term Debt}}{\text{Net Worth}}$$

4. **Gross profit to sales** This ratio is determined by dividing gross profit or gross margin by net sales. Gross profit is determined by deducting costs of goods sold from net sales. No general guidelines exist for this ratio, or even among companies within an industry, as it can vary substantially.

$$\text{Gross-Profit-to-Sales Ratio} = \frac{\text{Gross Profit}}{\text{Net Sales}}$$

5. **Net profit to sales** This ratio is calculated by dividing net profit by net sales. You may use net profit either before or after taxes. As with the previous ratio, no general guidelines exist because of the variability among companies and industries. This figure can be as low as 1 percent or less for retail food stores and supermarkets, and as high as 8 or 9 percent in some service sectors.

However, you might evaluate how these ratios compare with those of other, similar companies or how they have been changing over time. If the ratio has recently been declining, why? This may indicate that the firm's costs have been increasing without a commensurate increase in prices, or perhaps competition may have increased and the company is forced to keep its prices low in order to compete.

$$\text{Net-Profit-to-Sales Ratio} = \frac{\text{Net Profit (Before or After Taxes)}}{\text{Net Sales}}$$

6. **Return on assets** This ratio is determined by dividing net profit (before or after taxes) by total assets. It is an excellent indicator of whether all the firm's assets are contributing to its profits and how effectively the assets are being employed — the real test of economic success or failure. Unfortunately, this is not an easy ratio to apply, because it is a measure of the movement of assets in relation to sales and profits during a particular period of time. The methods used by accountants to determine the level of total assets in the business can have a great effect on this ratio, and there are no real general or convenient rules of thumb for finding out whether the current return on assets is acceptable.

$$\text{Return on Assets} = \frac{\text{Net Profit (Before or After Taxes)}}{\text{Total Assets}}$$

7. **Sales to Inventory** This ratio is determined by dividing annual net sales by the average value of inventories. This does not indicate actual physical turnover since inventories are usually valued at cost while sales are based on selling prices, including markups, but this ratio does provide a reasonable yardstick for comparing stock-to-sales ratios of one business with another or with the average values for the industry.

$$\text{Sales to Inventory Ratio} = \frac{\text{Net Sales}}{(\text{Beginning Inventory} + \text{Ending Inventory}) / 2}$$

8. **Collection Period** To determine the average collection period for the business' outstanding accounts receivable, annual net sales are divided by 365 days to determine the business' average daily credit sales. These average daily credit sales are then divided into accounts receivable to obtain the average collection period. This ratio is helpful in assessing the collectability of any outstanding receivables.

$$\text{Average Collection Period} = \frac{\text{Accounts Receivable}}{\text{Net Sales} / 365}$$

All these ratios are calculated from information on the firm's income statement or balance sheet. Figures 4.1 and 4.2 illustrate simplified financial statements for a hypothetical firm called The Campbell Co. The value of each of these ratios for that company would be as follows:

1. Current ratio $= \dfrac{\$158,000}{\$95,000} = 1.66$

2. Quick ratio $= \dfrac{\$78,000}{\$95,000} = 0.82$

3. Debt to net worth $= \dfrac{\$135,000}{\$50,000} = 2.70$

4. Gross profit to sales $= \dfrac{\$133,000}{\$425,000} = 0.31 \text{ or } 31\%$

5. Net profit to sales $= \dfrac{\$13,500}{\$425,000} = 0.03 \text{ or } 3\%$

6. Return on assets $= \dfrac{\$13,500}{\$185,000} = 0.07 \text{ or } 7\%$

7. Sales to Inventory Ratio $= \dfrac{\$425{,}000}{(\$75{,}000 + 80{,}000)/2} = 5.48$

8. Average Collection Period $= \dfrac{\$53{,}000}{\$425{,}000/365} = 45$ days

It would appear from these ratios that The Campbell Co. is in reasonably sound shape financially. Its debt-to-net-worth ratio is within acceptable limits, and the business is quite solvent as indicated by the current and quick ratios. The other ratios are more difficult to evaluate, but they would be quite acceptable for firms in many lines of business.

FIGURE 4.1   EXAMPLE OF SIMPLIFIED BALANCE SHEET

THE CAMPBELL CO.
BALANCE SHEET
AS OF DECEMBER 31, 200Y

ASSETS		(000s)	
Current Assets			
Cash		$ 25	
Accounts receivable		53	
Inventory		80	
Total current assets			$ 158 **(A)**
Fixed Assets			
Machinery	$ 40		
Less: Accumulated depreciation	25	15	
Equipment and fixtures	30		
Less: Accumulated depreciation	18	12	
Total fixed assets			27 **(B)**
Total Assets (C = A + B)			$ 185 **(C)**
LIABILITIES AND OWNER'S EQUITY			
Current Liabilities			
Accounts payable	$ 60		
Notes payable	35		
Total current liabilities		95	
Long-Term Liabilities			
Notes payable†	$ 40		
Total long-term liabilities		40	
Total liabilities			$ 135 **(D)**
OWNER'S EQUITY			
Capital investment		20	
Retained earnings		30	
Total owner's equity			50 **(E)**
Total Liabilities and Owner's Equity (F = D + E)			$ 185 **(F)**

* Debt is due within 12 months.
† Debt is due after 1 year.

| FIGURE 4.2 | EXAMPLE OF SIMPLIFIED INCOME STATEMENT |

THE CAMPBELL CO.
INCOME STATEMENT
FOR YEAR ENDING DECEMBER 31, 200Y

		(000s)	
Gross sales	$428		
Less: Returns	3		
Net Sales		**$425**	**(A)**
Cost of goods sold:			
Beginning inventory	$ 75		
Plus: Net purchases	297		
Cost of goods available	372		
Less: Ending inventory	80		
Cost of Goods Sold		292	**(B)**
Gross Profit (C = A − B)		**$133**	**(C)**
Selling expenses		**$ 29**	**(D)**
Administrative expenses:			
Office salaries	$ 60		
Interest	9		
Depreciation	10		
Other administrative expenses	7		
Total Administrative Expenses		86	**(E)**
Profit Before Income Tax (F = C − D − E)		**$ 18**	**(F)**
Income Tax (G = 25% of F)		4.5	**(G)**
Net Profit (G = F − G)		**$ 13.5**	**(H)**

To illustrate the range of possible values for each of these ratios, some typical examples for Canadian companies in a number of industries are shown in Table 4.1. Notice that there can be considerable variation in the value of each ratio within economic sectors as well as between sectors. Within a sector these ratios represent an average for each industry code and, therefore, may be somewhat misleading. These figures include a range of firms, some of which may be doing extremely well and others that may be on the verge of bankruptcy. The variations from sector to sector are largely due to structural differences that impact the financial profile of firms in each line of business in quite different ways.

This data as well as other detailed financial and employment data on small businesses by industry in Canada is available from the Small Business Profiles database of Industry Canada at strategis.ic.gc.ca/cgi-bin/sbp/sbp-cgi. These profiles are usually produced every two years with 1995 being the most current available. These data can provide performance benchmarks for the financial planning of both startup and established business.

Keep in mind that financial ratios are open to wide interpretation and should only be relied on to get a general perspective on the relative financial health of the business, to measure the financial progress of the business from one time period to another, or to flag major deviations from an industry or sector norm.

Value of Tangible Assets

In assessing the balance sheet of the prospective acquisition, you must determine the actual or real value of the tangible assets. A physical count of the inventory must be taken to determine if the actual level corresponds to the level stated on the balance sheet. This inventory must also be appraised in terms of its age, quality, saleability, style, condition, balance, freshness, etc. Most large inventories will have some obsolescence. You must determine whether the present inventory is consistent with current market conditions. Also, take care that the seller does not sell this inventory after you have checked it. Any consignment goods in inventory should be clearly identified as well. This evaluation is best performed by someone with considerable experience in the industry involved. Perhaps you can hire the services of the owner of a similar but non-competing firm to assist you in this appraisal.

You must also check the age of any outstanding accounts receivable. Some businesses continue to carry accounts receivable on their books that should have been charged off to bad debts, resulting in an overstatement of the firm's profit and value. Generally, the older the receivables, the lower their value. Old outstanding accounts may reveal a slack credit policy by the present owner. These old accounts will have to be discounted in determining the present value of the business.

The fixed assets of the business must also be scrutinized. You should determine if the furniture, fixtures, equipment, and building are stated at their market or depreciated value. Some questions you should ask include: How modern are these assets? Are they in operating condition? How much will it cost to keep these assets in operation? Are the assets all paid for? You must be aware of any liens or chattel mortgages which may have been placed against these assets. This pledging of assets to secure a debt is a normal business practice; however, you should know about any such mortgages. Other liabilities such as unpaid bills, back taxes, back pay to employees, and so on, may be hidden; you must be aware of the possibility of their existence, and contract with the seller that all claims not shown on the balance sheet will be assumed by him or her.

Value of Intangible Assets

In addition to the more obvious physical goods and equipment, certain intangible assets may also have a real value to a prospective purchaser. Among the most important of these are goodwill, franchise and licensing rights, and patents, trademarks, and copyrights.

You must be very realistic in determining what you can afford or are prepared to pay for goodwill. Is the public's present attitude toward the business a valuable asset that is worth money, or is it a liability? Typically, few businesses that are for sale have much goodwill value. Is any goodwill associated with the business personal to the owner or largely commercial due to the location, reputation, and other characteristics of the business? If largely personal, this goodwill may not be transferable to a new owner so you should not pay very much for it. Many business owners, however, often have very unrealistic and inflated ideas of the goodwill associated with their business because they have built it up over the years with their own "sweat equity" and, therefore, are not very objective. So you should be careful, and talk to customers, suppliers, neighbours, employees, and perhaps even competitors, to determine if this level of goodwill in fact exists.

In fact, quite often things are not always as they appear. When Jeanne Lawrence bought what she thought was a reputable and thriving fashion design business and retail store, she expected business to carry on as usual. It was only after she had taken over the firm that she discovered that the company's once reputable name had become tarnished in the past year. She was bombarded with a litany of customer service complaints ranging from poor workmanship, to ill-fitting clothing, to people who had paid in full for work that hadn't been done. The situation was so bad she was spending all the money she was taking in on new business repairing the damage that had been done before she took over the company. Eventually Lawrence realized that she could repair the merchandise that had been sold before she took over but she couldn't repair the reputation of the business, so she changed the name (Entrepreneurs in Action #11).

TABLE 4.1 KEY BUSINESS RATIOS IN CANADA — CORPORATIONS

Line of Business	I Current Ratio (Times)	III Debt/ Net Worth (Times)	IV Gross Profit/ Sales (%)	V Net Profit/ Sales (%)	VI Return on Assets (%)	VII Sales to Inventory (Times)	VIII Collection Period (Days)
TOTAL ALL INDUSTRIES	1.2	2.0	40.1	5.4	7.2	11.9	42.7
RETAIL TRADE	1.5	2.8	21.9	1.0	5.5	6.4	15.9
Books & stationery stores	1.2	3.6	20.7	0.2	—	4.1	18.0
Women's clothing stores	1.3	6.4	24.2	1.4	7.4	4.4	17.9
Florists, lawn and garden centres	1.6	9.1	23.2	0.3	—	6.7	17.8
Household furnishing stores	1.5	3.1	24.3	2.9	7.1	2.7	18.6
Shoe stores	1.6	2.6	22.3	2.5	7.1	3.0	7.1
WHOLESALE TRADE	1.5	2.7	17.6	1.9	6.4	7.6	45.6
Food	1.3	5.5	11.2	0.3	3.5	14.0	32.9
Metal and metal products	1.6	1.3	19.6	4.8	11.5	9.4	53.3
Petroleum products	1.5	1.3	19.4	3.3	9.7	25.2	46.3
MANUFACTURERS	1.5	2.0	23.7	3.1	7.8	8.5	53.6
Bakery products	0.9	5.7	26.0	—	—	17.5	26.7
Women's clothing	1.6	1.9	19.5	2.4	8.2	9.0	51.0
Fruit and vegetable industries	1.9	2.8	20.2	0.1	—	5.5	38.0
Heating equipment	1.9	1.6	23.7	3.1	8.5	6.8	53.1
Metal fabricating	1.7	1.3	22.6	3.5	7.2	7.5	60.1
Sawmill and planing mill	1.6	1.8	23.7	3.3	8.4	6.7	32.8
CONSTRUCTION INDUSTRIES	1.4	2.6	41.2	1.9	5.7	9.2	50.5
Residential building	1.5	2.7	17.9	1.3	4.3	4.1	40.0
BUSINESS SERVICES	1.5	1.7	50.2	9.0	13.2	379.6	71.4
Funeral services	1.4	2.1	65.1	10.3	6.7	163.3	53.0
Hotels and motor hotels	0.6	3.8	47.6	−2.4	3.9	76.4	14.5
Sports and recreation services	1.6	5.1	57.3	−2.7	2.5	54.1	19.8
TRANSPORTATION AND STORAGE	0.9	2.6	58.9	3.2	8.4	638.0	39.6
Radio broadcasting	3.0	0.6	49.4	16.4	25.3	—	35.8
Taxicab industry	1.1	2.0	49.3	0.6	2.9	—	63.5
Truck transport	1.0	2.6	59.3	3.1	9.4	—	37.1

Source: 1995 Small Business Profiles — Canada (strategis.ic.gc.ca/cgi-bin/sbp/sbp-cgi)

If franchise, licensing, or other rights are involved in the business, you should make certain that you understand the terms and conditions associated with such rights, and that these rights will be in fact transferred to you upon acquisition of the company. An effort should also be made to determine the market value of any patents, trademarks, or copyrights the company may hold, and make sure these are part of the sale — i.e., do not remain with the current owner upon completion of the transaction.

Cash Flow

You must also observe the cash flows generated by the operation. A business can be very profitable, but chronically low in cash due to overly generous credit terms, excessive inventory levels, or heavy fixed interest payments. You must assure yourself that upon your entry into the

ENTREPRENEURS IN *ACTION*

Buyer Beware Doesn't Only Apply to Customers

Clothing store owner bought bad reputation

When Jeanne Lawrence bought a reputable and thriving company this year, she expected business would carry on as usual.

Lawrence bought a fashion design and retail store earlier this fall that specializes in made-to-order evening wear, bridal gowns and daytime apparel. Clothing ranges from $100 lingerie sets to $2,000 evening gowns. Lawrence is a designer with 25 years' experience and has also operated a store before.

Service complaints

But when she took over from the previous owner she was bombarded with a litany of customer service complaints. So many in fact that she says she's spending all the money she's taking in on new business repairing damage done before she took control Nov. 1.

"I've been trying to repair the reputation this place had at one time," says Lawrence.

Lawrence says customer complaints range from poor workmanship to poor-fitting clothing, to people who paid in full for work that hadn't been done. Since she has taken over, Lawrence discovered the business's once reputable name has fallen in the last year.

Lawrence estimates about 75 per cent of the clientele was lost in the last year or two.

"Complaints were never redressed. I've been contacted by the Better Business Bureau with horror stories."

Lawrence wouldn't reveal the purchase price of the business but said it was considerable. She said she thought she was also buying the goodwill that went with the company's name.

"To buy a name that's reputable — that doesn't come cheap," she comments.

Marty Eakins is a partner with the Winnipeg office of KPMG. Eakins says when buying a business, it's very much caveat emptor.

"The whole notion of due diligence is critical."

He says that means hiring an experienced financial person to review financial statements both current and past. But Eakins says even at that, no firm can give 100 per cent assurance that what you're buying is solid gold.

Lawrence says she had her accountant look at the books (her accountant recommended she buy the company). And financially, the business was solid. It was the company's reputation that wasn't what she expected.

Eakins says goodwill is difficult to assess. In purely financial terms, goodwill is the excess of the purchase price over the tangible assets. Eakins says if a company has assets valued at $500,000 and someone pays $1 million, then the goodwill they've purchased is $500,000.

Eakins says prospective buyers should learn as much about the business they're buying as possible, looking at macroeconomic factors such as the industry and the national economy as well as the business itself. He says checking customer lists and talking to a few customers is also helpful.

Lawrence is sticking with the business, but she's already made changes. Along with her associate, designer Karen Dolan, she's bringing in

WAYNE GLOWACKI/WINNIPEG FREE PRESS

more seasonal wear and gift items. Lawrence says they've even started selling ready-to-wear that's 80 percent completed and then can be altered to the individual.

Changed the name

Most importantly, Lawrence realizes that she can repair merchandise sold previously, but she can't repair the reputation associated with the name. So the store name has been changed to Loiselle.

Unfortunately, Lawrence has spent so much money fixing mistakes that for the moment she can't afford a new sign.

Source: Paul McKie, "Clothing Store Owner Bought Bad Reputation," *Winnipeg Free Press*, December 1, 1997, p. B5. © Winnipeg Free Press. Reprinted with permission.

business you would have sufficient inflows of cash to meet your cash outflow requirements. Constant cash problems can indicate that the business is possibly being run by ineffective management or that the firm's resources have generally been badly allocated. You must ask yourself if you have the know-how to overcome this misallocation of resources. If the firm's cash flow is very low, and the long-term debt is quite high, the business may be eating up its capital to pay the debt, or possibly defaulting on its debt. If you are to contend with such issues, you may have to increase the firm's debt or be prepared to invest more capital in the business in order to ease the cash flow problem.

Marketing Considerations

The previous section deals with the internal aspects of the firm's profitability; there has been no discussion of the external determinants of these conditions. But you must be concerned with analyzing markets, customers, competition, and various other aspects of the company's operating environment.

You must carefully examine the company's current market situation. Each market segment served by the firm must be analyzed and understood. Studying maps, customer lists, traffic patterns, and other factors can help you to determine the normal market size for the business. Once the market and its various segments are understood, the composition of these segments should be determined in order to identify the approximate number of customers in the total market. As a buyer, you should be concerned with:

1. The company's trading area
2. Population demographics
3. The trend and size of the market
4. Recent changes in the market
5. Future market patterns

All these factors help in determining whether the firm's market area is changing, or there is a declining relevant population, or technological or other changes may be creating an obsolete operation.

This kind of information can assist you in assessing trends in the level of the business' market penetration. For example, if its market share has been increasing, then perhaps you should anticipate further growth. But if the business' market penetration has been declining or static, you should be aware that something could be wrong with the operation. It may be that the business is nearing the end of its life cycle. A shrewd seller, aware that the operation is approaching a natural decline, may be bailing out.

Competition facing the business must also be evaluated and understood. First and foremost, you should make sure that the present owner will not remain in competition with you.

Very often an owner will dispose of a business only to open up a similar operation. If the business is largely based on the personality and contacts of the owner, you may be hard pressed to maintain the necessary rapport with customers, suppliers, and financial sources. A legal agreement may help ensure that the vendor will not go on to compete with you.

Another aspect of assessing competition is to look at that presently faced by the firm. You should be aware of the business' major competitors and what trends can be foreseen in the nature of their activity. Most of this information can be obtained either from direct observation or by talking with other people in the business.

Other aspects of the environment also should not be overlooked. You must be tuned in to developments in the economy, changes in technology, government policy and regulations, and trends in society at large that can affect your business situation. Your banker or other professionals may be able to tell you what the experts are saying about such variables. Both national and regional economic factors must be studied in order to develop accurate projections as to the size of the market opportunity available to the business.

Human Factors

When a business is being purchased, manpower must be considered equal in importance to financial and marketing factors, for usually it is desirable to retain certain key people to provide some continuity. As a prospective buyer, you should assess the value of the company's personnel and try to become acquainted with the attitudes of the present employees. For example, will key employees continue to work for the firm under your management? If these key people are likely to leave, you must anticipate the consequences.

Both the quality and the quantity of trained personnel must be evaluated. The skill level of the employees has some bearing on the sale value of the business. Highly trained staff, for example, can increase the seller's bargaining power. On the other hand, inefficient and poorly trained staff may permit you to negotiate a lower purchase price because of the long-term expense involved in retraining or hiring additional employees.

Other Concerns

In assessing a business to buy, you will also have to take into account a number of other factors. These include various legal considerations as well as past company policies. The legal aspects of doing business are becoming increasingly more complex and the use of a lawyer is practically a fact of business life. A lawyer can help you in such areas as deciding on an appropriate form of legal organization; identifying real estate documents such as zoning restrictions and covenants that may put you at a disadvantage; labour laws and union regulations; complying with all licensing and permit requirements; the transferability of intangible assets such as copyrights, patents, dealerships, and franchises; and whether buying the shares or the assets of the firm is the most advantageous way of purchasing the company.

You should also have some understanding of the historical practices of the firm relating to employees, customers, and suppliers if future policies are to enhance your opportunities for business growth. An evaluation of these practices and policies will determine if you should continue with past practices or make modifications. If you fail to do so, you may eventually find yourself in a situation where you have to continue policies that are ill-advised in the long run. For example, it may be necessary to tighten credit policies or make a change in labour practices, even though this may cause a short-term loss of customers or employees.

How to Determine an Appropriate Price to Pay for a Business

Buying a business is a serious matter involving a substantial financial and personal investment. A business bought at the wrong price, or at the wrong time, can cost you and your family much more than just the dollars you have invested and lost. After you have thoroughly investigated a business opportunity according to the factors in the previous section, weighed the wealth of information you have gathered, and decided that your expectations have been suitably fulfilled, a price must be agreed upon with the seller.

Determining an appropriate price to pay for a business is a complex and technical process. If you are making this determination on your own, you should either have a sound knowledge of general accounting principles and evaluation techniques or use the services of a professional accountant.

Setting the purchase price for a going concern typically involves two separate kinds of evaluations:

1. **Balance sheet methods** — evaluation of the firm's tangible net assets
2. **Earnings-based methods** — evaluation of the firm's expected future earnings

The balance sheet methods are generally less reliant on estimates and forecasts than the earnings-based methods; however, it should be remembered that they totally ignore the future earnings capability of the business.

Balance Sheet Methods

If the company has a balance sheet, the quickest means of determining a valuation figure is to look at its net worth as indicated there. You simply take the total assets as shown in the financial statement and subtract total liabilities to get the *net book value*. The advantage of this method is that for most firms the numbers are readily available.

Its drawbacks, however, are numerous. The company's accounting practices will have a big impact on its book value. Similarly, book value does not necessarily reflect the fair market value of the assets or the liabilities. For example, buildings and equipment shown on the balance sheet may be depreciated below their actual market value, or land may have appreciated above its original cost. These differences will not be reflected on the company's balance sheet. Despite these drawbacks, however, net book value may be useful in establishing a reference point when considering the asset valuation of a business. This approach is illustrated in Section I of Figure 4.3 on the basis of the balance sheet for The Campbell Company presented in Figure 4.1.

To correct for differences from the real situation, you may wish to make some modifications to create a *modified book value*. This is simply the book value adjusted for major differences between the stated book value and the fair market value of the company's fixed assets and liabilities. This refinement of the plain book value approach still has a number of drawbacks, but it does, however, give a more accurate representation of the value of the company's assets at current market value than book value does. The application of this method is illustrated in Section II of Figure 4.3.

A third approach is to go beyond the books of the company to get a more detailed evaluation of specific assets. Generally this involves determining the *liquidation value* of the assets or how much the seller could get for the business or any part of it if it were suddenly thrown onto the market. This approach is ordinarily a highly conservative evaluation and, as such, is frequently useful in determining the lowest valuation in a range of values to be considered. The liquidation value approach is presented in Section III of Figure 4.3.

FIGURE 4.3 APPLICATION OF BALANCE SHEET METHODS

BUSINESS VALUATION — THE CAMPBELL CO.
BALANCE SHEET METHODS

	(000s)
I. NET BOOK VALUE	
Total stockholder's equity*	$ 50
Net Book Value	**$ 50**
II. MODIFIED BOOK VALUE	
Net book value	$ 50
Plus:	
Excess of appraised market value of building and equipment over book value	25
Value of patent not on books	10
Modified Book Value	**$ 85**
III. LIQUIDATION VALUE	
Net book value	$ 50
Plus:	
Excess of appraised liquidation value of fixed assets over book value	9
Less:	
Deficit of appraised liquidation value of inventory over book value	(5)
Deficit due to liquidation of accounts receivable	(3)
Costs of liquidation and taxes due upon liquidation	(8)
Liquidation Value	**$ 43**

* Item E from Figure 4.1.

Earnings Methods

In most cases a going concern is much more than just the sum of its physical assets. While the cost of reproducing or liquidating these assets can be closely determined, the cost of duplicating the firm's experience, management, technical know-how, and reputation is not so easily determined. These intangible factors will be reflected in the firm's past and expected future earnings.

To study past earnings trends, it is important to select a time period that is true and representative. A period of five years is generally considered to be an appropriate length of time to observe an earnings trend; however, economic cycles and other factors must be taken into consideration.

Once earnings have been determined, various approaches can be used in order to determine an appropriate price. The most popular approach is a simple *capitalization of an average of past profits* or *capitalization of earnings*. In this method, the profits for a selected period of years are adjusted for unusual items and an appropriate capitalization rate is applied to the average profit level derived. (See Figure 4.4, and Section I of Figure 4.6.)

A variation on this method is to weight the earnings of prior years to give greater emphasis to more recent profit levels (for example, the most recent year is given a weight of 5, the previous year 4, the next previous year 3, and so on).

The major advantage of this approach is that it is easy to use. However, the selection of an appropriate capitalization rate or multiple to apply to past or expected future earnings is not a simple, straightforward process. For illustrative purposes we have selected a desired rate of return of 16 percent, or approximately six times earnings in Figure 4.6.

The rate that can be earned on secure investments usually serves as the "base" rate or minimum capitalization rate that would be used. The chosen capitalization rate is really an assessment of the risk you perceive to be related to the business in comparison to the risk related to obtaining the "base" rate. It is an indication of the rate of return you are prepared to accept for assuming that risk in relation to the rates of return you could earn from other, more secure investments such as bonds, guaranteed income certificates, etc.

The selection of a capitalization rate can have a large impact on your evaluation of a business. If, for example, your desired rate of return is increased from 16 percent to 20 percent in Figure 4.6, the estimated value of The Campbell Co. based on capitalization of their past earnings would be reduced from $60,000 to $48,000. The estimated values using discounted future earnings and discounted cash flow would be similarly reduced if we were to use a 20 percent rather than a 16 percent expected rate of return.

The *discounted future earnings* approach requires estimating after-tax earnings for a number of years in the future as well as determining an appropriate rate of return for the investor. Each future year's earnings are then discounted by the desired rate of return. A higher discount rate might be considered in this case since the estimates are based on projections of future earnings rather than historical results and may be very subjective in nature. In addition, since net earnings, after tax, are used as the basis for the projection, the discount rate used should be net of tax as well. The sum of these discounted values is the estimated present value of the company (Figure 4.5 and Section II of Figure 4.6).

FIGURE 4.4   EXAMPLE OF SUMMARY OF EARNINGS SHEET

THE CAMPBELL CO.
SUMMARY OF EARNINGS FOR PAST FOUR YEARS

Year	Earnings After Taxes (000s)
200Y	$13.5
200Y–1	12.1
200Y–2	10.8
200Y–3	7.2
200Y–4	4.6

FIGURE 4.5   EXAMPLE OF PROJECTED INCOME SHEET

THE CAMPBELL CO.
PROJECTED FIVE-YEAR EARNINGS AND CASH FLOW

Year	Projected Earnings After Taxes (000s)	Projected Cash Flow (000s)
200Y+1	$14.0	$16.9
200Y+2	16.8	21.1
200Y+3	20.2	26.4
200Y+4	24.2	33.0
200Y+5	29.0	41.2

Assumptions:
1. Earnings are expected to grow at a rate of 20% per year.
2. Cash flow is expected to grow at a rate of 25% per year.

FIGURE 4.6 APPLICATION OF EARNINGS METHODS

BUSINESS VALUATION — THE CAMPBELL CO.
EARNINGS METHODS

I. CAPITALIZATION OF EARNINGS

	Average Earnings Over Past Five Years (Figures 4.2 and 4.4) (000s)
200Y–4	$ 4.6
200Y–3	7.2
200Y–2	10.8
200Y–1	12.1
200Y	13.5
Total	$48.2 in the previous 5 years

Average Earnings = $9.6

Divided By: Investor's desired rate of return = 16%*

Value of Company Based on Capitalization of Past Earnings = 9.6 x 100/16 = $60.0

II. DISCOUNTED FUTURE EARNINGS

	Projected After-Tax Earnings (Figure 3.5) (000s)	x	Present Value Factor Assuming 16% Return	=	Present Value of After-Tax Earnings (000s)
200Y+1	$ 14.0		0.862		$12.1
200Y+2	16.8		0.743		12.5
200Y+3	20.2		0.641		13.0
200Y+4	24.2		0.552		13.4
200Y+5	29.0		0.476		13.8
Total	$104.2			**Total**	$64.8

Value of Company Based on Discounted Future Earnings = $64.8

III. DISCOUNTED CASH FLOW

	Projected Cash Flow (Figure 3.5) (000s)	x	Present Value Factor Assuming 16% Return	=	Present Value of Cash Flow (000s)
200Y+1	$ 16.9		0.862		$14.6
200Y+2	21.1		0.743		15.7
200Y+3	26.4		0.641		16.9
200Y+4	33.0		0.552		18.2
200Y+5	41.2		0.476		19.6
Total	$138.6				$85.0

Value of Company Based on Discounted Cash Flow = $85.0

---

* The actual rate of return to use depends upon your cost of capital, as well as the perceived risk inherent in the investment.

The advantage of this approach is that future earnings potential becomes the principal investment criterion, taking into account the time value of money. The principal disadvantage is that in many situations, future earnings cannot be projected with any real accuracy because of the uncertainties of the operating environment and the marketplace.

The *discounted cash flow* approach is essentially the same as the discounted future earnings one, except that future anticipated cash flows rather than earnings are used in the computation, as can be seen in Section III of Figure 4.6. The difference between earnings and cash flow is that earnings will include provision for depreciation, amortization, deferred taxes, and similar "non-cash" expenses. Like the discounted future earnings approach, this method of valuation also depends upon highly uncertain estimates and assumptions. Many people feel, however, that this method and the discounted future earnings method typically provide the most reasonable estimates of a company's value.

Each of these evaluation methods is illustrated for the case of Campbell. The following assumptions are reflected in these calculations:

1. Future earnings are estimated with new management in place.

2. Earnings are expected to grow at a rate of 20 percent per year.

3. The income tax rate, including federal and state or provincial income taxes, is 20 percent.

4. Your desired return on investment is 16 percent.

As illustrated in Figure 4.7, the values of The Campbell Company vary widely according to the valuation method used. The actual value of the company will depend upon which method is most appropriate for the circumstances. For example, the seller will argue that the valuation method yielding the highest value — modified book value or discounted cash flow — is the most appropriate one. However, you would argue that the one reflecting the lowest value for the business — liquidation value — is probably the most appropriate. The price actually agreed upon will result from extensive negotiation between you and the prospective seller, and will involve considering not only these formal evaluation methods but a host of other business and personal considerations as well.

FIGURE 4.7 CAMPBELL CO. VALUATIONS ACCORDING TO DIFFERENT METHODS

Method	Estimated Value (000s)
Net book value (Figure 4.3, I)	$50.0
Modified book value (Figure 4.3, II)	85.0
Liquidation value (Figure 4.3, III)	43.0
Capitalization of earnings (Figure 4.6, I)	60.0
Discounted future earnings (Figure 4.6, II)	64.8
Discounted cash flow (Figure 4.6, III)	85.0

Rule-of-Thumb Approaches

In some situations, especially the purchase of service industries, certain rules of thumb have been developed to serve as useful guides for the valuation of a business. They typically rely on the idea of a "price multiplier." One common rule of thumb in firms where there are substantial assets is to add up the fair market value of the company's fixed assets, plus the owner's cost of current inventory, plus approximately 90 percent of what appear to be good accounts receivable, plus a percentage of the company's net income before taxes as goodwill. In companies where there are relatively few tangible assets, another rule of thumb is to calculate the selling price as a percentage of the net or gross annual receipts of the business. This method is illustrated in Table 4.2 for various types of businesses. In this table, other important conditions to consider, and key things to watch out for, are listed as well.

Using one of these rules of thumb does not mean that the balance sheet and the income statement for the business can be ignored. These rules are merely a starting point for business valuation and must be reviewed in the context of the other business factors discussed earlier in this section.

What to Buy — Assets or Shares?

The acquisition of a business may be structured under one of two basic formats:

1. You can purchase the seller's stock or shares in the business.
2. You can purchase part or all of the business' assets.

Although these alternatives are treated somewhat the same for financial reporting purposes, the tax consequences can differ significantly. A major consideration in the purchase or sale of a business may be the effect on the tax liability of both the buyer and the seller. The "best" form of a particular transaction will depend on the facts and circumstances of each case. Since the tax implications of acquiring or disposing of a business can be very complex, and a poorly structured transaction can be disastrous for both parties, it is suggested that you seek competent tax advice from your accountant or lawyer regarding this matter. Another factor to consider in deciding whether to buy assets or shares are "contingent liabilities." If assets are acquired, in most instances the buyer takes no responsibility for any contingencies that may arise subsequent to the sale such as lawsuits, environmental liabilities, or tax reassessments.

In some cases there may not be any choice. If the company is a sole proprietorship, for example, there are no shares, only assets and liabilities accumulated in the course of doing business which belong to the proprietor personally. So when acquiring the company, you and the owner must decide which of these assets and liabilities are to be transferred and which are to stay with the present owner. You may feel that some of the assets are not really essential to carry on the business and the seller may desire to keep something — often the real estate, which you may be able to lease rather than buy from him. This may be one way of reducing the cost of the business to you. These are matters which would have to be discussed in detail between you and the prospective seller.

Advantages and Disadvantages of Buying an Existing Business

The case for buying an existing firm, as against setting up a new one of your own, is not clear-cut either way. Each situation must be decided on its merits. There are distinct advantages and disadvantages to each course of action. You must consider how well your personal preferences fit into each of these options.

Reasons for Buying an Established Business

Here are some reasons why one *should* consider buying an established business:

1. Buying an existing business can reduce the risk. The existing business is already a proven entity. And it is often easier to obtain financing for an established operation than for a new one.
2. Acquiring a "going concern" with a good past history increases the likelihood of a successful operation for the new owner.

TABLE 4.2   VALUING A SMALL BUSINESS BY RULE OF THUMB

Business	Price Multiplier	Important Conditions	Watch For:
Apparel stores	0.75 to 1.5 times net plus equipment and inventory	Location, competition, reputation, specialization	Unfavourable shopping patterns, inadequate parking, outdated inventory
Beauty salons	0.25 to 0.75 times gross plus equipment and inventory	Location, reputation, boutique image	Excessive staff turnover
Car dealerships	1.25 to 2 times net plus equipment	Type of dealership, location, reputation of company	Brand new manufacturers, factory allocation policy
Employment agencies	0.75 to 1 times gross, equipment included	Reputation, specialization, client relations	Excessive staff turnover
Fast food stores	1 to 1.25 times net	Location, competition, neatness of premises, lease terms	Inadequate street traffic, inadequate servicing space or seating area
Gas stations	$1.25 to $2 per gallon pumped per month, equipment included	Gallons/month, lease terms, location, competition, other services	Poor traffic pattern, short lease
Grocery stores	0.25 to 0.33 times gross, equipment included	Location, lease terms, presence of liquor, condition of facilities	Nearby supermarkets or convenience stores
Insurance agencies	1 to 2 times annual renewal commissions	Client demographics and transferability, carrier characteristics	Agent turnover, account mix
Newspapers	0.75 to 1.25 times gross, equipment included	Location, demographics, economic conditions, competition, lease terms	Stagnant or declining area
Real estate offices	0.75 to 1.5 times gross, equipment included	Tenure of salespeople, franchised office, reputation	Intensity of competition
Restaurants	0.25 to 0.5 times gross, equipment included	Competition, location, reputation	Predecessor failures
Travel agencies	0.04 to 0.1 times gross, equipment included	Revenue mix, location, reputation, lease terms	Negative climate for international travel
Video shops	1 to 2 times net plus equipment	Location, competition, inventory	Obsolescence of tapes, match of tapes to customers

Excerpted from S. M. Pollan and M. Levine, *Playing to Win: The Small Business Guide to Survival & Growth*, advertising supplement to *U.S. News & World Report* and *The Atlantic*, 1988. Used by permission.

3. The established business has a proven location for successful operation.

4. The established firm already has a product or service that is presently being produced, distributed, and sold.

5. A clientele has already been developed for the product or service of the existing company.

6. Financial relationships have already been established with banks, trade creditors, and other sources of financial support.

7. The equipment needed for production is already available and its limitations and capabilities are known in advance.

8. An existing firm can often be acquired at a good price. The owner may be forced to sell the operation at a low price relative to the value of the assets in the business.

Disadvantages of Buying an Established Business

Here are some reasons why one may decide *not* to buy an existing business:

1. The physical facilities (the building and equipment) and product line may be old and obsolete.

2. Union/management relationships may be poor.

3. Present personnel may be unproductive and have a poor track record.

4. The inventory may contain a large amount of "dead" stock.

5. A high percentage of the assets may be in poor-quality accounts receivable.

6. The location of the business may be bad.

7. The financial condition of the business, and its relationships with financial institutions, may be poor.

8. As a buyer, you inherit any ill will that may exist toward the established firm among customers or suppliers.

9. As an entrepreneur, you have more freedom of choice in defining the nature of the business if you start one of your own than if you purchase an existing firm.

As you can see, there are both pluses and minuses in choosing to acquire an established business. You should view this option in terms of whether it will enable you to achieve your personal objectives. How do these advantages/disadvantages compare with those of starting a new business of your own? In buying an existing business do you see a reasonable opportunity to succeed? No one else can really advise you what to do. Instead, you must "do your own thing" and match the alternatives with your abilities and interests.

Checklist for a Business Acquisition

Should you start a new business or buy an existing one? At this point in your deliberations, this is the critical question. The material in the Business Acquisition Questionnaire, Figure 4.8, will aid you in making this choice.

If, after answering the questions in Part A, you decide to enter an established business rather than to start one of your own, then you should proceed to the questions in Part B. You may want to reproduce these pages and answer the same questions for several businesses you have in mind. Go through the questionnaire and answer the questions concerning each business as conscientiously as you can.

FIGURE 4.8 BUSINESS ACQUISITION QUESTIONNAIRE

PART A

Before deciding whether you will purchase an established business, you need to give consideration to the positive and negative features of this alternative. You should rate each point in the questionnaire as you perceive its significance and importance to you.

1. How would you define the nature of the business in which you are interested?

_____

_____

_____

2. How important are each of the following factors to you in electing to buy an established business? Indicate the importance of each factor to you on a scale ranging from 0 (not important at all) to 10 (extremely important):

a. Having a business with a proven performance record in sales, reliability, service, and profits _____

b. Avoiding the problems associated with assembling the composite resources — including location, building, equipment, material, and people _____

c. Avoiding the necessity of selecting and training a new workforce _____

d. Having an established product line _____

e. Avoiding production problems typically associated with the start-up of a new business _____

f. Having an established channel of distribution to market your product _____

g. Having a basic accounting and control system already in place _____

h. Avoiding the difficulty of having to work out the "bugs" that commonly develop in the initial operation of a new business _____

i. Having established relationships with suppliers and financial institutions _____

j. Being able to acquire the assets of the business for less than their replacement value _____

Total _____

3. In checking back over the points covered in question 2, the closer your total score on all items is to 100, the more purchasing an established business is likely to be of interest to you as a means of going into business for yourself.

PART B

The following is a set of considerations to be assessed in evaluating an established business. Your responses, information from the present owner, and other information concerning the status of the business should guide you to a comfortable decision as to whether this business is for you.

1. Why is the Business for Sale?

_____

_____

_____

_____

continued

Business Aquisition Questionnaire — continued

2. Financial Factors

  a. Recent sales trend:
  - _____ Increasing substantially
  - _____ Increasing marginally
  - _____ Relatively stable
  - _____ Decreasing marginally
  - _____ Decreasing substantially

  b. Recent trend in net profit:
  - _____ Increasing substantially
  - _____ Increasing marginally
  - _____ Relatively stable
  - _____ Decreasing marginally
  - _____ Decreasing substantially

  c. Are the financial statements audited?

  Yes _____   No _____

  d. Apparent validity of financial statements:

  Accurate _____   Overstated _____   Understated _____

  Check the following:
  - Relationship of book value of fixed assets to market price or replacement cost
  - Average age of accounts receivable and percentage over 90 days
  - Bad debts written off in the past 6 months, 12 months

  e. Ratio analysis:

	Industry Standard	This Company Year To Date	Last Year	Two Years Ago
Current ratio	_____	_____	_____	_____
Quick ratio	_____	_____	_____	_____
Debt-to-net-worth ratio	_____	_____	_____	_____
Gross-profit-to-sales ratio	_____	_____	_____	_____
Net-income-to-sales ratio	_____	_____	_____	_____
Return on assets	_____	_____	_____	_____

3. Tangible Assets

  a. Are the land and buildings adequate for the business?

  Yes _____   No _____

  b. Is the location acceptable?

  Yes _____   No _____

  c. Is the machinery and equipment worn and out of date?

  Yes _____   No _____

  d. How does it compare with the latest available?

  _____

  _____

  _____

Business Aquisition Questionnaire — continued

   e. What is the maintenance status of the plant and equipment?

      Excellent _____ Good _____ Fair _____ Poor _____

   f. Is the plant of sufficient size and design to meet your current and projected requirements?

      Yes _____ No _____

   g. Does the plant appear to be well laid out for the efficient use of people, machines, and material?

      Yes _____ No _____

   h. What is the approximate value of the company's inventory?

      Raw material $ _____

      Work-in-process $ _____

      Finished goods $ _____

      Total $ _____

   i. Does the inventory contain a high proportion of obsolete or "dead" stock?

      Yes   No

4. Intangible Assets

   a. Does the company name or any of its trade names have any value?

      Yes _____ No _____

   b. What kind of reputation does the business have with its customers?

      Positive _____ Neutral _____ Negative _____

   c. What kind of reputation does the business have with its suppliers?

      Positive _____ Neutral _____ Negative _____

   d. Are any franchise, licensing, or other rights part of the business?

      Yes _____ No _____

      Are they included in the deal?

      Yes _____ No _____

   e. Are any patents, copyrights, or trademarks part of the business?

      Yes _____ No _____

      Are they included in the deal?

      Yes _____ No _____

5. Marketing Factors

   a. Is the market for the firm's product/service:

      _____ Increasing?

      _____ Stable?

      _____ Declining?   If *declining*, this is principally attributable to:

                  _____ i. Decreasing demand due to lower popularity

                  _____ ii. A changing neighbourhood

                  _____ iii. A declining target population

                  _____ iv. Technological change

                  _____ v. Lack of effort by present owner

                  _____ vi. Other factors

6. Human Factors

   a. Is the present owner in good health?

      Yes _____ No _____

continued

Business Aquisition Questionnaire — continued

  b. Does the present owner plan to establish a new business or acquire another business that would compete with yours?

  Yes _____ No _____ Uncertain _____

  What are the intentions of the present owner?

  _____

  _____

  _____

  c. How efficient are current personnel?

   i. What is the rate of labour turnover? _____ %

   ii. What is the rate of absenteeism? _____ %

   iii. What proportion of production is completed without rejects? _____ %

   iv. Can you accurately determine the cost of producing an individual unit of the product or service? Yes _____ No _____

   v. How has this changed in the past year?
      Increased _____ Stayed the same _____ Decreased _____

  d. Has a union recently won an election to serve as a bargaining agent for the company's employees?
     Yes _____ No _____

  e. Will most of the key employees continue to work for the firm under your management?
     Yes _____ No _____

  f. Will you have to incur considerable costs in retraining or hiring additional employees?
     Yes _____ No _____

7. Other Considerations

  a. Are there any zoning restrictions or caveats on the property that may put you at a competitive disadvantage?
     Yes _____ No _____

  b. Can you satisfy all the federal and provincial licensing and permit requirements?
     Yes _____ No _____

  c. Have you considered what would be the most advantageous way of purchasing the company?
     Buy shares _____ Buy assets _____ Don't know _____

  d. Have you had a lawyer and an accountant review the material you received from the vendor and any other information you may have regarding the business?
     Lawyer   Yes _____ No _____
     Accountant Yes _____ No _____

8. Your Evaluation of the Business

  What have you determined to be the approximate value of the business based on the following valuation approaches?

  a. Net book value $ _____
  b. Modified book value $ _____
  c. Liquidation value $ _____
  d. Capitalization of past earnings $ _____
  e. Discounted future earnings $ _____
  f. Discounted cash flow $ _____

The areas covered by this checklist are not meant to be exhaustive; they are presented merely to guide and stimulate your own thinking about buying an existing business. The more information you can compile to assist you in making this decision the better.

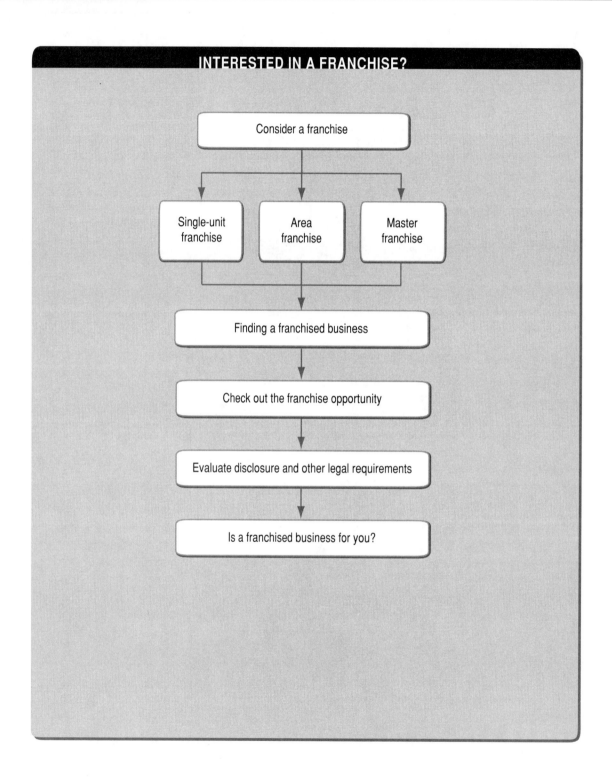

INTERESTED IN A FRANCHISE?

Consider a franchise

Single-unit franchise

Area franchise

Master franchise

Finding a franchised business

Check out the franchise opportunity

Evaluate disclosure and other legal requirements

Is a franchised business for you?

Considering a Franchise

I n addition to exploring the possibilities of starting your own business or buying an existing one, you may want to investigate the opportunities presented by *franchising*. Franchising allows you to go into business for yourself, and at the same time be part of a larger organization. This reduces your chances of failure, because of the support that the established company can provide. If this appears to be an attractive situation, then a franchise may be the answer for you. Let's look at what this means in the context of starting a business of your own.

An Introduction to Franchising

Franchising has often been referred to as an industry or a business. However, it is neither. It can best be described as *a method of doing business* — a means of marketing a product and/or service which has been adopted and used by a wide variety of industries and businesses.

What Is Franchising?

There is no single, simple definition of franchising. For example, Statistics Canada defines it as "A system of distribution in which one enterprise (the franchisor) grants to another (the franchisee) the right or privilege to merchandise a product or service." The International Franchise Association, the major trade association in the field, defines it as "A continuing relationship in which the franchisor provides a licensed privilege to do business, plus assistance in organizing, training, merchandising, and management in return for consideration from the franchisee." These are just two of the many definitions that have been offered.

Regardless of the formal definition, however, it is best to think of franchising as a legal and commercial relationship between the owner of a trademark, trade name, or advertising symbol and an individual or group of people seeking the right to use that identification in a business. A franchisee generally sells goods and services supplied by the franchisor or that meet the franchisor's quality standards. Franchising is based on mutual trust and a legal relationship between the two parties. The franchisor provides business expertise such as a proven product or service offering, an operating system, a marketing plan, site location, training, and financial controls that otherwise would not be available to the franchisee. The franchisee brings to the franchise operation the motivation, entrepreneurial spirit, and often the money, to make the franchise a success.

Virtually all franchise arrangements contain the following elements:

1. A continuing relationship between two parties
2. A legal contract which describes the responsibilities and obligations of each party
3. Tangible and intangible assets (such as services, trademarks, and expertise) provided by the franchisor for a fee
4. The operation of the business by the franchisee under the franchisor's trade name and managerial guidance

Franchise arrangements can be subdivided into two broad classes:

1. **Product distribution arrangements**, in which the dealer is to some degree, but not entirely, identified with the manufacturer/supplier
2. **Entire-business-format franchising**, in which there is complete identification of the dealer with the supplier

In a *product distribution arrangement*, the franchised dealer concentrates on one company's product line, and to some extent identifies his or her business with that company. Typical of this type of franchise are automobile and truck dealers, gasoline service stations, and soft drink bottlers.

Entire-business-format franchising is characterized by an ongoing business relationship between franchisor and franchisee that includes not only the product, service, and trademark, but the entire business format — a marketing strategy and plan, operating manuals and standards, quality control, and continuing two-way communications. Restaurants, personal and business services, rental services, real estate services, and many other businesses fall into this category.

Entire-business-format franchising has been primarily responsible for most of the growth of franchising since 1950. Most of our comments will relate to this form of franchising.

Advantages of Franchising

As has been pointed out, franchising is one means for you (the *franchisee*) to go into business for yourself, but yet at the same time also be part of a chain, with the support of an established company (the *franchisor*) behind you. This can enable you to compete with other chains through the use of a well-known trademark or trade name. In addition, the franchisor may provide you with assistance in such areas as site selection, equipment purchasing, national advertising, bookkeeping, the acquisition of supplies and materials, business counselling, and employee training.

As a franchisee you will have the opportunity to buy into an established concept with reduced risk of failure. Statistics show that a typical franchisee has an 80 percent chance of success. Several factors may explain this result. First, your risk is reduced because you are supposedly buying a successful concept. This package includes proven and profitable product or service lines, professionally developed advertising, a known and generally recognized brand name, the standardized design or construction of a typical outlet, and a proven and market-tested operating system. Second, you are often provided with training for your new job and continuing management support. You have the ongoing assistance of a franchisor, who can afford to hire specialists in such areas as cost accounting, marketing and sales, and research and development. These are important assets usually not available to the small, independent businessperson.

As a franchisee you may also be able to take advantage of the lower cost of large-scale, centralized buying. You may be able to purchase supplies at reduced cost, since the franchisor can purchase in bulk and pass the savings along. You may also have access to financing and credit arrangements that would not otherwise be available to an independent business. Banks and other lending institutions are usually more willing to lend money to a franchisee who has the backing of a large, successful franchisor than they are to a completely independent business.

A franchisee has the opportunity to acquire a proven system which has already been developed, tested and refined, with all of the bugs already worked out. This allows you to avoid a lot of the start-up problems typically associated with starting an independent business. Downhill ski racer Todd Brooker, for example, served 2,000 customers in the first couple of days after the opening of his Wendy's franchise in Collingwood, Ont. (Entrepreneurs in Action #12). Brooker had first coveted a McDonald's franchise but when faced with their rigid franchise contract and a pervasive corporate culture, went with Wendy's instead. While still having to deal with many of the operational problems of starting a new business like overseeing construction, interviewing prospective employees, and setting up the payroll, the affiliation with a company like Wendy's undoubtedly enabled him to jump start his business more quickly than otherwise would have been the case.

12   ENTREPRENEURS IN ACTION

Through the Gate

How to Jump-Start a New Franchise

Downhill ski racer Todd Brooker is accustomed to making split-second decisions at high speed, so he was in his element last winter when he opened his Wendy's restaurant in Collingwood, Ont. Looking back at his first months, however, he displays the perfectionism that served him well as a World Cup skier: "Now I know why everyone wants a second franchise," he says. "Everything you've done, you figure you could do better if you had another chance."

Don't be misled. Brooker's Wendy's franchise served 2,000 customers in the first couple of days after its December opening. Always competitive, he attributes the success of his grand opening to hard work and good technique.

After buying the land on a corner of Collingwood's main drag, Brooker got dirty quickly. Once Wendy's approved his blueprints, he found a contractor and donned a hard hat, appearing at the building site each day. By November, he was interviewing for the 90 positions he figured he needed for the first month over Christmas. "Drawing up a schedule was a big pain in the neck," he says. "You don't know how strong anyone will be, so you just schedule everyone three hours at a time."

Soon, it was time to ramp up to the Dec. 15 opening. "Cleaning was the big thing," he recalls. "Drywall dust just gets into everything." By Dec. 9, he started bringing in paper goods, cooking supplies and utensils, putting together tables and arranging the menu boards. Two days later, the food arrived — another Wendy's franchisee passed along his opening food supplies order as a guide — and Brooker was finally ready for three days of "practice runs."

Over the previous weeks he had made the rounds of every local business he could find, passing out free lunch and dinner coupons for the days leading up to the opening. "I told them to come over and help us train our employees," Brooker recalls. "Every coupon came back. I gave away $2,500 worth of food a day." The third day, he also invited the mayor, deputy mayor, councillors and municipal economic development people for a VIP dinner.

Opening day, the lineups went out the door. Brooker was thrilled. Then an employee asked when they would be paid. "I hadn't even thought about how to pay everyone," Brooker laughs. He quickly drove to the bank to set up a payroll, and calculated deductions and tax remissions by hand for about four months until he joined the bank's fully automated program. "Doing things the stupid way gives you an education about what it's all about," he says. "If I just went to the bank, I wouldn't understand half this stuff. So I'm glad I did it that way, but I'm also glad I'm not doing it any more."

Source: Canadian Franchising Association.

Disadvantages of Franchising

While franchising has a considerable number of advantages, there are also several disadvantages of which you should be aware. One of the principal complaints is the degree of control which franchisors exert over their franchisees. While you will be an independent businessperson, in effect you do not have complete autonomy and must operate within the operating system as defined by the franchisor. You are usually in a subordinate position to the franchisor and must abide by the often extremely rigid terms and conditions of the franchise agreement. All franchise contracts give the franchisor either an open right to terminate the contract or the right to terminate upon breach of the agreement. As a result, you may find yourself in a weak bargaining position.

Franchisees also have certain reporting obligations to the franchisor and may be subject to frequent inspection and constant supervision. To fit comfortably into such an arrangement, you must accept the necessity of such controls. These restrictions, however, may be unacceptable to some individuals. You must seriously assess your personal suitability for the role of a franchisee.

Another disadvantage of franchising is that the cost of the services provided to you by the franchisor is based on your total sales revenue. These costs can amount to 10 percent or more of your total revenue or an even larger share of your profits. A related complaint is that the markup which the franchisor may add to the products you must buy from them can increase your operating costs, particularly if equally good products could be purchased elsewhere at lower prices. While you might initially feel that your operating costs are likely to be lower as a result of the franchisor's central purchasing program, it may not become apparent until later that you are actually paying a huge markup on the material, equipment, and supplies you acquire.

Acquiring a franchise is not necessarily a licence to print money. Besides an initial franchise fee, you will probably also have to make periodic royalty payments and advertising contributions based on a percentage of your gross revenues. Even with these expenditures, you still run the risk of not achieving the expected sales, and thus the profit, which the franchisor stated was possible.

It should also be remembered that, as a matter of fact, the benefits available through franchising have not always materialized. Franchisors have not always supplied the services they promised or truthfully disclosed the amount of time and effort the franchisee would have to commit to the franchise. Termination policies of many franchisors have given franchisees little or no security in many cases.

Types of Franchises

Franchise Formats

There are three major ways a franchise can be formatted:

- **Single-unit franchise** This is the most popular and simplest format. In it, the franchisor grants you the right to establish and operate a business at a single location. This has been the most popular means of franchise expansion and the method by which many independent entrepreneurs have become involved in franchise distribution.

- **Area franchise** This format involves a franchisor's granting you the right to establish more than one outlet within a specified territory. This territory can be as large as an entire state, a province, or even a country, or it can be as small as part of a city. To assure that this territory is adequately serviced, the franchisor will usually require the construction and operation of a specific number of outlets within a period of time. Area franchising may be a means of achieving certain economies of scale, and perhaps a lower average franchise cost. On the other hand, it requires a larger total capital outlay for plant and equipment. Area franchisees with a large number of outlets can sometimes acquire greater financial strength than their franchisors. This has happened in a number of instances in the fast food industry.

- **Master franchise** In this format, a franchisor grants you (the *master franchisee*) the right, not only to operate an outlet in a specific territory, but also to sell subfranchises to others within that same territory. Granting master franchises is the fastest way for a franchisor to expand, but it is also very complex and results in a division of fees and royalties between the franchisor and subfranchisor. A master franchisee may not need as much initial capital as an area franchisee, but he or she must learn not only how to open and operate a franchise business but also how to sell franchises.

Range of Available Franchises

To give you an idea of the current scope of franchising, *Opportunities Canada* in their franchise and dealership guide[1], provides information on over 1500 different franchisor organizations in 32 product/service categories. The range of possibilities available to a prospective franchisee includes opportunities in the following areas:

- Accounting and financial services
- Automotive products and services
- Beauty, health, and personal services
- Building products and services
- Business related/communication services
- Car rental and limo services
- Computer products and services
- Convenience & grocery stores and bakeries
- Educational and training systems
- Employment and personnel services
- Fast food: takeout/sit-in
- Food retail: candy, coffee, yogurt, etc.
- Health aids and services and water treatment
- Hotels, motels, and campgrounds
- Interior decorating products and services
- Lawn care, landscaping, and hydroponic services
- Maid and janitorial services
- Maintenance, repair, restoration, and cleaning products
- Pet products and services
- Photography, art products, and services
- Printing, copying, and typesetting
- Publishing
- Real estate
- Recreation, sporting goods, and related services
- Restaurants: dining rooms/bars
- Retail apparel: footwear and fashion accessories
- Retail miscellaneous
- Security systems
- Support services: franchise and dealerships
- Travel
- Vending and dispensing machine systems
- Video retail

Within this broad spectrum of available opportunities, the most popular areas have been fast food (takeout/sit-in), food retail (candy, coffee, yogurt, etc.), automotive products and services, and business related/communication services.

At the individual franchisor level, the Top 10 franchise organizations for 1999 based on an evaluation by *Entrepreneur*[2] magazine were:

1. Yogen Früz Worldwide — Frozen yogurt & ice cream (www.yogenfruz.com)

2. McDonald's — Hamburgers, chicken, salad (www.mcdonalds.com)

---

[1] *Opportunities Canada*, Vol. 6, No. 2, Fall-Winter 1996-97.

[2] *Entrepreneur*, Vol. 27, No. 1, January 1999. The evaluation is based on a number of factors including length of time in business and number of years franchising, number of franchised units and company-owned operating units, start-up costs, growth rate, percentage of terminations, and financial stability of the company.

3. Subway — Submarine sandwiches and salads (www.subway.com)

4. Wendy's Int'l Inc. — Quick-service restaurant (www.wendys.com)

5. Jackson Hewitt Tax Service — Computerized tax preparation (www.jacksonhewitt.com)

6. KFC — Chicken (www.kfc.com)

7. Mail Boxes Inc. — Postal/business/communication services (www.mbe.com)

8. TCBY Treats — Frozen yogurt, ice cream, sorbet (www.tcby.com)

9. Taco Bell Corp. — Mexican quick-service restaurant (www.tacobell.com)

10. Jani-King — Commercial cleaning services (www.janiking.com)

Legal Aspects of Franchising

Canadian Legislation and Disclosure Requirements

Many states in the U.S. have laws and regulations governing franchise companies, but the same is not true for provinces in Canada. Only Alberta has a Franchise Act.

The Alberta legislation did require franchisors wishing to sell franchises in that province to disclose the material facts involved in operating a franchise. This involved filing a prospectus as well as a set of audited financial statements with the Alberta Securities Commission.

Many franchisors, however, complained that the Alberta legislation was incredibly oner- ous. It took a long time to prepare the required material, and the legal costs of complying were prohibitive for small, first-time franchisors. To address these concerns, the Alberta legislature passed a new Franchise Act in the spring of 1995, which relaxed some of the more stringent demands on franchisors.

Instead of having to file documents or register with a government agency, franchisors (with some exceptions) must provide prospective franchisees with a disclosure document containing copies of all franchise agreements, financial statements, and other related mate- rial. This disclosure document must be provided to a prospective franchisee at least 14 days before any agreement is signed or any payments are made related to the franchise. These financial statements no longer need to be audited but must be prepared in accordance with generally accepted accounting standards. Further information on the legislation and regula- tions can be obtained from Alberta Department of Municipal Affairs, Industry Standards, Housing and Consumer Affairs Division at (403) 422-1588 (www.gov.ab.ca./~ma). This change will put more onus on franchisees, not only in Alberta but elsewhere in Canada as well, to take more responsibility for their business investments.

Beyond Alberta, Canada is known as the "Wild West" of franchising. Ontario has pro- posed franchise legislation for a number of years and did introduce legislation similar to that in Alberta in the spring of 1998, but it was never passed. Approval of such legislation might prevent further situations like that of Fereshteh Vahdati and her husband in Entrepreneur in Action #13 who spent more than $100,000 to buy a Toronto pizza franchise and another $100,000 in legal costs in a court battle against the pizza-chain owner, and ended up losing it all. In all other provinces, franchisors are under no obligation to provide any specific informa- tion or file any material with a government agency or department. As a franchisee, you are on your own for the most part. If your potential franchisor does operate in Alberta, however, you should request a copy of the disclosure material they are obliged to provide to prospective franchisees in that province.

13

ENTREPRENEURS IN ACTION

Taken to the Cleaners

Fereshteh Vahdati and her husband spent more than $100,000 to buy a Toronto pizza franchise, invested thousands more on various fees—and worked 17 hours a day.

Their payoff?

"We didn't make any money," said a despondent Vahdati on Thursday.

"Everything goes to (the chain) ... These people cheat us and we've lost everything."

Vahdati said she and her husband spent $100,000 on legal costs in a fruitless court fight against the pizza-chain owner.

The couple immigrated from Iran eight years ago and heard about the business from an Iranian community newspaper here.

The owner, also of Iranian descent, asked them to pay a 10 per cent royalty and four per cent of sales for advertising, Vahdati said.

But after they bought the stores, they were told they also had to spend $65,000 a year to buy flyers from the owner.

They eventually ran out of money and the company seized the stores from them, Vahdati said.

Source: Adapted from Tom Blackwell, "New Bill Aims to Protect Franchise Owners." *Canadian Press Newswire*, Dec. 3, 1998.

The U.S. Situation

Since 1979 the U.S. Federal Trade Commission (FTC) has required that every franchisor offering franchises in the U.S. have a *disclosure statement* called a "Uniform Franchise Offering Circular" (UFOC) ready to offer a prospective franchisee. A copy of any disclosure statement can be obtained from the Federal Trade Commission, Washington, DC 20580. This document discloses 20 categories of information:

1. Identifying information about the franchisor
2. Business experience of the franchisor's directors and key executives
3. The franchisor's business experience
4. Litigation history of the franchisor and its directors and key executives
5. Bankruptcy history of the franchisor and its directors and key executives
6. Description of the franchise
7. Money required to be paid by the franchisee to obtain or commence the franchise operation
8. Continuing expenses to the franchisee in operating the franchise business that are payable in full or in part to the franchisor or to a person affiliated with the franchisor
9. A list of persons who represent either the franchisor or any of its affiliates, with whom the franchisee is required or advised to do business
10. Real estate, services, supplies, products, inventories, signs, fixtures, or equipment which the franchisee is required to purchase, lease, or rent, and a list of any persons with whom such transactions must be made
11. Descriptions of consideration paid (such as royalties, commissions, etc.) by third parties to the franchisor or any of its affiliates as a result of a franchisee's purchase from such third parties
12. Description of any franchisor assistance in financing the purchase of a franchise
13. Restrictions placed on a franchisee's conduct of the business

14. Required personal participation by the franchisee

15. Information about termination, cancellation, and renewal of the franchise

16. Statistical information about the number of franchises and their rate of termination or failure

17. Franchisor's right to select or approve a site for the franchise

18. Training programs for the franchisee

19. Celebrity involvement with the franchise

20. Financial information about the franchisor

The FTC regulations also require that if the franchisor makes any claims regarding the level of earnings you might realize as a result of owning its franchise, a reasonable basis must exist to support the accuracy of these claims. When such claims are made, the franchisor must have prepared an "Earnings Disclosure Document" for prospective franchisees, explaining the basis and material assumptions on which the claims are made.

If the franchise you are investigating currently operates in the U.S., this information should be readily available.

The Franchise Agreement

Because two independent parties participate in a franchise relationship, the primary vehicle for obtaining central coordination and control over the efforts of both participants is a formal contract. This *franchise agreement* is the heart of the franchise relationship. It differs from the typical contract in that it contains restrictive clauses peculiar to franchising which limit your rights and powers in the conduct of the business. Franchisors argue that these controls are necessary in order to protect their trademark and to maintain a common identity for their outlets.

A franchise agreement should cover a variety of matters. There should be provisions that cover such subjects as:

- The full initial costs, and what they cover
- Use of the franchisor's trademarks by the franchisee
- Licensing fees
- Land purchase or lease requirements
- Building construction or renovation
- Equipment needs
- Initial training provided
- Starting inventory
- Promotional fees or allowances
- Use of operations manuals
- Royalties
- Other payments related to the franchisor
- Ongoing training
- Cooperative advertising fees
- Insurance requirements
- Interest charges on financing
- Requirements regarding purchasing supplies from the franchisor, and competitiveness of prices with those of other suppliers
- Restrictions that apply to competition with other franchisees
- Terms covering termination of the franchise, renewal rights, passing the franchise on to other family members, resale of the franchise, and similar topics

In considering any franchise proposition, you should pay a great deal of attention to the franchise contract. Since it is a key part of the relationship, it should he thoroughly understood. The rest of this section discusses the evaluation of an agreement for a single-unit franchise within a business format franchise system. It is important to realize, however, that this is not a "typical" franchise agreement; there is really no such thing. While agreements may follow a fairly standard approach in terms of format, they do not do so in terms of content. Every agreement is specially drafted by the franchisor to reflect its particular objectives and the future of the business.

Obligations Undertaken by the Franchisor

The obligations undertaken by the franchisor may include any or all of the following:

1. To provide basic business training to you and your employees. This includes training in bookkeeping skills, staff selection, staff management, business procedures, and the systems necessary to control the operation. In addition, the franchisor may provide you with training relating to the operational aspects of the business.

2. To investigate and evaluate sites for the location of your franchise. You will be advised as to whether or not the site meets the franchisor's standards and what sort of performance might be expected at that location. In addition you may be assisted in the design and layout of your franchise operation.

3. To provide either the equipment or the specifications for any necessary equipment and furniture you require.

4. To provide promotional and advertising material to you, and some guidance and training on marketing and promotional principles.

5. The franchisor may provide you with a statement indicating the amount of opening inventory required, and may make arrangements for you to purchase inventory either from the franchisor's own purchasing department or from particular suppliers established for this purpose.

6. The franchisor may provide you with on-site assistance for the opening of your franchise outlet. Quite often the franchisor will provide a team of two to three people to assist you in getting the business off the ground.

7. The franchisor may also provide business operating manuals explaining the details of operating the franchise system and a bookkeeping/accounting system for you to follow. There may also be additional support through such things as business consultation, supervisory visits to your premises, and staff retraining.

Obligations Imposed Upon a Franchisee

Your obligations as a franchisee may include any or all of the following:

1. To build your franchise outlet according to the plan or specifications provided by the franchisor

2. To maintain construction and opening schedules established by the franchisor

3. To abide by the lease commitments for your franchise outlet

4. To observe certain minimum opening hours for your franchise

5. To pay the franchise fees and other fees specified in the franchise agreement

6. To follow the accounting system specified by the franchisor and to provide financial reports and payments of amounts due promptly

7. To participate in all regional or national cooperative advertising and to use and display such point-of-sale or advertising material as the franchisor stipulates (this would include having all your advertising materials approved by the franchisor)

8. To maintain your premises in clean, sanitary condition and redecorate when required to do so by the franchisor

9. To maintain the required level of business insurance coverage

10. To permit the franchisor's staff to enter your premises to inspect and see whether the franchisor's standards are being maintained

11. To purchase specific goods or services from the franchisor or specified suppliers

12. To train all staff in the franchisor's method and to ensure that they are neatly and appropriately dressed

13. Not to assign the franchise contract without the franchisor's consent

14. To maintain adequate levels of working capital and abide by the operations manual provided by the franchisor

These are only examples of some of the obligations you might expect to incur. There will probably also be clauses involving bankruptcy, transfer of the business, and renewal of the contract, and provisions for the payment of royalties and other financial considerations.

Franchise Fees and Royalties

In most cases you will be required to pay an initial franchise fee on signing the franchise agreement. This fee generally pays for the right to use the trade name, licences, and operating procedures of the franchisor, some initial training, and perhaps even assistance in site selection for your franchise outlet. The amount of the fee varies tremendously, according to the type of franchise business. For a large restaurant operation or hotel, for example, the fee may be as high as $50,000 or $60,000, but for a small service franchise (such as maid service or lawn care) it may be only $5,000 to $10,000. This fee is not all profit for the franchisor, as it must go to pay for franchisee recruitment, training, assistance with site selection, and other services normally provided to you. Some franchisors will charge a separate training fee, but this is usually established merely to recover the cost of providing the training to you and your employees.

In addition to this initial fee, ongoing fees may also be provided for in the franchise agreement. These will generally consist of royalties payable for ongoing rights and privileges granted by the franchisor. Royalties are usually calculated as a percentage of the gross sales, not profits, generated by your franchise. They may be paid either weekly, monthly, or quarterly, and represent the main profit centre for most franchisors. These royalties must continue to be paid even though the franchise may be losing money. For a fast food franchise, typical royalties range from 3 percent to 8 percent. For some service franchises, the royalty may run from 10 to 20 percent or even higher.

While some franchisees come to resent having to continue to pay ongoing royalties to their franchisor, this payment may be preferable to the franchisor charging a higher initial fee to the franchisee. Ongoing royalty payments at least imply a continuing commitment to the success of the franchise by the franchisor, to the ultimate benefit of both parties.

As well as royalty fees, many franchise agreements require you to contribute a proportion of your business' gross revenues to a regional or national cooperative advertising fund. This contribution may be an additional 2 to 4 percent of gross sales. These payments are used to develop and distribute advertising material and to run regional and national advertising campaigns. These, too, are typically not a source of profit for the franchisor.

The administration of these advertising funds has often been the subject of considerable concern to franchisees and one of the areas of greatest dispute between franchisors and franchisees. The advertising fund should be maintained as a separate trust account by the franchisor and not intermixed with its general operating revenues. The purpose of this fund should be specified in the franchise agreement. In addition, the agreement should also state how and by whom the fund will be administered.

In addition to requiring you to support a regional or a national advertising program, a franchisor may require you to support your own *local* advertising. Typically you must spend a specific amount on a periodic basis, calculated either on the basis of a percentage of gross sales or in terms of a fixed amount. Local advertising devised by you will normally require the prior approval of the franchisor.

In some cases the franchisor also provides you with special services such as bookkeeping, accounting, and management consulting services which are billed on a fee-for-service basis. Before acquiring a franchise, you should be sure that you understand all the fees that will be payable, including any extra fees that may not be mentioned in the franchise agreement.

Purchase of Products and Supplies

A key element in the success of many franchise organizations is the sameness of each of the franchise outlets. Therefore, the franchisor will work to ensure the maintenance of a certain quality of product or service and to make sure that uniform standards are employed throughout their system. Consequently, many franchisors, in an attempt to exercise complete control over their operation, require you to purchase products and services from them or from designated sources. In some cases the approved suppliers may include affiliates of the franchisor. You may also be able to purchase items from other sources of supply, provided the franchisor has approved each of those sources in advance.

If the franchisor exerts tight control over such supplies, you should try to ensure beforehand that supplies are going to be readily available when required, that they are sold to you at fair market value and on reasonable terms, and that you have the ability to choose alternative sources for any non-proprietary items if the franchisor or the designated supplier is unable to provide them to you when required.

Many franchisors earn a profit from providing supplies to their franchisees. Often, however, because franchisors exercise enormous buying power they can supply goods and services at prices and under terms which are better than those you could negotiate for yourself. You should shop around to compare prices for comparable merchandise. If the prices being charged by the franchisor are out of line, this added cost can dramatically affect your business' future earnings.

Volume rebates are often paid to franchisors by suppliers of particular products. Rather than pocket the money themselves or distribute it back to their franchisees, some franchisors will contribute this to the advertising fund. As a potential franchisee you should ask how these rebates will be handled, as a considerable amount of money may be involved.

Leased Premises

Many franchise operations require the use of physical facilities such as land and buildings. Where these premises are leased rather than owned by the franchisee, there are a number of ways in which this lease arrangement can be set up:

1. The franchisor may own the land and/or buildings and lease it to you.
2. You may lease the land and/or building directly from a third party.
3. You may own the property, sell it to the franchisor, and lease it back under a *sale leaseback* agreement.
4. A third party may own the property and lease it to the franchisor, who then sublets it to you.

The franchise agreement should spell out who is responsible, you or the franchisor, for negotiating the lease, equipping the premises, and paying the related costs. If a lease is involved, its terms and renewal clauses should be stated and should correspond with the terms of the franchise. You must be careful not to have a 20-year lease on a building and only a 5-year franchise agreement, or vice versa.

Franchisors generally want to maintain control of the franchise premises. Accordingly they will often own or lease the property on which the franchise business is located, and then sublet these premises to you. In other situations the franchisor may assign a lease to you subject to a conditional reassignment of the lease back to the franchisor upon termination of the franchise for any reason.

With respect to other leasehold improvements, you may also be required to purchase, or lease from the franchisor or from suppliers designated by the franchisor, certain fixtures, furnishings, equipment, and signs that the franchisor has approved as meeting their specifications and standards.

Territorial Protection

In many cases the franchise agreement provision with respect to your territory and protection of that territory may be subject to considerable negotiation prior to inclusion in the agreement. You will generally want to have the franchisor agree not to operate or grant a franchise to operate another franchised outlet too close to your operation. This restriction may be confined to a designated territory, or may be confined to a predetermined geographic radius from your premises.

Franchisors, on the other hand, like to see exclusive territorial protection kept to a minimum. As a result, some franchisors may restrict the protection provided to you to a grant of first refusal to acquire an additional franchise within your territory, or may subject you to a performance quota in terms of a prescribed number of outlet openings in order to maintain exclusivity within your territory. Another approach taken by some franchisors is to limit exclusivity to a formula based on population, with the result that when the population within your territory exceeds a certain number, the franchisor may either itself operate, or grant a franchise to operate, an additional outlet in the territory.

Some questions you might like to have answered in the franchise agreement are as follows:

1. Exactly what are the geographic boundaries of your territory, and are they marked on a map as part of the contract?
2. Do you have a choice of other territories?
3. What direct competition is there in your territory, and how many more franchises does the franchisor expect to sell in that area within the next five years?
4. If the territory is an exclusive one, what are the guarantees of this exclusivity?
5. Even with these guarantees, will you be permitted to open another franchise in the same territory?
6. Can your territory be reduced at any time by the franchisor?
7. Has the franchisor prepared a market survey of your territory? (If so, ask for a copy of it and study it.)
8. Has the specific site for the franchise within the territory been decided on? (If not, how and when will this be done?)

Training and Operating Assistance

Virtually every franchise agreement deals with the question of training the franchisee. Training programs may involve training schools, field experience, training manuals, or on-location training.

The franchise agreement should have some provision for an initial training program for you, and should specify the duration and location of this training and who is responsible for your related transportation, accommodation, and living expenses. This initial training is generally provided for you and the manager of your franchise business. The franchisor will usually require you and your managers to complete the training program successfully prior to the opening of your franchise business. If for some reason you should fail to complete the training program, the franchisor often reserves the right to terminate the agreement and refund all fees, less any costs incurred so far.

Many franchise agreements also provide for start-up advisory training at the franchise premises prior to or during the opening of the business. This typically involves a program lasting a prespecified number of days. The agreement should indicate who is expected to bear the cost for such start-up training, including who will be responsible for the payment of travel, meals, accommodation, and other expenses of the franchisor's supervisory personnel.

The franchise agreement may also make reference to periodic refresher training. It should specify whether attendance at such programs is optional or mandatory. If they are mandatory, you should ensure that a specified maximum number of such programs is indicated for each year of the franchise agreement. The duration and location of these programs should also be specified.

Most franchisors want tight control over the day-to-day operations of the franchise, and accordingly they provide extensive operating assistance to their franchisees. This assistance is often in the form of a copyrighted operations manual that spells out, procedure by procedure, how you are expected to run the business. The manual will include such information as the franchisor's policies and procedures, and cover such details as the hours you must remain open, record-keeping methods and procedures, procedures for hiring and training employees, and, in a restaurant franchise, such matters as recipes, portion sizes, food storage and handling procedures, and menu mix and prices. The franchise agreement may also indicate that operating assistance will be provided in relation to:

1. The selection of inventory for your franchise business
2. Inspections and evaluation of your performance
3. Periodic advice with respect to hiring personnel, implementing advertising and promotional programs, and evaluating improvements in the franchise system
4. Purchasing goods, supplies, and services
5. Bookkeeping and accounting services
6. Hiring and training of employees
7. Formulation and implementation of advertising and promotional programs
8. Financial advice and consultation
9. Such additional assistance as you may require from time to time

Contract Duration, Termination, and Renewal

The duration of your franchise agreement may be as short as one year or as long as 40 to 50 years. However, the majority of franchise contracts run from 10 to 20 years. Most agreements also contain some provision for renewal of the contract. Be sure you understand these renewal provisions and what the terms, conditions, and costs of renewal will be. Renewal provisions commonly contain requirements for the payment of additional fees and upgrading of the franchise facilities to standards required by the franchisor at that time. The cost of upgrading is usually borne by the franchisee.

You should be aware, however, that not all agreements necessarily contain provisions for their renewal at the expiration of the initial term. Some agreements merely expire at the end of this term, and the rights revert to the franchisor.

The part of the franchise agreement usually considered most offensive by many prospective franchisees are those sections relating to termination of the agreement. Franchisors typically wish to develop a detailed list of conditions in which you might be considered in default of the agreement. *Events of default* typically fall into two categories: (1) critical or material events which would allow for termination of the agreement without notice by the franchisor and (2) events upon which you would first be given written notice with an opportunity to correct the situation.

Most franchise agreements also allow the franchisor the right, upon termination or expiration, to purchase from you all inventory, supplies, equipment, furnishings, leasehold improvements, and fixtures used in connection with the franchise business. The method of calculating the purchase price of such items is entirely negotiable by the parties prior to the execution of the franchise agreement. This has been another area of considerable disagreement between franchisors and franchisees.

When renewing franchise agreements, many franchisors do not require the payment of an additional fee, but they may require franchisees to pay the current, and usually higher, royalty fees and advertising contributions. These increases, of course, reduce your income. In addition, the franchisor may require you to make substantial leasehold improvements, update signage, and make other renovations to your outlet in order to conform to current franchise system standards. These capital expenditures can be expensive, so it should be clear from the beginning what improvements might be required upon renewal.

Selling or Transferring Your Franchise

With respect to the transfer or sale of your franchise, most franchise agreements indicate that you are granted rights under the agreement based on the franchisor's investigation of your qualifications. These rights are typically considered to be personal to you as a franchisee. The contract will usually state that transfers of ownership are prohibited without the approval of the franchisor, but you should attempt to have the franchisor agree that such consent will not be unreasonably withheld.

For self-protection, you should be sure that the agreement contains provisions for the transfer of the franchise to your spouse or an adult child upon your death. Also, it should be possible to transfer the franchise to a corporation which is 100 percent owned by you and has been set up solely to operate the franchise. These transfers should be possible without the payment of additional fees.

Most franchisors, however, require transfer of your franchise to an external party who meets their normal criteria of technical competence, capital, and character. You may be able to enhance the marketability of your franchise by anticipating these and other problems in the initial negotiations.

Another common provision is for the franchisor to have a *right of first refusal* — the option to purchase your franchise in the event that you receive an offer from an independent third party to acquire your rights. In such a situation you may be required to first offer such rights back to the franchisor under the same terms and conditions offered by the independent third party. If the franchisor declines to acquire your rights within a specified period of time after receipt of your notice of such an offer, you can proceed to complete the sale or transfer to the third-party purchaser.

One problem with this right of first refusal is the response time the franchisor has to exercise this right. In some agreements the allowable period is several months, during which the third-party buyer is left on hold. In your original agreement, you should try to negotiate for a more reasonable period of 15 to 30 days for the exercise of this right of first refusal.

Some Examples

As mentioned above, the specific terms included in a franchise agreement can vary substantially from situation to situation. For example, under the terms of the Nutri-Lawn, Ecology Friendly Lawn Care franchise agreement for their residential and commercial lawn care franchise, franchisees pay $15,000 for an initial franchise fee plus a monthly royalty of 6% of gross sales and 2% of gross sales for the corporate advertising program. The minimum total investment required of the franchisee to get into the business is approximately $45,000 – $15,000 for the franchise fee, $15,000 for the necessary equipment and $15,000 in working capital to launch the business. For this fee the franchisee receives the use of the company's trademark and tradenames. There is also a two-week initial training program plus some ongoing training and marketing support, including a defined territory.

In contrast, franchisees of The Great Canadian Bagel Company can expect to make a total investment of about $300,000 to open a typical outlet. In addition they will need further funds for the rental deposit on their property, security deposits of various kinds, and money for working capital. This includes their standard franchise fee of $30,000. In addition, royalties amount to six percent of gross sales paid monthly and the advertising contribution is a further one and one-half percent of sales. Of the total amount, franchisees are required to have at least $100,000 in unencumbered cash. The rest can be financed through one of the national bank franchise programs. Franchisees receive four weeks of classroom and in-store training, assistance in store design and site selection, on-site pre-opening assistance and training and ongoing support in store operations, marketing, purchasing and other aspects of running the business.

The Keg Steakhouse and Bar bills itself as Canada's leading steakhouse. A typical new, stand-alone Keg restaurant requires an investment of $1.8 million to build the facility and cover the necessary start-up costs. This includes the franchise fee of $50,000. Franchisees also pay a royalty of 5% of their gross sales each month and contribute 2.5% to a corporate advertising fund. This enables them to use the "Keg" brand name on their restaurant and the company provides them with training and other support before they open their location and ongoing support in accounting, marketing, menu development, personnel management, and financial planning.[3]

A sampling of some other popular franchisors indicating their initial franchise or dealership fee, royalty rate, required advertising contribution, and their approximate total average investment to open a typical outlet is shown in Table 5.1.

Buying a Franchise

Finding a Franchise Business

Perhaps the most common source of preliminary information regarding available franchises is newspaper advertisements. Major business newspapers such as *The National Post*, and *The Globe and Mail* all have special sections devoted to franchise advertisements. The "Business" or "Business Opportunities" section of the classified advertisements in your local newspaper can also be an important place to look for prospective franchise situations. Business journals and trade magazines may also contain ads for many franchise organizations. Recommendations from friends, trade shows and seminars, and business opportunity shows often held in our larger cities can also be excellent means of contacting franchisors.

Another important source of information is franchise directories, which list franchisors' names and addresses along with information on the type of franchise offered, the costs involved, and other useful information. Some useful directories are the *Franchise Annual* published by Info Press Inc. (728 Center St., Lewiston, NY 14092 or P.O. Box 670, 9 Duke St., St. Catharines, Ont. L2R 6W8), (infonews.com.franchise) and *Opportunities Canada* published by the Type People Inc. (2550 Goldenridge Road, Unit 42, Mississauga, Ontario, L4X 2S3).

---

[3] For further information on these and other franchise opportunities see *The 1999 Franchise Annual*, or *The Canadian Business Franchise Handbook*, Third Edition, CGB Publishing Ltd., Victoria, B.C., V8Z 3R1.

TABLE 5.1 A SAMPLING OF CANADIAN FRANCHISORS

Franchisor	Number of Owned Units	Number of Franchisees /Dealers	Initial Fee	Royalty	Advertising	Approximate Investment Required
Boston Pizza	1	100	$45,000	7%	2.5%	$650-725,000
Dollar Rent-a-Car	—	46	$15-59,000	7	2	$90-150,000
Great Canadian Dollar Store	—	42	$15,000	4	—	$65,000
Molly Maid	—	160	$14,000	6	—	$18,000
Dairy Queen Canada	—	504	$35,000	4	3-6	$450-1,200,000
We Care Home Health Services	—	43	$25,000	5	2	$50,000
McDonald's Restaurants of Canada	335	727	$45,000	17% including rent, service fees and advertising	—	$600-800,000
Midas Muffler	20	230	$25,000	5	5	$225,000
Yogen Fruz	108	4654	$15-25,000	6	2	$100-150,000
Second Cup Coffee Co.	11	360	$20,000	9	—	$170-225,000
Tim Hortons	25	1500	$50,000	3	—	$275-360,000
Kwik-Kopy Printing	—	76	$25,000	6	3	$200,000
Shred-It	12	33	$45,000 US	5	1.5	$500,000

Source: Adapted from *The 1999 Franchise Annual*, Info Franchise News Inc., 1999.

Checking Out the Franchise Opportunity

After sifting through the various choices available, most prospective franchisees narrow their selection down to one or two possibilities. The next step is requesting a promotional kit from each of these franchisors. Normally this kit contains basic information about the company — its philosophy, a brief history, a listing of the number of outlets, where they do business, etc. Most kits also contain an *application form* requesting your name and address, and information about your past business experience, the value of your net assets, and other data; for the process to continue with the franchisor, you must complete it in detail. The form may have any one of a number of titles:

- Confidential Information Form
- Personal History
- Confidential Application
- Franchise Application
- Pre-interview Form
- Qualification Report
- Credit Application
- Application for Interview Form
- Request for Interview

Regardless of which of these titles is used, they are all different ways of describing the same thing and request much the same information. For example, you may be asked for:

1. Personal data such as your name, address, telephone number, age, health and physical impairments, marital status and number of dependents, and the name of any fraternal, business, or civic organizations to which you might belong

2. Business data such as your present business or corporation, your position, the name and address of your employer, how long you have been involved in this business, your present annual salary, and any previous business history you may have

3. References such as your present bank and the name and address of your bank manager, and any other references you may care to provide

4. Financial data such as your average annual income for the past five years, and a total declaration of your current assets and liabilities to establish your net worth

5. Additional data that relate to your particular interest in the franchise

The application form normally requires you to provide a deposit, typically in the range of $2,000 to $5,000. In most cases the form will state that this deposit will be credited toward the initial franchise fee without interest or deduction if the transaction should proceed. However, you should make sure that if you are turned down, all or most of this deposit will be refundable, especially if it is a large amount of money and the franchise is new and unproven.

If your application is approved, the franchisor will interview you to determine your suitability as a franchisee. The focus of this interview will be on assessing your capability according to various objective criteria that have been established by the franchisor. Every franchisor has its own established criteria based on previous experience with various kinds of people. For example, many franchisors will not consider absentee owners and refuse to grant franchises strictly for investment purposes. They feel that the success of their system rests on the motivation created by individually owned and managed outlets.

The personal characteristics desired by the franchisor will vary with the type of business. For example, a different level of education is necessary to operate a management consulting service than is needed to operate a carpet cleaning firm. Research on these selection criteria indicates that many franchisors tend to rank them in the following order:

1. Credit and financial standing
2. Personal ability to manage the operation
3. Previous work experience
4. Personality
5. Health
6. Educational background

While other factors may also be considered by particular franchisors, these criteria tend to dominate the selection process.

This interview is also an opportunity for you to raise questions about the franchisor's financial stability, trademark protection policy, the ongoing services provided to franchisees, information regarding any financial packages that may have been arranged with particular banks, the names and addresses of current franchisees, and any other questions that may occur to you. This is an opportunity for you and the franchisor to assess each other and see if you can work together on a long-term basis.

At this interview, the franchisor will also provide you with a copy of the franchise agreement. At this point, you must evaluate all the available information with the help of your accountant, your bank manager, and your lawyer in order to ensure that you feel comfortable with the franchisor and that you are happy your investment is secure. If you have any remaining questions or doubts, now is the time to resolve them. Then, if you are still not completely sure in your own mind that you wish to proceed, you should ask for a refund of your deposit.

Well-established and popular franchisors are unlikely to change their arrangements or legal documentation very much in response to a prospective franchisee's requests. They have successful systems in which many would-be franchisees would like to participate. For them, it's a seller's market.

If one of these franchisors accepts you as a franchisee, you may have to make up your mind very quickly. It is important to be decisive. If you are comfortable with the franchisor and the franchise agreement, you should be ready to sign. If not, you should ask for a refund and pursue other opportunities.

Some franchisors will expect you to sign the contract right away. Others wait until they have found a suitable location for your outlet, usually within a predetermined period of time. In some cases, it can take weeks, perhaps even months, for a suitable site to be found or a lease negotiated before you actually sign. It should also be remembered that popular franchisors often have long waiting lists of prospective franchisees, so that one or more years can pass before you will be in business.

Franchise Financing

One of the first steps in evaluating any franchise opportunity is to determine the total cost of getting into the business. This could include the initial franchise fee, real estate rental, equipment costs, start-up inventories and expenses, and initial working capital requirements. This total commitment can be substantial. A recent study released by the International Franchise Association in the United States indicated the following average initial investment to start a franchised outlet by industry category. These figures are in U.S. dollars and do not include the cost of real estate.[4]

Baked Goods	$170,000
Business Services	$72,000
Fast Food	$180,000
Lodging	$1,800,000
Printing	$207,000
Restaurant	$559,000
Service Business	$121,000
Sports & Recreation	$471,000
Travel	$73,000

Then you must determine how much of this amount must be put up as an initial investment and what kind of terms might be arranged for handling the balance. Most franchisors expect the franchisee to put up 30 to 50 percent of the total franchise package cost as an initial investment. You must ask yourself whether you have enough unencumbered capital to cover this amount.

Financing of the remainder can sometimes be done through the franchisor, or the franchisor may have previously arranged a standardized financing package for prospective franchisees through one of the major banks or trust companies. Subway, the successful submarine sandwich franchise, offers its new franchisees financing via an in-house equipment leasing program.

---

[4] "The Profile of Franchising: A Statistical Abstract of 1996 UFOC (Uniform Franchise Offering Circulars), Info Franchise Newsletter, International Franchise Association Educational Foundation.

Moneysworth & Best Shoe Repair Inc. also has an in-house financing program for franchisees in conjunction with one of the major banks. These programs may be somewhat more expensive for the franchisee than arranging an independent bank loan, but they can be more convenient.

The initial investment required for a restaurant franchise can be substantial. A typical fast food take-out restaurant such as Koya Japan has an initial franchise fee of $25,000 and an average total investment of $175,000. The cost of a full service restaurant such as Swiss Chalet Chicken & Ribs includes a franchise fee of $75,000 and a total investment ranging from $1.1 million to $1.4 million. In these cases, equipment and leasehold improvements tend to make up the largest component of the total cost.

In the retail sector, the size of the total investment will vary depending on the nature and location of the outlet. For example, a video store like Jumbo Video will require a franchise fee of $50,000 and a total investment of roughly $400,000, with the franchisee having to provide $150,000 in cash. A computer store like Compucentre has a franchise fee of $25,000 with an average investment of $275,000, while a retail building supply dealership like Windsor Plywood has an initial fee of $35,000 and a total required investment upwards to $1 million. Most of these investments are typically in inventory.

The investment required for a service franchise is usually much lower. Many service franchises can be established for a total investment of less than $50,000. For example, Scharecorp, Canada's largest franchise organization and the operator of Good Turn Systems coin-operated vendors bearing the Muscular Dystrophy Association name and logo, has a franchise fee of $17,500 and a total average investment of $35,000. Similarly, Jani-King Canada, the world's largest commercial cleaning franchise, offers their franchises for a fee ranging from $9,900 to $24,900 depending on the territory, with a nominal additional amount of financing for equipment, supplies, and initial working capital. A residential cleaning and maid service franchise like Molly Maid can be established for a franchise fee of $14,000 plus $4-5,000 in working capital. At the other extreme, opening a franchised hotel or motel may involve a total investment of several million dollars, although the initial amount of money required may be much less since the land and buildings for the hotel or motel can often be externally financed.

Future Trends in Franchising

A number of trends have emerged in the past few years and are likely to continue for several years across the U.S. and Canada. Among the most important of these are:

1. The growth in *conversion franchising*, the conversion of an independent business to a franchise. The idea is not new, and in the past has been used extensively in the franchising of real estate and travel agencies. The movement to conversion franchising is expected to be evident in many other areas, however, especially in construction, home repair and remodelling services, all types of business services, non-food retailing, hotels and restaurants.

2. Women have become involved in franchising in numbers larger than ever before, both as franchisors and as franchisees. Franchising offers new opportunities for women who are entering the professional and management ranks and want to be part of the business world or to invest in an independent business career. Starting their own businesses through franchising decreases the risk factor for women with little or no previous business experience. Furthermore, women often excel in businesses that cater specifically to the needs or interests of other women.

3. Changing consumer lifestyles and the new status of working women in society have influenced the growth of franchising, particularly in terms of non-food retail stores that provide a variety of services for the home. Accelerated growth is expected in franchise stores providing home

furnishings, decorating, picture framing, and other types of accessories for the home. Growth is also expected to take place in all types of general merchandise, video, and electronic stores.

4. Computer technology is having a dramatic impact on the service sector, especially franchising. The computer industry has established new businesses in the form of franchised retail stores and this trend is expected to continue. Although competition will intensify and other distribution channels emerge, franchisors of computer stores will focus on two areas: (1) computer stores specializing in home computers, video games, software, and hardware, and (2) stores providing support services and systems for business.

5. Dental health care and other medical services have become an integral part of franchising as franchised centres have spread to all regions of Canada and the U.S. This trend is expected to continue to develop rapidly as medical expenditures rise and the application of modern business methods by franchisors provide increased efficiency, greater service, and lower fees, while meeting the needs of the huge, untapped market.

6. Franchised restaurants of all types are expected to continue to be the most popular sector of franchising. Increased activity is expected in the upscaling of franchised restaurants in terms of exterior and interior decor, service, and quality and variety of food items served. Franchisors of restaurants have been among the fastest-growing, and this trend is expected to continue for the next few years.

7. Franchises that specialize in automotive repairs will continue to grow in many areas of the huge automotive "after-market." This trend will continue to expand through the next decade. Traditional sources of automotive repair are disappearing with the continuing decline of new-car dealerships and full-service gasoline service stations. In addition, the automobile population is growing annually in both number and variety and, on average, cars on the road are getting older. Franchise growth will be in specialized automotive centres providing services in tuneup, quick lube, muffler repair and replacement, transmissions, brakes, painting, electrical repairs, and general car care.

8. Other areas of franchising that bear watching over the next few years are automobile leasing, packaging and rapid delivery of parcels, home building, medical centres, temporary health services, and business brokers.

9. Convenience stores, emphasizing speed and service, provide the multiple "fill-in" items that consumers need between their regular trips to the supermarket. In order to increase their sales volume and compete with fast food restaurants, many convenience stores are offering a wide variety of take-out foods. This segment of the franchise industry is expected to continue to grow dramatically.

10. Businesses engaged in franchising educational services are becoming highly specialized. For example, increased leisure time has created a growing market for dietary, tanning and exercise training centres that has been successfully exploited by franchise systems. Franchisors have also entered the growing field of early childhood education. Sales of this segment of the franchise industry, too, are expected to continue to increase dramatically.

Evaluating a Franchise — a Checklist

The checklist shown in Figure 5.1 can serve as an effective tool for you to use in evaluating a franchise opportunity. Reading through the questions, you will notice that some of them require you to do a little homework before you can reasonably respond. For example, you and/or your lawyer will have to review the franchise agreement in order to assess the acceptability of the various clauses and conditions. You will also have to give some thought to how much capital you have personally and where you might raise additional financing.

Some questions call for further research. Ask the franchisor for the names and addresses of a number of current franchisees. Select a sample of them and contact them to discuss their views of the franchisor and the franchise agreement. Make certain your interview takes place without the franchisor or his representative present. Check the length of time that franchisee has operated in that particular location in comparison to the length of time that franchise has been in existence. If there is a difference try to determine what happened to the earlier franchisee(s). If you have been provided with pro forma financial statements or other information by the franchisor indicating the level of sales and financial performance you might expect, ask these franchisees to confirm that they are reasonably close to reality. In addition, what you may feel you require in terms of training, advertising and promotion support, and ongoing operating assistance may be a function of the type of franchise you are evaluating.

Make a copy of this checklist for each franchise you intend to evaluate. By using a similar outline to assess each opportunity, it will be much easier for you to compare them.

FIGURE 5.1 CHECKLIST FOR EVALUATING A FRANCHISE

THE FRANCHISOR

1. What is the name and address of the franchise company?
   Name _____
   Address _____
   _____

2. The franchise company is: Public _____ Private _____

3. What is the name and address of the parent company (if different from that of the franchise company)?
   Name _____
   Address _____
   _____

4. The parent company is: Public _____ Private _____

5. On what date was the company founded and when was the first franchise awarded?
   Company founded _____ First franchise awarded _____

6. How many outlets does the franchise currently have in operation or under construction? _____
   a. Of these outlets, how many are franchised and how many are company-owned?
      Franchised _____ Company-owned _____
   b. How many franchises have failed? _____
   c. How many of these failures have been within the past two years? _____
   d. Why did these franchises fail?
      Franchisor's reasons _____
      _____
      _____
      Franchisee's reasons_____
      _____
      _____

7. How many new outlets does the franchisor plan to open within the next 12 months? Where will they open?
   How many _____ Where _____
   _____

continued

Checklist for Evaluating a Franchise — continued

8. a. Who are the key principals in the day-to-day operation of the franchisor's business?

Name	Title	Background
_____	_____	_____
_____	_____	_____
_____	_____	_____
_____	_____	_____

   b. Who are the directors of the company, other than those individuals named above?

Name	Business Background
_____	_____
_____	_____
_____	_____

   c. Who are the consultants to the company?

Name	Business Specialty
_____	_____
_____	_____
_____	_____

THE FRANCHISE

1. Fill in the following data on each of several present franchisees.

Franchise 1

Owner _____

Address _____

_____

Telephone _____

Date started _____

Franchise 2

Owner _____

Address _____

_____

Telephone _____

Date started _____

Franchise 3

Owner _____

Address _____

_____

Telephone _____

Date started _____

2. Has a franchise ever been awarded in your area?   Yes _____   No _____

   a. If Yes, and it is *still in operation*, provide details.

   Owner _____

   Address _____

   Telephone _____

   Date started _____

Checklist for Evaluating a Franchise — continued

    b. If Yes, and it is *no longer in operation*, provide details.

Person involved _____

Address _____

Date opened _____

Date closed _____

Reason for failure _____

3. Is the product or service offered by the franchise:

    a. Part of a growing market?   Yes _____ No _____

    b. Needed in your area?   Yes _____ No _____

    c. Of interest to you?   Yes _____ No _____

    d. Safe for the consumer?   Yes _____ No _____

    e. Protected by a guarantee or warranty?   Yes _____ No _____

    f. Associated with a well-known trademark or personality?   Yes _____ No _____

    g. Accompanied by a trademark that is adequately protected? Yes _____ No _____

4. Will you be acquiring:

    a. A single-unit franchise?   _____

    b. An area franchise?   _____

    c. A master franchise?   _____

5. The franchise is: Exclusive _____   Non-exclusive _____

6. What facilities will be required and will you have to own or lease?

    a. Business can be operated out of home?   Yes _____ No _____

    b. Facilities required:

	Yes	*No*	*Own*	*Lease*
Office	_____	_____	_____	_____
Retail outlet	_____	_____	_____	_____
Manufacturing facility	_____	_____	_____	_____
Warehouse	_____	_____	_____	_____
Other (specify)	_____	_____	_____	_____

7. Who will be responsible for:

	Franchisor	*Franchisee*
a. Location feasibility study?	_____	_____
b. Facility design and layout?	_____	_____
c. Construction?	_____	_____
d. Furnishing?	_____	_____
e. Arranging financing?	_____	_____

FRANCHISE COSTS

1. Is a forecast of expected income and expenses provided?   Yes _____ No _____

    a. If Yes, is it:

       i. Based on actual franchisee operations? _____

       ii. Based on a franchisor-owned outlet? _____

       iii. Based strictly on estimated performance? _____

    b. If Yes, does the forecast:

       i. Relate directly to your market area? Yes _____ No _____

       ii. Satisfy your personal goals? Yes _____ No _____

       iii. Provide for an acceptable return on investment? Yes _____ No _____

       iv. Provide for an adequate level of promotion and personal expenses? Yes _____ No _____

continued

Checklist for Evaluating a Franchise — continued

2. How much money will it require to get started in the business? Itemize.

Item	Amount
a. Franchise fee	$ _____
b. Franchisor-provided services	_____
c. Supplies and opening inventory	_____
d. Real estate	_____
e. Machinery and equipment	_____
f. Furniture and fixtures	_____
g. Opening expenses	_____
h. Other	_____
Total Initial Investment	$ _____ (A)

3. How much other money will be required:

a. To defray operating losses for first few months of operation? $ _____ (B)

b. To cover your personal expenses for the first year of operation? $ _____ (C)

4. Total financial requirements (A + B + C = D) $ _____ (D)

5. How much of these total financial requirements do you personally have available? $ _____ (E)

6. If the franchisor provides any financial assistance:

a. How much? $ _____ (F)

b. What does this represent as a percentage of your total estimated costs? _____ %

c. What is the interest rate on this financing? _____ %

d. When does the money have to be paid back? _____

7. Where will you be able to obtain the rest of the required funds?
Specify sources from the following list:

a. Banks, credit unions or other financial institutions	$ _____
b. Finance companies	_____
c. Friends, relatives, and neighbours	_____
d. Other private sources	_____
e. Leasing arrangements	_____
f. Suppliers' credit	_____
g. Government assistance programs	_____
h. Other (specify)	$ _____
Total	$ _____ (G)

8. Total funds available from all sources (E + F + G = H)

Grand Total $ _____ (H)

9. How do the funds available compare with your total estimated requirements? (D – H) $ _____

THE FRANCHISE AGREEMENT

1. Have you obtained a copy of the franchise agreement? Yes _____ No _____

2. Have you given a copy to your lawyer and accountant to review?

Lawyer   Yes _____ No _____

Accountant Yes _____ No _____

Checklist for Evaluating a Franchise — continued

3. Does the agreement contain clauses that relate to the following areas and activities and are the specified terms and conditions acceptable or unacceptable to you?

	Yes	No	If Yes Acceptable	Unacceptable
a. Franchise fee	_____	_____	_____	_____
b. Commissions and royalties	_____	_____	_____	_____
c. Purchase of products and supplies	_____	_____	_____	_____
d. Lease of premises	_____	_____	_____	_____
e. Territorial protection	_____	_____	_____	_____
f. Training assistance	_____	_____	_____	_____
g. Termination	_____	_____	_____	_____
h. Renewal	_____	_____	_____	_____
i. Selling and transferring	_____	_____	_____	_____
j. Advertising and promotion	_____	_____	_____	_____
k. Operating assistance	_____	_____	_____	_____
l. Trademark protection	_____	_____	_____	_____

RUNNING YOUR FRANCHISE OPERATION

1. Does the franchisor provide you with an initial formal training program? Yes _____ No _____

If Yes: a. How long does it last? _____ days

b. Is cost included in the franchise fee? Yes _____ No _____ Partially _____

If No or Partially, specify how much you will have to pay for:

    i. Training course $ _____

    ii. Training materials   _____

    iii. Transportation   _____

    iv. Room and board   _____

    v. Other   _____

    Total Costs $ _____

c. Does the training course cover any of the following subjects?

i. Franchise operations	Yes _____	No _____
ii. Sales	Yes _____	No _____
iii. Financial management	Yes _____	No _____
iv. Advertising and promotion	Yes _____	No _____
v. Personnel management	Yes _____	No _____
vi. Manufacturing methods	Yes _____	No _____
vii. Maintenance	Yes _____	No _____
viii. Operations	Yes _____	No _____
ix. Employee training	Yes _____	No _____
x. Other (specify) _____		
_____	Yes _____	No _____

2. How do you train your initial staff?

a. Is the training program provided by the franchisor? Yes _____ No _____

b. Does the franchisor make a staff member available from head office to assist you? Yes _____ No _____

c. What materials are included in the staff training program?

_____

_____

_____

continued

Checklist for Evaluating a Franchise — continued

3. Is there any requirement for you to participate in a continuing training program?
Yes _____ No _____
If Yes:
    a. Who pays the cost of this program?   Franchisee _____ Franchisor _____
    b. If you have to pay for this continuing training, how much does it cost? $ _____

4. Is the product or service of the franchise normally sold by any of the following means?

a. In customer's home — by appointment	Yes _____ No _____
b. In customer's home — by cold-calling	Yes _____ No _____
c. By telephone	Yes _____ No _____
d. In a store or other place of business	Yes _____ No _____
e. At customer's business — by appointment	Yes _____ No _____
f. At customer's business — by cold-calling	Yes _____ No _____
g. By direct mail	Yes _____ No _____
h. Other (specify) _____	Yes _____ No _____

5. How do you get sales leads and customers?

a. Provided by franchisor	Yes _____ No _____
b. Self-generated	Yes _____ No _____
c. Through advertising	Yes _____ No _____
d. By direct mail	Yes _____ No _____
e. By telephone	Yes _____ No _____
f. Through trade shows	Yes _____ No _____
g. Other _____	Yes _____ No _____

6. Give a brief profile of the types of customers you feel are the best prospects for the products or services offered by the franchise.

_____
_____
_____

7. a. What is the national advertising budget of the franchisor? $ _____
b. How is this budget distributed among the primary advertising media?

TV	_____%
Radio	_____
Newspaper	_____
Outdoor	_____
Magazines	_____
Direct mail	_____
Other (specify) _____	_____
Total	**100%**

8. What kind of advertising and promotion support is available from the franchisor for the local franchisee?

	Yes	No	If Yes, Cost
a. Prepackaged local advertising program	_____	_____	$ _____
b. Cooperative advertising program	_____	_____	$ _____
c. Grand-opening package	_____	_____	$ _____

9. Do you need the services of an advertising agency?   Yes _____ No _____

Checklist for Evaluating a Franchise — continued

10. a. Who are your principal competitors? Name them in order of importance.

1. _____

2. _____

3. _____

b. Describe what you know about each and how each compares with your franchise.

Competitor 1

Owner _____

Address _____

_____

Description _____

_____

_____

Competitor 2

Owner _____

Address _____

_____

Description _____

_____

_____

Competitor 3

Owner _____

Address _____

_____

Description _____

_____

_____

11. What operating assistance is available from the franchisor if you should need it?

a. Finance and accounting	Yes _____	No _____
b. Advertising and promotion	Yes _____	No _____
c. Research and development	Yes _____	No _____
d. Sales	Yes _____	No _____
e. Real estate	Yes _____	No _____
f. Construction	Yes _____	No _____
g. Personnel and training	Yes _____	No _____
h. Manufacturing and operations	Yes _____	No _____
i. Purchasing	Yes _____	No _____
j. Other (specify) _____	Yes _____	No _____

12. Does the franchisor have a field supervisor assigned to work with a number of franchises?

Yes _____ No _____

If Yes: a. How many franchises are they assigned to?

b. Who would be assigned to your franchise?

Name _____

Address _____

_____

Telephone _____

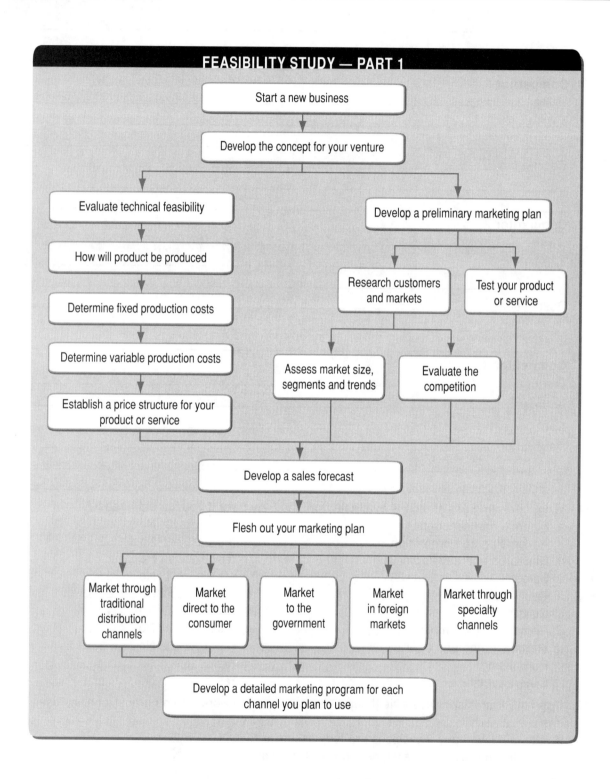

FEASIBILITY STUDY — PART 1

Start a new business

Develop the concept for your venture

Evaluate technical feasibility

How will product be produced

Determine fixed production costs

Determine variable production costs

Establish a price structure for your product or service

Develop a preliminary marketing plan

Research customers and markets

Test your product or service

Assess market size, segments and trends

Evaluate the competition

Develop a sales forecast

Flesh out your marketing plan

Market through traditional distribution channels

Market direct to the consumer

Market to the government

Market in foreign markets

Market through specialty channels

Develop a detailed marketing program for each channel you plan to use

Conducting a Feasibility Study

Part 1:
Technical and Market Assessment

So far, we have considered and evaluated your new venture primarily from a conceptual point of view. That is, we have concentrated on the following questions:

1. What product/service businesses would you be interested in pursuing?
2. How attractive are these venture ideas?
3. What options should you consider in getting into a business of your own?
4. How should your business be organized?
5. How can you protect your idea or concept?

Now, in Stage Six, a step-by-step process will be presented to help you transform your *chosen* venture concept from the idea stage to the marketplace. This is accomplished by means of a *feasibility study*.

Before starting a new business you should first conduct a feasibility study to determine whether your idea could turn into a profitable business venture. In many cases, the opposite is true. People get all excited about the prospects of a new business without giving careful consideration to its prospects or thoroughly researching and evaluating its potential. Some time later they may discover that while the idea was good, the market was too small, the profit margins too narrow, the competition too tough, the financing insufficient or there are other mitigating reasons that cause the business to fail. If the individuals involved had thoroughly researched their idea and conducted a feasibility study before starting, many of these failed businesses would never have been started in the first place.

A feasibility study is the first comprehensive plan you need in contemplating any new venture. It proves both to yourself and others that your new venture concept can become a profitable reality. If the feasibility study indicates that the business idea has potential, write a business plan. A typical feasibility study considers the following areas:

1. The concept for your venture
2. The technical feasibility of your idea
3. An assessment of your market
4. The supply situation

5. Cost-profit analysis
6. Your plans for future action

The first four of these topics will be discussed in this Stage; the last two will be addressed in Stage Seven. Much of the same information can be incorporated into your subsequent business plan (see Stage Eleven) if it appears that your venture warrants commercial development.

The contents of a typical feasibility study are outlined in Figure 6.1. You can use this guide to assist you in evaluating the feasibility of your new venture idea.

Your Venture Concept

It is critical that you be able to clearly and concisely explain, verbally, the principal concept underlying your venture — what sets it apart from other businesses of similar character. If you have difficulty explaining to other people precisely what it is your business proposes to do, it is a clear sign that your concept still needs development and refinement.

An idea is not yet a concept, only the beginning of one. A fully developed concept includes not only some notion as to the product or service the business plans to provide, but also a description of the proposed pricing strategy, promotional program, and distribution plans. It will also consider such aspects of the business as what is unique or proprietary about your product or service idea, any innovative technology involved in its production or sale, and the principal benefits it is expected to deliver to customers.

Developing a good description of your concept can be difficult. Many concepts are too broad and general, not clearly communicating the really distinctive elements of the venture — for example, "a retail sporting goods outlet" or "a tool and equipment rental store." Other concepts may use words like "better service," "higher quality," "new," "improved," or "precision machined," which are either ambiguous or likely to have different meanings for different people. It is much better to have a detailed, clear, definitive statement — for example, "a retail outlet providing top-of-the-line hunting and fishing equipment and supplies for the serious outdoors person" or "a tool and equipment rental business for the professional, commercial and residential building contractor." Such descriptions are easier to visualize and allow the uninformed to really understand what it is you propose to do.

Your business concept is not necessarily etched in stone. It may need to change and evolve over time as you come to better understand the needs of the marketplace and the economics of the business. Sharpening and refining of your concept is normal and to be expected.

Technical Feasibility

You should keep in mind that not all businesses are started on the basis of new or original ideas. Many, in fact, merely attempt to copy successful ventures. To simplify matters, all product and service ideas can be placed along a continuum according to their degree of innovativeness or may be placed into one of the following categories:

1. **New invention** This is something created for the first time through a high degree of innovation, creativity, and experimentation. Examples are fibre optics, laser surgery, and computer bubble memories.

2. **Highly innovative** This term means that the product is somewhat new and as yet not widely known or used. Examples are cellular phone systems and light rail transit train systems.

3. **Moderately innovative** This refers to a product which is a significant modification of an existing product or service or combines different areas of technology, methods, or processes.

FIGURE 6.1   A TYPICAL FEASIBILITY STUDY

Feasibility Study Contents

Concept for your venture
- Explain clearly and concisely the principal concept underlying your venture and what sets it apart from other businesses.

Technical feasibility of your Idea
- Indicate the degree of innovativeness of your venture idea and the risks associated with it.
- Does it need to be subjected to some form of technical evaluation or assessment?

Market assessment
- Describe the profile of your principal target customers.
- Indicate current market size, trends and seasonal patterns.
- How do you plan to test your idea?
- Describe any market research or customer surveys you plan to conduct.
- Assess the nature of your competition.
- Estimate your expected sales and market share.

Your marketing plan
- Detail the marketing strategy you plan to use.
- Describe your marketing plan including your sales strategy, advertising and promotion plans, pricing policy, and channels of distribution.

Managing the supply situation
- How do you plan to assure continuing access to critical supplies of raw materials and component parts at reasonable prices?
- Will you produce or subcontract your production?

Conduct cost and profitability assessment
- Determine the funds required to set up your business.
- Develop short-term financial projections including:
  - Cash flow forecasts
  - Pro forma profit and loss statements
  - Pro forma balance sheet
  - Breakeven analysis

Plan for future action
- What were the strong and weak points of your venture idea?
- Did your assessment indicate the business was likely to be profitable?
- Is it sufficiently attractive to proceed with the development of a complete business plan?

Examples include microprocessors used to control automobile fuel injection systems or single-person cars. The term could also refer to such ideas as the redesign of bicycles to make them easier to ride by handicapped or physically disabled people, thus developing a new market.

4. **Slightly innovative** This term means that a small, yet significant, modification is made to an established product or service, as in larger-scale or more exotic recreational water slides.

5. **"Copycatting"** This is simply imitating someone else's business idea.

The degree of innovation inherent in a business idea has strong implications for the risk, difficulty in evaluation, and profit potential of the venture. *Risk* refers to the probability of the product or service's failing in the marketplace. *Evaluation* is the ability to determine its worth or significance. *Profit potential* is the level of return or compensation that you might expect for assuming the risks associated with investing in this business.

In general, the following relationships hold:

1. New inventions are risky and difficult to evaluate, but if they are accepted in the marketplace they can provide enormous profits.

2. For moderately innovative and slightly innovative ideas, the risks are lower and evaluation is less difficult, but profit potential tends to be more limited.

3. In the "copycat" category, risks are often very high and profit potential tends to be quite low. Such businesses usually show no growth, or very slow growth, and there is little opportunity for profit beyond basic wages.

Every new product must also be subject to some form of analysis to ensure that the benefits promised prospective customers will indeed be delivered. In developing a working prototype or an operating model with this in mind, some of the more important technical requirements to consider are:

1. **Keep it as simple as possible** Keep it simple to build, to transport, to maintain, and above all to use.

2. **Make it flexible** There are many examples of products that were unsuccessful in the application for which they were originally developed but were able to be redesigned to satisfy the needs of an entirely different market.

3. **Build a product that will work as intended without failing** Quality assurance, or eliminating the need for regular and constant service, is becoming more important to consumers. They are more inclined than ever before to look for products that are durable, reliable, safe, and easily maintained.

If a product does not meet these technical qualifications it should be reworked until it does.

One key approach for testing a new product is to subject it to the toughest conditions that might be experienced during actual use. In addition to this kind of test there may be standard engineering tests to which the product will have to be subjected to receive Canadian Standards Association (CSA) or Underwriters Laboratory (UL) certification. You might also undertake an evaluation of alternative materials from which the product might be made. Further assistance in conducting a technical evaluation may be available from various agencies of your provincial government as well as some colleges and universities.

Market Assessment

Assessing the potential market for your concept is a critical part of any feasibility study. At the very least, you need to demonstrate that a market does in fact exist, or there is not much point in developing a full-scale business plan. In some cases the potential market may be large and obvious; in others, considerable research and investigation may be required to demonstrate there is likely to be any significant level of demand. It is essential to determine that there is a sufficiently large market to make the concept financially viable.

Who is Your Customer?

In order to tailor your marketing program to the needs of your market, you must have a very clear idea of who your customers are likely to be. To do this you will need to conduct some thorough research in the marketplace. The more information you have about your target market, the better you will be able to develop a successful marketing plan.

The first thing to recognize is that the term "market" does not only refer to a single type of possible customer. A number of different types of markets exist such as:

1. The consumer market, consisting of individual users of products and services such as you and I.
2. The institutional market, consisting of organizations such as hospitals, personal care homes, schools, universities, and similar types of institutions.
3. The industrial market, comprised of other firms and businesses in your community and across the country.
4. The government market, consisting of various agencies and departments of the municipal, provincial, and federal governments.
5. The international market, composed of markets similar to the above examples outside the national boundaries of the country.

Very few businesses initially operate in all of these markets. Most analyze the possibilities available to them in each situation in order to determine which offers the best potential. This involves asking such broad questions as:

1. How big is the market?
2. Where is it located geographically?
3. How fast is it growing?
4. What organizations and/or individuals buy this kind of product or service?
5. Why do they buy it?
6. Where and how do they buy it?
7. How often do they buy it?
8. What are their principal requirements in selecting a product or service of this type?

This kind of assessment will serve to identify some broad areas of opportunity for you.

In addition to doing this broad analysis, you might also question whether within these major market types there are groups of potential buyers with different preferences, requirements, or purchasing practices. For example, toddlers, teenagers, business people, and older adults all have quite different clothing needs. A manufacturer must take these into account in developing and marketing their product line. Each of these groups should well be considered as a separate *target market*. This process of breaking large, heterogeneous consumer or industrial markets down into more homogeneous groups is known as *market segmentation*. Most markets can be segmented on the basis of a number of variables:

1. Their geographic location, such as part of a city, or town, county, province, region, or country.
2. Their demographic description such as age, sex, marital status, family size, race, religion, education level, and occupation. Non-consumer markets might be classified on the basis of their total purchases or sales, number of employees, or type of organizational activity.

3.　A variety of sociological factors, such as their lifestyle, user status, usage rate, timing, and means of purchasing, and reasons for buying products or services similar to yours.

Figure 6.2 at the back of this Stage provides a framework you can complete to develop a *market profile* of your prospective customers.

Estimating Total Market Size and Trends

A large part of market assessment is determining the volume of *unit sales* or *dollar revenue* that might flow from a market and what proportion of this you might expect to capture. At first glance "unit sales" seems to mean simply how many potential customers there are in the market for your product/service. However, this would overlook the possibility that some customers may buy more than

"Business is lousy. Maybe I should have done more market research first."

© Randy Glasbergen. Reprinted with permission from www.glasbergen.com

one unit of the product/service. Estimates of total market size must take these *repeat purchases* into account. Total demand is determined by multiplying the number of customers who will buy by the average number of units each might be expected to purchase. To determine the total market size in dollars, simply multiply this total number of units by the average selling price.

Figure 6.3 at the back of this Stage provides a form you can complete to estimate the approximate total market size (past, present, and future) and the expected trends for your product/service type.

Customer and Market Research

Sources of Market Information

There are a number of sources you might consult to get a handle on the approximate size of the market you are considering entering. Some of these sources are Statistics Canada publications; various industry reports, trade journals, and investment journals; and financial statements of your leading competitors. You must be careful to make some provision for error in your estimate of market size. Most of the information sources you will consult will not be able to provide complete up-to-date figures, and forecasts of future sales are always subject to error. Statistics Canada, for example, breaks the country up into 36 Census Metropolitan Areas (CMA). (www.statcan.ca/english/census96/list.htm) For each CMA there are a series of referenced maps providing an index for which it is possible to get a *tract number* for almost any neighbourhood in the country. From this tract number you can get a detailed breakdown of the number of people and their characteristics within a single local neighbourhood or for a combination of tracts comprising a region of a city or for the entire metropolitan area. This data can be a valuable resource providing a wide variety of information on a large number of geographic markets. The major drawback, however, is that it is largely derived from census data and may be a little stale. This should not be surprising, given the constantly changing tastes of consumers and ongoing technological advancement.

Following are listings of some of the more popular sources of market information. Much of this material is available at your local public, college, or university library. In most situations the best place to start is with *the trade publications and trade associations for the industry in which your business will compete.*

Trade Publications　Just to give you an idea of the number and diversity of the trade publications produced in Canada, take a minute to review Table 6.1. It is by no means a listing of *all* trade-oriented publications, merely a sampling of the range of material available to you. Depending on the nature of your new venture, any one or more of innumerable publications could represent a source of market-related information or a means for you to communicate with potential customers.

General Publications   In addition to trade publications there are numerous general publications that can be extremely useful in compiling relevant market data. Some of the more important of these are listed in Table 6.2 at the back of this Stage. In addition to all these publications, sources that you should look to for information include:

1. Your local chamber of commerce
2. Your city or municipal hall
3. Local or regional development corporations
4. District school board offices
5. Provincial government offices
6. Downtown business associations
7. Shopping centre developers
8. Advertising agencies
9. Newspapers, radio, and television stations
10. Competitors
11. Sales representatives and trade suppliers
12. Similar businesses in another location
13. Other business associates

TABLE 6.1   SOME TRADE PUBLICATIONS PRODUCED IN CANADA

Aerospace & Defence Technology	Canadian Mining Journal	Jobber News
Applied Arts	Canadian Music Trade	Lighting Magazine
Architecture Concept	Canadian Oil & Gas Handbook	Luggage, Leathergoods & Accessories
Atlantic Fisherman	Canadian Pharmaceutical Journal	L'Automobile
Aviation Trade	Canadian Pool & Spa Marketing	Machinery & Equipment MRO
Bakers Journal	Canadian Premiums & Incentives	Masthead
Bath & Kitchen Marketer	Canadian Security	Medicine North America
Benefits Canada	Canadian Vending	Modern Purchasing
Boating Business	Computer Dealer News	Motel/Hotel Lodging
Bodyshop	Construction Canada	Office Equipment & Methods
Building Renovation	Cosmetics	Plant Engineering & Maintenance
Business to Business Marketing	Dental Practice Management	
CAD/CAM & Robotics	Design Engineering	Plastics Business
Canadian Apparel Manufacturer	Eastern Trucker	Quill and Quire
Canadian Beverage Review	Electrical Equipment News	Sanitation Canada
Canadian Building Owner & Property Manager	Farm Equipment Quarterly	Service Station & Garage Management
Canadian Doctor	Fleur Design	Shopping Centre Canada
Canadian Food & Drug	Floor Covering News	Software Report
Canadian Forest Industries	Food in Canada	Sports Business
Canadian Funeral News	Food & Drug Packaging News	The Bottom Line
Canadian Grocer	Footwear Forum	The Business and Professional Woman
Canadian Hairdresser	Fur Trade Journal	The Western Investor
Canadian Heavy Equipment Guide	Gardenland	Trade Asia Magazine
Canadian Hotel & Restaurant	Gifts and Tablewares	Transportation Business
Canadian Industry Shows & Exhibitions	Greenhouse Canada	Visual Communications
Canadian Jeweler	Group Travel	Water & Pollution Control
Canadian Machinery & Metal-working	Hardware Merchandising	Woodworking
	Health Care	
	Industrial Distributor News	
	Industrial Product Ideas	

Canada Business Service Centres

One prospective source of market information that should not be overlooked is your provincial Canada Business Service Centre (CBSC). The CBSCs are a collaborative effort between federal, provincial, and private sector organizations designed to provide business people with access to a wide range of information on government services, programs, and regulations. Each CBSC offers a broad range of products and services tailored to meet the needs of its particular clients. These include:

- a toll-free telephone information and referral service
- the Business Information System (BIS) database containing information on the services and programs of the participating departments and organizations
- faxables: condensed versions of the BIS products accessed through an automated FaxBack system
- pathfinders: a set of documents that provide brief descriptions of services and programs related to a particular topic (e.g., exporting, tourism)
- a collection of other business services which could include interactive diagnostic software, videos, business directories, how-to manuals, CD-ROM library search capability, and external database access

CBSCs are located in one major urban centre in each province. A complete listing of the location of each Centre and the numbers for telephone referral and FaxBack service at each site can be found in the listing of Useful Contacts at the back of this book.

The Internet

Another place where you may be able to find a good deal of information about any idea you plan to pursue is the Internet. Not everything is available on the Net yet. In fact, it has been described as a "Work in Progress." But, with a little practice now even new users can skim the Net's millions of Web pages and thousands of Usenet newsgroups for topics of general interest and also to home in on precise bits of specific data.

What has simplified the job of culling information from the millions of Web pages and Usenet groups is the development of a variety of search tools that enable the user to search rapidly through a variety of searchable directories or the nooks and crannies of the Web itself to create in seconds indexes of information related to a particular topic.

The two most popular types of search tools for the Internet are directories and search engines. An Internet directory allows you to search for Internet sites by category. You should use a directory if you are looking for Web sites on a particular topic such as home-based business, a particular company or business such as Imperial Oil, or if you are looking for a general subject guide to resources available over the Internet. The most comprehensive Internet directory for Canada is Yahoo! Canada (www.yahoo.ca). It contains tens of thousands of web sites organized into 14 main categories such as travel, sports and food, and hundreds of subcategories.

While a directory like Yahoo! Canada organizes Web sites into a number of neat categories, "search engines" enable you to search the entire contents of all the sites on the World Wide Web (WWW). These search engines help you look for specific words or phrases within Web sites. The most popular search engines include AltaVista (www.altavista.digital.com) or (www.altavista.ca) for Canadian sites and sources, Lycos (www.lycos.com), Infoseek (www.infoseek.com), OpenText (www.opentext.com), Excite (www.excite.com), Hotbot (www.hotbot.com) and WebCrawler (www.webcrawler.com).

Search engines have two primary advantages over directories. The first is that the search is conducted over a much broader base of information. A search engine sends out software agents or "spiders" that explore the entire Internet instead of just the Web pages that have been indexed for the directory. Secondly, since search engines are automated, they are more successful in finding and indexing new Web pages. However, search engines are not very discriminating, so sorting through the thousands of matches that may result from any search can be a real chore. The differences between search engines and directories, however, are becoming clouded as each starts to take on more of the characteristics of the other.

In addition to these basic directories and search engines, there are a number of other search tools you should consider. These include:

- All-in-one or "parallel" search engines such as SavvySearch (guaraldi.cs.colostate.edu) and MetaCrawler (metacrawler.ca.washington.edu). These search engines simultaneously submit your search request to several other search engines and combine the results into one report.

- Specialty search engines such as Search.com (www.search.com) and Deja News (www.dejanews.com) only search the contents of special databases instead of searching the entire Internet. These databases are usually carefully selected and screened to provide quality information on very specialized topics.

- Review Indices like Excite Power Search (www.excite.com), Magellan Internet Guide (www.mckinley.com), Lycos Top 5% (www.lycos.com) and Webcrawler (www.webcrawler.com). These review indices are often incorporated into conventional search engines and are separate, searchable databases composed of a number of specially selected, premium quality sites.

- Subject guides can be an excellent source of information about a particular topic since someone who has a lot of knowledge about the subject usually prepares the index. There are literally thousands of subject guides that contain links to a number of other Web sites and many of them can be found by searching in directories like Yahoo! Canada. Some of the best ones for information relevant to small business include the Industry Canada Web site (www.strategis.ic.gc.ca), the Web Site of the Canadian Youth Business Foundation (CYBF) (www.cybf.ca), the Web Site of *Profit Magazine* (www.PROFITguide.com) and EntreWorld's Web site (www.entreworld.org). These guides can be excellent starting points to begin your search for other, more specific information.

- City guides such as City Net (www.city.net) and World City Guide (cityguide.lycos.com) provide information about various cities and towns and can be used to locate other Internet resources that can provide you with very specific and detailed information about those communities.[1]

Most directories and search engines provide basic instructions as to how to initiate a search as part of their home page. For a beginner, it all starts with you entering a "query." A "query" consists of one or more key words — a company name, a city or country, or any other topic likely to appear either in the title or the body of a Web page. Most search programs employ Boolean logic, expanding or limiting a search by including "and," "but," and "or" as part of the search process. The more precise your query, the better. For example: if you are interested in a topic like antique automobiles, typing in "antique and automobiles" instead of just "automobiles" will direct you to information regarding older cars although you may also get sites for antique dealers in general and other related subjects.

With most search engines the process starts with the click of your mouse once you have entered your query. Within seconds, a list of matches is produced, usually in batches of 10, with a brief description and the home page address. A further click on one of the matches gets you to that page or Usenet group.

---

[1] For a more detailed discussion of the use of these search tools see Jim Carroll, Rick Broadhead, Don Cassel, *1998 Canadian Internet Handbook, Educational Edition*, Prentice Hall Canada Inc., 1998.

The most popular search engines can also be accessed from the home pages of the two most popular Web browsers, Netscape Navigator and Microsoft's Internet Explorer.

Market-testing Your Idea

There are a number of methods for testing the market prospects of your idea. These include prototype development, obtaining opinions from prospective buyers, comparing your idea with competitors' offerings, conducting in-store tests, and demonstrating it at trade shows.

One or more of these techniques can be employed to assess how the market is likely to react to your concept or idea. The young owners of Spin Master Toys, for example, used a variety of methods to refine and test the idea of the Air Hog, their World War II-era toy jet fighter that flies on compressed air. The English inventors who developed the concept had put together a crude prototype to demonstrate the idea. It was described as "a Canada Dry ginger ale bottle with foam wings" and didn't fly. Subsequent prototypes "flew some of the time — kind of" until after myriad versions, a year and a half and half a million dollars later they finally had what appeared to be a market-ready product. (See Entrepreneurs in Action #14).

At the same time as this product development was taking place, one of the owners took an early prototype of the product to a buyer for Canadian Tire stores. The response was very positive and while the company was not prepared to meet the timeliness for delivery required by the buyer and turned down the sale, the experience did confirm that retailers would be behind their product if they could produce an acceptable, working version.

The company also conducted some focus groups with actual kids to see what they thought of the Air Hog and to assess their ability to use it properly. The initial results were disastrous. The kids couldn't figure out the plane's air-pump system, they turned the propeller the wrong way, and had a variety of other problems. To overcome these difficulties, the company came up with a couple of solutions. One was to set up a 1-800 number to serve as a help line for kids experiencing problems. The other was to include an instructional video with every Air Hog explaining the proper way to use the toy.

All this testing seems to have paid off. The Air Hog was ranked as one of the hottest toys of the 1998 Christmas season by *Time* magazine and touted as one of the year's top achievements in science and technology by *Popular Science*. Three hundred and fifty thousand Air Hogs literally flew off the shelves of major U.S. retailers over that season and the company expects to sell one million more during 1999.[2]

Developing a Prototype   A *prototype* is a "working model" of your product. If you are considering selling a product that, when mass-produced, could cost you $5 per unit to manufacture, prototypes may cost you over $200 each. However, this could be an inexpensive investment, because with just one prototype you can get photographs, make up a brochure or circular, show the idea to prospective buyers, and put out publicity releases. You don't need a thousand or ten thousand units at this stage.

Even though you are only interested in producing, at most, a few units at this point, it is still important to get manufacturing prices from a number of (around five) different suppliers. You should find out how much it will cost to produce various quantities of the product (1,000 units, 5,000 units, 10,000 units) and what the terms, conditions, and costs of the production process would be. Once you have this information you will be able to approach buyers and intelligently and confidently discuss all aspects of the product.

Obtaining Opinions from Prospective Buyers   A second way to test your product idea is to ask a professional buyer's personal opinion. For example, most major department stores and other retail chains are organized into departments, each department having its own buyer. After arranging

---

[2]   Shawna Steinberg and Joe Chidley, "Fun for the Money," *Canadian Business*, December 11, 1998, pp. 44-52.

14

Cashing in on Kids

Like a pilot in a death spiral, Ben Varadi was having one of those gut-checking moments. As head of product development for Spin Master Toys, he had flown last January to Scottsdale, Ariz., to film a commercial for a new product that had a lot riding on it. Even though Spin Master had yet to put it in production, the Air Hog promised to be a coup not only for the budding Toronto-based company, but for the industry as a whole: a toy airplane that would run on compressed air rather than gas or rubber bands, and would fly for hundreds of yards rather than piddling out after just a few. In theory, at least, this is what should have happened: the weather should have been cloudless and dry (Varadi chose Arizona as a location because it hardly gets any rain), and the prototype should have flown through the air with the greatest of ease.

So Varadi and the crew are out on a Holiday Inn golf course in Scottsdale — and the sky is cloudy. Too bad, but not awful — who's going to worry about clouds, even a little rain, once this baby is airborne? They get set to fire up the Air Hog, a purple-and-yellow flying machine that otherwise resembles a World War II-era fighter plane. The sophisticated air-compressor engine is primed, the cameras are rolling, the tousle-haired kid hired to star in the ad lets the Air Hog go and — well, a mere four seconds later, the toy's sputtering film début comes to an end on the hard track of the fairway. Crash and burn, baby.

It's a rule in toy advertising that you can't make a product appear to do things in a commercial that it can't do in reality. Trouble was, as with most new toys in the preproduction stage, the Air Hog's abilities were still unknown. Varadi, who's 28, and his Spin Master cohorts, president Anton Rabie and CEO Ronnen Harary, both 27, knew what it was *supposed* to do; they just weren't quite sure that it could actually *do* it. "Until you're in production, all you've got are theories," Varadi says. "You can spend all this money and at the end of the day, it still doesn't work."

So your company is spending $100,000 filming this commercial — and the Air Hog is performing like a pig. What do you do? You get creative. You shoot the commercial, cutting shots of the plane's brief flights so that it *looks* like it's flying

100 yards a pop, like it's twisting and turning through the air just the way you want it to. There's nothing dishonest about that — as long as the product, once it's on the market and the object of every 10-year-old boy's desire, lives up to its billing. "So we had a challenge," Varadi says. "We had to make the thing fly like it did in the commercial."

The inverted logic must have worked, because the Air Hog is soaring these days. In an industry dominated by giants such as Hasbro, Mattel and Irwin, five-year-old Spin Master Toys seems to have come up with a bona fide hit. As the Christmas buying season — which accounts for between 60% and 70% of toy sales in North America — gears up, the Air Hog seems poised to be one of the most talked about toys of the year. In October, *Time* magazine put it next to Tiger Electronics' Furby (an interactive fuzzy doll that is this year's equivalent of Tickle Me Elmo), Hasbro's Teletubbies (with a hit kids' show behind them) and Lego's MindStorms (a computerized robot kit) as the season's hottest new toys. *Popular Science* magazine stuck the plane on its December "Best of What's New" cover, trumpeting the toy as one of the year's top 100 achievements in science and technology. The Air Hog even made it onto US network television, when the *Today* show featured it in a pre-Christmas "Gadget Guru" segment.

Maybe not surprisingly, the Air Hog has been flying off the shelves of US specialty stores such as FAO Schwarz and Noodle Kidoodle. Since June, Spin Master has sold 350,000 Air Hogs to retailers, who sell it for US$29.99 to US$39.99 ($49.99 in Canada); by next August, Rabie, Harary and Varadi expect to sell a million more, sending Spin Master's 1998-'99 revenue soaring to $30 million — triple what it was in 1997-'98. Not bad for a product that the major toy companies thought would never fly. And the TV commercial hasn't even aired yet.

They might have been college buddies, but you couldn't ask for three men who seem less like one another to run a company. Varadi, the toymaster, is fittingly a bit of a prankster, his lean face wearing a mischievous perma-grin. Harary? As operations head, he's sort of dour, all business. And Rabie, the ringleader, is the face of Spin Master — all buff and youthful, with a look that could have been ripped from the pages of *GQ*. Their dynamic is a strangely seamless one — they even finish each other's sentences. But that's not to say they think alike. And as business partners, it's like different pieces of a puzzle coming together to complete the picture.

The history of Spin Master Toys is part Wright brothers, part Roots — a tale of what happens when innovation meets savvy marketing. Childhood pals who met at summer camp a few years after their families moved to Toronto from South Africa, Rabie and Harary both attended the University of Western Ontario in London, where the future company president studied business and Harary took political science. While at school, where they also met biz-student Varadi, the pair established a business under the name Seiger Marketing. Their idea: a campus poster adorned with frosh-week photos and advertising from local businesses. After graduating, Rabie and Harary, then 23, had $10,000 in their pockets from poster sales; all they needed was a product. And when Harary's grandmother brought back a novelty gift from Israel in 1994 — a sawdust-filled stocking with a face that sprouted grass for hair-they knew they had found it. The Earth Buddy was born.

With the Earth Buddy's vaguely environmental cachet, Rabie figured it would be a perfect fit for the urban-adventurer image espoused by Roots Canada Ltd., a company founded by Michael Budman and Don Green (who, coincidentally, also met at summer camp). Budman bit, allowing Rabie and Harary to test-market the nouveaux Chia Pets in Roots stores. The little guys were, in short, a hit. In the US, K-Mart ordered 500,000 Buddies. Operations moved from Harary's kitchen to a factory staffed by 200 employees working around the clock. In six months, the Earth Buddy generated $1.8 million in sales. That's a lot of sawdust and socks.

One hit wonder? No way. In 1994 the company launched a three-rod juggling game called Spin Master Devil Sticks — a higher-tech version of a product Harary sold from the back of his VW Microbus at Grateful Dead concerts when he was 17. In the spring of 1995, the Devil Sticks became the No. 1 non-promoted toy in Canada, selling more than 250,000 units in six months. It broke the company into the US, positioning it for continent-wide distribution, and it gave Rabie and Harary's business a new name — Spin Master — which has proven to be appropriate in more ways than one.

The Air Hog flew onto the scene in February 1996, at the Toy Fair, an annual get-together in New York that attracts hundreds of toymakers, retailers and inventors. There, Varadi was approached by inventors from the English firm Dixon-Manning Ltd., who pitched an idea they had for a plane that ran on air power. Varadi and Harary arranged to meet with Dixon-Manning at 5 p.m. that day to discuss details, but when they arrived, they found the inventors had optioned the concept for 30 days to a major US toy company. "So I made a note to call them in 30 days and see if they passed — and sure enough, they did," recalls Harary. "And when [Dixon-Manning] sent the item to us, I saw why."

THOMAS FRICKE PHOTOGRAPHY

Basically, the prototype the inventors sent to Toronto was, Harary says, "a Canada Dry ginger ale bottle with foam wings — it still had the label on it." But the partners at Spin Master saw opportunity. "The one thing that did appeal to me wasn't so much the item itself as the state of the category," Varadi says. Here's the reason: the toy-airplane market didn't have a middle. On the top end were gasoline-powered planes that sold for $80 and up; on the low end were $3 rubber-band-and-balsa-wood "aircraft." Varadi figured that, in that niche market, "there's got to be something in the middle." And the air-pressure technology was something new, holding out the promise of a whole line of toys that ran off its simple-sounding, but hard-to-produce, pneumatic engine. "If we could pull this off, we'd be like pioneers in this category," Varadi says. "We also realized that this would elevate the level of the company in terms of how people saw us."

The trio started talking to buyers within two months of taking on the project in July 1996. Harary took a prototype to a Canadian Tire buyer in October, who said she would place "a big order"— *if* he could ship it for spring. "I had this nagging feeling, what if we make this commitment and can't keep it — will it risk the reputation of the company?" he says. "I looked them in the face and said, 'I don't think we can make it.' No one wants to turn down a challenge, but it was probably one of the best things we've done." Egos still intact, the boys now had confidence that retailers were behind their product. But talking to the buyers led to another revelation: Hasbro, Mattel and, as Varadi says, "everybody and his uncle" had turned down the Air Hog. "You're thinking, if a company like Hasbro turned it down, what were they thinking that we were missing?"

That was gut check No. 1. And for a time, it must have seemed that the no-takers were right. The first prototype Spin Master received from Dixon-Manning didn't fly; the second "flew some of the time — kind of," Harary says.

The three had planned on the development phase taking six months. It ended up taking a year and a half — and costing half a million dollars, money they say came exclusively from company coffers. Rabie remembers getting frantic eureka-style calls from Harary and Varadi, who would be out in a park somewhere testing one of myriad versions of the Air Hog. "There's been another breakthrough!" Varadi would proclaim. Rabie would run out to the park with a camcorder to make a tape to show buyers and — it wouldn't fly, again. "It was Murphy's Law," Rabie says. Meanwhile, focus-group results with actual kids were disastrous: they couldn't figure out the plane's air-pump system, they turned the propeller the wrong way — you name it. Rabie and his team came up with two solutions. One was to set up a 1-800 help line for fledgling pilots; the other was to produce an instructional video (now included with every Air Hog). By showing the video, Varadi says, "we went from a terrible focus group, where one out of five could do it, to a focus group where every kid could do it."

At the end of 1997, Harary was taking his third trip to Asia, learning everything he could about toy manufacturing and negotiating a production deal with a factory in Hong Kong. The next step was to make the moulds for all the parts and set up the machinery to manufacture the planes — a tooling-up that would cost $100,000. Time for another gut check. "It's easy to make one thing work," Harary says, "but to make half a million things work is a totally different ball game." Having already missed one anticipated spring launch, and with another just months away, Rabie, Harary and Varadi decided it was time to fly or get off the plane. But would it work? "When we made the decision to go ahead with it, we didn't know," Rabie says, "We just said, '"OK, we're going to tool and debug."'"

The plan was to launch Air Hogs in May 1998 — since it's an outdoor toy, the Spin Masters figured it would be ideal for a spring début. So they made the ad in Arizona, fixed the design bugs and simultaneously tested two distribution paths in Minneapolis: specialty chains such as Noodle Kidoodle, which concentrate on high-end educational toys, and Target department stores in the area. With air support from the commercial, the plane beat expectations under both retailing models, selling more than 25 units per store per week (eight to 12 units in that price category is considered good). In the end, Spin Master decided to stick with a conservative distribution plan, leaving the Air Hog in specialty stores and as a Sears catalogue item for a year, then releasing it in the mass market with a national ad campaign in the spring of 1999 through major retailers, who usually book their product line a year in advance anyway. "We could go to mass retailers after Minneapolis and say, 'It works!'" Rabie says. "Now we're coming into 1999 with every major retailer's support when we do our TV campaign."

Source: Shawna Steinberg and Joe Chidley, "Fun for the Money," *Canadian Business*, December 11, 1998, pp. 44-520. Reprinted with permission.

to see the buyer representing the product area in which you are interested, arm yourself with the cost information you received from potential suppliers. Remember, a buyer is a very astute person. He or she has seen thousands of items before yours, and in most cases will be able to tell you if products resembling yours have ever been on the market, how well they sold, what their flaws were, etc. You can get a tremendous amount of free information from a buyer, so it is advisable to solicit his or her independent opinion before you become too involved with your product.

Comparing with Competitors' Products   Most of us have only limited exposure to the vast array of products available in the marketplace and thus could end up spending a lot of money producing a "new" product which is already being marketed by someone else. Test your product idea by comparing it with other products already on the market, before you invest your money.

One-Store Test   Another way to test your product is to run a *one-store test*. This can be done by arranging with a store owner or manager to put a dozen units of your product on display. The purpose of this test is to learn what the public thinks about your product. You can often get the store owner's cooperation, because the store doesn't have to put any money up front to purchase your product. However, there can be problems associated with such tests. If you are very friendly with the owner, he or she may affect the results of the test in your product's favour by putting it in a preferred location or by personally promoting it to store customers. You should request that your product be treated like any other, because you are looking for unbiased information.

Also, you should keep in mind that one store does not constitute a market; the one store in which you test may not be representative of the marketplace in general. Nevertheless, the one-store test is a good way to gather information on your product.

Trade Shows   Another excellent way to test your product idea is at a trade show. It makes no difference what your field is — there is a trade show involving it. At a trade show you will have your product on display and you can get immediate feedback from sophisticated and knowledgeable buyers — people who know what will sell and what will not. There are approximately 15,000 trade shows in Canada and the U.S. every year, covering every imaginable product area. There is bound to be one that could serve as a reasonable test site for you.

Conducting a Customer Survey

A critical factor in successfully launching a new venture is understanding who your customers are and what needs your product or service might satisfy. It is important to consider that not all potential customers are alike or have similar needs for a given product. For example, some people buy a toothpaste primarily to prevent cavities, while others want a toothpaste that promotes whiter teeth, fresher breath, or "sex appeal," or has been designed specifically for smokers or denture wearers. You have to determine which of these segments (i.e., cavity prevention, whiter teeth, etc.) your product or service can best satisfy.

As previously mentioned, most major markets can be broken down into more homogeneous groups or *segments* on the basis of a number of different types of variables. In developing a plan for your proposed business venture you must consider who your potential customers are and how they might be classified, as in the toothpaste example, into somewhat more homogeneous market segments. You should be clear in your own mind just which of these segments your venture is attempting to serve. A product or service that is sharply focussed to satisfy the needs and wants of a specifically defined customer group is typically far more successful than one that tries to compromise and cut across the widely divergent requirements of many customer types. Small businesses are often in a position to search for "holes" in the market representing the requirements of particular customer types that larger companies are unwilling or unable to satisfy.

In order to be successful, you should seek a *competitive advantage* over other firms — look for something especially desirable from the customer's perspective, something that sets you apart and gives you an edge. This may be the quality of your product, the speed of your service, the diversity of your product line, the effectiveness of your promotion, your personality, your location, the distinctiveness of your offering, or perhaps even your price.

To accomplish all this may require some basic market research. This might be thought of as one of the first steps in testing your product or service idea with potential customers.

Since you will want to provide as good a description of your offering as possible (preferably via a prototype), personal, face-to-face interviews are the best method for gathering the information.

Figure 6.4 at the back of this Stage provides an outline for a survey you might conduct. It would be wise to interview at least 30 to 40 potential customers to help ensure that the responses you receive are probably representative of the marketplace in general. This approach can be used effectively for either consumer or industrial products/services.

This customer survey will provide you with important information that will allow you to further develop and fine-tune your marketing strategy. For example, if you discover that the most customers will pay for your product is $10, and you had planned on charging $12, you will have to reconsider your pricing strategy. Similarly, if customers prefer to purchase products like yours by mail, you will have to keep that in mind as you set up a distribution system. The responses to each of the questions posed in the survey should be analyzed and their impact on areas of marketing strategy noted. These will be brought together later in your preliminary marketing plan.

The Nature of Your Competition

Unless your product or service is a "new to the world" innovation, which is unlikely, it will have to compete with other products or services that perform a similar function. In the customer survey, your respondents probably identified the names of a number of firms that offer products or services designed to meet the same customer needs as yours. Now, you must ask specific and detailed questions concerning your likely competition. The answers will help you get a better understanding of the sales and market share you could achieve, and changes or improvements you should make in your marketing program (pricing, promotion, distribution, etc.).

You should also be on the lookout for areas where you can gain a sustainable competitive advantage. In other words: Can you provide the best-quality, the lowest-cost, the most innovative, or the better-serviced product?

Figure 6.5 at the back of this Stage provides a form to help you organize your evaluation. Fill out a copy of this form for each major competitor you have identified. Unfortunately, competitors will probably not cooperate in providing you with this information directly. Sources that can be useful in getting the information, however, include published industry reports, trade association reports and publications, corporate annual reports, and your own personal investigation.

Developing a Sales Forecast

Sales forecasting is the process of organizing and analyzing all the information you have gathered to date in a way that makes it possible to estimate what your expected sales will be. For your business plan, these figures for your first year of operation should be monthly, while the estimates for subsequent years can be quarterly. A serious miscalculation many aspiring entrepreneurs make is to assume that because their new product or service appeals to *them*, other consumers will buy it as well. It is important to be aware of this tendency. This type of thinking is often reflected in what is known as the "2 percent" syndrome. This syndrome follows a line of reasoning such as, "The total market for a product is $100 million. If my firm can pick up just 2 percent of this market, it will have sales of $2 million per year."

There are, however, two things wrong with this line of reasoning. The first is that it may be extremely difficult for you to capture 2 percent of this market unless your business has a unique competitive advantage. The second is that a 2 percent market share may still be unprofitable, since competing firms with greater market share may benefit from *economies of scale* — lower unit cost due to mass-production — and other cost advantages unavailable to your firm.

There are a number of external factors that can affect your sales. These include:

- seasonal changes
- holidays

- special events
- political activities and events
- general economic conditions
- weather
- fashion trends and cycles
- population shifts
- changes in the retail mix

In addition, there are a number of internal factors that must be considered as well, such as:

- level of your promotional effort
- your ability to manage inventory levels effectively
- the distribution channels you decide to use
- your price level relative to the competition
- any labour and personnel problem you might encounter.

It is impossible to predict all these situations but you should try to take them into account in developing your sales forecast.

One approach to gaining some insight into your business' potential market is to follow the example laid out in Figure 6.6. Refer to the *market profile* you developed in Figure 6.2. How do you feel your prospective customers would decide whether or not to buy your offering. This estimate should also consider the likely frequency and volume of a typical customer's purchases over a certain period of time.

In implementing this process, you should think about how prospective customers will likely hear about the opportunity to buy your product/service, whether from a salesperson, from an advertisement, or through a chain of middlemen. Estimates can then be made of how many of the people you have described are good prospects, and consequently what your total sales volume might be. This can be an "armchair" procedure involving the use of some library references or personal knowledge of similar businesses. The estimate of market potential developed using this method can be quite crude; however, it is important that you think your way through such a process and not sidestep it in favour of simply hoping a market exists for you.

Selecting a Location

It is often said that the three most important factors in the success of any retail business are "location, location, and location." Every new business faces the problem of where to locate its facilities. This problem is much more critical to retailers than to other types of businesses. Much of their business typically comes from people who are walking or driving by. As a consequence, a customer's decision to shop or not shop at a particular store may depend on such factors as what side of the street you are on, ease of access and egress, availability of parking, or similar concerns. This means that in determining the best location for your business you will have to concern yourself with a variety of issues.

1. **Zoning Regulations** Zoning bylaws govern the kind of activities that can be carried on in any given area. Classifications vary from locality to locality, but many municipalities categorize activities as residential, commercial office, commercial retail, institutional, and industrial. When considering a location, make certain the business activities you plan to pursue are permitted under the zoning restrictions for that area.

2. **Municipal Licences and Taxes** Businesses must typically buy a municipal business licence. In the city of Winnipeg, for example, more than 115 types of businesses require a licence, which costs from $15 to over $2,000. In general, businesses in some amusement fields or that affect public health and safety require a licence.

Businesses, like homeowners, must usually pay a "business tax" — a tax assessed as a percentage of the rental value of the premises or on the basis of a standard assessment per square foot of space utilized. These requirements vary from municipality to municipality.

3. **Municipal Services** You should make sure that municipal services such as police and fire protection, adequate sewer and water supplies, public transit facilities, and an adequate road network are available to meet your business' requirements.

4. **Other Considerations** Other things to consider are such site-specific issues as:
   - Cost
   - The volume and timing of traffic past the location
   - The nature of the location, whether on a downtown street, in a strip mall, or in an enclosed mall
   - The nature of the area surrounding your location and its compatibility with your business
   - The kind and relative location of surrounding businesses
   - The volume of customer traffic generated by these other firms and the proportion that might "spin off" to your store
   - The growth potential of the area or community
   - The number and location of curb cuts and turnoffs

Figure 6.7 at the back of this Stage provides a rating form you can use to help choose the most favourable location for a retail business.

Most of these same location factors also apply to service businesses, although perhaps not to the same degree. If your service business requires you to visit prospective customers at their home or place of business, a central location providing easy access to all parts of your market area may be preferred.

Location has a quite different meaning for manufacturing firms. Manufacturers are principally concerned about locating their plant where their operations will be most efficient. This means considering such issues as the following:

1. General proximity to primary market areas
2. Access to required raw materials and supplies
3. Availability of a suitable labour force
4. Accessibility and relative cost of transportation and storage facilities
5. Availability and relative cost of power, water, and fuel supplies
6. Financial incentives and other inducements available from municipal, provincial, or federal government agencies

The importance of each of these factors in the location decision will depend on the nature of your manufacturing business and your own preferences and requirements.

Buying or Leasing Facilities

Many new businesses already own or decide to purchase the land and building in which their ventures are located or the machinery and equipment they will require to operate. With today's extremely high costs, however, this may not be a wise decision. The majority of new firms are not principally in the business of speculating in real estate and should not acquire their own property. During their early stages most businesses tend to be short of cash and many have failed because they had their capital tied up in land and buildings when it could have been more effectively used to provide needed working capital for the business itself. In addition, a business that owns its own building may be more difficult to sell at a later date, since a smaller number of potential buyers will have enough capital to buy both the business and the property.

If you are planning to rent or lease your facilities it is probably a good idea to have your lawyer review the terms and conditions of the agreement. You will want to ensure satisfactory arrangements in such matters as:

1. **The duration of the agreement** A business lease can last a year, three years, five years, or any other mutually agreed-upon term. A short-term lease may be preferable if your situation is likely to change soon. However, the lease conditions can be a valuable asset of your business, and a short-term lease may reduce the sale value of your business (if you ever sell it) because of loss of the goodwill associated with maintaining your present location. The ideal lease arrangement should enable you to stay in the location for some time, in case your venture is successful, but give you the flexibility to move after a reasonable period of time if it doesn't work out.

    You also need to consider the terms and conditions for renewing the lease. Are there provisions for automatic renewal? Is there a maximum to any rent increase applied upon renewal of your lease?

2. **The rent** Rental costs for commercial property are commonly stated in terms of the annual cost per square foot of floor space. For example, a 1500 square foot location rented for $8 per square foot will cost $12,000 a year, or $1000 per month. This may be a *net lease*, in which you pay a single monthly fee which is all-inclusive (rent, utilities, maintenance costs, property taxes, etc.), or a "net-net-net" or *triple net lease*, in which you pay a base rent plus a share of all the other expenses incurred by the landlord in operating the building. In the latter situation your operating costs may fluctuate each year because of changing tax, maintenance, insurance, and other costs.

    In retail shopping malls, *participating* (or *percentage*) *leases* are common. Instead of a fixed monthly rent, the landlord receives some percentage of your sales or net profit. There are several types of participating leases. You may pay either a percentage of the total monthly sales of your business, a base rent plus some percentage of your gross sales, or a percentage of your net profit before interest and taxes. Shopping centre leases can be quite complex documents, so be certain to check with your accountant and lawyer before committing yourself.

3. **The ownership of any additions or improvements you might make to the facilities** Under the terms of most leases, all improvements and fixtures that you add to the premises are considered as belonging to the landlord. They immediately become part of the building and cannot be removed without his or her consent. If you need to install expensive fixtures to launch your business, you should try right up front to negotiate permission to remove specific items.

4. **Any restrictions on the use of the property** Most leases specify the kind of business activity you can carry on in the location. Before signing, you should think not only about the activities you now plan to engage in, but also about those you might wish to engage in in the future. Many leases also contain a non-competition clause to protect you from competitive firms' coming into the premises and taking away your business.

5. **Whether you are permitted to sublet some or all of the property to a third party** This is commonly permitted, but only with the prior written consent of the landlord, and it is subject to any use restrictions and non-competition clauses in your agreement.

    A closely related issue is your ability to assign any remaining time left on your lease to another party. If you decide to sell your business, this can be an attractive part of the package. In some cases, assignment of the lease is not permitted; in others, an assignment may be acceptable with the prior written consent of the landlord, which may then not be unreasonably withheld.

6. **The nature of any default and penalty clauses** The lease will spell out the situations which constitute a breach of its conditions and the recourse available to the landlord. Obvious grounds for default include failure on your part to pay the rent, the bankruptcy of your business, violation of the use conditions or non-competition clauses, and so on. Should you default on the lease, the landlord may be able to claim accelerated rent for the time remaining on the lease. For example, if you were to move out two years before your lease expires, the landlord may claim the full two years' rent. In this situation, however, the landlord legally must try to limit his or her damages by renting out your space to another party as soon as possible.

   Your lease may or may not contain a *penalty clause* limiting your exposure should you breach the lease. A penalty of three months' rent is common in many situations, although the landlord will want you or the directors of an incorporated business to sign personal guarantees for the amount of the penalty.

Of course, building your own facility enables you to more carefully tailor the property to the specific requirements of your business but tends to be a much more costly alternative.

Home-Based Businesses

For many kinds of businesses, working out of the home has become a very popular and attractive option. There are a number of advantages to running your business out of your home, the most obvious of which is the cost.

Not only can you save on the rent for your business premises by operating in this manner; Revenue Canada will also let you write off part of your home expenses for income tax purposes. Possible writeoffs are utility costs, mortgage interest, municipal taxes, and other expenses related to maintaining that part of your premises used for your business. You can also save on the cost and time of travelling to and from work every day, and you have greater flexibility in planning and organizing your work and personal life. In addition, a home-based business may have a number of other benefits such as letting you wear more comfortable clothes and giving you more time to look after and be with your family.

There are, however, a number of disadvantages.

1. It takes a lot of self-discipline to sustain a regular work schedule and resist distractions from family, friends, television, and other sources. You may find that there are too many interruptions to work effectively, that you tend to mix work with family life too much, or become distracted by household chores. Conversely, you may find it very difficult to get away from your work when you would like to, since it is so close at hand, and you may have trouble quitting after a full day.

2. Suppliers and prospective customers may not take you as seriously. You may have to rent a post office box or make other arrangements to give the appearance of operating from a more conventional commercial location.

3. The space available in your home may not be appropriate for your business, and you may not have access to facilities and equipment such as computers and fax machines that you need to conduct your business effectively.

4. If your house is in a typical residential area, operating a business from your home will probably contravene local zoning bylaws.

   It is true that most municipal governments have become reasonably flexible in this regard and do not go looking for violations; they will, however, respond to complaints from immediate neighbours and others in the vicinity. It is probably a good idea to check with these people before starting any kind of visible business activity from your home. Activities that may lead to complaints are posting a large sign on the front lawn, constant noise, a steady stream of customers, suppliers, or others in and out of your home, or the clutter of parked vehicles in your yard or on the street.

In the end, operating a home-based business is really a very personal decision. From a legal perspective, you can probably do what you want, as long as no one complains. However, this mode of operation is not suitable for all types of businesses, and for many people may not be a comfortable decision.

Fleshing Out Your Marketing Program

The purpose of this section is to bring together what you have learned about the total market potential for your product or service, customer attitudes toward your particular offering, and the nature of the competitive environment you will be facing. The goal is to put down on paper a preliminary marketing strategy or plan for your new venture concept. This involves making some decisions regarding what you feel is an appropriate *marketing mix* for your business. Put simply, the principal ingredients of your marketing program that must be blended together to form your overall strategy can be grouped under the following headings:

1. Product or service offering
2. Pricing program
3. Promotional plans
4. Method of distribution

Product or Service Offering

The product area involves the planning and development of the product or service you are planning to offer in the marketplace. This involves defining the breadth and depth of your offering, the length of your line, how it will be packaged and branded, the variety of colours and other product features, and the range of complementary services (delivery, repair, warranties, etc.) that will be made available to the customer.

Pricing Program

Your pricing strategy involves establishing the right base price for your offering so that it is appealing to customers and profitable to you. This base price may be adjusted to meet the needs of particular situations, such as to encourage early acceptance of your offering during its introductory stages, to meet aggressive or exceptional competition, to provide for trade, functional, seasonal, and other discounts, or to introduce your product/service into new market situations.

One of the most commonly used strategies by retailers and small manufacturers is *markup pricing*. The cost of your product or service is determined and used as the base, and then a markup is added to determine what your selling price should be. *Markups* are generally expressed as a percentage of the selling price — for example, a product costing $2.50 and selling for $5 has a 50 percent markup.

To illustrate, let's assume you've come up with a new formula for an automobile engine treatment that will be sold through auto parts jobbers to service stations for use in consumers' cars. Table 6.3 illustrates what the price markup chain for this product might look like.

As you can see, in this illustration a product with a factory cost of $1.50 has a retail selling price of $5 to the final consumer. The markup percentages shown here are merely examples of a typical situation, but in most wholesale and retail businesses standard markups tend to prevail in different industry sectors. Food products and other staple items usually have a low unit cost and high inventory turnover, so the markups tend to be fairly low, 15 to 25 percent: products such as jewelry and highly advertised specialty products typically have higher markups, perhaps as much as 50 or 60 percent or even more.

TABLE 6.3	PRICE MARKUP CHAIN		
		Per Bottle	Markup
Direct factory costs		$1.00	
Indirect factory costs		0.50	
Total factory cost		$1.50	
Manufacturer's markup		0.50	25%
Manufacturer's selling price		$2.00	
Jobber's markup		0.50	20%
Jobber's selling price		$2.50	
Service station markup		2.50	50%
Service station selling price		$5.00	

This type of markup pricing is simple and easy to apply and can be very successful if all competitors have similar costs of doing business and use similar percentages. On the other hand, this approach does not take into account variations in the demand for the product that may occur with a different final price. For example, how much more or less of the engine treatment would be sold at a price of $4 or $6 rather than the $5 price determined by the standard markup chain?

Most manufacturers do not employ markup pricing in the same way that many wholesalers and retailers do. However, if you plan to manufacture a product that will be sold through wholesalers and various types of retail outlets, it is important for you to know the markups these distributors will likely apply to your product. For instance, in the above example if the manufacturer of the engine treatment thinks $5 is the right retail price, he or she can work backwards and determine that it must be able to sell profitably to the jobbers for $2 in order to succeed. If that is not possible, perhaps the overall marketing strategy for the product should be reconsidered.

In addition to establishing a base price for your product or service line, you may permit some customers to pay less than this amount in certain circumstances or provide them with a discount. The principal types of discounts are quantity discounts, cash discounts, and seasonal discounts. *Quantity discounts* are commonly provided to customers who buy more than some minimum quantity or dollar value of products or services from you. This discount may be based either on the quantity or value of each individual order (non-cumulative) or on the total value of their purchases over a certain period of time, such as a month (cumulative).

Cash discounts are based on the typical terms of trade within an industry and permit the customer to deduct a certain percentage amount from the net cost of their purchases if payment is made in cash at the time of purchase or full payment is made within a specified number of days. Different types of businesses have their own customary cash discounts. For example, a typical discount is expressed as "2/10 net 30." In this situation, a customer who is invoiced on October 1 for an outstanding bill of $2000 need only pay $1960 if payment is made before October 10. This is a 2 percent cash discount for making payment within the 10 days. Otherwise the full face value of the invoice ($2,000) is due by October 31 or 30 days after the invoice date.

Seasonal discounts of 10 percent, 15 percent, 20 percent, or more on your normal base price may be offered to your customers if their purchases are made during your slow or off-season. This gives you a method of moving inventories that you may otherwise have to carry over to the following year or of providing your dealers, agents, and other distributors with some incentive to stock up on your products well in advance of the prime selling season.

Promotional Plans

The budget that you allocate for the promotion of your new venture must be distributed across the following activities:

1. Advertising
2. Sales promotion
3. Public relations
4. Personal selling

Each of these activities differs along a number of important dimensions such as their cost to reach a member of the target audience and the degree of interaction that can take place with that audience. Table 6.4 summarizes how these activities compare on a number of different criteria.

TABLE 6.4	A COMPARISON OF VARIOUS PROMOTIONAL ACTIVITIES*			
	Advertising	Sales Promotion	Public Relations	Personal Selling
Cost per Audience Member	Low	Low	Very Low	Very High
Focus on Target Markets	Poor to Good	Good	Moderate	Very Good
Ability to Deliver a Complicated Message	Poor to Good	Poor	Poor to Good	Very Good
Interchange With Audience	None	None	Low to Moderate	Very Good
Credibility	Low	Low	High	Moderate to High

*Adapted from Gerald E. Hills, "Market Opportunities and Marketing," in William D. Bygrave. *The Portable MBA in Entrepreneurship*, Second Edition, John Wiley & Sons, Inc. 1999.

The distribution of your expenditures should be made to obtain the maximum results for your particular circumstances. It is impossible to generalize about the optimum distribution of your dollars to each of these activities. Different businesses use quite different combinations. Some companies put most of their money into hiring a sales force and their sales promotion program; others put most of their budget into a media advertising campaign. The proper combination for you will depend on a careful study of the relative costs and effectiveness of each of these types of promotion and the unique requirements of your business.

We often think of promotion as being directed strictly toward our final prospective customer, and in fact the largest share of most promotional activity is channelled in that direction. However, promotion can also be used to influence your dealers, your distributors, and other members of your distribution channel. This may persuade them to adopt your offering more rapidly and broaden the breadth of your distribution coverage.

Advertising

Advertising is one of the principal means you have of informing potential customers about the availability and special features of your product or service. Properly conceived messages presented in the appropriate media can greatly stimulate demand for your business and its offerings. A wide range of advertising media are available to carry your messages, of which the most important are those listed in Table 6.5. Which of these media you should choose for your advertising program

TABLE 6.5 THE MOST COMMON ADVERTISING MEDIA

1. **MAGAZINES**
   a. Consumer magazines
   b. Trade or business publications
   c. Farm publications
   d. Professional magazines

2. **NEWSPAPERS**
   a. Daily newspapers
   b. Weekly newspapers
   c. Shopping guides
   d. Special-interest newspapers

3. **TELEVISION**
   a. Local TV
   b. Network TV
   c. Special-interest cable TV

4. **RADIO**
   a. Local stations
   b. Network radio

5. **DIRECTORY**
   a. Yellow Pages
   b. Community
   c. Special-interest

6. **DIRECT MAIL ADVERTISING**
   a. Letters
   b. Catalogues

7. **OUTDOOR ADVERTISING**
   a. Billboards
   b. Posters

8. **TRANSPORTATION ADVERTISING**
   a. Interior car cards
   b. Station posters
   c. Exterior cards on vehicles

9. **POINT-OF-PURCHASE DISPLAYS**

10. **ADVERTISING NOVELTIES AND SPECIALTIES**

11. **THE INTERNET**

will depend on the consumers you are trying to reach, the size of the budget you have available, the nature of your product or service, and the particular message you hope to communicate.

Advertising on the Internet One form of advertising that is rapidly increasing in popularity is the use of the Internet. The World Wide Web is open for business and small firms, particularly retail businesses, are jumping aboard in ever increasing numbers. Before joining this throng, however, you should consider whether a Web presence will really serve your business interests. If so, you need to formulate a clear strategy or plan, rather than just developing another Web page to join the millions that already exist on the Net.

Should you decide to proceed with implementing a Web site, remember that the Web is not a passive delivery system like most other media but is an active system where the user expects to participate in the experience. Your virtual storefront must be genuinely interesting and the interactivity of the Web should be used to your advantage to attract and hold the ongoing interest of your target consumers.

Opening a successful Web site is not as complicated as it may appear but it can be expensive to do the job right. You can do it yourself or enlist the expertise of a multimedia production house. Production costs depend entirely upon the size and interactivity of your site, running anywhere from $500 on the cheap to $100,000 for a full-blown corporate site. Maintenance costs are minimal but materials and other aspects of the site's operation should be updated regularly, such as once a month. To find out more about Canadian multimedia houses, a listing is provided at http://www.ideaguy.com.

Once your page is developed, it is important that you get a domain name and file a registration request. You will also want a reliable Web server to house your site. Try to get as many links leading to your site as possible by listing with directories, hotlinks, and so on where consumers will be able to find you quite easily. You might also give some consideration to joining a Cybermall.

Personal Selling

Personal selling involves direct, face-to-face contact with your prospective customer. A personal salesperson's primary function is usually more concerned with obtaining orders than informing your customers about the nature of your offering as in the case of advertising. Other types of salespeople are principally involved in providing support to different components of your business or filling routine orders rather than more persuasive kinds of selling. The basic steps involved in the selling process are as follows:

1. **Prospecting and qualifying** Identifying prospective customers
2. **The sales approach** The initial contact with the prospective customer
3. **Presentation** The actual sales message presented to a prospective customer
4. **Demonstration** of the capabilities and features or most important characteristics of the product or service being sold
5. **Handling any objections or concerns** the prospective customer may have regarding your offering
6. **Closing the sale** Asking the prospective customer for the order
7. **Postsales activities** Follow-up to determine if customers are satisfied with their purchase and to pursue any additional possible sales

Sales Promotion

Sales promotion includes a broad range of promotional activities other than advertising and personal selling that stimulate consumer or dealer interest in your offering. While advertising and personal selling tend to be ongoing activities, most sales promotion is sporadic or irregular in nature. Sales promotion includes activities related to:

1. Free product samples
2. Discount coupons
3. Contests
4. Special deals and premiums
5. Gifts
6. Special exhibits and displays
7. Participation in trade shows
8. Off-price specials
9. Floats in parades and similar events

As you can see, sales promotion consists of a long list of what are typically non-recurring activities. They are intended to make your advertising and personal selling effort more effective and may be very intimately involved with them. For example, your advertising may be used to promote a consumer contest, or certain special deals and incentives may be offered to your salespeople to encourage them to increase their sales to your dealers or final consumers. These activities can be an effective way for businesses with a small budget and some imagination to reach potential sales prospects and develop a considerable volume of business.

Public Relations

Public relations relates to your business' general communications and relationships with its various interest groups such as your employees, stockholders, the government, and society at large, as well as your customers. It is concerned primarily with such issues as the image of you and your business within the community rather than trying to sell any particular product or service. Publicity releases, product introduction notices, news items, appearances on radio and television, and similar activities are all part of your public relations program.

Method of Distribution

Your *channel of distribution* is the path your products or service take to market. Physical products typically follow one or more complex paths in getting from the point at which they are produced into the hands of their final consumer. These paths involve the use of several different kinds of wholesalers and retailers who perform a variety of functions that are essential to making this flow of products reasonably efficient. These functions include buying, selling, transporting, storing, financing, risk-taking, and several others.

Distribution channels consist of channel members who are independent firms that facilitate this flow of merchandise. There are many different kinds and they have quite different names, but the functions they perform may not be that dramatically different. For example, wholesalers are generally classified according to whether they actually take title or ownership of the products they handle (*merchant wholesalers*) or not (*agents*). Merchant wholesalers are further classified as *full-service, limited-function, drop shippers, truck wholesalers,* and *rack jobbers*. Agents are commonly referred to as *brokers, manufacturer's agents, selling agents, food* or *drug brokers,* etc. For a small manufacturer all of these types of wholesalers, alone or in combination, represent possible paths for getting their product to market.

Retailers, too, cover a very broad spectrum, starting with the large department stores that carry a broad product selection and provide an extensive range of customer services, through specialty stores such as electronics, men's clothing, and furniture stores, on down to discount department stores, grocery stores, drug stores, catalogue retailers, and convenience stores. All represent possible members that could be included in your channel of distribution.

In addition to opportunities for marketing your products or services in conjunction with these traditional and conventional distribution channel members, you should not overlook more unconventional possibilities for reaching your potential customers. For example, over the past few years we have seen tremendous growth of various forms of non-store retailing, including:

1. Mail order catalogues
2. Direct response advertising on television, and in newspapers and magazines
3. Direct selling door to door
4. Party plan or home demonstration party selling
5. Direct mail solicitations
6. Vending machines
7. Trade shows
8. Fairs and exhibitions

You should also be aware of market opportunities that may exist for your venture in foreign markets. These may be accessed by direct exporting, using the services of a trading company, licensing or franchising a firm in that market to produce and sell your product or service, setting up a joint venture with a local firm, or some similar strategy.

Managing the Supply Situation

A key factor in the success of any new venture is some assurance of continuing access to critical supplies of raw material and component parts at reasonable prices. Many new businesses have floundered due to changing supply situations that impacted their ability to provide products of acceptable quality or drastically increased their costs of production. These conditions are seldom correctable and tend to be terminal for the smaller firm. It is critical that you investigate the range of possible sources for these key elements well in advance of starting your venture.

Assessing your supply situation requires an understanding of the manufacturing cycle for your product or service and an in-depth appreciation of the market for equipment, materials, and parts. One strategy being followed by more and more smaller firms is to subcontract their production requirements instead of making their own products. This strategy has a number of significant advantages:

- Your business can use the subcontractor's money instead of having to raise the funds to build your own production facilities.

- You can take advantage of the expertise and technical knowledge possessed by the subcontractor without having to develop it yourself.

- Using a subcontractor may enable you to bring your business on stream more rapidly. There is no need to delay while your production facilities are being built and broken in.

- You can concentrate your time on developing a market for your products and running your business rather than on trying to produce a satisfactory product.

- You may be able to benefit from the reputation and credibility of the subcontractor; having your products produced by a firm with an established reputation will rub off on your business.

- A reliable subcontractor can also keep you up to date with technical advances in that field so that your products don't become obsolete.

- Perhaps the most important advantage of using a subcontractor is that it establishes your costs of production in advance, reducing the uncertainty and unpredictability of setting up your own facilities. A firm, fixed price contract from a reliable subcontractor nails down one of your most important costs of doing business and facilitates your entire planning process.

As you can see, there are a number of strong advantages to subcontracting certain aspects of your operations but that does not necessarily mean this strategy should be employed in all situations. There are a number of disadvantages that should be considered as well:

- The cost of having a job done by a subcontractor may not be as low as if you did the work yourself. The subcontractor may have antiquated equipment, high cost, unionized labour, or other problems to deal with that make their operations very expensive. Subcontractors also factor in some margin of profit for themselves into a job. The end result may be a total production cost which would make it very difficult for you to successfully compete.

- Your business may be jeopardized if the subcontractor should fail to meet commitments to you or divulge critical trade secrets about your product or process.

In any case, sometimes a suitable subcontractor is just not available. If you want your product produced, you may have no alternative but to do it yourself.

Regardless of the approach you decide to take, to cover your supply situation there are a number of key factors that have to be considered. These include:

- Delivered cost (total cost including transportation, etc.)
- Quality
- Delivery schedules
- Service level

All have to be at an acceptable level in order for you to have confidence your supply situation is under reasonable control.

| TABLE 6.2 | OTHER PUBLISHED SOURCES OF MARKET INFORMATION |

GENERAL

Gale Directory of Publication and Business Media
    Gale Research, Inc.
    835 Penobscot Bldg.
    645 Griswold Street
    Detroit, MI., 48226
    (www.gale.com)

The Standard Periodical Directory
    Oxbridge Communications Inc.
    150 Fifth Avenue
    New York, NY 10011
    (www.mediafinder.com)

Ulrich's International Periodicals Directory
    R.R. Bowker Company
    245 West 17th Street
    New York, NY 10011
    (www.bowker.com)

Indexes to books and magazine articles on a wide variety of business, industrial, and economic topics:

Bibliographic Index: A Cumulative Bibliography of Bibliographies
    H.W. Wilson Co.
    950 University Avenue
    New York, NY 10452
    (www.hwwilson.com)

Business Periodicals Index
    H.W. Wilson Co.
    950 University Avenue
    New York, NY 10452
    (www.hwwilson.com)

Canadian Business Index
    Micromedia Limited
    158 Pearl Street
    Toronto, Ontario M5H 1L3
    (www.mmltd.com)

A detailed listing of source books, periodicals, directories, handbooks, and other sources of information on a variety of business topics:

Directory of Industry Data Sources
    Ballinger Publishing Co.
    54 Church Street
    Box 281
    Cambridge, MA 02138

Encyclopedia of Business Information Sources
    Gale Research Company
    835 Penobscot Bldg.
    645 Griswold St.
    Detroit, MI 48226
    (www.gale.com)

A general guide to business publications:

Business Information: How to Find it, How to Use it
    Oryx Press
    2214 North Central Avenue
    Phoenix, AZ 85004-1483
    (www.oryxpress.com)

Business Information Sources
    University of California Press
    2120 Berkeley Way
    Berkeley, CA 94720
    (www.ucpress.edu)

Directories of business oriented databases:

Gale Directory of Databases
    Gale Research Inc.
    835 Penobscot Building
    645 Griswold St.
    Detroit, MI. 48226
    (www.gale.com)

LEXIS/NEXIS
    Reed Elsevier
    P.O. Box 933
    Dayton, OH 45401
    (www.lexis-nexis.com)

Other Published Sources of Market Information — continued

INDUSTRY AND MARKET INFORMATION

Data on income, population, expenditures, etc. by major market area:

Survey of Buying Power (annual special issue of *Sales and Marketing Management*)
　　Bill Communications, Inc.
　　633 Third Avenue
　　New York, NY 10017
　　(www.billcom.com)

Information on population size and growth, income, expenditures, prices, and similar data by market area:

FP Markets—Canadian Demographics
　　Financial Post Data Group
　　333 King Street East
　　Toronto, ON M5A 4N2
　　(www.fpmarkets.com)

Market Research Handbook
　　Statistics Canada
　　Ottawa, Ontario K1A 0T6
　　(www.fedpubs.com/mkthdbk.htm)

COMPANY INFORMATION

Detailed information on most major corporations:

Dun & Bradstreet Reference Book of American Business
　　Dun & Bradstreet Inc.
　　99 Church St.
　　New York, NY 10007
　　(www.dnb.com)

Wall Street Research Net
　　(www.wsrn.com)

Moody's Manuals and Investors Services
　　99 Church Street
　　New York, NY 10007
　　(www.moodys.com)

Listings of Canadian manufacturers by location and product category:

Fraser's Canadian Trade Directory
　　Maclean Hunter Limited
　　777 Bay Street
　　Toronto, Ontario M5W 1A7
　　(www.frasers.com)

Scott's Trade Directory: Metropolitan Toronto and Toronto Vicinity
　　Scott's Directories Southam Ltd.
　　Box 365
　　75 Thomas Street
　　Oakville, Ontario L6J 5M5
　　(www.scottsinfo.com)

　　Scott's Industrial Directories:
　　• Western Manufacturers
　　• Ontario Manufacturers
　　• Quebec Manufacturers
　　• Atlantic Manufacturers

Other Published Sources of Market Information — continued

MARKETING INFORMATION

Listings of rates and other information on radio, television, consumer magazines, trade magazines, direct mail, and newspapers:

Standard Rate & Data Media Publications
    Standard Rate & Data Service
    5201 Old Orchard Rd.
    Skokie, IL 60077
    (www.srds.com)

Canadian Advertising Rates & Data
    Maclean Hunter Research Bureau
    777 Bay Street
    Toronto, Ontario M5W 1A7
    (www.cardmedia.com)

A listing of agents and firms representing manufacturers of all types:

Verified Directory of Manufacturer's Representatives
    MacRae's Industrial Directories
    87 Terminal Drive
    Plainview, NY 11803

Manufacturer's Agents National Association Directory of Members
    Manufacturer's Agents National Association
    20316 Mill Creek Road
    P.O. Box 3467
    Laguna Hills, CA 92654

Comprehensive listings of U.S. and Canadian meetings, conventions, trade shows, and expositions:

Conventions & Meetings Canada
    Maclean Hunter Limited
    777 Bay Street
    Toronto, Ontario M5W 1A7
    (www.meetingscanada.com)

Directory of Conventions
    Sales and Marketing Management Magazine
    Bill Communications, Inc.
    633 Third Avenue
    New York, NY 10017
    (www.billcom.com)

Trade Shows Worldwide
ExpoWorld.net
(www.expoworld.net)

A comprehensive listing of mail order firms:

Mail Order Product Guide
    B. Klein Publications
    P.O. Box 8503
    Coral Springs, FL 33065

Directory of Mail Order Catalogs
    Grey House Publishing
    Pocket Knife Square
    Lakeville, CT 06039
    (www.greyhouse.com)

Catalogue of Canadian Catalogues
    Alpel Publishing
    P.O. Box 203
    Chambly, QC J3L 4B3
    (www.total.net/nalpelie/)

A comprehensive listing of all trade and professional associations in Canada:

Directory of Associations in Canada
    Micromedia Ltd.
    158 Pearl Street
    Toronto, Ontario M5H 1L3
    (www.mmltd.com)

FIGURE 6.2   DEVELOPING A MARKET OR CUSTOMER PROFILE

1. Define your target customers in terms of geography, demographic characteristics, or other factors.

_____

_____

_____

_____

_____

2. How many of these target customers are in your trading or relevant market area?

_____

_____

_____

_____

_____

3. What are the principal factors these customers consider in the purchase of a product/service like yours?

_____

_____

_____

_____

_____

4. Why will they buy your product rather than your competitors'?

_____

_____

_____

_____

_____

FIGURE 6.3   FORM FOR ESTIMATING MARKET SIZE

ESTIMATED TOTAL MARKET SIZE

1. DESCRIPTION OF PRINCIPAL MARKET

_____

_____

	200A	200B	200C	200D	200E
Estimated sales in units	_____	_____	_____	_____	_____
Estimated sales in $000	_____	_____	_____	_____	_____

2. OVERVIEW OF MAJOR SEGMENTS

   a. Description of segment: _____

_____

	200A	200B	200C	200D	200E
Estimated sales in units	_____	_____	_____	_____	_____
Estimated sales in $000	_____	_____	_____	_____	_____

   b. Description of segment: _____

_____

	200A	200B	200C	200D	200E
Estimated sales in units	_____	_____	_____	_____	_____
Estimated sales in $000	_____	_____	_____	_____	_____

FIGURE 6.4   OUTLINE FOR A CUSTOMER SURVEY

Name of Customer _____

1. NATURE OF THE CUSTOMER'S BUSINESS OR ROLE

_____

_____

_____

2. CUSTOMER'S REACTION TO YOUR PRODUCT OR SERVICE

   a. What advantages/benefits do they see?

_____

_____

   b. What disadvantages do they see?

_____

_____

   c. What questions do they raise?

_____

_____

_____

Outline for a Customer Survey — continued

3. SPECIFIC NEEDS AND USES

a. What needs and uses do they have for a product/service such as yours?

_____

_____

_____

4. SELLING PRICE, SERVICE, AND SUPPORT

a. What do you believe would be an acceptable selling price?

_____

_____

b. What level of service and support would they expect?

_____

_____

_____

c. What other terms would they expect?

_____

_____

_____

5. CURRENT PURCHASING PRACTICES

a. Where do potential customers currently buy this type of product or service (retailer, wholesaler, direct mail, broker, etc.)?

_____

_____

_____

_____

6. NAME OF COMPETITIVE FIRMS

a. What competing firms' products and services are they currently using?

_____

_____

_____

FIGURE 6.5   FORM FOR ANALYZING YOUR COMPETITORS

Name of Competitor _____   **Estimated Market Share** _____%

1. PRODUCT OR SERVICE

a. How does the company's product or service differ from other products and services in the marketplace? _____

_____

_____

_____

b. Do they offer a broad or narrow product line? _____

_____

c. Do they emphasize quality? _____

2. PRICE

a. What is their average selling price? _____

b. What is their profit margin? _____

c. What type of discounts do they offer? _____

d. Do they emphasize a low selling price? _____

3. PROMOTION

a. How much do they spend on advertising and trade promotion? _____

b. How well known are they (brand recognition)? _____

c. Through which media do they advertise? _____

_____

d. What other types of promotion do they use? _____

_____

e. How many salespeople do they have? _____

4. DISTRIBUTION/LOCATION

a. What type of distribution intermediaries do they use (brokers, company sales force, direct to wholesaler, etc.)? _____

_____

_____

b. Where are they located? _____

c. Is location very important in this industry? _____

5. MARKETING STRATEGY

a. Does the company cater to any particular segment of the market? _____

_____

b. Does the company offer some unique product or service that makes it different from other competitors? _____

_____

_____

Form for Analyzing Your Competitors — continued

    c. Do they offer a particularly low price?_____

    d. What is the principal factor that accounts for the success of this firm?_____

6. MARKET POSITION

    a. What is their market share?_____

    b. Have their sales been growing? Stable? Declining?_____

    _____

    c. How successful are they?_____

    _____

7. MAJOR STRENGTHS AND WEAKNESSES

    a. What are their major strengths?_____

    _____

    _____

    b. What are their major weaknesses?_____

    _____

    _____

FIGURE 6.6   DEVELOPING A SALES FORECAST

1. Provide a summary overview of typical individuals, companies, or organizations that are likely prospects for your product/service offering as described in the market profile you prepared in Figure 6.2. Ask yourself such questions as: How old would these customers be? Where do they live? In what types of activities would they participate? What primary benefits are they looking for in my product or service? Etc.

    _____

    _____

    _____

    _____

    _____

2. How many of the people or organizations you have described as good prospects are in your trading area?

    _____

    _____

    _____

3. Describe how you feel these individuals or organizations would go about deciding whether to purchase your product/service rather than a competitor's offering. Would these potential customers be principally concerned with price, convenience, quality, or some other factor?

    _____

    _____

    _____

    _____

Developing a Sales Forecast — continued

4. How often would prospective buyers purchase your product or service? Daily? Weekly? Monthly? Etc. Where would they look for it or expect to buy it? What kind of seasonal or other patterns are likely to influence sales? How will holidays or other special events affect sales patterns within a month? A year?

_____

_____

_____

_____

5. How much (in dollars and/or units) would a typical customer purchase on each buying occasion?

_____

_____

6. How would your customers likely hear about your product/service offering? Through newspapers? TV or radio advertisements? Word of mouth? Salespeople? Middlemen? Etc.

_____

_____

_____

7. From the above information, estimate your expected annual sales in terms of *dollars* and/or *number of units:*

a. By week for each month for the first year of operation of your business.

	Week 1	Week 2	Week 3	Week 4
January				
February				
March				
April				
May				
June				
July				
August				
September				
October				
November				
December				

b. By month for each of the next two years.

	2nd year	3rd year
January		
February		
March		
April		
May		
June		
July		
August		
September		
October		
November		
December		

FIGURE 6.7   RATING FORM FOR SELECTING A RETAIL LOCATION

FACTOR A: PRIMARY ACCEPTANCE OR REJECTION FACTORS
(RATE YES OR NO)

	Location No.			
	1	2	3	4
1. Will municipal zoning allow the proposed business?	____	____	____	____
2. Does this site meet the minimum operating needs of the proposed business?	____	____	____	____
3. Do existing buildings meet minimum initial needs?	____	____	____	____
4. Is the rent for this location within your proposed operating budget?	____	____	____	____
5. Is the rent for this location, with or without buildings, reasonable?	____	____	____	____

One "No" answer may be sufficient reason not to proceed with further investigation unless some modification can be achieved.

FACTOR B: SITE EVALUATION
(USE PERCENTAGE SCALE 0 TO 100)

	Location No.			
	1	2	3	4
6. How does this location compare with the best possible location available?	____	____	____	____
7. What rating would you give the present buildings on the site?	____	____	____	____
8. How would you rate the overall environment of this location with the best environment existing within your trading area?	____	____	____	____
9. How would you rate the availability of parking for automobiles?	____	____	____	____
10. How would you rate the nature and quantity of combined foot and auto traffic passing your location?	____	____	____	____
11. What is the improvement potential of this location?	____	____	____	____
Total	____	____	____	____

FACTOR C: TREND ANALYSIS
(COMPARE THE ANSWER FOR EACH LOCATION AND RANK EACH BY NUMBER FROM AMONG THOSE REVIEWED — i.e., 1ST, 2ND, 3RD, OR 4TH)

	Location No.			
	1	2	3	4
12. Has the location shown improvement through the years?	____	____	____	____
13. Is the owner and/or landlord progressive and cooperative?	____	____	____	____
14. What major patterns of change are affecting this location?	____	____	____	____
a. Streets: speed limits, paving	____	____	____	____
b. Shopping centres	____	____	____	____
c. Zoning	____	____	____	____
d. Financial investment	____	____	____	____
e. Dynamic leadership and action	____	____	____	____
f. Type of shopper or other potential customer	____	____	____	____
15. What businesses have occupied this location over the past 10 years?	____	____	____	____
16. Have the businesses identified in question 15 (above) been successful?	____	____	____	____
17. Why is this location now available?	____	____	____	____
18. Are a number of other suitable locations available?	____	____	____	____

Rating Form for Selecting a Retail Location — continued

FACTOR D: PRICE-VALUE DETERMINATION

	Location No.			
	1	**2**	**3**	**4**

19. What is the asking rent for each location? ____ ____ ____ ____

20. What numerical total for each site is developed through questions 6 to 11? ____ ____ ____ ____

21. Is there a "No" answer to any of questions 1 to 5? ____ ____ ____ ____

22. Do the answers to questions 12 to 18 develop a pattern which is: ____ ____ ____ ____

   a. Highly favourable? ____ ____ ____ ____

   b. Average? ____ ____ ____ ____

   c. Fair? ____ ____ ____ ____

   d. Questionable? ____ ____ ____ ____

   e. Not acceptable? ____ ____ ____ ____

Rank each location according to numerical totals and preferences as to subjective Factors C and D. ____ ____ ____ ____

Adapted from M. Archer and J. White, *Starting and Managing Your Own Small Business* (Toronto: Macmillan Company of Canada, 1978), pp. 38–40. Reproduced by permission.

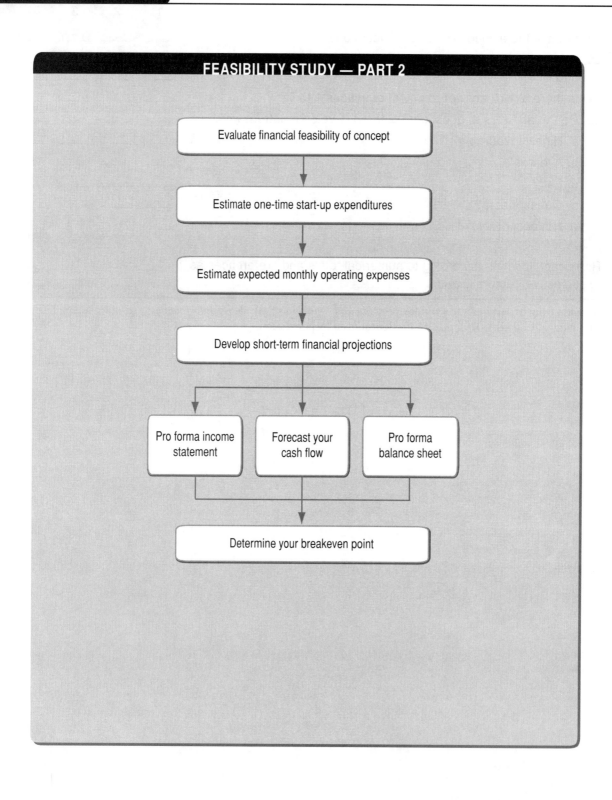

FEASIBILITY STUDY — PART 2

Evaluate financial feasibility of concept

↓

Estimate one-time start-up expenditures

↓

Estimate expected monthly operating expenses

↓

Develop short-term financial projections

↓

Pro forma income statement | Forecast your cash flow | Pro forma balance sheet

↓

Determine your breakeven point

Conducting a Feasibility Study

Part 2:
Cost and Profitability Assessment

In addition to determining the size and nature of the market for your new venture idea, it is also important to consider the financial components of your business. The costs associated with operating your business may include labour, materials, rent, machinery, etc. Collecting potential sales and cost information should put you in a better position to make reasonably accurate financial forecasts that can be used not only as a check on the advisability of proceeding with the venture but also for raising capital, if required.

Determine Your Start-up Financial Requirements

The process of financial analysis begins with an estimate of the funds required to set up your business. Start-up financial requirements can be broken down into two components:

1. **One-time expenditures** that must be made before your business can open its doors. This includes such expenses as the purchase or lease of furniture, fixtures, and equipment; utility deposits and fees; and pre-opening advertising and promotion expenses. In the case of retailing and manufacturing businesses these requirements can be considerable, while a

Cathy © 1998 Cathy Guisewite. Reprinted with permission of UNIVERSAL PRESS SYNDICATE. All rights reserved.

service business may not require a very large initial expenditure to get started. A typical example showing the estimated one-time financial requirements for the start-up of a sporting goods store is illustrated in Figure 7.1

2. **Operating expenses** such as payments for owner and employee wages, raw materials, rent, supplies and postage, and other expenses that must be made until the business begins to show a profit. Many new businesses take several months or even years before they operate "in the black." Sufficient funds should be available to cover a *minimum* of two to three months' operation and provide a cash reserve for emergency situations. As a typical situation, your cash requirements may be reduced if your business gets started with firm orders in hand, or even a down payment from some customers, which may start to generate considerable cash flow from the moment you open your doors. On the other hand, a business that is going to build up slowly, or a high tech business requiring a lot of initial research and development, may need to have sufficient working capital available to carry it for four or six months or even longer. A typical example showing the estimated funds required to cover these initial operating expenses for a sporting goods store is also illustrated in Figure 7.1.

Note that a sporting goods store, like many retail businesses, is a relatively capital-intensive business to start. The bulk of the money is required to finance the initial inventory you will need to stock the store, while most of the remaining one-time funds go to decorating and providing the necessary fixtures for the store. In addition, you should have approximately $40,000 available to cover your estimated monthly expenses until the business starts generating a positive cash flow. You do not necessarily have to have that much money available strictly from your own resources; $100,000 – 150,000 may be sufficient. Suppliers may be prepared to grant you credit terms so that you do not necessarily have to pay for some of your stock for 30 or 60 days. Or the bank may be prepared to extend a line of credit to you that you can draw on to meet some of your working capital requirements as they arise.

Insufficient financing is a major cause of new business failure, so you should be certain you have sufficient financing to cover both your estimated one-time and your initial operating expenses.

Develop Short-term Financial Projections

Pro Forma Income Statement

The next step is to estimate your total expected revenue and expenses for at least the first year of operation of your business. This projected operating statement, or *pro forma income statement*, should show:

1. Your predicted sales volume for the first year of operation of your business
2. How much it will cost to produce or purchase the products you will sell
3. Your fixed monthly operating expenses such as rent, utilities, insurance premiums, and interest costs
4. Your controllable monthly operating expenses such as advertising and promotion expenses, wages and salaries, and delivery expenses
5. Your expected net operating profit or loss

One means of developing a pro forma income statement for your business is to follow the Desired Income Approach suggested by Szonyi and Steinhoff.[1] This approach enables you to

---

[1] A. J. Szonyi and D. Steinhoff, *Small Business Management Fundamentals*, 3rd Canadian ed. (Toronto: McGraw-Hill Ryerson, 1988), pp. 58-65.

FIGURE 7.1	ESTIMATED START-UP REQUIREMENTS FOR A SPORTING GOODS STORE

ESTIMATED MONTHLY EXPENSES

Item	Your estimate of monthly expenses based on sales of $ 600,000 per year Column 1	Your estimate of how much cash you need to start your business (see column 3.) Column 2	What to put in column 2 (these figures are typical for one kind of business. You will have to decide how many months to allow for in your business.) Column 3
Salary of owner-manager	$ 3,000	$ 6,000	2 times column 1
All other salaries, wages and benefits	4,000	12,000	3 times column 1
Rent	1,500	4,500	3 times column 1
Advertising	1,000	3,000	3 times column 1
Delivery expense	350	1,050	3 times column 1
Supplies	200	600	3 times column 1
Telephone	150	450	3 times column 1
Other utilities	400	1,200	3 times column 1
Insurance	300	600	Payment required by insurance company
Interest	1,000	3,000	3 times column 1
Maintenance	400	1,200	3 times column 1
Legal and other professional fees	250	750	3 times column 1
Miscellaneous	2,000	6,000	3 times column 1
ONE-TIME FINANCIAL REQUIREMENTS			Leave column 2 blank
Fixtures and equipment		20,000	
Decorating and remodelling		10,000	
Installation of fixtures and equipment		5,600	
Starting inventory		160,000	
Deposits with public utilities		2,000	
Legal and other professional fees		1,500	
Licences and permits		800	
Advertising and promotion for opening		2,500	
Accounts receivable		8,000	
Cash		5,000	
Other		5,000	
TOTAL ESTIMATED CASH YOU NEED TO START WITH		$ 255,750	Add up all the numbers in column 2

develop financial projections on the basis of the actual operating performance of firms similar to the business you are contemplating. It also suggests that your business should provide you with not only a return for the time you will spend running the business but also a return on the personal funds you have to invest to launch the business. For example, you could keep your present job or obtain another one and earn a salary working for someone else. You could also invest your money in common stocks, bonds, guaranteed income certificates, or other investments, where it would yield some kind of return. Both possibilities should be kept in mind in determining your expected minimum level of acceptable profit performance of your new venture.

To illustrate this approach, assume you are considering the possibility of opening a retail sporting goods store like the one we discussed before. You have determined that you would like to have a salary of $40,000/year from the business, plus $10,000 as a reasonable return on the investment you will have to make in the business. These represent your desired income and return levels. By referring to Dun & Bradstreet Canada information, Robert Morris and Associates Industry Statement Studies, or the Statistics Canada Small Business Profiles you can obtain comprehensive financial data on sporting goods stores as well as dozens of other different lines of business.

Combining the information about your desired income and return goals with some of this published data will enable you to develop a pro forma income statement highlighting the level of operations you will have to reach in order to achieve your goals. The additional information you require is:

- **The average inventory turnover for this type of business** is the number of times a typical firm's inventory is sold each year. If the business carries an inventory of $25,000 and its overall cost of goods sold is $150,000, inventory turnover is six times per year.

- **The average gross margin** is the difference between the firm's net sales and cost of goods sold, expressed as a percentage. For example, if the business' net sales are $200,000 while cost of goods sold total $140,000, its gross margin is $60,000 or 30 percent.

- **Net profit as a percentage of sales** is relatively self-explanatory. It can be determined either before or after the application of any federal or provincial taxes. In the case of the Statistics Canada Small Business Profiles, it is shown before the application of any taxes.

Developing the Statement

With this data and an estimate of your desired salary and return levels, you can construct a pro forma income statement for a sporting goods store. Checking the 1995 Statistics Canada Small Business Profiles for SIC code J6541 – Sporting Goods Stores (www.strategis.ic.gc.ca/cgi-bin/sbp/sbp.cgi) provides us with the following information:

Inventory turnover	2.9 times per year
Gross margin	34.1% of sales
Net profit as a percentage of sales	1.9%

Figure 7.2 illustrates how this data, along with the information about your desired salary and return can be used to develop a pro forma income statement. This statement indicates the minimum level of sales your business will have to generate in order to provide you with your desired salary and level of profitability. Sales above this level will probably provide a higher level of profits while lower sales will likely mean you will not make as much money as you had hoped. It is assumed in this evaluation that your business will be operated as efficiently, and in a similar manner to, other sporting goods stores across the country.

All the figures in this statement have been computed from our ratio data and our stated desired salary and return on investment. For example:

1. Our $10,000 desired profit is inserted on line (E).

2. Profits for a retail sporting goods store are very slim at only 1.9% of sales. In order to determine the sales level required to provide our desired level of profitability, we divide $10,000 by 0.019 to obtain our estimate of the required level of $526,000 for net sales on line (A).

3. Our statistics indicate that sporting goods stores typically have an average gross margin of 34.1 percent of net sales. In our situation this would provide a gross margin estimate of $179,000 on line (C).

4. The difference between our estimated net sales and gross margin has to provide for our cost of goods sold. In this example our cost of goods sold will be $526,000 – $179,000 = $347,000 on line (B).

5. Sporting goods stores have a relatively low level of inventory turnover in comparison with other types of retail business. A typical retail firm will turn over its inventory from six to seven times per year while our statistics indicate a turnover ratio of only 2.9 times for our sporting goods store. This means we need to have more money tied up in inventory to support our estimated level of net sales than most other retailers. Our projected average inventory level can be determined by dividing our net sales revenue by the inventory turnover rate or $526,000/2.9 = $181,000.

6. The difference between our expected gross margin and the net operating profit (before taxes) necessary to provide our desired income level represents our total operating expenses in line (D). In this case $179,000 – $10,000 = $169,000 should be available to cover such expenses as our salary and that of our employees, rent, insurance, promotion, interest, and similar expenses. Note that our expected salary of $40,000 has to be included in this amount.

FIGURE 7.2	SAMPLE PRO FORMA INCOME STATEMENT FOR A RETAIL STORE

TOUGH GUYS SPORTING GOODS
PRO FORMA INCOME STATEMENT
For the year ending [date]

Net sales		$526,000 **(A)**
Less: Cost of goods sold:		
Beginning inventory	$167,000	
Plus: Net purchases	361,000	
Goods available for sale	$528,000	
Less: Ending inventory	181,000	
Cost of goods sold		347,000 **(B)**
Gross margin		$179,000 **(C)**
Operating expenses		169,000 **(D)**
Net Profit (Loss) Before Income Tax		**$ 10,000 (E)**

This pro forma statement shows you the level of sales, investment in inventory, and similar information you need to know in order to generate the indicated level of desired income you feel you need to obtain from the business.

The statement constructed in Figure 7.2 is based upon the distinct financial characteristics of a small, retail sporting goods business and relates only to that situation. A pro forma income statement for a store in another line of business could look very different due to variations in inventory turnover, gross margin percentage, and other factors reflecting the different character of that business.

This is even more true if we are considering the start-up of a service business or a manufacturing company. Service firms, like drycleaners and management consultants, typically do not carry an inventory of goods for resale and so don't have a "cost of goods sold" section on their income statement. Manufacturing companies, on the other hand, may have several types of inventory — raw materials, work in process, and finished goods. Appropriate levels for all three types of inventories should be determined and reflected in the projected income statement. The statement also tries to determine the value of raw materials and components, direct labour, factory overhead, and other inputs required to manufacture a product suitable for sale. This "cost of goods manufactured" replaces the cost of goods sold component on the pro forma statement.

Determining Reasonable Operating Expenses

So far, our pro forma income statement has lumped all our business' projected operating expenses together under a single heading. For example, Figure 7.2 shows our overall, estimated operating expenses to be $169,000. This means that all operating expenses must be covered by this amount if we are to achieve our desired level of profitability.

The same statistical sources used to obtain the data for our overall pro forma statement can be used to obtain a breakdown of the typical operating expenses for our type of business. For example, the Statistics Canada Small Business Profiles provide data on the operating results of sporting goods stores. It indicates the following breakdown of operating expenses as a percentage of sales for the average firm:

Advertising	1.9%
Delivery expenses	0.7%
Depreciation	1.2%
Wages, salaries, and benefits	15.4%
Insurance	0.5%
Interest and bank charges	1.9%
Professional fees	0.5%
Rent	2.9%
Repairs and maintenance	0.8%
Fuel	0.5%
Utilities	1.1%
Other expenses	4.8%

These expenses total approximately 32.2% of sales. If we translate these percentages to our pro forma income statement, we can obtain an approximation of the detailed breakdown of our operating expenses in dollar terms. Our finalized pro forma income statement would look like Figure 7.3.

This complete pro forma statement can now serve as part of your plan for outlining the requirements of your proposed new business venture or as a guide or schedule to monitor the ongoing performance of your new business during its early stages.

A typical pro forma statement that you can use for projecting the first-year operating performance of your new business is illustrated in the Outline for a Feasibility Study (Figure 7.7) at the back of this Stage.

Forecast Your Cash Flow

Your next step is to bring the operating profit or loss you have projected closer to reality by developing a *cash flow forecast*. This cash flow analysis is the most important document you will compile in assessing the financial feasibility of your business idea. It is also the most important tool available to you for contemplating and controlling the financial affairs of your business. As illustrated in Entrepreneurs in Action #15, failure to plan adequately for their future cash requirements is one of the principal reasons small businesses don't survive. Greg and Kate Williams' failure to estimate accurately the incoming revenue for the one-hour photo shop they purchased caused them not only to lose the business and the money they had invested in it but have to declare personal bankruptcy as well. An accurate cash flow forecast can be your best means of ensuring continued financial solvency and the survival of your business.

15

Over the Edge

Greg and Kate Williams (their names have been changed) were only in their early fifties when Greg took early retirement. Still youthful and vigorous, the Williams had a mortgage to repay, car payments to make and three children in their twenties who still relied on their parents for the occasional handout between jobs. The Williams weren't rich, but they weren't worried either. They'd arrived in Canada from Scotland in 1966 with just $132 between them. Within days of their arrival, they were hard at work. A draughtsman by training, Kate found a job with the provincial government. Greg worked in a beer store, laid floor tile, maintained an apartment building and worked for Sears. Then, in 1969, he joined the city police force. "I was 26 and fit as a fiddle," he recalls.

As the years passed, the Williams saved their money, bought a new house for $19,000, sold it for $30,000 and moved to a larger house farther out of the city. By the late 1970s, their family included two daughters and a son. To earn more money, they opened a video store in the mid-1980s. "It went very well," Kate says, "but with three kids at home, we had to choose finally between running the business and raising our children. The kids were getting neglected."

By then, Greg was within sight of early retirement. He'd served the police force well, as an officer on the beat, a detective and an undercover officer. In 1988, Greg and Kate moved to a resort community about two hours from the city. They paid $119,000 for their one-year-old house, just as real-estate prices in the province began to soar. For the next seven years, until June, 1995, Greg drove back and forth to work.

Before he left the police force "with exemplary service," Greg and Kate found a retail venture that would keep them busy and make some money to augment their savings and pension income. They met the owner of a one-hour photo shop in a nearby town, who wanted to sell out. For $60,000—less than half the price of new equipment alone—the Williams bought the business lock, stock and barrel. the former owner taught them how to operate the developing unit, and the Williams took over in May, 1995. In June, Greg retired. And in November,

when the lease expired, the Williams moved the shop from its original location to a newly built shopping mall in their home town.

The move was part of the Williams' plan. Before they invested in the business, they'd learned from their town planners that a photo shop was one of about a dozen businesses the town would need as it expanded over the next few years. Based on the current population of the town — about 11,000 — the Williams calculated the shop could break even if only one in four people in town used their shop to develop photographs, buy film and purchase the occasional picture frame, battery, camera strap or lens. Based on their business plan, the Williams had arranged financing through a local economic-development corporation, which provided a loan of $40,000, and through a local finance company, which provided another $10,000 to cover leasehold improvements. They raised $10,000 privately and scraped together the same amount from their own money. By the time they opened the new store, it had cost the Williams almost $75,000. "The store was beautiful," Kate says. "It was a treat for people to come into."

Unfortunately, not many people came. A couple of local real-estate agents used it to prepare photos and brochures for advertising. But with the resort closed down for the winter, there just weren't enough people walking through the door.

As 1996 began, the Williams realized they were in trouble. Rent alone cost them $1,400 a month. On top of that, they paid taxes and utilities. The Williams also realized they weren't competing on a level field with other one-hour photo services in the area. Department, grocery and drug-store chains have a steady demand for their services; they also pay far less for their equipment and supplies than the Williams since they buy in volume. A roll of developing paper, for example, for which the Williams paid $142 costs the chains about $60. And because of the volume of photographs the big chains develop, they receive the same equipment as the Williams $60,000 unit free of charge. No wonder they could develop a roll of film for $2 to $3 less than the Williams charged.

The fewer people who patronized the shop, the more expensive it became to run the place.

The chemicals in the developing unit, which sat unused for days at a time, went bad and had to be replaced almost monthly, at a cost of $600. The rent had to be paid, whether there were customers or not. Greg began siphoning money from a retirement account he'd set up with the contributory surplus from his police pension, then had to find more money to cover the income tax on the withdrawals. By November, 1996, Greg and Kate knew they were in trouble. "Everything that was coming in was going out again," says Greg, "but it still wasn't enough."

A financial consultant suggested they close the store and enjoy their Christmas, but the Williams hung on until February, 1997, when they finally closed the store for good. Even then, they owed only $71,000, excluding their house and equipment. But as Diane Hessel of A. Farber & Partners Inc., observes, "It might as well have been $71 million for the Williams."

Besides, they didn't distinguish between their personal and business debts. No matter how you described it to them, a debt was a debt, and they had a lot of them. In addition to their loan from the local economic-development corporation, they owed another $17,000 to the credit union that had advanced them funds for a previous debt and leasehold improvements, more than $9,500 to their equipment supplier and another $11,000 to Revenue Canada for tax on their previous video business. Along with their own personal debts on their van and house, the Williams owed a total of $229,000; their assets amounted to about $158,000.

On February 27, 1997, the Williams filed for bankruptcy. They expected their bankruptcy to proceed smoothly through the courts, but in October, two of their creditors opposed the Williams' application for discharge—which meant that, unlike the other creditors, they insisted on a court hearing, when they would seek some form of compensation from the estate. Under the stress of their financial predicament and after 25 years of police work, Greg Williams suffered an angina attack. In January, 1998, he underwent triple bypass surgery. The following month, the Williams appeared in bankruptcy court to explain why they could not repay every dollar they owed to their creditors.

After hearing their case, the judge ordered each of the Williams to repay $50 a month for distribution to their unpaid creditors, for a total payment of $2,500, as a condition of the terms for discharge from bankruptcy. They also had to come up with about $4,000 for Revenue Canada, which they arranged to pay off in installments. They can incur further debt, but they have to wait for seven years to have the bankruptcy removed from their credit record. "Pensions are exempt from seizure under the Pension Benefits Act," Hessel points out. "So they're much better off than most bankrupts. And remember, bankruptcy is not a punitive act. It's intended to get people back on their feet."

Slowly but surely, the Williams are doing just that. After closing their shop, Greg found part-time work as a security guard. A couple of months after their appearance in court, he received an invitation to work part-time for the provincial police force. Kate worked long hours in a donut shop for several months until the franchise was sold to a new owner. Now she collects Employment Insurance, which will run out shortly, "the first time in 30 years I've ever claimed it."

"I'm only 56," Greg says optimistically, "but retirement is out the window, at least for another few years. In any case," he adds, "sitting back playing golf and going fishing really wasn't for me."

Source: Bruce McDougall, "Over the Edge," *The Financial Post Magazine*, November, 1998, pp. 51-53. Reprinted with permission.

Cash flow statements are similar to but differ from income statements in a number of ways. Cash flow is exactly as the name implies. The statement only measures the flow of cash into and out of the business. Non-cash accounting entries that may show up on an income statement such as depreciation, amortization, and asset transfers are ignored in forecasting the cash flow statement. Similarly, expenses that have been incurred but not yet paid and income that has been earned but not yet received are not included in the cash flow statement either.

The need for a cash flow analysis originates from the reality that in most businesses there is a time discrepancy between when your expenditures are incurred and when the cash is actually realized from the sale of the products or services you provide.

In a typical small business, sales revenue and expenses vary throughout the year. Your cash flow forecast tries to predict all the funds that you will receive and disburse within a certain period of time — e.g., a month, quarter, or year — and the resulting surplus or deficit. It allows you to estimate the total amount of cash you actually expect to receive each period and the actual bills that have to be paid. At times your cash inflows will exceed your outflows; at other times your cash outflows will exceed your inflows. Knowing your expected position and cash

FIGURE 7.3	SAMPLE COMPLETED PRO FORMA INCOME STATEMENT WITH BREAKDOWN OF OPERATING EXPENSES

TOUGH GUYS SPORTING GOODS
PRO FORMA INCOME STATEMENT
For the Year (date)

1. Gross Sales		$526,000
2. Less: Cash Discounts		0
A. NET SALES		**$526,000**
Cost of Goods Sold:		
3. Beginning Inventory	$167,000	
4. Plus: Net Purchases	361,000	
5. Total Available for Sale	$528,000	
6. Less: Ending Inventory	181,000	
B. COST OF GOODS SOLD		**$347,000**
C. GROSS MARGIN		**$179,000**
Less: Variable Expenses		
7. Owner's Salary		40,000
8. Employee's Wages and Salaries		41,000
9. Supplies and Postage		0
10. Advertising and Promotion		10,000
11. Delivery Expense		3,700
12. Bad Debt Expense		0
13. Travel		0
14. Legal and Accounting Fees		2,600
15. Vehicle Expense		0
16. Miscellaneous Expenses		24,700
D. TOTAL VARIABLE EXPENSES		**$122,000**
Less: Fixed Expenses		
17. Rent		15,300
18. Repairs and Maintenance		4,200
19. Utilities (Heat, Light, Power)		4,800
20. Telephone		1,000
21. Taxes and Licences		1,000
22. Depreciation		5,300
23. Interest		10,000
24. Insurance		2,600
25. Other Fixed Expenses		2,600
E. TOTAL FIXED EXPENSES		**$ 46,800**
F. TOTAL OPERATING EXPENSES		**$169,000***
G. NET OPERATING PROFIT (LOSS)		**$ 10,000**

* Numbers may not match operating expense percentages exactly due to rounding.

balance will enable you to plan your cash requirements and negotiate a line of credit with your bank or arrange other external financing.

Your completed cash flow forecast will clearly show to the bank loans officer what additional working capital, if any, your business may need and demonstrate that there will be sufficient cash on hand to make the interest payments on a line of credit or a term loan for purchasing additional machinery or equipment or expanding the business.

Estimate Your Revenues

In most small businesses, not all sales are for cash. It is normal practice to take credit cards or to extend terms to many customers. As a result, the revenue from a sale may not be realized until 30 days, 60 days, or even longer after the actual sale is made. In developing your cash flow forecast you must take into account such factors as:

- Your ratio of cash to credit card or credit sales
- Your normal terms of trade for credit customers
- The paying habits of your customers
- Proceedings from the sale of any auxiliary items or other assets of the business

Sales should only be entered on the cash flow forecast when the money has actually been received in payment.

Determine Your Expenditures

To estimate your cash outflow you must consider:

- How promptly you will be required to pay for your material and supplies. It is not uncommon that a new business will have to pay for its inventory and supplies up front on a cash on delivery (COD) basis until it establishes a reputation for meeting its financial commitments. Then it may be able to obtain more favourable credit terms from its trade suppliers. These terms of trade should be reflected in the cash flow forecast. For example, if you have to pay your suppliers' invoices right away, the cash payouts would be reflected in the cash flow forecast during the same month in which the purchases were made. However, if you have to pay your suppliers' invoices within 30 days, the cash payouts for July's purchases will not be shown until August. In some cases, even longer-term trade credit can be negotiated, and then cash outlays may not be shown for two or even three months after the purchase has been received and invoiced. You must know:

- How you will pay your employees' wages and salaries (weekly, biweekly, or monthly).

- When you must pay your rent, utility bills, and other expenses. For example, your rent, telephone, utilities, and other occupancy costs are normally paid every month. Other expenses like insurance and licence fees may be estimated as monthly expenses but not treated that way for cash flow purposes. Your insurance premium of $1200 annually may have to be paid in three instalments: $400 in April, August, and December. That is how it must be entered on the cash flow worksheet. Your license fees might be an annual expense incurred in January of each year and would be reflected as part of your estimated disbursements for that month.

- The interest and principal payments that you must make each month on any outstanding loans.

- Your plans for increasing your inventory requirements or acquiring additional assets.

Reconciling Your Cash Revenues and Cash Expenditures

To illustrate, let us consider the situation of Tough Guys Sporting Goods, a small retail store, in Figure 7.4. Tough Guys plans to open its doors at the beginning of the new year. Its owner, Bill Buckwold, wants to develop a monthly cash flow forecast for the expected first year of operation of the business and has made the following forecasts.

- Total sales for the year are projected to be $526,000 with a strong seasonal pattern peaking in June and July.

- Of the stores monthly sales, 60 percent are cash sales and 40 percent are credit card sales for which the cash is received in the following month.

- Inventory is purchased one month in advance of when it is likely to be sold. It is paid for in the month it is sold. Purchases equal 66 percent of projected sales for the next month.

- Cash expenses have been estimated for such items as the owner's salary and employees' wages and salaries, advertising and promotion expenses, delivery expense, rent, utilities, taxes and licenses, insurance, and other expenses.

- The stores *beginning* cash balance is $10,000 and $5,000 is the *minimum* cash balance that should be available at the beginning of every month.

- The store has negotiated a line of credit with the bank at an interest rate of 10 percent annually but the interest due has to be paid monthly. This line of credit can be drawn on in order to ensure the business has its $5,000 minimum cash balance available each month up to a limit of $50,000.

At the end of each month it shows the cash balance that is available to be carried over to the next month's operations. To this it adds the total of the next month's cash receipts and subtracts the total of the next month's cash expenditures to determine the adjusted balance to be carried forward to the following month. In summary form this relationship can be demonstrated by the following formula:

Forecasted Cash Flow in Month (x) = Cash Balance Carried Over from Month ($x - 1$) + Expected Cash Inflow in Month (x) – Estimated Cash Expenditures in Month (x).

As you can see, cumulative cash surpluses or shortfalls are clearly evident well in advance of their actual occurrence. Knowing this information in advance can assist you in scheduling your initial capital expenditures, monitoring your accounts receivable, avoiding temporary cash shortages, and can enable you to plan your short-term cash requirements well in advance. Tough Guys, for example, does not achieve a positive cash flow until May. The business will be forced to draw on its line of credit in January, February, March and April in order to make certain it will have the necessary minimum cash balance available to continue to run the business. Preparing a pro forma cash flow forecast enabled Bill to anticipate these needs and avoid the possibility of any nasty surprises.

A typical cash flow forecast that you can use to project your anticipated cash surplus or shortfall at the end of each month of the first year of operation of your business is illustrated in the Outline for a Feasibility Study (Figure 7.7) at the back of this Stage.

FIGURE 7.4   SAMPLE CASH FLOW FORECAST

Pro Forma Cash Flow Forecast for Tough Guys Sporting Goods
12 - Month Cash Flow Projections

Minimum Cash Balance Required = 5,000

	January	February	March	April	May	June	July	August	September	October	November	December	YEAR 1 TOTAL
Cash Flow From Operations (during month)													
1. Cash Sales	12,000	18,000	22,200	28,800	30,000	36,600	39,000	30,000	24,000	24,000	21,000	30,000	315600
2. Payments for Credit Sales	0	8,000	12,000	14,800	19,200	20000	24,400	26,000	20,000	16,000	16,000	14,000	190400
3. Investment Income	0	0	0	0	0	0	0	0	0	0	0	0	0
4. Other Cash Income	0	0	0	0	0	0	0	0	0	0	0	0	0
A. TOTAL CASH ON HAND	$12,000	$26,000	$34,200	$43,600	$49,200	$56,600	$63,400	$56,000	$44,000	$40,000	$37,000	$44,000	$506,000
Less Expenses Paid (during month) [1]													
5. Inventory or New Material	-13,200	-19,800	-24,420	-31,680	-33000	-40,260	-42,900	-33,000	-26,400	-26,400	-23,100	-33,000	-314160
6. Owner's Salary	-3,000	-3,000	-3,000	-3,000	-3,000	-3,000	-3,000	-3,000	-3,000	-3,000	-3,000	-3,000	-36000
7. Employee's Wages and Salaries	-2,000	-3,000	-3,000	-3,500	-4,300	-4,300	-4,500	-4,500	-3,000	-2,500	-2,500	-3,900	-41000
8. Supplies and Postage	0	0	0	0	0	0	0	0	0	0	0	0	0
9. Advertising and Promotion	-2,000	-1,000	-500	-700	-700	-700	-800	-1,000	-500	-800	-800	-1,500	-11000
10. Delivery Expense	-200	-250	-250	-300	-300	-400	-400	-500	-300	-300	-300	-500	-4000
11. Travel	0	0	0	0	0	0	0	0	0	0	0	0	0
12. Legal and Accounting Fees	-500	-250	-250	-250	-250	-250	-250	-250	-250	-250	-250	-250	-3250
13. Vehicle Expense	0	0	0	0	0	0	0	0	0	0	0	0	0
14. Maintenance Expense	-1,000	0	0	-800	0	-1000	0	-500	-1,000	0	-700	0	-5000
15. Rent	-1,100	-1,100	-1,100	-1,100	-1,100	-1,100	-1,100	-1,100	-1,100	-1,100	-1,100	-1,100	-13200
16. Utilities	-450	-450	-450	-450	-450	-450	-450	-450	-450	-450	-450	-450	-5400
17. Telephone	0	0	0	0	0	0	0	0	0	0	0	0	0
18. Taxes and Licenses	-1,000	0	0	0	0	0	0	0	0	0	0	0	-1000
19. Interest Payments	0	-50	-53	-93	-100	-107	-107	-107	-107	-107	-107	-107	-1,046
20. Insurance	-600	0	0	-600	0	0	-600	0	0	-600	0	0	-2,400
21. Other Cash Expenses	-2,000	-2,000	-2,000	-2,000	-2,000	-2,000	-2,000	-2,000	-2,000	-2,000	-2,000	-2,000	-24000
B. TOTAL EXPENDITURES	(27,050)	(30,900)	(35,023)	(44,473)	(45,200)	(53,567)	(56,107)	(46,407)	(38,107)	(37,507)	(34,307)	(45,807)	(494,456)
Capital													
Purchase of Fixed Assets	0	0	0	0	0	0	0	0	0	0	0	0	0
Sale of Fixed Assets	0	0	0	0	0	0	0	0	0	0	0	0	0
C. CHANGE IN CASH FROM PURCHASE OR SALE OF ASSETS	$0	$0	$0	$0	$0	$0	$0	$0	$0	$0	$0	$0	$0
Financing													
Payment of Principal of Loan	0	0	0	0	0	0	0	0	0	0	0	0	0
Inflow of Cash From Bank Loan	6000	4150	4800	813	851	0	0	0	0	0	0	0	16614
Issuance of Equity Positions	0	0	0	0	0	0	0	0	0	0	0	0	0
Repurchase of Outstanding Equity	0	0	0	0	0	0	0	0	0	0	0	0	0
D. CHANGE IN CASH FROM FINANCING	$6,000	$4,150	$4,800	$813	$851	$0	$0	$0	$0	$0	$0	$0	$16,614
E. INCREASE (DECREASE) IN CASH	($9,050)	($750)	$3,977	($60)	$4,851	$3,033	$7,293	$9,593	$5,893	$2,493	$2,693	($1,807)	$28,158
F. CASH AT BEGINNING OF PERIOD	$10,000	$950	$200	$4,177	$4,116	$8,967	$12,000	$19,293	$28,886	$34,779	$37,272	$39,965	$10,000 [2]
G. CASH AT END OF PERIOD	$950	$200	$4,177	$4,116	$8,967	$12,000	$19,293	$28,886	$34,779	$37,272	$39,965	$38,158	$38,158
MEET MINIMUM CASH BALANCE	FINANCE	FINANCE	FINANCE	FINANCE	ACCEPTABLE	ACCEPTABLE	ACCEPTABLE	ACCEPTABLE	ACCEPTABLE	ACCEPTABLE	ACCEPTABLE	ACCEPTABLE	ACCEPTABLE

[1]   Expenses and other payments should be entered as negative (–) numbers.

[2]   This entry should be the same amount as for the beginning of the year. All other rows will be the total for the entire year.

Pro Forma Balance Sheet

One more financial statement should also be developed — a *pro forma balance sheet* listing what you forecast your business will own (assets) minus what it will owe to other people, companies, and financial institutions (liabilities) to determine its net worth at any particular point in time. A typical pro forma balance sheet is illustrated in Figure 7.5.

Current assets would include an estimate of your expected average accounts receivable, start-up inventory requirements, available cash, and similar items. *Fixed assets* are typically items like buildings, fixtures, machinery and equipment, automobiles, and other capital items which you will need to operate your business and that typically get used up over a number of years, and therefore must be *depreciated* in value gradually.

Current liabilities are debts you expect to incur that will fall due in less than 12 months. These usually include bills from your suppliers for the supplies and raw materials you will need for your initial inventory, short-term loans from banks and other financial institutions, any portion of your long-term debt that must be repaid during your initial year of operation, and so on. *Long-term liabilities* include outstanding mortgages on land and buildings, notes on machinery and equipment, loans made to the business by you, your partners, and other stockholders, and any other outstanding loans of a long-term nature.

To help choose among several business options you might consider evaluating them on the basis of their expected *return on investment* (ROI). For example, will the rate of return on the money you will have invested in your business be greater than the rate of return you might expect on your money if you invested it elsewhere? ROI can be determined by dividing your expected net profit (before tax) for the first year (as determined in Figure 7.2) by the expected net worth of your business at the end of the year (from Figure 7.5). For example,

$$\text{ROI} = \frac{\text{Net Profit (Before Taxes)}}{\text{Net Worth}}$$

A ratio of 10 to 25 percent might be sufficient to provide for the future growth of your business. If your expected return is less than this, your money could probably be better used elsewhere.

Determine Your Breakeven Point

As your preliminary financial forecasts begin to clarify the size of the potential opportunity you are investigating, there is one other key question to explore: What sales volume will be required for your business to break even? This *breakeven point* indicates the level of operation of the business at which your total costs equal your total revenue. The breakeven point is important, because it indicates when your business begins to make a profit. If your sales level is less than the breakeven point, your business will suffer a loss.

The breakeven point is affected by several factors — among them your fixed and variable costs and your selling price. *Fixed costs* are those that remain constant regardless of your level of sales or production. *Variable costs* vary directly with the amount of business you do. For example, your rent is a fixed cost, because it remains the same regardless of your level of sales. Your cost of goods sold, however, is variable, because the amount you spend is directly related to how much you sell. Fixed costs typically include insurance, licences and permits, property taxes, rent, and similar expenses. Variable costs include supplies, salaries and wages, raw material, utilities, and delivery expenses. Variable costs are usually determined on a per-unit or per-dollar of sales basis.

FIGURE 7.5   SAMPLE PRO FORMA BALANCE SHEET

TOUGH GUYS SPORTING GOODS BALANCE SHEET
End of year 1

ASSETS

Current Assets:

1. Cash	9,000	
2. Accounts Receivable	17,000	
3. Inventory	185,000	
4. Other Current Assets	27,000	
A.Total Current Assets		**$238,000**

Fixed Assets:

5. Land and Buildings	0		
less depreciation		0	
6. Furniture and Fixtures	40,000		
less depreciation		40,000	
7. Equipment	0		
less depreciation		0	
8. Trucks and Automobiles	0		
less depreciation		0	
9. Other Fixed Assets	18,000		
less depreciation		18,000	
B.Total Fixed Assets			**$ 58,000**
C.Total Assets (C = A + B)			**$296,000**

LIABILITIES

Current Liabilities (due within 12 months)

10. Accounts Payable	97,000	
11. Bank Loans/Other Loans	29,000	
12. Taxes Owed		
D.Total Current Liabilities		**$126,000**

Long-term Liabilities

13. Notes Payable (due after one year)	100,000	
14. Other Long-Term Liabilities	59,000	
E.Total Long-Term Liabilities		**$159,000**
F.Total Liabilities (F = D + E)		**$285,000**

NET WORTH (CAPITAL)

SHARE CAPITAL

Common Shares	1,000
Preferred Shares	0
RETAINED EARNINGS	10,000
G.Total Net Worth (G = C − F)	**$ 11,000**
H.Total Liabilities and Net Worth (H = F + G)	**$296,000**

The breakeven point can be determined algebraically. The basic formula is:

$$\text{Breakeven Point (Units)} = \frac{\text{Total Fixed Costs}}{\text{Contribution Margin per Unit}}$$

where:

Contribution Margin per Unit = Selling Price per Unit – Variable Cost per Unit

The following simple hypothetical example may help illustrate the breakeven concept. Suppose a recently graduated college student has an opportunity to rent a kiosk near a popular beach area to sell ice cream cones. It will cost him $500 per month to rent the kiosk, including the cost of utilities. In order to set up his business he borrows $1000 to acquire the necessary freezers and other fixtures, a loan that has to be paid back at a rate of $100 per month.

He plans to sell his ice cream cones for $1 each. He estimates that his direct costs of supplies for each cone he sells will be:

Ice cream	$0.50
Cones	0.05
Napkins, etc.	0.05
Total Cost	$0.60

Rather than plan for a regular salary, he has decided to pocket any net profit the business might earn as his income.

In this example the student receives $1 for each ice cream cone he sells but must use supplies worth $0.60 (his variable cost) to earn it. Therefore, he keeps $0.40 (this $0.40 is called his *contribution margin*) to cover his fixed costs (in this case, his rent is his only fixed cost). His contribution margin per unit can then be expressed as follows:

$$\begin{aligned} \text{Contribution Margin per Unit} &= \text{Selling Price} - \text{Total Variable Cost} \\ &= \$1 - \$0.60 \\ &= \$0.40 \end{aligned}$$

For determining the number of ice cream cones he will have to sell each month to break even, the formula is as follows:

$$\frac{\text{Total Fixed Costs}}{\text{Contribution Margin per Unit}} = \text{Breakeven Volume (units)}$$

or, in this case:

$$\frac{\$500}{\$0.40} = 1250 \text{ ice cream cones per month}$$

Therefore, the student must sell a minimum of 1250 ice cream cones each month in order to cover his fixed costs of doing business. Even at this level of operation, he does not earn any income for himself. It is only after his sales exceed this level that the business starts to generate sufficient revenue to provide him with some compensation for his time and effort. In addition, this calculation does not consider any interest charges on the $1000 he had to borrow to start the business. These charges would normally be considered a fixed cost as well.

Relating this notion to our retail sporting goods store we can determine the volume of sales required to breakeven, If we assume all our operating expenses indicated in Figure 7.3

are fixed in the short term, including such items as our salaries and wages and our advertising and promotional expenditures, our financial statement can be summarized as follows:

Projected sales $526,000

Projected fixed expenses $169,000

Projected variable expenses $347,000
(basically our cost of goods sold)

Total sales needs to breakeven $\text{Fixed Expenses} \div 1 - \left(\dfrac{\text{Variable Expenses}}{\text{Sales}} \right)$

$\$169,000 \div 1 - \left(\dfrac{\$347,000}{\$526,000} \right)$

$\$169,000 \div (1 - .66)$

$\$169,000 \div .34$

$\underline{\$497,058}$

Therefore, the store needs to sell at least $497,000-worth of merchandise each year to break even based on our estimate of its average gross margin percentage and other variable costs. This concept is illustrated in Figure 7.6 as well.

The value of breakeven analysis is that it can be used to determine whether some planned course of action — for example, starting a new business, opening a new store, or adding a new item to your product line — has a chance of being profitable. Once you have estimated the breakeven point for the action, you are in a better position to assess whether such a sales volume can be achieved and how long it will take to reach it.

It is essential that you determine the breakeven level of operation for your business before you proceed very far with its implementation. Bankers and other financial people will expect to see this information as part of the financial documentation for your venture. In addition, if it appears that the breakeven volume is not achievable, the business idea is probably destined to fail and should be abandoned before any money is invested.

FIGURE 7.6   GRAPHICAL REPRESENTATION OF THE BREAKEVEN POINT FOR TOUGH GUYS SPORTING GOODS

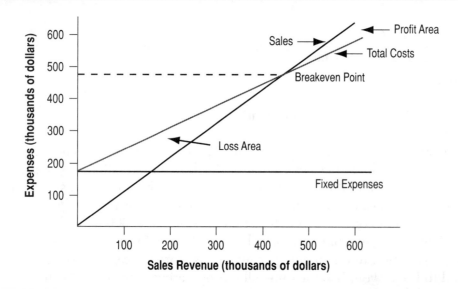

Conduct a Comprehensive Feasibility Study

Figure 7.7 provides a detailed framework that you can use to conduct a comprehensive feasibility assessment of your own new venture idea. When you have completed this evaluation, you need to give some thought to where you go from here. Does the business look sufficiently viable to proceed with the development of a comprehensive business plan? Have you identified all the potential flaws and pitfalls that might negatively impact your business? What role do you expect to play in the growth of the venture? Do you plan to produce and market the concept yourself, or do you hope to sell or license the idea to someone else? How much external money do you need and where do you think you can obtain it? These are the kinds of issues that need to be carefully considered and resolved before you will be in a position to move forward.

In most cases, the next stage is to write out a complete *business plan*. This, however, requires a major commitment of time, effort, and money. Make sure your feasibility study indicates that your concept is clearly viable and that a reasonable profit can be expected.

And don't be too disappointed if your feasibility assessment indicates that your concept is not likely to be profitable. Think of all the time and money you have saved by not going forward with the implementation of a business that has a low probability of succeeding. That's why a preliminary assessment is so essential.

FIGURE 7.7   OUTLINE FOR FEASIBILITY STUDY

YOUR CONCEPT

1. Describe the principal concept underlying your product or service idea.

2. What is unique or distinctive about your idea? How does it differ from similar concepts already being employed in the marketplace?

3. Who will be the primary customers of your concept and what are the principal benefits your concept will deliver to them?

4. How innovative is your concept? How would you categorize it along the continuum from "copycatting" to being an entirely new invention?

continued

Outline for Feasibility Study — continued

5. Is your idea technically feasible? Have you built a working model or prototype? Will you have to obtain Canadian Standards Association (CSA) approval or other permissions, before the concept can be marketed?

_____

_____

_____

_____

PRELIMINARY MARKETING PLAN

Products and Services

1. What products or services will you sell? (Be specific.)

_____

_____

_____

_____

_____

2. What additional customer services (delivery, repair, warranties, etc.) will you offer?

_____

_____

_____

_____

_____

3. What is unique about your total product or service offering?

_____

_____

_____

_____

Customers

1. Define your target customers. (Who are they?)

_____

_____

_____

_____

_____

2. How many target customers are in your trading area?

_____

_____

_____

_____

3. Why will they buy your product?

_____

_____

_____

_____

Outline for Feasibility Study — continued
Competition

1. Who are your principal competitors? What is their market position? Have their sales been growing? Stable? Declining?

    a. _____

    _____

    b. _____

    _____

    c. _____

    _____

    d. _____

    _____

2. How does your concept differ from each of these other products or services?

    _____

    _____

    _____

    _____

Location

1. What location have you selected for your business?

    _____

    _____

    _____

    _____

2. Why did you choose that location?

    _____

    _____

    _____

    _____

Pricing

1. Describe your pricing strategy.

    _____

    _____

    _____

    _____

2. Complete the following chain of markups from manufacturer to final customer:

Cost to manufacture	_____	(A)
Manufacturer's markup	_____	(B)
Manufacturer's selling price (C = A + B)	_____	(C)
Agent's commission (if applicable)	_____	(D)
Wholesaler's cost (E = C + D)	_____	(E)
Wholesaler's markup	_____	(F)
Wholesaler's selling price (G = E + F)	_____	(G)
Retailer's markup	_____	(H)
Retailer's selling price (I = G + H)	_____	(I)

continued

Outline for Feasibility Study — continued

3. How do your planned price levels compare to your competitors'?

_____

_____

_____

_____

_____

Promotion

1. What will your primary promotional message to potential customers be?

_____

_____

_____

_____

_____

2. What will your promotion budget be?

_____

_____

_____

_____

_____

3. What media will you use for your advertising program?

_____

_____

_____

_____

_____

4. Will you have a cooperative advertising program? Describe it.

_____

_____

_____

_____

_____

5. Describe your trade promotion program.

_____

_____

_____

_____

_____

6. Describe any publicity, public relations, or sales promotion program you will have.

_____

_____

_____

_____

_____

Outline for Feasibility Study — continued
Distribution

1. How do you plan to distribute your product? Direct to the consumer? Through traditional distribution channels? Through specialty channels such as exhibitions, mail order, or trade shows?

_____

_____

_____

_____

_____

2. Will you employ your own sales force or rely on the services of agents or brokers? How many?

_____

_____

_____

_____

_____

_____

THE SUPPLY SITUATION

1. What raw materials or component parts will you require to produce your product or service? What volume of these materials will you require? Who will be your major source of supply? Do you have alternative supply arrangements or other sources that can meet your requirements?

_____

_____

_____

_____

2. What will be the cost of these materials and components? Are prices guaranteed for any length of time? Are volume or quantity discounts available? What credit terms will your suppliers make available to you?

_____

_____

_____

_____

3. Describe your manufacturing requirements. Will you manufacture the product yourself or use subcontractors? What will it cost to establish your own manufacturing facility?

_____

_____

_____

_____

4. If you are planning to use subcontractors, what alternatives are available? What are their capabilities and comparative costs? Will you have to incur any other costs — e.g., for moulds, etc.? Do any of these contractors provide additional services?

_____

_____

_____

_____

continued

Outline for Feasibility Study — continued

COST/PROFITABILITY ANALYSIS

1. What do you estimate your costs would be and the funds required to get your business successfully launched?

   a. Complete the following chart to determine your one-time financial requirements.

   Estimated One-time Start-up Financial Requirements

Item	Total Original Cost	Estimated Cash Required
1. Land	$_____	$_____
2. Building	_____	_____
3. Improvements:		
I Mechanical	_____	_____
II Electrical	_____	_____
III Construction	_____	_____
4. Machinery and equipment	_____	_____
5. Installation of equipment	_____	_____
6. Shop tools and supplies	_____	_____
7. Office equipment and supplies	_____	_____
8. Vehicles	_____	_____
9. Starting inventory	_____	_____
10. Utility hookup and installation fees	_____	_____
11. Licences and permits	_____	_____
12. Pre-opening advertising and promotion	_____	_____
13. Accounts payable	_____	_____
14. Cash for unexpected expenses	_____	_____
15. Other cash requirements	_____	_____
Total Estimated One-Time Cash Requirements (1+ ... +15)		$_____

   b. Do you have this much money available or have some ideas as to where you might be able to obtain it?

2. What do you estimate your sales will be, by product or service category, for your first 12 months? What will it cost you to produce those products or provide that service? What do you estimate your gross margin will be for each product or service? How does this compare with the norm for your industry? What operating expenses for such items as rent, travel, advertising, insurance, and utilities do you expect to incur? What profit do you estimate your business will show for its first 12 months?

   Complete the following pro forma income statement for your first year of operation.

3. How are your sales and expenses expected to vary throughout the year? What proportion of your sales will be for cash? On credit? What credit terms, if any, will you provide to your customers? What credit terms do you expect to receive from your suppliers? What other expenses will you have to pay on a regular, ongoing basis?

   a. Complete the following table to estimate your cash flow surplus or deficit for each month of your first year in business.

Outline for Feasibility Study — continued

PRO FORMA INCOME STATEMENT
For the period ending _____

		1	2	3	4	5	6	7	8	9	10	11	12	Total
Gross sales														
Less Cash discounts														
Net Sales	**(A)**													
Cost of goods sold:														
Beginning inventory														
Plus: Net purchases														
Total goods available for sale														
Less: Ending inventory														
Cost of Goods Sold	**(B)**													
Gross Margin (C = A – B)	**(C)**													
Less: Variable expenses														
Owner's salary														
Employees' wages and salaries														
Supplies and postage														
Advertising and promotion														
Delivery expense														
Bad debt allowance														
Travel														
Legal and accounting fees														
Vehicle expenses														
Miscellaneous expenses														
Total Variable Expenses	**(D)**													
Less: Fixed expenses														
Rent														
Utilities (heat, light, water, power)														
Telephone														
Taxes and licences														
Depreciation or Capital Cost Allowance														
Interest														
Insurance														
Other Fixed Expenses														
Total Fixed Expenses	**(E)**													
Total Operating Expenses (F = D + E)	**(F)**													
Net Operating Profit (Loss) (G = C – F)	**(G)**													
Income Taxes (estimated)	**(H)**													
Net Profit (Loss) After Income Tax (I = G – H)	**(I)**													

continued

TWELVE-MONTH CASH FLOW PROJECTIONS

	Month 1	Month 2	Month 3	Month 4	Month 5	Month 6	Month 7	Month 8	Month 9	Month 10	Month 11	Month 12	Year 1 TOTAL
Cash Flow From Operations (during month)													
1. Cash Sales													
2. Payments for Credit Sales													
3. Investment Income													
4. Other Cash Income													
A. TOTAL CASH FLOW ON HAND	$	$	$	$	$	$	$	$	$	$	$	$	$
Less Expenses Paid (during month)[1]													
5. Inventory or New Material													
6. Owners' Salaries													
7. Employees' Wages and Salaries													
8. Supplies and Postage													
9. Advertising and Promotion													
10. Delivery Expense													
11. Travel													
12. Legal and Accounting Fees													
13. Vehicle Expense													
14. Maintenance Expense													
15. Rent													
16. Utilities													
17. Telephone													
18. Taxes and Licences													
19. Interest Payments													
20. Insurance													
21. Other Cash Expenses													
B. TOTAL EXPENDITURES	$	$	$	$	$	$	$	$	$	$	$	$	$
Capital													
Purchase of Fixed Assets													
Sale of Fixed Assets													
C. CHANGE IN CASH FROM PURCHASE OR SALE OF ASSETS	$	$	$	$	$	$	$	$	$	$	$	$	$
Financing													
Payment of Principal of Loan													
Inflow of Cash From Bank Loan													
Issuance of Equity Positions													
Repurchase of Outstanding Equity													
D. CHANGE IN CASH FROM FINANCING	$	$	$	$	$	$	$	$	$	$	$	$	$
E. INCREASE (DECREASE) IN CASH	$	$	$	$	$	$	$	$	$	$	$	$	$
F. CASH AT BEGINNING OF PERIOD	$	$	$	$	$	$	$	$	$	$	$	$	$[2]
G. CASH AT END OF PERIOD	$	$	$	$	$	$	$	$	$	$	$	$	$
MEET MINIMUM CASH BALANCE	Acceptable	Acceptable	Acceptable	Acceptable	Acceptable	Acceptable	Acceptable	Acceptable	Acceptable	Acceptable	Acceptable	Acceptable	Acceptable

[1] Expenses and other payments should be entered as negative (−) numbers.

[2] This entry should be the same amount as for the beginning of the year. All other rows will be the total for the entire year.

Outline for Feasibility Study — continued

b. Can you arrange for more favourable terms from your suppliers, accelerate the collection of your outstanding accounts receivable, negotiate a line of credit with your bank, or take other action to enable your business to continue to operate if cash flow is insufficient?

4. What do you estimate your total fixed costs will be for your first year of operation? What did you estimate your average gross margin to be as a percentage of your total sales in preparing your pro forma income statement in question 2? (This amount is also known as your *contribution margin per dollar of sales*.)

Compute your breakeven level of sales by means of the following formula:

$$\text{Breakeven Point (\$ sales)} = \frac{\text{Total Fixed Costs}}{\text{Contribution Margin per \$ of Sales}}$$

When do you expect to attain this level of sales? During your first year of business? Your second year? Your third year?

PLANS FOR FUTURE ACTION

1. According to your feasibility study, what were the strong points and weak points of your new venture idea? Can the weak points and potential problems be successfully overcome?

_____

_____

_____

_____

2. Does the feasibility assessment indicate that the business is likely to be profitable? Does it look sufficiently attractive that you should write a comprehensive business plan? What other information do you have to obtain, or what additional research do you have to do, in order to develop this plan?

_____

_____

_____

_____

3. If you decide not to proceed with the development of a business plan, indicate the reasons why.

_____

_____

_____

_____

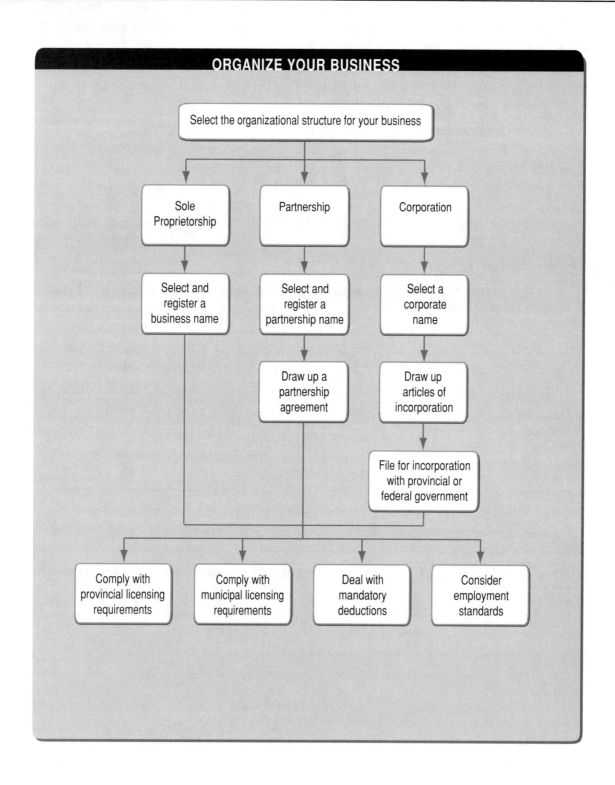

ORGANIZE YOUR BUSINESS

Select the organizational structure for your business

Sole Proprietorship	Partnership	Corporation

Select and register a business name

Select and register a partnership name

Select a corporate name

Draw up a partnership agreement

Draw up articles of incorporation

File for incorporation with provincial or federal government

Comply with provincial licensing requirements	Comply with municipal licensing requirements	Deal with mandatory deductions	Consider employment standards

Organizing Your Business

One of the key issues you must resolve when starting your new venture is the legal form of organization the business should adopt. Making that decision means you should consider such factors as:

1. The complexity and expense associated with organizing and operating your business in one way or another

2. The extent of your personal liability

3. Your need to obtain start-up capital and operating funds from other sources

4. The extent to which you wish ownership, control, and management of your business to be shared with others (if at all)

5. The distribution of your business' profits and losses

6. The extent of government regulation you are willing to accept

7. Tax considerations and implications

8. The need to involve other principals in your venture

The most prevalent forms your business might take are:

- **An individual or sole proprietorship**
- **A partnership (general partnership or limited partnership)**
- **A corporation**

Individual Or Sole Proprietorship

The *individual* or *sole proprietorship* is the oldest and simplest form of business organization. As owner or proprietor, you have complete control over the conduct and management of your business. You alone are accountable for all business activities and their consequences. You assume the business' profits and are liable for its debts. You and the business are one and the same. The sole proprietorship is the most common form or organization for small businesses, particularly in the early stages of their development.

Advantages of Sole Proprietorship

- **Simple and inexpensive to start** A sole proprietorship is both simple and inexpensive to create and dissolve. It can be brought into existence with a minimum of legal formalities and terminated just as readily. Start-up costs are minimal — usually they are confined to registering your business name with the appropriate authorities and obtaining the necessary licences.

- **Individual control over operations** The operation of the business is coordinated in the mind and actions of a single individual. You are literally your own boss. If the business is not successful you are free to dissolve it. And if the business does well, you can have a strong personal sense of accomplishment.

- **All profits to the owner** If the business does well you will reap the benefits of your efforts; no one will share in the profits of the business. You work for yourself and determine your own destiny. In addition, if your business should incur a loss during its early stages, that loss is deductible from any other income you may have.

Disadvantages of Sole Proprietorship

- **Unlimited liability** Since the business and the proprietor are not recognized as being separate by law, you can be held personally liable for all the debts of your business. That means you may have to satisfy business debts with personal assets such as your house and car if the business is unable to meet its obligations. You may be able to protect some personal assets by putting them in your spouse's name before starting your venture but there is no real guarantee against domestic breakdown.

- **More difficult to obtain financing** The business' capital will be limited to what you, as the owner, can personally secure. This is typically less than $50,000 unless substantial security is available. With a sole proprietorship you are not in a position to share ownership with others who could contribute additional funds needed by the business.

- **Limited resources and opportunity** A sole proprietorship usually holds limited opportunity and incentive for employees, as it is not a form of ownership conducive to growth. One person can only do so much and may not have all the skills and knowledge necessary to run all phases of the business. Employees may have to be hired to perform these tasks. The life of the business in a proprietorship is limited to the life of the proprietor. If you should die, become ill, or encounter serious personal problems, your business is immediately affected, and unless other provisions are made, your business will die with you. This could lead to a forced sale of the business' assets by your beneficiaries, perhaps at a substantial loss.

Partnership

A *partnership* is an association of two or more individuals carrying on a business for profit. The *principals* (partners) should jointly prepare a written partnership agreement outlining the following issues in terms that are clearly understood and mutually acceptable to all of them:

1. The rights and responsibilities of each partner
2. The amount and nature of their respective capital contributions to the business
3. The division of the business' profits and losses
4. The management responsibilities of each partner involved in the operation of the business
5. Provision for termination, retirement, disability, or death of a partner
6. Means for dissolving or liquidating the partnership

Partnerships fall into two categories: *general partnership* and *limited partnership*.

General Partnership

A *general partnership* is similar to a sole proprietorship except that responsibility for the business rests with two or more people, the partners. In a general partnership all the partners are liable for the obligations of the partnership and share in both profits and losses according to the terms of their partnership agreement.

Advantages of a General Partnership

- **Pooling of financial resources and talents** The partnership is useful for bringing together two or more people who can combine their skills, abilities, and resources into an effective group. Management of the business is shared among the principals.

- **Simplicity and ease of organization** A partnership, like a sole proprietorship, is easy and inexpensive to establish and is subject to a minimum amount of regulation.

- **Increased ability to obtain capital** The combined financial resources of all the partners can be used to raise additional capital for the business. Income from the partnership is taxed as part of the personal income of each of the partners.

- **Potential for growth** A partnership has a higher potential for growth than a proprietorship, since a valuable employee may be offered a partnership to dissuade him or her from leaving the firm. Growth, however, is still quite restricted compared to that possible with a limited company.

Disadvantages of a General Partnership

- **Unlimited liability** Partners are personally liable for all the debts and obligations of their business and for any negligence on the part of any of them occurring in the conduct of the business. This is similar to the situation with a sole proprietorship, except that the partners are liable both as a group and individually — i.e., not only for their own actions (*severally*) but also for the actions of all others in the partnership (*jointly*).

- **Divided authority** There is less control for an individual entrepreneur in a partnership with divided authority. There may be possible conflicts of views among partners which are difficult to resolve and could affect the conduct of the business.

Limited Partnership

In a *limited partnership*, the partners' share in the liability of the business *is limited to the extent of their contribution to the capital* of the business. In such a partnership, however, there must also be one or more *general* partners, i.e., partners with *unlimited* liability.

The limited partners may not participate in the day-to-day management of the business of the partnership or they risk losing their limited-liability status. Also, a limited partner is entitled to interest on his or her capital of no more than 5 percent per year and some agreed-upon share of the profits. Limited partners have one major power — the ability to remove the general partner(s).

Advantages of a Limited Partnership

- **Limited liability** If properly established and registered the liability of the limited partners is restricted to the extent of their investment. Thus, you may find it easier to recruit investors.

Disadvantages of a Limited Partnership

- **Centralized management** In a limited partnership only a small subgroup of the owners — the general partners — have decision-making authority and can participate in the management of the business.

- **Difficulty in changing ownership** It is generally difficult to change ownership in a partnership, since the partnership must be dissolved and reconstituted every time a partner dies or wants to retire. So it is important that the procedure for dealing with this issue be laid out in a partnership agreement.

Corporation

The *corporation* is the most formal and complex of the various forms of business organization. A firm that is *incorporated* is a separate legal entity from its owners — that is, legally, it is regarded as a "person" with a separate, continuous life. As a legal person, a corporation has rights and duties of its own: it can own property and other assets, it can sue or be sued, and it files its own tax return. Ownership of a corporation is recognized through the purchase of *shares*, or *stock*, which can be held by as few as one or as many as thousands of *shareholders*.

A business need not be large to be incorporated. A sole proprietorship regularly earning in excess of $40,000 to $50,000 of taxable income annually probably should be incorporated.

Advantages of a Corporation

- **Limited liability** The owner or shareholder of a corporation is liable only for the amount he or she paid or owes for the shares. In case of bankruptcy, creditors are not able to sue shareholders for outstanding debts of the business.

- **Continuity of the business even if the owner dies** Since it is an entity under the law, a corporation is not affected by the death or withdrawal of any shareholder. The shares of its stock can be sold or transferred to other individuals without difficulty. This ease of transfer allows for perpetual succession of the corporation, which is not the case with a sole proprietorship or partnership.

- **Easier to raise capital** Incorporation makes it easier to raise capital, which is done by selling stock. In addition, corporations with some history and a track record can negotiate more effectively with outside sources of financing than either a proprietorship or a partnership.

- **Employee benefits** A corporation has a better opportunity to provide benefits to employees and stockholders in a variety of ways such as salaries, dividends, and profit-sharing plans.

- **Tax advantages** Being an independent entity in the eyes of the law, a corporation receives different tax treatment than either a proprietorship or a partnership, and is taxed separately on its business profits. This may provide you with some opportunity for tax deferral, income-splitting, or the reduction of your actual tax costs through the deductibility of certain personal fringe benefits.

Disadvantages of a Corporation

- **Cost** Corporations are more expensive to start and operate. Initially, incorporation can cost in excess of $1000 in legal and regulatory fees. In addition, a lawyer may charge upwards of $300 a year to maintain the registered office and keep the corporate *book*, i.e., the record of annual meetings, directors' meetings, etc.

- **Legal formalities** A corporation is subject to more-numerous and complicated regulatory requirements than a proprietorship or partnership. Corporations must typically file annual reports, hold annual meetings, and file federal and provincial tax returns. This can be very expensive and time-consuming for a small-businessperson, and may require the ongoing services of an accountant and a lawyer.

- **Inability to flow losses through** It is not uncommon for a new business to incur substantial start-up costs and operating losses during its first few years. These losses are "locked in" — a corporation must accumulate them for its own use in future years, and cannot use them to offset income a shareholder may have from other sources. If your business should never become very profitable, it is conceivable that its losses could never be used to reduce your tax liability.

    This is in contrast to a proprietorship or partnership, whose early losses would "flow through" to the owners of the business, to be deducted on their personal income tax returns in the year they were incurred. Therefore, it may be more beneficial financially not to incorporate, so you can offset other income for tax purposes. This can improve your overall cash flow when your business is just getting started and cash flow is most critical. You can always decide to incorporate later without any tax consequences.

- **Guarantee** Lenders often require a personal *guarantee*. This largely negates the advantage of limited liability.

Registration and Incorporation — Making it Legal

For a sole proprietorship, no formal, legal *registration* is required as long as the business is operated under your own name. However, if a specific business name like "Regal Dry Cleaners" or "Excel Construction" is used, or if more than one owner is implied by the use of "and Associates" or "and Sons" in conjunction with your name, your business must be logged with the Registrar of Companies or the Corporations Branch of the province in which the business is located. Registration is a relatively simple and inexpensive process that you can probably take care of yourself. Partnerships must be registered in a similar fashion.

Incorporation is a more complicated and considerably more expensive process that usually requires the services of a lawyer. If your business activities will initially be confined to a single province, you need only incorporate as a provincial company. Should your business plans include expansion to other provinces, however, you will be required to register in each province in which you wish to do business as an extra-provincial company, or register as a federally incorporated company.

Companies can be classified as either private or public. *Public companies* are those like Alcan and Great West Life which trade their shares on one of the country's public stock exchanges and with which most of us are familiar. They typically employ professional managers, external directors, and a number of shareholders who are the owners of the business.

Private companies, on the other hand, tend to have only one shareholder, or at most a small number of shareholders. There is some restriction on the transfer of their shares in their *articles of incorporation*, and their shares cannot be offered for sale to the public. A private corporation is sometimes called an *incorporated partnership*, because it usually consists of one, two, or three people who are personal friends, business associates, or family members, each of whom may play two or three roles, serving, for example, as an officer, director, and a shareholder of the company all at the same time.

Calories restaurant highlighted in Entrepreneurs in Action # 16 is a good example of an incorporated partnership. Janis and Remi Cousyns own 50 percent of the business and their partner Janet Palmer owns the other 50 percent. All three work in the business and have quite different responsibilities. Janet is the General Manager while Janis serves as the Maître d' and Remi the principal chef.

If you choose to incorporate, a private corporation is probably the type you will establish.

She was a young ballet dancer when he spotted her on the train to Nice 10 years ago. Remi Cousyn, a chef at an exclusive hotel in Switzerland, cast aside his inhibitions and decided to talk to the young, blond Canadian. "I remember thinking I might never get a chance like this again," he recalls. Janis, who had attended the National Ballet School in Toronto and danced with the Royal Winnipeg Ballet, was travelling in Europe. Over the next few years, Remi and Janis spent time together in France, but by 1991, they had moved to Montreal. That same year, they got married in Janis's home town of Saskatoon.

The Cousyns, both 29, spent four years in Montreal, but they eventually returned to Saskatoon, where they now run a restaurant that is not only establishing new culinary standards but turning a profit, too. In fact, their time in Montreal was in many ways a preparation for their current way of life. While Remi worked as a chef, Janis went to university and completed an undergraduate degree in business administration at Concordia. "I knew we would be doing something on our own and I wanted to have a basic knowledge of business," she recalls.

In 1996, during a brief stay in Whistler, B.C., where they worked together in the same restaurant, Janis received the phone call that drew the young couple back to the prairies. In years past, she had waitressed at a café in Saskatoon called Calories. Her former boss, Janet Palmer, who had subsequently become Janis's friend, telephoned to ask her and Remi to come aboard as partners. "Janet said her partner wasn't interested in the business any more and we could slide right in," recalls Janis. "The restaurant wasn't in great shape financially, and I think Janet understood we would be able to provide what was lacking." Janis, who was pregnant at the time with daughter Gabrielle, longed to return home, and Remi, keen to be "master of my own kitchen," also welcomed the move.

Within a year of forming a partnership in 1996, the three had transformed the coffee house into a money-making restaurant. In their first year as partners, Calories went from being in the red to a modest net profit of $9,000; the following year, that figure jumped to $32,000. With a growing clientele and expanded menu, it became clear that more space and a better-equipped kitchen were needed. After preparing a 45-page business plan, the Calories partners applied to a credit union for a loan. To their surprise, they received $175,000 — 90% of the projected renovation costs.

Janis attributes their success to a modest yet sound business plan. "It's pretty well known in the industry that banks aren't interested in financing restaurants. In fact, the credit-union board said they don't lend money to restaurants—ever. But with Calories, the decision to approve the loan was unanimous. We documented how we would cover the costs of paying back the loan in the worst case scenario, and they liked that." Calories is repaying the loan in monthly payments of $3,200 at a fixed rate of 9.8%. On top of the loan, the partners secured another $50,000 for the reno costs through a shareholding plan in which customers bought shares, each valued at $5,000 with a 4% annual yield. The business has no obligation to buy the shares back.

The completed renovations — which include a dining room and new commercial gas stove — made an immediate impact on Calories' bottom line. Not only have the regular theatre and university crowds remained loyal, Remi says they also "see a lot more suits" — a more affluent dinner crowd with money to spend on his international dishes. In March, the first full month after renovating, the business made $75,000, an increase of about 20% over the last full month. Despite being closed for eight weeks for the reno, this year's annual gross for their fiscal year ending in June reached $600,000, compared to $515,000 in 1997. Net profit jumped to $40,000, which is being pumped back into the business "for loans and equipment," reports Remi.

The team uses 30% of the restaurant's gross for food and another 30% goes to paying staff — besides the part-timers, full-time waiters and dishwashers on the payroll, Calories employs a kitchen manager, a bookkeeper, two cooks, a baker and a cleaner. The Cousyns own 50% of the business while Janet Palmer owns the other half. Palmer is general manager, Janis is maître d'hôtel and Remi is chef de cuisine.

The Cousyns are satisfied with the business as it presently exists. "When we first started, sales were about $35,000 a month and we expected $45,000 to be a fairly decent number," says Remi. "Now we've surpassed that—our first month after the renovations we sold $75,000." Janis suggests expanding Calories' small catering line, which now constitutes about 5% of their business, or combining a restaurant with an art gallery, or even franchising, noting that "Calories is a very transportable concept. It appeals to a wide range of people and it has good food." Although they don't own the building Calories occupies, they have made an offer on it, rationalizing that it is smarter to build equity, but they feel that at $300,000, its price is too high.

It's true that running a restaurant comes with long hours and is physically demanding, but both Remi and Janis are happy. It's the independence they find appealing. Remi has always wanted autonomy in the kitchen, and Janis finds the restaurant business gives her a sense of personal control that ballet never did. "In the ballet, if a director doesn't like your style as a dancer, you're finished." In the restaurant business, on the other hand, a strong concept, creative-cooking and a flair for service can make you captain of your own ship. And with the right financial decisions, it can also provide enough money to live a comfortable lifestyle—now and in retirement.

Source: Hugh Lockhart, "Recipe for Success," *The Financial Post Magazine*, September, 1998, pp. 81-84. Reprinted with permission.

Choosing a Name

Like people, all businesses must have a name. The simplest procedure is to name the business after yourself — Harry Brown's Printing, for example. This type of name does not require formal registration for a sole proprietorship, but it does have disadvantages. For example, you might get people phoning you at home at all hours if you and your business' name are the same. In addition, your personal reputation may be tarnished should you experience some financial problems and be forced into receivership or bankruptcy. And if you should ever sell your business, your name would go with it, and the new owner's actions could reflect negatively on your reputation.

For businesses to be registered or incorporated, the most important consideration in selecting a name is that it be acceptable to the Registrar of Companies in your province. All provinces require that a search be conducted of proposed names. Any name that is similar to a name already registered will be rejected to avoid public confusion. It is not uncommon to have to submit several names before one is finally approved. To avoid this problem some individuals use a series of numbers rather than letters for the name of their corporation. On acceptance, the name is typically reserved for your exclusive use for 90 days, so that you can proceed with your registration or the filing of your articles of incorporation.

The best approach is usually to choose a distinctive name for the firm that *accurately describes* the type of business you plan to carry on. That is, a name like "Speedy Courier Service" or "Super-clean Automobile Washing" is probably much better than one like "Universal Enterprises" or "General Distributing." A good way to check out names is to go through the Yellow Pages or local business directories and get some idea of the range of names currently in use in your business area and perhaps some inspiration for a brilliant new possibility.

Names that are likely to be rejected and which should be avoided are those that:

1. Imply any connection with or approval of the Royal Family, such as names that include the word "Imperial" or "Royal"

2. Imply approval or sponsorship of the business by some unit of government, such as names containing "Parliamentary," "Premier's," or "Legislative"

3. Might be interpreted as obscene or not really descriptive of the nature of the firm's business

4. Are similar to or contractions of the names of companies already in business, even though they may be in a different field, such as "IBM Tailors" or "Chrysler Electronics"

The firm's name can become one of your most valuable assets if your business is successful, as has happened in the case of companies like McDonald's and Holiday Inn. Don't go for the first name that comes to mind. Think it over very carefully.

By permission of Johnny Hart and Creators Syndicate, Inc.

Other Legal Requirements and Taxes

Once you have determined the most appropriate form of organization for your business, you also need to consider a number of other legal and regulatory requirements that relate to such issues as the kinds of licences you may require, your obligations regarding the collection and payment of different employee contributions and taxes, and the current standards for employment that exist in your province.

Licences and Permits

You may require a municipal as well as a provincial licence to operate your business. Your need for the former depends on the location and nature of your business; requirements for the latter depend solely on the nature of your business.

Municipal

Not all types of businesses require a municipal licence. Every municipality regulates businesses established within its boundaries and sets its own licensing requirements and fees. In Winnipeg, for example, 114 types of businesses and occupations require a licence. In general, these are amusement operations or ones that may affect public health and safety. The licensing fees can be as high as several thousand dollars, but in most cases the fees are quite nominal — a few dollars.

In addition, all businesses — whether or not they require a licence — must conform to local zoning regulations and bylaw requirements. In fact, zoning approval is usually a prerequisite to licence approval. Companies operating in their own facilities in most cities must also pay a business tax, assessed as a percentage of the rental value of their business facilities.

Provincial

Various provincial authorities also require a licence or permit. For example, in Ontario all establishments providing accommodation to the public, such as hotels, motels, lodges, tourist resorts, and campgrounds, must be licensed by the province. Businesses planning to serve liquor, operate long-haul cartage and transport operations, process food products, produce optical lenses, or manufacture upholstered furniture or stuffed toys may also require licensing. You should check with the local authorities to determine the types of licences and permits your business might require.

Mandatory Deductions and Taxes

If your business has a payroll you will be required to make regular deductions from employees' paychecks for income tax, employment insurance (EI), and the Canada Pension Plan (CPP). These deductions must be remitted to Revenue Canada every month.

In addition, you may also be required to pay an assessment to your provincial Workers' Compensation Board. The size of your payment will be based on the nature of your business and its risk classification as well as the estimated size of your annual payroll. These funds are used to meet medical, salary, and the rehabilitation costs of any of your employees who may be injured on the job.

Depending on the size of your venture, you may also be responsible for remitting taxes of various kinds to either the provincial or the federal government. All provinces, except Alberta, apply a retail sales tax to almost all products and services sold to the ultimate consumer. Exceptions in some provinces include food, books, children's clothing, and medicine. The size and the application of these taxes varies from province to province, but if your business sells to final consumers you must obtain a permit and are responsible for collecting this tax and remitting it to the government on a regular basis.

Federal taxes largely fall into the categories of the Goods and Services Tax (GST) and income tax. Several provinces have integrated their provincial sales tax with the federal government's Goods and Services Tax (GST) to create a Harmonized Sales Tax (HST). The GST/HST is levied on virtually all products and services sold in Canada. There are some minor exceptions for certain types of products. If your taxable revenues do not exceed $30,000 you do not have to register for the GST or HST, but you can still choose to register voluntarily even if your revenues are below this level. You should check and see whether these taxes apply in your business. If so, you will be required to obtain a Business Number (BN) and remit any taxes collected on a regular basis.

How income tax is collected depends on the form of organization of your business. Sole proprietorships and partnerships file income tax returns as individuals and the same regulations apply. Federal and provincial taxes are paid together and only one personal income tax form is required annually for both, although payments may have to be remitted quarterly on the basis of your estimated annual earnings.

Corporations are treated as a separate entity for income tax purposes and taxed individually. The rules, tax rates, and regulations that apply to corporations are very complex and quite different from those that apply to individuals. You should obtain professional advice or keep in touch with the local tax authorities to determine your obligations under the Income Tax Act and to keep the amount of tax you have to pay to a minimum.

Employment Standards

All provinces have standards for employment and occupational health and safety that must be adhered to by all businesses within their jurisdiction. These requirements deal with such matters as:

1. Hours of work
2. Minimum wages
3. Statutory holidays
4. Overtime pay
5. Equal pay for equal work
6. Termination of employment
7. Severance pay
8. Working conditions
9. Health and safety concerns

You should contact the office of your provincial Ministry of Labour or its equivalent and request a copy of the Employment Standards Act in effect in your province as well as a copy of the Guide to the Act. This will provide you with specific information on all of these topics, or you can use the services of an accountant or lawyer.

Conclusion

There is no pat answer to the question of the legal form of organization you should adopt. A lot will depend on such issues as the expected size and growth rate of your new venture, your desire to limit your personal liability, whether you plan to start the business on a part-time or a full-time basis, whether you expect to lose or make money from a tax point of view during your first one or two years of operation, your need for other skills or additional capital, and so forth. Take a look at Figure 8.1. It summarizes many of the important differences between the various forms of organization available to you and may help you make your decision.

One word of caution: if you are considering any type of *partnership* arrangement, be extremely careful. In hard reality, partners should fulfil at least one of two major needs for you: they should provide either needed *money* or needed *skills*. If you allow any other factors to overshadow these two essential criteria, you may be taking an unnecessary risk.

One of the primary reasons new venture teams often fail is ill-advised partnerships. Partnerships entered into principally for reasons of friendship, shared ideas, or similar factors can create considerable stress for both the partnership and the individuals involved. It has often been said that a partner should be chosen with as much care as you would choose an ideal spouse. However, in contemporary society, perhaps even greater care should be exercised, since a partnership may be even more difficult to dissolve than a marriage. An unhappy partnership can dissolve your business much faster than you can dissolve the partnership.

FIGURE 8.1   WHICH FORM OF BUSINESS ORGANIZATION IS BEST FOR YOU?

Figure 8.1 summarizes many of the important differences between the various forms of business available to you. Review each of the alternatives on the dimensions indicated and select which one best fits with your particular circumstances. This may vary from characteristic to characteristic since there are pros and cons of each form. Once you have reviewed all dimensions, you should be able to select the organizational form that appears to be the best overall for your particular situation.

Form of Organization	Initial Requirements and Costs	Liability of Owners	Control	Taxes	Transfer of Ownership	Continuity	Ability to Raise Money
Sole Proprietorship	Minimum requirements. Perhaps only registration of your business name	Unlimited liability	Absolute control over operations	Income from business taxed as personal income	May transfer ownership of assets	Business ceases to exist when owner quits or dies	Limited to what the owner can personally secure
General Partnership	Easy and inexpensive to establish	Each partner is personally liable for all debts of the partnership	Requires majority vote of all general partners	Income from business is taxed as personal income of the partners	Requires agreement of all partners	Dissolved upon withdrawal or death of partner unless specified in partnership agreement	Combined resources of all the partners can be used to raise capital
Limited Partnership	Moderate requirements. Should be registered provincially	Liability limited to the extent of their individual investment	May not participate in the day-to-day management of the business	Same as general partners	May sell interest in the company	Same as general partnership	Limited liability may make it easier to raise capital but can be complicated
Corporation	Most expensive. Usually requires a lawyer to file Articles of Incorporation	Liability limited to investment in company	Control rests with shareholders	Corporation taxed on its income and shareholders taxed on dividends received	Easily transferred by selling shares of stock	Not affected by the death or withdrawal of any shareholder	The most attractive form for raising capital

Which form best
meets your needs
on each dimension
(Select One) _____ _____ _____ _____ _____ _____ _____

Which form of organization do you feel best meets your overall needs? _____

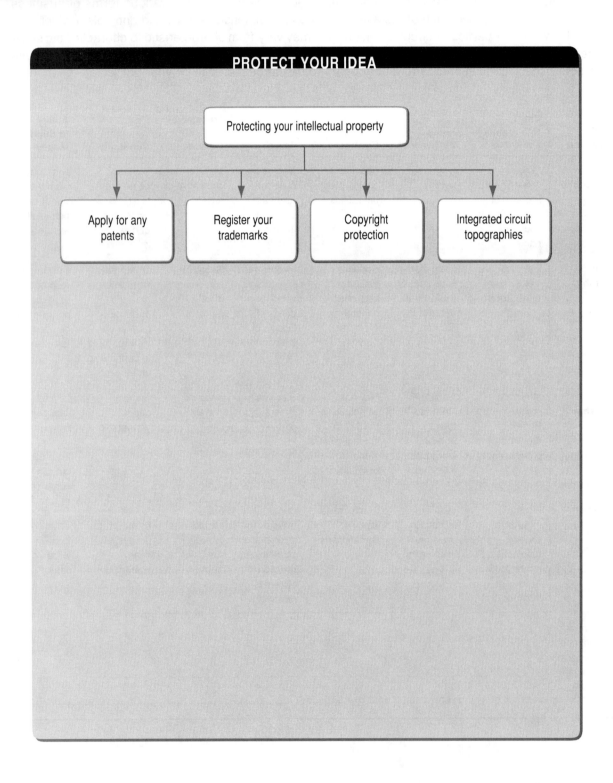

PROTECT YOUR IDEA

Protecting your intellectual property

Apply for any patents

Register your trademarks

Copyright protection

Integrated circuit topographies

Protecting Your Idea

Many entrepreneurs are also inventors. One of the primary problems faced by these inventor/entrepreneurs is how to protect the idea, invention, concept, system, design, name, or symbol that they feel may be the key to their business success. Legislators have long recognized that society should provide some protection for the creators of this "intellectual property." The laws they have developed provide a form of limited monopoly to the creators of intellectual property in return for their disclosure of the details of the property to the public.

Intellectual property is broken down into five components under the law:

1. Patents
2. Trademarks
3. Copyrights
4. Industrial designs
5. Integrated Circuit Topographies

Protection of your intellectual property can be expensive. While government costs may range from only a small fee for registration of a copyright to several hundred dollars for registration of a patent, many of the procedures can be quite complex and require you to obtain the services of a registered *patent agent*. This can increase the total cost of obtaining a patent to as much as $10,000, the cost depending on the complexity of the application. Therefore, it is important that you understand the advantages and disadvantages provided by this protection, and its likely impact on the success and financial viability of your business.

Applying for a Patent

A *patent* is a government grant that gives you the right to take legal action, if necessary, against other individuals who without your consent make, use, or sell the invention covered by your patent during the time the patent is in force. Patents are granted for 20 years from the date on which the application was first filed and are not renewable. On expiration of its patent, a patented device falls into the *public domain* — i.e., anyone may make, use, or sell the invention.

To be patentable, your device must:

1. Have "absolute novelty"
2. Be useful
3. Not be easily thought of by anyone skilled in the area of the invention's application

A patent may be granted to the inventor of any new and useful product, chemical composition, machine, or manufacturing process.

Patents will *not* be granted for any of the following:

1. An improvement to a known device that would be obvious to a person familiar with the known device
2. An improvement to a known device whose only difference from the original is a change in size, shape, or degree
3. A device whose prime purpose is illegal or illicit
4. A device that has no useful function or that doesn't work
5. Printed material
6. An idea or suggestion that is not completely developed
7. A scientific principle
8. A method of doing business
9. New works of art
10. A medical treatment
11. Recipes for dishes or drinks
12. A previously unknown substance that occurs naturally
13. A computer program
14. A process that depends entirely on artistic skill and leads to an ornamental effect

A patent may only be applied for by the *legal owner(s) of an invention*. You cannot apply for a patent for an invention you may have seen in another country even though that invention may never have been patented, described, or offered for sale in Canada.

Patents are now awarded to the *first inventor to file an application* with the Canadian Patent Office, rather than on the basis of the "first to invent" system previously used in Canada. This means you should file as soon as possible after completing your invention (though not prematurely so that certain key elements or features of your idea will be missing from your application). It is also important that you not advertise or display or publish information on your invention too soon, as this may jeopardize your ability to obtain a valid patent later on. There is a one-year grace period for disclosure by an applicant but it is suggested that the following rule of thumb be adopted: *Your application for a patent should be filed before your product is offered for public sale, shown at a trade show, or otherwise made public.*

How to Apply

If your idea is patentable and you wish to obtain patent protection, you should take the following steps:

1. **Find a patent agent** The preparation and *prosecution* (assessment) of patent applications is quite complex. You should consult a patent agent trained in this specialized practice and registered to practise before the Commissioner of Patents. Though hiring such an agent is not mandatory, it is highly recommended. A list of such individuals can be found in the publication *List of Registered Agents*, available from The Commissioner of Patents, The

Canadian Intellectual Property Office, 50 Victoria Street, Place du Portage, Phase I, Hull, Que. K1A 0C9 (www.cipo.gc.ca).

2. **Conduct a preliminary search** The first step your agent will recommend is a preliminary search of existing patents to see if anything similar to your idea has already been patented, in which case you may conclude the process immediately. This can save you a lot of time and money that might otherwise be spent pursuing a futile application. The search can be conducted at the Patent Office in Hull, Quebec or at your local public library.

An recently established Web site will make it easier for you to search for patent information. Instead of paying a lawyer to research patents or spending days in the library yourself, you can now do much of the legwork electronically. The Canadian Patent Database (patent1.ic.gc.ca) contains the full content of all patent files going back to 1920 freely available with downloadable text and drawings.

3. **Prepare a patent application** A patent application consists of an abstract, a specification, and drawings.

An *abstract* is a brief summary of the material in the specification. The *specification* is a document that contains (1) a complete description of the invention and its purpose and (2) *claims*, which are an explicit statement of what your invention is and the boundaries of the patent protection you are seeking. *Drawings* must be included whenever the invention can be described pictorially. Typically, all inventions except chemical compositions and some processes can be described by means of drawings.

4. **File your application** Filing your application means submitting it along with a petition asking the Commissioner of Patents to grant you a patent. In Canada, filing must be done within one year of any use or public disclosure of the invention.

If your application is accepted, you will be required to pay an annual maintenance fee to keep it in effect. Independent inventors and small businesses whose gross annual revenues are less than $2 million pay lower maintenance fees than businesses classified as "other than small." Fees range from zero in the first year to $200 in years 15 to 19 of the patent's life.

5. **Request examination** Your application will not automatically be examined simply because you have filed it. You must formally request examination and submit the appropriate fee. This request can be made any time within seven years of your filing date.

Filing an application and not requesting examination can be a cheap and effective way of obtaining some protection for your invention without necessarily incurring all the costs of obtaining a patent. For example, let's assume you want to protect your idea but don't wish to spend all the money required to obtain a patent while you assess the financial feasibility of your invention. Filing an application establishes your rights to the invention and publication of the application by the Patent Office informs other people of your claim to the product or process. Should they infringe on your invention after your application is published, you have seven years to decide whether to pursue the grant of a patent and seek retroactive compensation.

Requesting an examination, however, is no guarantee that a patent will be granted. And if it is not, you will have no grounds to claim damages for infringing on your idea.

The Canadian Patent Office receives over 35,000 applications a year, mostly from American inventors and companies. As a result, the examination process can be very slow, commonly taking two to three years to complete.

6. **If necessary, file amendment letters** Upon your requesting an examination, the patent examiner will assess your claims and either approve or reject your application. If your application is rejected, you can respond by filing an *amendment letter* with the Commissioner of

Patents. The letter will be studied by the examiner. If the patent is not then granted, there may be a request for further amendments. This process will continue until either the patent is granted, your application is withdrawn, or your application is finally rejected.

Protection Provided by Your Patent

As you can see, the patenting process is complex, costly, and time-consuming. If you have a patent application in process and are concerned that someone else may attempt to patent your invention, you may use the label "Patent Pending" or "Patent Applied For" to inform the public that your application for a patent has been filed. This, however, has no legal significance and does not mean that a patent will necessarily be granted. Of course, it is illegal to use this term if in fact no application is on file.

If your patent application is granted, the onus will be entirely on you to protect your rights under the patent, for the Patent Office has no authority to prosecute for patent infringement. If infringement occurs, you may (1) bring legal action to compel the offender to account for any profits made, (2) seek an injunction to prevent further use of your patent, or (3) obtain a court order for the destruction of any materials produced which infringe on your rights. This, however, can be a very expensive and time-consuming process, which may prohibit a small business from enforcing its rights.

A patent granted in Canada or the U.S. provides you with no protection outside the country in which it was originally granted. To obtain protection in other countries, you must register your patent in each country within the time limit permitted by law (typically one year from your initial application). You can apply for a foreign patent either from within Canada via the Canadian Patent Office, or directly through the patent office of the country or countries concerned. Under the terms of the Patent Cooperation Treaty, it is possible to file for a patent in as many as 43 countries, including the U.S., Japan, and most of Europe, by completing a single, standardized application which can be filed in Canada. Ask your patent agent about these procedures before you decide to file in another country.

You should realize that holding a patent on a worthy idea does not necessarily mean commercial success. Dan Knight and Rick Hilton, whose case is described in Entrepreneurs in Action #17, appear to have an interesting idea with their patented Golf Bag Cooler, but they may never even recover the cost of obtaining their patents.

They are in a similar situation to Mich Delaquis and Fred Coakes and their state-of-the-art, self-draining cookware discussed in Entrepreneurs in Action #18. They have secured patents in the United States and Canada for the locking mechanism on the lid of their pots and invested virtually all of their life's savings and a good portion of their families' and friends' savings. Even though they have managed to interest The Shopping Channel in demonstrating their product, they still need to raise another $100,000 to get the cookware sets produced in Hong Kong, and they are still a long way from making a profit on their idea.

An invention succeeds by acceptance in the marketplace. Your patent may be perfectly valid and properly related to your invention but commercially worthless. Thousands of patents are issued each year that fall into this category. A patent does not necessarily contribute to the economic success of an invention. In some high-technology fields, for example, innovations can become obsolete long before your patent is issued, effectively making the patent worthless.

Holding a patent may improve your profitability by keeping similar products off the market, giving you an edge. But there is no guarantee you will be able to prevent all competition. Litigation, if it becomes necessary, can require considerable financial resources, and the outcome is by no means assured. A high percentage of patent infringements challenged in court result in decisions unfavourable to the patent holder.

17 ENTREPRENEURS IN *ACTION*

A Cool Idea for the Golf Bag

Happiness is pulling a cold beverage out of your golf bag when the clubhouse is four fairways away.

Working up a sweat to get to golf course clubhouses for a cool sip is what prompted Dan Knight and Rick Hilton to invent their Golf Bag Cooler.

It's a skinny tube that fits inside a golf bag and holds six cans. A spring made out of musical instrument wire pushes a fresh can of pop (or beer) to the top of the bag every time one is taken out.

"It was Rick's idea about five years ago. I had an old doodle art tube at home and we tried to come up with a calibrated spring for it," says Knight. "For a while, until we got the right spring, we thought we'd have to put a caution label on the tube in case it shot cans out."

What keeps the cans cold — even in 98 degree Fahrenheit weather — is the air space between two PVC tubes fit one into the other, and small hockey puck-like objects filled with freezable gel which fit in between the cans. "It was the spring and the disks which got us the patent," says Hilton. "There's lots of elongated tube coolers out there, but these two things made ours unique. We got the idea for the disks from a toy hockey puck which we drilled a hole into and filled with gel. We had to use a turkey baster."

They had to turn to engineering companies and a couple of professors at the University of Manitoba to find out what material to build the coolers out of. The parts are manufactured in Boucherville, Quebec and then shipped to Winnipeg.

But as any inventor soon learns, there are three stages to any invention — dreaming it up, getting the patent and then getting it on the market.

Knight and Hilton along with partner Russ Glow have American and Canadian patents on the Golf Bag cooler but they're still trying to find a market with which to share their slice of heaven.

Source: Excerpted from Susie Strachan, "Dreaming of A Cool Million: Inventors Perceive Need, Seek to Cash-in on Fulfilling It," *Winnipeg Free Press*, February 18, 1992. © *Winnipeg Free Press*. Reprinted with permission.

However, there are many instances where patenting a product concept or idea has led to commercial success. Bill Laidlaw noticed an economic and environmental problem his employer, BC Hydro, was experiencing and invented "Replugs" to solve it (Entrepreneurs in Action #19). Replug sales have gone from $37,000 in 1992 to over $350,000 in 1997 with 75 percent coming from the U.S. Even more impressive has been the market performance of Gary Eklund's drive-through farm gate illustrated in Entrepreneurs in Action #20. To date, Eklund has sold over 10,000 gates, realizing over $2 million in sales, and exported his product to Japan, Chile, Sweden, Australia, and the U.S. Not bad performance for a product he developed largely to eliminate some of the frustration he experienced in his own job.

Bob Dickie of Spark Innovations Inc. has built his whole business around patentable products. He holds 80 patents for his inventions and thinks patent protection is crucial to business success in the 90s. Bob's first product was the FlatPlug, billed as the first innovation in electrical plug design in 75 years. The FlatPlug lies flat against the wall, unlike a conventional electrical plug which sticks out perpendicular to the wall. As a result, it doesn't waste space behind furniture and is more difficult for children to pry out. Bob got the idea when he saw his daughter reach through her crib bars for a conventional plug. FlatPlug is protected by eight U.S. and worldwide patents. Even the package — a cardboard sleeve that keeps the extension cord and the plug in place — is patented.

18

ENTREPRENEURS IN ACTION

Feeling the Strain

Pot inventors refuse to give up on a dream

Take two east-end boys who made their living in a city snowmobile plant, lock them in a basement for three years and what do you get?

For Mich Delaquis and Fred Coakes, the answer is a state-of-the-art, self-draining cookware set.

Along the way, the two men exhausted their life savings and a sizable portion of their family's and friends', were knee-deep in flawed designs, fruitlessly wore out welcome mats at city banks, and were turned away by every cookware manufacturer in North America.

But come Feb. 15, the two partners will proudly display their eight-piece EasyStrain Cookware set on The Shopping Channel, every hustling entrepreneur's Valhalla.

"After all we've been through, it feels really good to know we've got a product that's not only good but others see that too," said Delaquis, 30, who has kept his day job as a warranty analyst at Polaris Industries Ltd.

What Delaquis and Coakes have produced is a set of pots and pans that are self-draining and with lids that lock on tight.

The design is simple. When cooking, the straining holes are covered. When it's time to strain, you line up the arrows on the lid with a matching arrow on the handle and turn clockwise; this locks the lid and exposes the holes.

The products are heavy-duty stainless steel with a thick bottom. The larger pots and pans come with an extra handle, making straining easier.

"What struck us was the quality and the unique feature," said Maureen McDermott, merchandise manager at The Shopping Channel. "It's a pretty-looking set. They've used 0.9-millimetre stainless steel. They haven't scrimped on quality.

"It's safe and it's good for either left-handed or right-handed people. I think we'll sell a lot of them."

Delaquis and Coakes are your typical entrepreneurs. Delaquis is the tinkerer; Coakes, the hustler and deal-maker. They saw a need and

went about their way to find a product to fill that need.

Delaquis remembers the day three years ago when, still single and living on his own, he scalded his hand while straining a pot of pasta.

"I didn't have a strainer and I had to do it with just lifting the lid a little bit," Delaquis said. "The idea popped into my head that it would be

MARC GALLANT/WINNIPEG FREE PRESS

a lot easier to do this if there was a strainer already inside the pot."

It was an idea that wouldn't go away. He went to Coakes, who was then head of the receiving department at Polaris, and told him of his plan.

They went into Coakes' basement and they tinkered. First, using snips and sheet metal, they tried to make their own pots and lids.

Then they concentrated on just designing the lid.

Their first design incorporated a spinning disc and a spring mechanism under the lid.

"The first five manufacturers we showed it to said it couldn't be made," said Coakes, 28. "We had to start all over again."

Along the way, the pair took a 10-week small business course from the Canada Business Service Centre. Then they found a helpful lawyer and an accountant.

Even when they came up with what they believed was a sure thing, they couldn't find anyone in North America to make it.

They secured patents in the United States and Canada for their locking mechanism and got the name trademarked, but 14 manufacturers turned them away.

"They either said it wouldn't work or they were too busy," Coakes said.

Both men credit staff at the Canada Business Service Centre with helping them find contacts in Hong Kong, as well as support here in Winnipeg.

It cost them $30,000 just to get the moulds designed.

"A year ago, I told Mich we've got to start selling some of these and stop writing all these cheques," said Coakes, who now sells Yellow Pages advertising for MTS Advanced.

But don't ask the pair to do a commercial for the Canadian banking industry. They've put $77,000 into the project to date and they need another $100,000 to make the minimum 1,250 sets the Hong Kong manufacturer will produce on a first order. All of that has been money from their own savings and that of family and friends.

"We'd be nowhere if it wasn't for the support and help from our family and friends," Delaquis said.

"One banker had the nerve to tell me that he so admired my tenacity he was certain I'd be a millionaire one day," Coakes said. "I told him I didn't need any lip service. We had two patents, a manufacturer, and now an agreement with The Shopping Channel but not one bank would help us. When we are millionaires, we won't be doing any business with him."

It's not over for Coakes and Delaquis. They're confident they'll find the investors necessary to bring the first 500 sets to The Shopping Channel in February. Once the sales take off, they're planning on larger pots and smaller pans.

After that, they will concentrate on direct marketing, with infomercials in the United States and trade shows. Then they'll go retail.

And Delaquis is not finished.

"I've got an idea or two for some other products."

Source: Aldo Santin, "Pot Inventors Refuse to Give Up on A Dream," *Winnipeg Free Press,* November 20, 1998, pp. B3 – B4. © Winnipeg Free Press. Reprinted with permission.

19 ENTREPRENEURS IN *ACTION*

"Plugging" Into the US Market

Bill Laidlaw of Victoria, British Columbia was employed with BC Hydro for 25 years in power line construction and maintenance. He noticed an economical and environmental problem his company was experiencing and invented "Replugs" to solve it. This product has proven its worth to BC Hydro and the novelty of Replugs is spreading to other industries.

The wooden poles used by Hydro companies require maintenance on a regular basis to control rot and insect infestation. Holes are drilled in the poles and preservatives or fumigants are poured into the holes, increasing the life of the pole. The holes then need to be sealed and, traditionally, wooden plugs have been used. Wooden plugs are difficult to pull out and new holes have to be drilled each time maintenance is required. Replugs are removable, reusable plastic plugs and have flexible

tapered threads that allow the plug to be pounded into the hole without damaging the hole. The plugs may be removed for maintenance and may be reused.

The result of using Replugs is an increase in the life of the poles—reducing costs. An effective maintenance program combined with the use of Replugs can result in average savings in excess of $5/pole/year for each wood pole subjected to the maintenance program. When the number of poles owned by a utility company is considered, dollar savings enter into the thousands (or even millions for large utilities.) There are an estimated 105 to 110 million wood poles in the United States!

After coming to the Canadian Innovation Centre in March of 1993, Laidlaw had a Critical Factor Assessment done. This assessment told him his product was feasible and recommended that he continue with the commercialization of Replugs.

Laidlaw took early leave from BC Hydro and established W.S. Laidlaw Products to market and manufacture his product. He subcontracted the manufacturing to Scott Plastics in BC and production began in 1990. A Renton, Washington distributor, Materials Procurement sells Replugs to the United States market. He markets them himself in Canada, saying, "it's really just in the starting phases." His market consists mostly of electrical utilities, but that is spreading as he recently filled an order for a jetty maintenance project at the Esquimalt Naval Base. Bill's company has now sold over *4 million* Replugs across North America.

Replugs have been tested and approved by BC Hydro. Cost analysis indicates that over the life of a wood pole, removable/reusable Replugs can save about $0.23/installed plug when compared to the wood plug alternative.

Laidlaw has experienced steady growth in sales. In 1992, Replug sales reached $37,000.

In 1997, sales were an impressive $350,000. To date, 75% of Laidlaw's sales are in the US, with only 25% in Canada.

Bill Laidlaw has not begun to penetrate middle and eastern Canada, and this is only due to the fact that there has not been a substantial marketing effort yet. As such, the opportunity to expand his market exists.

Laidlaw has the business foresight to see that organizations might not place considerable importance on replacing plugs. As a result, Laidlaw has published a paper which examines the method for evaluating the cost/benefits of wood pole maintenance. This paper serves to highlight the substantial savings a utility can realize.

A simple business idea, simply successful!

Source: "W.S. Laidlaw Products — A Canadian Business Plugging into the U.S. Market," *Eureka Magazine*, 1998. Reprinted with permission by the Canadian Innovation Centre.

In 1991, Bob set up Paige Innovations Inc. to commercialize FlatPlug. Sales in 1993 were about $6 million in Canada and the U.S. The company went public on the Toronto Stock Exchange in May 1994 with a market capitalization of $40 million.

Bob has a number of strict criteria he feels product ideas have to meet in order to have commercial potential:

- **It must be ten times better** Rather than evolutionary improvements in product design, he looks for concepts with enough of a "story" to make distribution channels take serious notice.

- **It must be patentable** "If we can't get a patent, the business is absolutely dead," says Mr. Dickie.

- **It must be a mass-production item** High-volume products have a higher turnover, reducing much of the risk of holding inventory.

- **It should be smaller than a bread box** Small items are easier to make and less costly to design, package, and transport.

- **It must lend itself to distribution through existing channels** Going through established market lines speeds the acceptance of a new product.

- **It should have no government involvement** Spark Innovations stays away from products that are motivated by or dependent on government support at any level.

- **It must be useful** Mr. Dickie only works with products that have long-term, practical usefulness. No novelties, fads or games.[1]

---

[1] Adapted from Ellen Roseman, "Spark of Genius," *The Globe and Mail*, September 26, 1994

20 ENTREPRENEURS IN *ACTION*

How to Build a Better Gate

Ecklund Drive-Thru Gates — A Canadian Solution to a Worldwide Problem

Gary Ecklund, as many business owners can confirm, innovated and developed his company based on personal experience.

In the early 80s, Ecklund was working at his family ranch in Saskatchewan. One of the more mundane requirements of his job was to watch, open and close the farm gate. His frustration with this "time wasting" job resulted in the biggest single improvement in drive through gates since first invented in 1924.

The gate — retailed at $237 — is designed such that there is a pressure release mechanism which allows the gate to "pop" open faster than a vehicle can bump into it. An electrically conductive rubber bumper sleeve offers a cushioning effect while maintaining a completely electrified gate. Ecklund's gate is adjustable in length, making it adaptable to many different gate sizes. Two patented processes include Ecklund's release mechanism, and the locking mechanism which ensures the gate is locked into place snugly once a vehicle passes through.

After three years of use at the Ecklund Ranch, Gary Ecklund felt that he had a product to bring to market. He first presented the drive through gate at the Canada Farm Progress Show in 1986. After this first show, Ecklund personally demonstrated his innovation through much travelling and cold calls. These initial gates are still in use 13 years later.

Ecklund's strategy has been to target, through price and promotion, to the top 3% of the market (that portion of the market willing to spend more on equipment). As a result, the Ecklund Drive-Thru gate has achieved a quality image.

To date, Ecklund has sold over 10,000 gates, achieving over $2 million in sales. His product has been exported to countries including: Japan, Chile, Sweden, Australia, and the US.

Source: "Eckland Drive-Thru Gates — A Canadian Solution to a Worldwide Problem," *Eureka Magazine,* 1998. Reprinted with permission by the Canadian Innovation Centre.

Registering Your Trademark

A *trademark* is a word, symbol, picture, design, or combination of these which distinguishes your goods and services from those of others in the marketplace. A trademark might also be thought of as a "brand name" or "identifier" that can be used to distinguish the product of your firm. For example, both the name "McDonald's" and the symbol of the golden arches are (among others) registered trademarks of the McDonald's Corporation.

To *register* a trademark means to file it with a government agency for the purpose of securing the following rights and benefits:

1. Exclusive permission to use the brand name or identifier in Canada

2. The right to sue anyone you suspect of infringing on your trademark to recover lost profits on sales made under your trade name, and for other damages and costs

3. The basis for filing an application in another country should you wish to export your product

To be registrable, a trademark must not be so similar in appearance, sound, or concept to a trademark already registered, or pending registration, as to be confused with it. For example, the following trademarks would not be registrable: "Cleanly Canadian" for a soft drink (too close to Clearly Canadian, a fruit-flavoured mineral water); "Extendo" for a utility knife (too close to Exacto).

The value of a trademark lies in the goodwill the market attaches to it and the fact that consumers will ask for your brand with the expectation of receiving the same quality product or service as previously. Therefore, unlike a patent, a trademark should be registered only if you have some long-term plans for it that will result in an accumulation of goodwill.

It is possible for you to use a trademark without registering it. Registration is not mandatory and unregistered marks have legal status. But registration is advised for most commonly used identifiers, since it does establish immediate, obvious proof of ownership.

How to Register Your Trademark

In Canada it is possible for you to register your trademark before you actually use it, but the mark will not be validated until it is actually put into service. Registration of a trademark involves the following steps:

1. **A search of previous and pending registrations** As with a patent, a search should be conducted to determine that your trademark does not conflict with others already in use. This search can also be conducted electronically at strategis.ic.gc.ca/sc_consu/trade-marks/engdoc/cover.html.

2. **An application to register your trademark** This involves filing an application for registration of your trademark.

Once your application is received, it is published in the *Trade Mark Journal* to see if anyone opposes your registration.

Even though registering a trademark is relatively simple compared with applying for a patent, it is recommended that you consult a *trademark agent* registered to practise before the Canadian Trade Marks Office.

Maintaining and Policing Your Trademark

It normally takes about a year from the date of application for a trademark to be registered. Registration is effective for 15 years, and may be renewed for a series of 15-year terms as long as the mark is still in use.

As with a patent, it is up to you to police the use of your trademark; the government provides no assistance in the enforcement of your trademark rights. It is your decision whether to take any legal action against an offender.

Registration of a trademark in Canada provides no protection of your trademark in other countries. If you are involved with or contemplating exporting to any other country, you should consider registering your trademark in that country.

Obtaining Copyright

A *copyright* gives you the right to preclude others from reproducing or copying your original published work. Materials protected by copyright include books, leaflets, periodicals and contributions to periodicals, lectures, sermons, musical or dramatic compositions, maps, works of art, photographs, drawings of a scientific or technical nature, motion pictures, sound recordings, and computer programs. A copyright exists for the duration of your life plus 50 years following your death.

How to Obtain a Copyright

In Canada, there is no legal requirement that your work be registered in order to obtain copyright; it is automatically acquired upon creation of an original work. Nevertheless, you may wish to apply for voluntary registration. When your work has been registered, a certificate is issued that can, if necessary, be used in court to establish your ownership of the work.

The Protection Provided by Copyright

Your copyright enables you to control the copying and dissemination of your own works. This includes publishing, producing, reproducing, and performing your material. As with patents and trademarks, the responsibility for policing your copyright rests with you.

It is important to understand some of the limitations of copyright protection as well. For example, for purposes of copyright protection, the term "computer program" refers to "a set of instructions or statements, expressed, fixed, embodied or stored in any manner, that is to be used directly or indirectly in a computer in order to bring about a specific result." This means that a *specific* computer program such as Microsoft Excel can be protected as a literary work but not the idea of *spreadsheet programs* in general. In addition, any accompanying documentation for a program, such as a user's guide, is considered a separate work and must be registered separately.

Unlike patents and trademarks, a copyright in Canada provides simultaneous protection in most other countries of the world.

Protecting Integrated Circuit Topographies

The circuits incorporated into an integrated circuit (IC) are embodied in a three-dimensional hill-and-valley configuration called a topography. These designs are protected by the Integrated Circuit Topography Act. IC products, commonly called "microchips" or "semiconductor chips" are incorporated into a variety of consumer and industrial products. The protection associated with the design of a topography is entirely distinct from that of any computer program embodied in the chip. Computer programs are subject to protection under the Copyright Act.

What Protection Does the Act provide?

The legislation provides exclusive rights in regard to:

- reproduction of a protected topography or any substantial part of it
- manufacturing an IC product incorporating the topography or any substantial part of it
- importation or commercial exploitation of a topography, or of an IC product which embodies a protected topography or any substantial part of it
- importation or commercial exploitation of an industrial article which incorporates an IC product that embodies a protected topography

The Act provides for a full range of civil remedies including injunctions and exemplary damages. Protection for registered integrated circuit topographies is provided for approximately 10 years.

How to Protect an IC Topography

To protect an IC topography you must apply to the Registrar of Topographies. Applications for "commercially exploited" topographies must be filed within two years of the date of first commercial exploitation anywhere. The application may be rejected if the topography was first exploited outside Canada. Owners must be Canadian or nationals of countries having reciprocal protection agreements with Canada.

For More Information on Intellectual Property

Further information on the protection of intellectual property can be obtained from:

Canadian Intellectual Property Office
Industry Canada
50 Victoria St.
Place du Portage, Phase 1
Hull, Quebec
K1A 0C9   Tel: (819) 997-1936 or at (cipo.gc.ca/)

or contact your local Industry Canada, Canada Business Services Centre.

The deadlines for filing, the length of time for which protection is provided, and the current registration fees for several types of intellectual property are summarized in Table 9.1.

TABLE 9.1	INFORMATION ABOUT PROTECTION OF INTELLECTUAL PROPERTY IN CANADA		
Type	**Application Deadline**	**Period of Coverage**	**Government Fees**

Patents	File within 1 year of publication (file before publication for most other countries)	20 years from filing of application	Filing fee $150
			Examination fee $150
			Allowance fee (Grant) $150
			Maintenance fee
			  Year 2, 3 & 4 $ 50
			  Year 5 to 9 $ 75
			  Year 10 to 14 $100
			  Year 15 to 19 $200

Trademarks	(None)	15 years; renewable indefinitely	Filing fee $150 Registration fee $200
Copyright	(None)	50 years plus life of author	Registration fee $ 65

Conclusion

As we have discussed, in addition to various *tangible* assets such as land, buildings, and equipment, your business may also own certain *intangible* assets, such as patents, trademarks, and copyrights. These can be just as important as, or even more important than, your tangible assets. And like tangible assets, with permission of their owner they can be bought, sold, licensed, or used by someone else.

Ideas that are not patentable, and are not otherwise protected, may be protected by contract law either by means of a written *non-disclosure agreement* or by treating them as *trade secrets*. This can be done by taking every precaution to keep valuable knowledge a secret and/or by placing specific provisions in any agreement you may have with your employees that they will neither disclose to anyone else nor use for their own purposes any trade secrets they may acquire while in your employ. The advantages of this type of protection may be even greater than those of patent protection. The success of this approach depends on your ability to control the access of outsiders to the information, as there are no *legal rights* in a trade secret. Typically, once confidential information has been publicly disclosed, it becomes very difficult to enforce any rights to it.

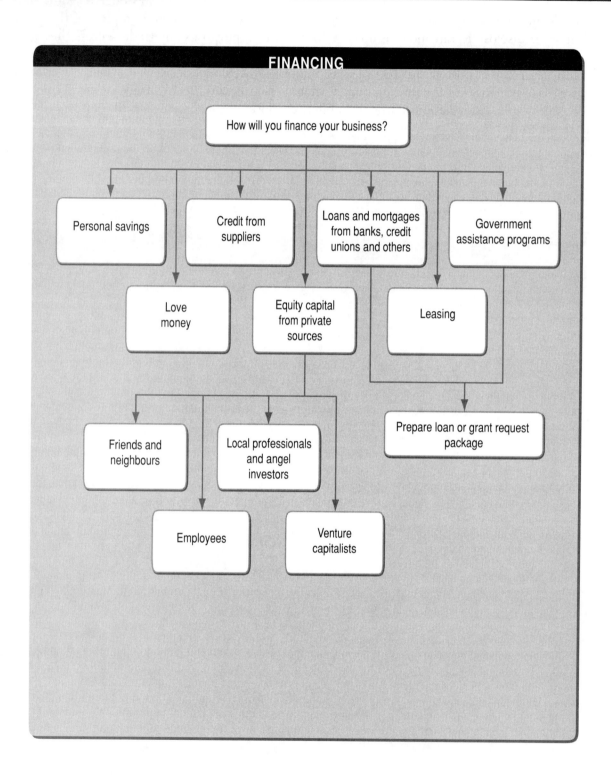

FINANCING

How will you finance your business?

- Personal savings
- Credit from suppliers
- Loans and mortgages from banks, credit unions and others
- Government assistance programs

- Love money
- Equity capital from private sources
- Leasing

- Friends and neighbours
- Local professionals and angel investors

- Employees
- Venture capitalists

Prepare loan or grant request package

Arranging Financing

Quite a number of sources of financing are available to established businesses. However, there are very few sources of *seed capital* for ventures that are just getting off the ground and have no track record. Obtaining such capital can require persistence and determination. Usually you must submit a formal proposal to a prospective lender, in which you outline your plans, needs, and schedule of repayment. Many financing proposals have to be revised several times before receiving a positive response. In addition, you may have to be prepared to combine financing from several sources in order to raise all the funds you require.

The major sources of funds for small-business start-ups are personal funds, "love money," banks, government agencies and programs, and venture capital.

Major Sources Of Funds

Personal Funds

The first place to look for money to start your business is your own pocket. This may mean cleaning out your savings account and other investments, selling your second car, postponing your holiday for this year, cashing in your RRSPs, extending your credit cards to the limit, mortgaging the cottage, taking out a second mortgage on the family home, or any other means you may have of raising cash.

"Love Money"

Once you have scraped together everything you can from your resources and personal savings, the next step is to talk to other people. Additional funds may come from your friends, family, and close personal relations. This is known as "love money."

Recent estimates indicate that, in fact, love money makes up more than 90 percent of the new business start-up capital in Canada. This personal funding is necessary because banks and other conventional sources usually will not lend money without extensive security. For example, Peter Oliver, whose case is described in Entrepreneurs in Action #21, was able to launch his successful chain of restaurants in Toronto only with the financial support of his wife's parents.

21   ENTREPRENEURS IN *ACTION*

Love Money — A Helluva Deal for Both Sides

"I've always wanted something I could build into something bigger," says Peter Oliver, explaining why in 1978 he gave up a lucrative career as a real estate agent, and opened Oliver's Old Fashioned Bakery in uptown Toronto. The something bigger is what the 38-year-old has today — four restaurants with anticipated 1987 sales of $12 million and gross profits of 8% to 12%. He also owns two of the four buildings that house his restaurants.

Oliver's success would not have been so swift without the financial support of his wife's parents. They provided the $40,000 down payment on the first building,, which was renovated with another $40,000 from Oliver's savings. In exchange for their investment, Oliver guaranteed his in-laws a minimum 12% annual return as well as half ownership in the building. The money has earned them almost 20% every year,

and the building has escalated in value from $160,000 to an estimated $1 million. ...

In the beginning he had no formal agreement with his in-laws. But as time went on and they invested more money in his company, proper documents were drawn up, both to arrange bank financing and give everyone concrete evidence of their investment. After nine years, Oliver has built a small empire on a base of love money. And his in-laws have made a superb return on their investments. Oliver sums it up beautifully: "They got a helluva deal," he says, "and I got a helluva deal."

Source: Excerpted from Larry Gaudet and Tony Leighton, "Setting Out with Buoyant Backing," *Canadian Business*, October 1987, pp. 76–77. By permission of the authors.

The biggest risk with this source of capital is that if your new business fails and the investors lose money, it can create considerable hard feelings among family and friends. This possibility can be reduced if you lay out all the terms and conditions of the investment in advance, just as you would for any other investors. You should explain the nature of your business, your detailed implementation plans, the risks associated with the venture, and other relevant factors. In fact, it is best if you give both yourself and your investors some measure of comfort by translating your understanding into a formal legal agreement, as Peter Oliver did with his in-laws. If the money is provided to you as a loan, another important reason for putting it into writing is that if, for some reason, you are unable to repay the money and your investor must write it off, the amount of a properly documented loan becomes a capital loss for income tax purposes and can be offset against any capital gains, thereby providing the investor with the potential for some tax relief from the loss.

This most basic kind of financing is often not enough to get the business started, but it is important for external funding sources to see that you and your family are prepared to invest most of your personal resources in the venture. Without a strong indication of this type of individual commitment, it will be extremely difficult to raise any other money. Why should someone not directly involved in the business risk money in your business if you are not prepared to put your own assets on the line?

Banks

Banks are the most popular and widely used *external* source of funds for new businesses. A visit to the local banker becomes almost a mandatory part of any new venture start-up situation. Banks historically have provided debt financing in the form of self-liquidating, short-term loans to cover small businesses' peak working capital requirements, usually in the form of an *operating loan* or *line of credit*.

An operating loan extends credit to you up to a prearranged limit *on an ongoing basis*, to cover your day-to-day expenses such as accounts receivable, payroll, inventory carrying costs, office supplies, and utility bills. If you happen to be in a highly seasonal or cyclical business, for example, such a "line of credit" can be used to purchase additional inventory in anticipation of your peak selling period. An operating loan is intended to *supplement your basic working capital*. It extends credit to you up to a prearranged amount *on an ongoing basis*, to cover your day-to-day expenses such as accounts receivable, payroll, inventory carrying costs, office supplies, and utility bills. An operating loan can also be used to bridge unexpected cash flow interruptions and/or shortfalls. It may give you the ability to take advantage of supplier discounts for prompt payment or, if you happen to be in a highly seasonal or cyclical business, to purchase additional inventory in anticipation of your peak selling period

Operating loans, however, can have some restrictions. For example, your banker may prohibit you from taking retained earnings out of your company during the early stages of your business. In addition, he or she may even veto the purchase of machinery, equipment, and other fixed assets above a certain amount. These operating loans are subject to annual review and renewal by mutual agreement but can often be terminated by the lender at its option unless specific conditions have been incorporated into the loan agreement. Interest on operating loans is usually *tied to the prime rate*. That means it can change either up or down as the prime rate changes. This can be an advantage when interest rates are declining but a major issue if rates are increasing rapidly.

Banks also provide *term loans* to small businesses — loans for the purchase of an existing business or to acquire fixed assets such as machinery, vehicles, and commercial buildings, which typically must be repaid in three to ten years. The "term" is usually linked to the expected lifespan of the asset. Three to four years is common for a truck or computer, while the term of a loan to acquire a building could be considerably longer. Term loans typically have a fixed interest rate for the full term. Therefore your interest cost is predetermined in advance and your budgeting process is simplified. However, the loan amount tends to be limited to a percentage of the value of the asset being financed. In addition, term loans often command a one-time processing fee of $1/2\%$ of the value of the loan.

You should realize that business bank loans, both operating and term loans are *demand* loans so that regardless of the term, the bank can and will demand they be paid back if it feels the company is getting into trouble. While this usually only occurs when the business has real problems, there is the potential for difficulties; what the banker may perceive as a serious situation may only be perceived as a temporary difficulty by the owner of the business.

Janine DeFreitas and Ken Fitzgerald, whose situation is described in Entrepreneurs in Action #22 and #23, are typical new business owners. Both were frustrated in their initial efforts to obtain financing from some of the major banks but both recognize they will need bank support to develop and grow their businesses beyond their current stage now that they are more firmly established. Janine, for example, was initially unable to obtain a bank loan despite the fact she had a business plan, love money provided by her father, and a commitment from her principal supplier to provide the necessary inventory for her store. When her request was finally approved on the third try, it was only because it was government guaranteed and co-signed by her father.

Similarly, Fitzgerald's request for start-up funding for his computer resale company was turned down by seven banks and he was forced initially to finance his business by running up charges on his credit card. It wasn't until several years later the company was finally successful in obtaining a line of credit from the Royal Bank. The line of credit has grown significantly over the years, but Fitzgerald and his wife both resent the fact that they

22

Controlling Interest

Janine DeFreitas
The Rubbery Inc., Mississauga, Ont.

Government guarantees, proven products, a 100-page business plan and cold hard cash sounds like a perfect recipe to lure bank financing. Janine DeFreitas knows otherwise.

After the former Rubbermaid Canada sales and merchandising manager watched the company's first full-line retail display sell out in just four weeks, DeFreitas got the urge to open a Rubbermaid-only store. Equipped with her business plan, $50,000 from her father and the promise of product from her supplier, DeFreitas was rebuffed by two banks—and two male loans officers—before a female lender at Toronto-Dominion issued a $110,000 loan. Still, the loan was government-guaranteed and co-signed by

DeFreitas' father. "They said I didn't put enough personal equity into it," she says.

The bank should have few worries now: at $3 million a year, sales have doubled projections. DeFreitas is now planning to go national within five years. She's considering franchising to finance out-of-province openings, but is looking at bank debt to fund up to five corporate stores in Ontario. "I wanted to open my own business so I wouldn't have to answer to anybody," DeFreitas explains. "If I go through an investor, I lose a certain amount of control."

Source: Excerpted from Charise Clark "How I Raised Funds," PROFIT: *The Magazine for Canadian Entrepreneurs*, November, 1998, pp. 35-36. © Charise Clark.

must still provide their personal guarantees for the loan despite the fact the business has sales over $5 million.[1]

The bank may ask for your personal guarantee of these loans as well as a pledge of collateral security for the full value of the loan or more. This means that even though your business might be incorporated, your personal liability is not necessarily limited to your investment in the business; you could lose your house, car, cottage, and other personal assets if the business should fail and you are unable to repay your loans to the bank.

In order to qualify for a loan you must have sufficient equity in your business and a strong personal credit rating. Banks do not take large risks. Their principal considerations in assessing a loan application are the safety of their depositors' money and the return they will earn on the loan. It is critical that you take these factors into account in preparing your loan proposal and try to look at your situation from the banker's point of view.

Government

Governments at all levels in Canada have developed a proliferation of financial assistance programs for small business. It is estimated there are more than 600 programs available from both the federal and provincial governments to help people begin a business or assist those that have already started. Many of these programs are aimed at companies in more advanced stages of their development who are looking to grow and expand, but quite a number can be utilized by firms in the start-up stage. Many of these programs offer financial assistance in the form of low-interest loans, loan guarantees, interest-free loans or even forgivable (non-repayable) loans. Others offer incentives like wage subsidies, whereby the government will pay an employee's wage for a certain period of time. These programs are too numerous to describe in any detail, but let us briefly look at several of the more important ones.

---

[1] *How I raised funds (How savvy entrepreneurs fight for the funding they need)*, PROFIT — *The Magazine for Canadian Entrepreneurs*, November, 1998, pp. 35-40.

23

ENTREPRENEURS IN *ACTION*

Will That Be Cash or Plastic?

Kevin Fitzgerald, President
Aurora Microsystems Distribution Inc.,
Sudbury, Ont.

In 1988, physics graduate Kevin Fitzgerald was looking to break into the booming computer resale industry, with a focus on the lucrative corporate, education and government markets. He had just one problem: he had $147 to his name.

Fitzgerald applied to seven banks for startup funds. "In not so many words, they told me I wouldn't succeed," he says. Undaunted, he founded Aurora Microsystems Distribution Inc. with credit cards acquired as a student. In his first year of operations, Fitzgerald ran up $60,000 in charges as he travelled around to drum up clients and bought basic consumables for the office. That figure more than doubled the following year as he put inventory on plastic. Sounds expensive, but by balancing 30-day terms from suppliers and 30 days from credit-card issuers with 60-day payments from customers, Fitzgerald generally paid off his cards promptly while avoiding steep interest charges. All told, Fitzgerald estimates he's charged $1 million in purchases since founding the company — and kept Aurora humming using little capital of his own.

"After years of running on vapor," says Fitzgerald, Aurora won a $50,000 line of credit from the Royal Bank in 1993. The LOC has grown to $500,000 over the years, but both Fitzgerald and his wife — an Aurora employee — guarantee it, despite Aurora's annual revenues of $5 million. That rankles: "If we screw up, the bank has the right to confiscate anything we own," says Fitzgerald. "If she doesn't sign, they pull the line. It's terrible. It's just not right." Fitzgerald was particularly dismayed by one banker with minimal knowledge of the computer business. After explaining that Aurora wanted to emulate Dell Computers, the manager replied, "Who's Dell?" Says Fitzgerald: "If they don't understand the business, how can they possibly understand why you should borrow money from them or how much or what you should do with it?"

As for alternatives, Fitzgerald says building a high-growth business on a shoestring budget leaves little time to scare up funds —a condition he blames for holding Aurora back. But that may soon change as Fitzgerald goes full-throttle to attract outside investors. He's already talked with two venture capitalists, but is willing to consider anyone who "will sit down and work with us," he says. And Fitzgerald figures Aurora would be an attractive investment: "We've never bounced a cheque."

Source: Excerpted from Charise Clark "How I Raised Funds," *PROFIT: The Magazine for Canadian Entrepreneurs*, November, 1998, p. 40.

Canada Small Business Financing Act

New and existing businesses whose gross revenues are less than $5 million may be eligible to obtain term loans from chartered banks, caisses populaires, credit unions or other lenders and have the loan partially guaranteed by the federal government under the Canada Small Business Financing Act (CSBFA) (previously known as the Small Business Loans Act (SBLA). These loans are provided at a reasonable rate of interest (prime plus no more than 3% for floating rate loans or the lender's residential mortgage rate plus 3% for a fixed-rate loan). In addition, lenders are required to pay a one-time loan registration fee to the government equal to 2% of the amount loaned. This fee is recoverable from the borrower. These loans may be used for any number of purposes, such as the purchase or renovation of machinery and equipment and the purchase and improvement of land and buildings for business purposes.

Loan proceeds may be used to finance up to 90 percent of the cost of the asset while the maximum value of loans a borrower may have outstanding under the CSBFA cannot exceed $250,000. For more information, contact any private sector lender or:

Small Business Loans Administration
Industry Canada
25 Queen Street
8th Floor East
Ottawa, Ontario K1A 0H5
Telephone: (613) 954-5540
(strategis.ic.gc.ca/csbfa)

Industrial Research Assistance Program (IRAP)

IRAP provides scientific and technical advice and limited financial assistance for projects designed to enhance a company's technical capability under two program elements:

1. Technology Enhancement (THE) provides financial support to cover up to 50 percent of the costs of subcontractors or consultants to a maximum of $15,000 for small-scale projects of a preliminary nature.

2. Research, Development and Adaptation (RDA) funds 50% of eligible project costs such as staff salaries up to $250,000 for a period of up to 36 months for larger-scale projects and more complex research and development activities.

    For more information contact:

National Research Council of Canada
Montreal Road
Ottawa, Ontario K1A 0R6
Telephone: (613) 993-7082
(pub.irap.nrc.ca/irap/web/irapcomm.nsf/)

Program for Export Market Development (PEMD)

PEMD is designed to increase export sales of Canadian goods and services by encouraging Canadian companies to become exporters and helping existing Canadian exporters to develop new markets. PEMD shares the cost of export market development activity these companies would not normally undertake on their own. Market Development Strategies supports a combination of visits, trade fair participation and market support activities with a repayable contribution ranging from $5,000 – 50,000. New exporters may be eligible to receive a maximum of $7,500 for either a market identification visit or for participation in an international trade fair.

    For more information contact:

Export Development Division
Department of Foreign Affairs and International Trade
125 Sussex Drive
Ottawa, Ontario K1A 0G2
Telephone: (613) 944-0018
(www.infoexport.gc.ca/section2/export/export_menu-e.asp)

Community Futures Program (CFP)

Community Futures is a community economic development program that provides economic planning services to communities as well as business counselling and loans to small business in non-metropolitan communities in Western Canada. Community Futures Development Corporations (CFDC) provide business loans up to $125,000 to assist existing businesses with expansion or to help entrepreneurs create new businesses. CFDCs also deliver two specialized loan programs:

1. The Western Youth Entrepreneurs Program provides loans of up to $25,000 to young entrepreneurs between the ages of 18 and 29.

2. The Entrepreneurs with Disabilities Program provides loans of up to $125,000 to entrepreneurs with disabilities.

> Western Economic Diversification Canada
> 1500-9700 Jasper Avenue
> Edmonton, Alberta T5J 4H7
> Telephone: (780) 495-7010
> (www.communityfutures.ca)

Women's Enterprise Initiative Loan Program

Western Economic Diversification, through the local Women's Enterprise Initiative in each western province, provides access to a loan fund for women entrepreneurs seeking financing for start-up or expansion of a business. To qualify the business must have a fully completed business plan and be 51 percent owned or controlled by a woman or women. Loans up to $100,000 are available.

For more information contact the Women's Enterprise Initiative in your province or (www.wd.gc.ca/eng/content/funds/weilp.html)

Aboriginal Business Canada—Youth Entrepreneurship

Canadian status and non-status Indians, Inuit, and Métis individuals between the ages of 18 and 29 are eligible for support with the preparation of business plans, marketing and financing the start-up, expansion, modernization, or acquisition of a commercially viable business. The maximum contribution possible is 60 percent of eligible capital and operating costs to a maximum contribution of $75,000. These contributions are non-repayable.

For more information contact:

> Aboriginal Business Canada
> 235 Queen Street
> Ottawa, Ontario K1A 0H5
> Telephone: (613) 964-4064
> (www.abc.gc.ca)

Business Development Bank of Canada (BDC)

The BDC is a federal Crown corporation that provides a wide range of financial, management counselling, and information services to small business through its broad network of over 80 branches across the country. Its financial services complement those of the private sector by providing funds for business projects that are not available from the commercial banks and other sources on reasonable terms. The BDC will provide term loans for the acquisition of fixed assets, working capital or operating loans, venture loans and venture capital. Its primary focus is on small- and medium-sized businesses operating in knowledge-based, growth-oriented indus-tries and export markets.

BDC offers an extensive variety of management and financial services including:

1. The Micro Business Program which combines personalized management support with term financing of up to $50,000 for existing businesses and up to $25,000 for start-ups.

2. The Young Entrepreneur Financing Program will provide term financing of up to $25,000 and 50 hours of business management support to young start-up entrepreneurs between the ages of 18 and 34 to enable them to get their business off the ground.

3. The Student Business Loans Program is offered through Human Resources Development Canada (HRDC) and offers loans up to $3,000 for student entrepreneurs to operate their own businesses during the summer months.

4. The CIBC/BDC Strategic Alliance (Aboriginal Owned Businesses) is one of a number of strategic alliances entered into by the BDC to focus on the special needs of a number of different markets. The CIBC alliance offers improved access to credit and support services for Aboriginal-owned businesses with total combined financing packages of up to $500,000.

For further information on these and other programs contact:

Head Office
Business Development Bank of Canada
5 Place Ville-Marie
Suite 400
Montreal, Quebec H3B 5E7
Telephone: Toll-free 1-888-463-6232
(www.bdc.ca)

Provincial Financial Assistance Programs

Most of the provincial governments provide a range of grants, loans, and other forms of assist-ance to small business. For example, Manitoba offers the Business Start Program that provides a loan guarantee for loans up to $10,000 along with an educational component to assist new entrepreneurs launching their new business. Similarly, Ontario provides the Young Entrepre-neurs Program. It is a financing and business training program operated in conjunction with the Royal Bank for youth 18-29 who are not attending school full-time and are interested in starting and operating a business in the province. Upon completion of the Young Entrepreneurs Busi-ness Training component, the program will provide them with a loan of up to $7,500 at prime plus 2%.

The number of these programs is much too extensive to discuss here, but you can obtain specific information on the programs offered in your province by contacting the appropriate government department listed among the Some Useful Contacts section (see page 330).

For More Information

For detailed information on specific federal or provincial programs, you might check the Industry Canada Strategis Web site at (strategis.ic.gc.ca/SSG/so01884e.html), contact your local Canada Business Services Centre, or check out one of the following publications at your local library.

Your Guide to Government Financial Assistance for Business
    Productive Publications
    P.O. Box 7200, Station A
    Toronto, Ontario, M5W 1X8
    Telephone: (416) 483-0634

Government Assistance Programs: A Practical Handbook
    CCH Canadian Ltd.
    6 Garamond Court
    Don Mills, Ontario, M3C 1Z5
    (www.ca.cch.com)

Government Assistance Programs and Subsidies (GAPS)
    Canada Pack
    P.O. Box 358
    Richmond Hill, Ontario, L4C 4Y6
    Telephone: (800) 667-6166

Venture Capital

Venture capital involves equity participation in a start-up or growing business situation. Conventional venture capital companies, however, really don't offer much opportunity for firms still in the concept or idea stage. These investors are generally looking for investment situations in proven firms requiring in excess of $1,000,000 and on which they can earn a 40 to 50 percent annual return. While these companies will often accept high-risk situations, most new venture start-ups don't meet their primary investment criteria. There are, however, a number of venture capital firms that may be prepared to consider smaller investments.

A number of them are listed in the Some Useful Contacts appendix at the back of this book. However, keep in mind that of 100 proposals considered by a typical venture capital firm, only four or five are selected for investment purposes. Therefore, the probability of receiving any financial assistance from this source is very slim. For more information, however, you can contact the:

    Canadian Venture Capital Association
    234 Eglinton Avenue East
    Suite 301
    Toronto, Ontario, Canada M4P 1K5
    Telephone: (416) 487-0519
    (www.cvca.ca)

Dilbert reprinted by permission of United Feature Syndicate, Inc.

A new business start-up probably has a better chance of obtaining equity capital from small, private venture capitalists — often called "angels" — or provincially supported venture capital programs. There may be doctors, dentists, lawyers, accountants, and other individuals within your community whom you can approach for investment funds. Many of these people may be looking for situations where they can invest small sums (less than $50,000) with the possibility of earning a larger return than that offered by more-conventional investments, and they are often prepared to invest in start-up situations.

A number of communities and organizations have programs to bring entrepreneurs together with private investors. York University and the MIT Alumni Club of Toronto as well as other organizations sponsor "enterprise forums" in which small companies get an opportunity to tell their story before a group of prospective investors and other experts. The Economic Innovation & Technology Council of the Province of Manitoba periodically sponsors the Invest Manitoba Venture Showcase where local firms who need capital and have a preliminary business plan get the opportunity to make a 10-minute presentation to an audience of prospective investors and others in the community who provide business financing (www.eitc.mb.ca/invest).

Similarly, the federal government started the Canadian Community Investment Program (CCIP) in 1996 as a means to improve access to risk capital for small- and medium-sized firms in smaller communities located some distance from the country's major financial centres. Each of the 22 demonstration projects across the country from Penticton, B.C. to Mount Pearl, Nfld. have developed various innovative strategies aimed at facilitating access to risk capital for their smaller firms. These include arranging investor forums, pre-screening proposals they receive before presenting them to investors, and making their entrepreneurs more investor-ready by offering coaching services and specific seminars (strategis.ic.gc.ca/growth).

Leon Rudanycz, who is profiled in Entrepreneurs in Action #24, is a typical "angel." He had a very successful business of his own, sold it, and used some of the proceeds to invest in other people's ideas. These investments gave him a way to keep involved, to continue to participate in the growth and development of these businesses, to contribute to major company decisions, and an opportunity to make a good financial return on his investments.

Obtaining money from private venture capital sources, however, may pose certain problems for you. You will probably have to give up at least partial ownership and control of your business. In addition, venture capitalists usually have limited resources, so additional funds may not be available if required later. Finally, as amateur investors, these people may not have the patience to wait out the situation if things don't work out as quickly as you originally planned.

Additional Sources of Financing

Personal Credit Cards

The credit limit extended by financial institutions on personal credit cards can provide you with ready access to a short-term loan but usually at interest rates that are considerably higher than more conventional financing (upwards of 18-22 percent). There may be occasions, however, where other sources of working capital are not available and drawing upon the personal line of credit associated with your cards may be the only source of funds available to sustain your business. This can be risky since you are personally liable for the expenditures on the card even though they may have been made for business purposes but it may be useful if you are expecting a major payment or other injection of cash into the business within a few days.

24

Looks Like an Angel

How do you find an angel? You might hear about him from your lawyer, from an investment company or from somebody at a cocktail party.

"You'd hear that Leon had a business and sold it, and invested in a couple of other ones successfully and has some money to invest," says Leon Rudanycz, a typical contributor to the largely unmeasured pool of informal investment capital that nurtures budding young companies.

Rudanycz, who has degrees in law and engineering, started up a computer distributing company in the mid-'80s. Now called Tech Data Canada Inc., it's one of the country's largest high-tech distributors. Rudanycz sold out, then became an angel by investing some of the proceeds in two other fledgling computer companies.

"Both were started out of people's homes, very lean and mean. I ended up selling my interest in both companies — one within four years, the other three. But they were both profitable from day one."

That's not always the case, and most venture capitalists make their money back when they take the company public, usually seeking an annual return of 30%-40%. In the crapshoot of angel investing, only a few ventures hit the big time, so the winners have to make up spectacularly for the many losers.

"Angel investing, by its nature, is less formal, involves smaller sums of money and usually does not involve a full-time position in the company," says Rudanycz. "It's generally more in the $100,000 range."

Carleton University has carried out the most extensive research into Canada's informal investment market, conducting a survey of 279 angels.

"The investors were found to be significantly more wealthy than most Canadians ... and occupy the top one percentile of wealth among Canadian households," says the Carleton report.

In plumbing the angel psychology, the research found that "investors tend to be men with an internal locus of control, very high needs for achievement and dominance."

Almost 90% expected to serve on a board of directors or advisers when investing. A third of them participate directly as an operating principal. And nearly two-thirds also stipulate some sort of operating covenants in the form of periodic reports, authorization of cash disbursements over a certain amount, and control of salaries and dividends.

Rudanycz fits the mould perfectly. "I demand a seat on the board, cheque-signing authority along with the owner, a good handle on the accounting and a hand in major decisions," he says.

His two subsequent high-tech investments were made in the form of a secured loan, and the shares were simply "the kicker, the bonus. I don't always do that, though." For example, Rudanycz says he's considering a straight equity investment in a clothing manufacture and design business. He'd get a piece of the action for a relatively measly $10,000.

"Projected sales in the first year are $100,000 and probably a million in the third, and for them this $10,000 is pivotal," says Rudanycz, describing a deal that's well beneath the threshold of the mainstream venture capital industry.

Excerpted from Gord MacLaughlin, "Divine Intervention," *The Financial Post*, May 6, 1995, p. 7. Reprinted with permission.

Suppliers Inventory Buying Plans

In some industries one way of obtaining working capital may be through supplier's financing. Suppliers may be prepared to extend payment terms to 60, 90, or even 120 days for some customers. Other suppliers may offer floor plan financing or factoring options to help their dealers finance inventory purchases, usually in advance of the peak selling season. In addition, many suppliers offer discounts off the face value of their invoice (typically 2 percent for payment within 10 days) or penalize slow paying customers with interest charges (often $1^{1}/_{2}$ percent a month). These programs can impact your financing requirements.

Leasing vs. Buying

In competitive equipment markets, specialized leasing and finance companies will arrange for the lease of such items as expensive pieces of equipment, vehicles, copiers, and computers. Leasing, often with an option to buy, rather than purchasing can free up your scarce capital for investment in other areas of your business. While the interest rates charged on the lease contract may be somewhat higher than you might pay through the bank, the lease expenses are usually fully deductible from your taxable income. A lease contract will fix your cost of having the equipment for a fixed term and may provide the flexibility to purchase the equipment at a later date at a predetermined price.

Leasehold Improvements

When locating your business in rented premises it is usually necessary to undertake a number of leasehold improvements in order to make the premises appropriate to your needs. Installing new electrical outlets, adding additional partitions and walls, laying carpet, painting, installing fixtures, and similar modifications can add considerably to the cost of launching your business. Sometimes it may be possible to get the landlord of your location to assist in making these improvements, particularly if there is a lot of other space available to rent. The landlord or property manager may agree to provide a portion (an allowance of a dollar amount per square foot of space) or cover all of your leasehold improvement in return for a longer-term lease (typically three to five years). Reducing your initial expenditures in this way can reduce the start-up cash and equity you require to launch your business, even though you will be paying for these improvements in your monthly rent over the course of the lease.

Advance Payment From Customers

It may be possible to negotiate a full or partial payment from some customers in advance to help finance the costs of taking on their business. In some industries, construction for example, it is customary to receive a partial payment at certain defined stages during the course of the project rather than waiting until completion. These payments can reduce the cash needs of running your business. Any work that involves special orders or custom designs for products specifically tailored to the requirements of one customer should require a significant deposit or full payment in advance.

With this extensive number of alternatives available to you as potential sources of financing, it may be useful for you to give some thought to the range of possibilities you might tap into in putting together the start-up requirements for your new venture. Figure 10.1 provides a framework for you to identify how much money you think you will need to launch your business and where you think that financing might possibly come from: your personal resources; friends, relations and other personal contacts; lending agencies; grant programs and other sources that may be available to you.

Evaluating Your Ability to Secure Financing

An important aspect of your financial condition is your ability to obtain financing. When seeking a loan, it is wise to shop around for the best available terms. In preparing to approach a banker regarding a loan, there are several suggestions you should keep in mind to increase your probability of getting the funds:

- Don't just drop in on your bank manager; make an appointment.
- Start your presentation by briefly describing your business and the exact reason you require a loan.

FIGURE 10.1   WHERE WILL YOU GET THE MONEY?

Starting a business usually requires some money. As we have pointed out in this Stage, there are any number of sources from which this financing can be obtained. You may need to give some thought to approximately how much money you think you will need to launch your business and just where you feel you will be able to obtain it. Completing a form like Figure 10.1 will give you a good estimate of roughly what your start-up financial requirements are likely to be.

How much money do you think you will need to launch your business? $ _____

Where can you get the funds?

SOURCE	POSSIBLE AMOUNT	
Personal Sources		
Cash	$ _____	
Stocks/bonds	_____	
Mutual Funds	_____	
Term Certificates	_____	
RRSPs	_____	
Cash Value of Life Insurance	_____	
Other Investments _____	_____	
Real Estate	_____	
Vehicles	_____	
Other Assets _____	_____	
Credit Card Limits	_____	
Other Personal Sources	_____	
Total Available from Personal Sources		$ _____
Personal contacts		
Family Members	$ _____	
Friends	_____	
Colleagues and Acquaintances	_____	
Partners	_____	
Other Private Investors _____	_____	
Total Available from Personal Contacts		$ _____
Lending Agencies		
Chartered Banks	$ _____	
Business Development Bank	_____	
Caisse Populaires and Credit Unions	_____	
Finance Companies	_____	
Government Agencies	_____	
Other Lending Agencies _____	_____	
Total Available from Lending Agencies		$ _____
Grant Programs		
Federal Government Programs	$ _____	
Provincial Government Programs	_____	
Municipal Programs	_____	
Other _____	_____	
Total Available from Grants		$ _____
Other Sources		
Suppliers Credit	$ _____	
Customers	_____	
Others _____	_____	
Total Available from Other Sources		$ _____
TOTAL AVAILABLE FROM ALL SOURCES		$ _____

- Be prepared to answer any questions your banker may have. He or she wants to determine how well you really understand your business. If you can't answer certain questions, explain why and say when you will be able to provide the information.

- Be prepared to discuss collateral and other security you may be required to provide.

- If your business is currently operating, invite the banker to stop by to see it first-hand.

- Ask when you can expect a reply to your request. If there is a delay, inquire whether there is additional information you need to provide.

A recent issue of *PROFIT* magazine asked entrepreneurs, bankers, and financial consultants their most successful time-tested secrets for getting the best from your banker. Here are their suggestions:

- **Know what your banker is looking for.** Before you set foot inside a bank, you should understand the ground rules of credit. Banks are not in the business of financing risk. Before they sign on the dotted line they need evidence you have a comprehensive plan and the management skills to successfully implement it. Ask yourself the question, "If I were a banker, would I lend money to me?" The bank needs to be reassured that you can repay your loan. The bank will also look for a strong base of equity investment in the company already. Don't expect the bank to invest in something you wouldn't invest in yourself. To reduce its risk the bank will want some form of collateral security. In many cases, the bank will require collateral worth two or three times the amount of the loan.

- **Don't "tell" your banker, "show him."** Don't just tell your banker about the great new product you have devised. Bring it or a prototype of it along to your banker and demonstrate what makes it so great. Bring in a sample of whatever it is you plan to sell and let them see it, taste it or try it firsthand.

- **Interview your banker.** There are no good banks, only good bankers. Be prepared to shop around. Make certain you are dealing with the right person and the right branch for you. Visit at least three different banks before making a decision. Ask your accountant, lawyer, customers, or suppliers for a referral.

- **Passion makes perfect.** The most persuasive thing an entrepreneur can do when he or she is negotiating a loan is to show how much passion they have for what they are doing. You should try to present the attitude that you are prepared to do everything possible to make the business succeed.

- **Ask for more money than you need.** One of the worst mistakes you can make is to not consider your future requirements when calculating the size of the loan or the line of credit you think you will need. If you have to go back to the bank in five or six months to ask for an increase, the bank is going to be very concerned. It reflects badly on your ability to plan and you are also making extra work for the bank that could be reflected in extra charges for your loan.

- **Get your banker involved in your business.** Invite your banker over, at least every six months, even if it's just for coffee. Make time to get to know your banker. Get them involved and ask them for advice. Take advantage of opportunities to network with bankers and their colleagues. If the bank holds a reception, or open house, make an effort to attend.

- **Increase your credit when you don't need it.** Many entrepreneurs only begin looking for outside financing when their own resources are tapped out. You should start to begin sourcing funds at least 12 months before you need it. Advanced planning will give you time to adequately explore all your options, meet with several banks, and ultimately work out the best deal for your business.

- **Make professional introductions.** Introduce your lawyer and your accountant to your banker. Make sure your accountant gets the bank's proposal outlining the terms and conditions of your loan or line of credit.

- **If all else fails, keep looking.** Finding the money to start or expand a business is hard work. Most entrepreneurs have been turned down many times for financing. The key is continuing to pursue every available means of securing the capital you need.[2]

A financial institution may turn down your loan application for any of a number of reasons, and it is important that you ask what they are. This knowledge may help you in future attempts to secure funding. Some of the most frequent reasons why a loan application can be rejected are as follows:

1. The business idea might be considered ill advised or just too risky.

2. You may not have offered sufficient collateral. Lenders want some assurance that they will be able to recover most or all of their money should you default on the payments.

3. The lender may feel there is insufficient financial commitment on your part.

4. You have not prepared a comprehensive and detailed business plan.

5. Your reason for requesting the loan is unclear or not acceptable to the lender. It is important that you specify the intended application of the requested funds and that this application be outlined in detail. This outline should also show your planned schedule for the repayment of the loan.

6. You do not appear confident, enthusiastic, well-informed, or realistic enough in your objectives. The lender's assessment of your character, personality, and stability are important considerations in their evaluation of your loan application.

The worksheet shown in Figure 10.2 will allow you to assess some of the critical factors that may affect your ability to secure external funding. It will also give you some indication of what aspects of your personal character, development of your business plans, or quality of the basic idea underlying your new venture could be improved. On the worksheet, indicate your assessment of your personal situation on each of the indicated factors as honestly as you can. How do you rate? Could some factors be improved on? What can you do to strengthen these areas, or how might you overcome this negative factor?

One question you should consider is, "How much can I possibly lose on my venture should it fail?" The losses in some types of businesses can wipe out virtually all of the funds you have invested or personally guaranteed. This tends to be true in situations like a financial planning and counselling business, a travel agency, or a hair salon, in which very little property or equipment is owned by the business. In other situations, such as manufacturing, construction, or real estate, there is usually an opportunity to sell the assets solely or partially owned by the business to recover at least part of your initial investment.

The way to explore this question is to consider alternative scenarios for different ways in which the business might fail and estimate the liquidation value of any residual assets. To the extent that this value falls short of the initial cost of those assets less any outstanding claims, you could lose that amount of money plus the opportunity cost of the time and effort you spent in trying to develop the business.

---

[2] Adapted from David Menzies, *Getting the Best From Your Bank*, PROFIT: *The Magazine for Canadian Entrepreneurs*, November, 1998, pp. 26-32. Reprinted with permission.

FIGURE 10.2   LOAN APPLICATION ASSESSMENT WORKSHEET

Assessment Factor	Poor 1	2	Good 3	Excellent 4	5
Personal credit rating	___	___	___	___	___
Capacity to pay back loan from personal assets if business fails	___	___	___	___	___
Collateral to pay back loan from personal assets if business fails	___	___	___	___	___
Character (as perceived in the community)	___	___	___	___	___
Commitment (your personal investment of time, energy, and money)	___	___	___	___	___
Clarity and completeness of your business plan	___	___	___	___	___
Viability of business concept (e.g., moderate risk)	___	___	___	___	___
Personal experience in the proposed business	___	___	___	___	___
Successful experience in your own business	___	___	___	___	___
Balanced management team available	___	___	___	___	___
Suitability of your personality to the pressures and responsibilities of the business	___	___	___	___	___

What can you do to improve the weak areas (where you have rated yourself 1 or 2)?

_____

_____

_____

_____

From D. A. Gray, *The Entrepreneur's Complete Self-Assessment Guide* (Vancouver: International Self-Counsel Press Ltd., 1986), p. 123.

Protecting Your Investment

One way to reduce some of the financial risks associated with your new venture is to obtain a *comprehensive insurance package*, one specifically designed to meet your business' protection requirements.

There are a number of different types of insurance you should consider obtaining for your business and discuss with your agent in arranging an appropriate program:

1. *General liability insurance* covers your liability to customers injured on your premises or off your premises by a product you have sold to them.
2. *Business premises insurance* will protect your business premises and equipment from loss due to fire, theft, and other perils.
3. *Business use vehicle insurance* must be obtained for cars and other vehicles used in the conduct of your business.
4. *Business interruption or loss-of-income insurance* will enable you to continue to pay the bills if your business should be closed down by damage due to fire, flood, or other catastrophe.

5. *Disability or accident and sickness insurance* can continue to provide you with a source of income if you should become seriously sick or disabled and unable to continue to run your business for a period of time.

6. *Key person insurance* can protect your business against the death of its key personnel. It is life insurance purchased by the business with the business being the sole beneficiary.

7. *Credit Insurance* protects you from extraordinary bad debt losses due to a customer going out of business.

8. *Surety and fidelity bonds* protect you from the failure of another firm or individual fulfilling its contractual obligations.

9. *Partnership insurance* can protect you against suits arising from actions taken by other partners in your business.

10. *Workers' compensation* provides coverage to your employees for compensation they receive due to illness or injuries related to their employment.

This kind of program won't protect you from *all* the risks associated with running your business, but it will provide you with some comfort against unpredictable occurrences in several areas that could threaten the survival of your venture.

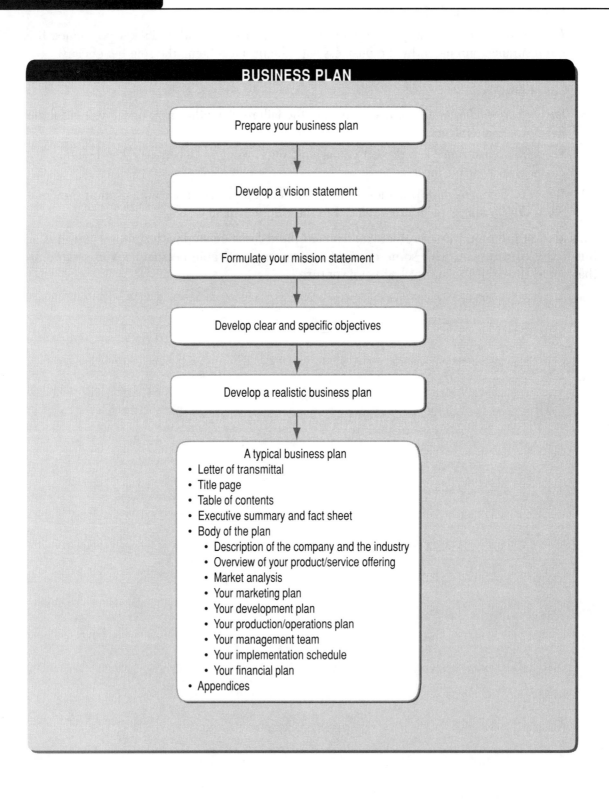

BUSINESS PLAN

Prepare your business plan

Develop a vision statement

Formulate your mission statement

Develop clear and specific objectives

Develop a realistic business plan

A typical business plan
- Letter of transmittal
- Title page
- Table of contents
- Executive summary and fact sheet
- Body of the plan
  - Description of the company and the industry
  - Overview of your product/service offering
  - Market analysis
  - Your marketing plan
  - Your development plan
  - Your production/operations plan
  - Your management team
  - Your implementation schedule
  - Your financial plan
- Appendices

Preparing Your Business Plan

The final stage in building a dream for a new venture of your own is developing your business plan. A *business plan* is a written document that describes all aspects of your business venture — your basic product or service, your prospective customers, the competition, your production and marketing methods, your management team, how the business will be financed, and all the other things necessary to implement your idea. It might be called the "game plan" of your business.

Business Planning — The "Big Picture"

Why Consider the "Big Picture"?

When you start your business you will find that there are many things that happen that you didn't expect, or didn't work out the way you expected. Don't worry. Your experience in this regard won't be unique. This happens to almost everyone. What is important is for you to be prepared for this to happen and ready to make adjustments. In making these changes it is important that you don't lose sight of what it is that you are really trying to do. This means that you need to keep the "Big Picture" in mind. The "Big Picture" is brought together in the business planning process.

The Steps in the Business Planning Process

The business planning process focuses on the future. It enables you to relate what you wish to achieve to what your business concept or idea can deliver. It entails working your way through each of the following steps in a logical and sequential way:

1. Develop a Vision Statement

A *Vision Statement* focuses on the *what* of your business. Your *Vision Statement* should describe your idealized perception of what your business will look like under perfect conditions, if all your goals and objectives have been met. It lays out the "Super Goal" that you would like your business to achieve. The key components of your *Vision Statement* will be:

- The name of your planned business venture

- The product/service offering you plan to provide
- The target market(s) you intend to serve

Your *Vision Statement* should be short (a sentence or two). It should also be easy to understand and easy to remember.

For example, a typical *Vision Statement* for a new sporting goods retailer might be:

"The Hockey House plans to provide a wide range of hockey-related products and services to casual skaters, minor hockey players, community clubs and organizations, and competitive hockey teams and players."

2. Formulate a Mission Statement

A *Mission Statement* focuses on the *how* of your business. It defines the purpose of your venture. It outlines the reason for the existence of your business and provides some understanding of how your business will be operated. It is, in fact, the "Super Strategy" of your business. The key components of your *Mission Statement* will describe:

- What your business will do
- Its market focus, niche, or particular image
- Your planned location and the geographic market served
- How you plan to grow the business
- Your sustainable uniqueness or what will distinguish your business from others and will continue to do so on a long-term basis

Your *Mission Statement* should be a series of short phrases that addresses each of these elements. For example, a *Mission Statement* for The Hockey House might state:

"The Hockey House will provide a broad range of skates, sticks, pads, sweaters, and other related hockey equipment and services intended to meet the requirements of ice and in-line hockey players at all levels of ability; from beginners to semi-professional and professionals. It will also sell related supplies and equipment such as goal nets and timers with a view to being the one-stop shop for hockey in Manitoba and northwestern Ontario. It will sell to individuals, teams, and community clubs through a retail outlet located adjacent to a major hockey complex in Winnipeg but will also produce a four-colour catalogue and call personally on groups in communities outside the city. Our principal competitive edge will be the breadth of selection we can offer and the quality of service we plan to provide."

3. Define the Fundamental Values By Which You Will Run Your Business

Many arguments, particularly in family businesses or partnerships, occur because the members do not share common values, even when they often assume that they do. For a new business to have a good chance of succeeding all principals should agree on a basic set of values by which they will operate. The process of discussing and trying to achieve agreement on these values is likely to identify points of difference that should be addressed before the business is started. This process can be conducted in two steps. Step 1 requires you and any other principals associated with the business to define their own personal values. Step 2 consolidates the common values by which the business will be operated.

An example of a statement of business values might look like the following:

"In conducting our business, we will implement our Vision by conducting our affairs so that our actions provide evidence of the high value we place on:

Integrity *by dealing honestly with our customers, employees, suppliers, and the community*

Responsibility *by taking into account the environment in which we do business, community views, and the common good*

Profitability by being conscious that an appropriate level of profit is necessary to sustain the business and allow our values to continue to be observed

Value by providing quality products that are recognized as delivering value for money

Employees by providing quality, equitable opportunities for development in a healthy workplace, with appropriate rewards"

4. Set Clear and Specific Objectives

Setting objectives for your business provides you with yardsticks with which to measure your ability to achieve your Vision. Objectives define measurable targets whose achievement can also contribute directly to the successful accomplishment of the mission of your business. Unlike "Goals," which provide a broad direction for your business, "Objectives" provide you with the means to measure directly the performance of your business.

Business objectives usually relate to such issues as:

- the return on investment the business should achieve
- a desired level of market position or market share
- projected stages of technological development
- specific levels of financial performance.

To be effective an objective should:

- refer to a specific outcome, not an activity
- be measurable
- be realistic and achievable based on the actual capabilities of the business
- contain a specific time deadline

For example, a reasonable set of objectives for The Hockey House might be:

1. *To generate $XXXX in sales by the end of year one*
2. *To achieve $YYY in after tax profits in year one*
3. *To increase inventory turnover from X times to Y times during year one.*

Figure 11.1 outlines a framework that will enable you to develop the "Big Picture" for your business.

5. Making It Happen! Develop a Realistic Business Plan.

Your business plan is the most important business document you will ever prepare and it is also probably the most difficult. It takes a lot of time, research, self-discipline, and commitment to complete properly and is not a lot of fun. However, regardless of whether you intend to start a small, part-time business in the basement of your home or launch a sophisticated, high-growth venture, you still need a business plan.

Your business plan is the culmination of all your self-evaluation, ideas, research, analysis, assessment, round-table discussions, bull sessions, schemes, and daydreams. It lays out for everyone to see precisely where you are now, where you are going, and how you plan to get there. It presents everything about you and what you intend to do — your goals and objectives, opportunities and threats facing you, your business strengths and weaknesses, and so on. It is a comprehensive but concise disclosure of all aspects of your business venture.

How you define your business plan, however, affects your approach to writing it. If you view it as a very complex and boring task, your plan will come across that way to any reader. As a result, many business plans are dry, rambling, and highly technical because the entrepreneurs behind them see them largely as some sort of formal academic exercise.

Your business plan should be viewed as a selling document, not unlike a piece of sales literature you would distribute about your company. Except with your business plan, rather than just promoting a particular product or service you are selling the whole company as a package. If you are really excited about your company and the idea upon which it is based, it should come through in your business plan. Your plan should convey to readers the excitement and promise that you feel about your venture.

FIGURE 11.1 DEVELOPING THE "BIG PICTURE"

1. DEVELOP YOUR VISION STATEMENT

   a. Write short phrases to describe each of the three elements in your Vision Statement:
   - the name of your planned venture
   - your product/service offering
   - the target market(s) you plan to serve

   b. Combine these phrases into a single sentence

   _____

   _____

   _____

   _____

   _____

2. FORMULATE YOUR MISSION STATEMENT

   a. Write short phrases to describe each of the following elements of your business:
   - what your business will do
   - its market focus, niche, or particular image
   - its planned location and geographic market served
   - how growth of the business will be achieved
   - your sustainable uniqueness or distinguishing characteristics

   b. Combine these phrases into short, linked sentences.

   _____

   _____

   _____

   _____

   _____

   _____

3. DEFINE THE FUNDAMENTAL VALUES BY WHICH YOUR BUSINESS WILL BE RUN

Step 1   Personal Values

Have each principal involved in the business complete the following framework for *five* values that they hold to be personally important.

   a. *Value:* Express as a single word _____

   What: A brief explanation of what the word means to you. _____

   _____

   _____

   Why? Outline why it is important that the business operate this way to you. _____

   _____

   _____

   b. *Value:* Express as a single word _____

What: A brief explanation of what the word means to you. _____

_____

_____

Why? Outline why it is important that the business operate this way to you. _____

_____

_____

c. *Value:* Express as a single word _____

   What: A brief explanation of what the word means to you. _____

_____

_____

   Why? Outline why it is important that the business operate this way to you. _____

_____

_____

d. *Value:* Express as a single word _____

   What: A brief explanation of what the word means to you. _____

_____

_____

   Why? Outline why it is important that the business operate this way to you. _____

_____

_____

e. *Value:* Express as a single word _____

   What: A brief explanation of what the word means to you. _____

_____

_____

   Why? Outline why it is important that the business operate this way to you. _____

_____

_____

Step 2   Values by Which the Business Will Be Managed

Complete Step 2 from the information provided by each of the principals in Step 1. Include only values that were *common to all principals*. Others should only be included after discussion, negotiation, and consensus among all individuals. Since some values will differ, it is necessary for all parties to agree which will be the common values used to guide the operations of the business. This list should contain five or six values at a maximum and it is important that they are compatible with each other. Each principal will then have to decide whether they will be able to work in a business where, perhaps, only some, or none of their personal values will be given expression.

a. *Value:* _____

   What: _____

_____

_____

_____

   Why? _____

_____

_____

_____

continued

Developing the "Big Picture" — continued

   b. *Value:* _____

      What: _____

      _____

      _____

      _____

      Why? _____

      _____

      _____

      _____

   c. *Value:* _____

      What: _____

      _____

      _____

      _____

      Why? _____

      _____

      _____

      _____

   d. *Value:* _____

      What: _____

      _____

      _____

      _____

      Why? _____

      _____

      _____

      _____

   e. *Value:* _____

      What: _____

      _____

      _____

      _____

      Why? _____

      _____

      _____

      _____

4. DEFINE YOUR OBJECTIVES

The business' Vision will be achieved when the following objectives have been attained:

   a. Objective _____

   b. Objective _____

   c. Objective _____

   d. Objective _____

   e. Objective _____

Notice in Entrepreneurs in Action #25 the time and effort Kent Groves dedicated to the development of his business plan. He spent over a year researching the mail-order industry, studying the competition, and asking questions of people who were experts in the business. Then, with the assistance of an accountant, he wrote his "road map" to guide him through every aspect of the implementation of his business. With the plan, he was also able to win the confidence of a banker who provided him with the necessary line of credit to carry his seasonal business over its slow periods. His business plan has become a combined operations manual/corporate bible that can be continually referred to so that he knows if, in fact, the business is evolving as he had originally anticipated.

25   ENTREPRENEURS IN *ACTION*

Business Plans: The Lies We Tell Our Bankers?

Some business people call them "the lies we tell our bankers." In this economy, however, a company looking for credit must put a lot more than creative writing in its business plan.

Kent Groves, president of catalogue retailer Maritime Trading Co. of Falmouth, N.S. and a former Nutrilawn International manager who spent a lot of time approving franchises, knows the importance of business plans. "Some of the best plans I saw were put together by people who totally ignored them once the loan was approved. And their franchises were in trouble."

Groves took a year to research the mail-order industry, studying catalogues, trade magazines and reports, and asking questions of industry experts. Then, with an accountant, he spent six weeks writing what he calls a "road map to guide you through every aspect of your operations."

The result: a 68-page plan with 16 appendices. Groves' Rand-McNally approach to mapping business highways offers an executive summary, mission statement ("we are the leader in the direct marketing of the highest quality Maritime products in the world"), profile, industry overview, and bibliography. And he provided details on sales and marketing, operations, and financing. "It helped to have an accountant who would say, 'Those figures don't make sense'," says Groves. "She asked the hard questions."

Most of Groves' efforts were geared to winning a line of credit — essential for a firm that makes all its money at Christmas. But the effort proved frustrating: MTC's application was rejected by Scotiabank, CIBC, and Hongkong Bank. The setback soured Groves: "The banks advertise 'We support small business.' Yeah, until you need money. What a crock!"

After moving to Nova Scotia full-time in June, Groves approached the Royal Bank in Halifax. There he met account manager Earl Covin, who got excited by his plan. "It was a breath of fresh air," says Covin. "I didn't have to do a lot of background work. It had more detail than most bankers ever expect, and it was very realistic." Once past the collateral hurdle — Groves' father helped out — the bank approved a $75,000 credit line in a day.

Beyond winning financial support, MTC's business plan has become a combined operations manual/corporate bible. Says Groves, "We continually check our expenses and they're right on track. We know where we stand." So when he saw catalogue costs coming in 25% below projections, he knew he could boost marketing spending 20%.

More importantly, revenue projections are also on budget. Another catalogue company, using one of the same mailing lists as Groves, received a 1.5% response rate — "dead on" for MTC's projections. MTC forecast an operating deficit of $49,200 at the end of September; the actual amount was $45,000. With his catalogues just hitting the market in October, Groves still expects sales to reach $100,000 by Dec. 31.

Like most road maps, MTC's business plan allows for dirt roads and detours. "When we stray," says Groves, "we know it and at what capacity we're varying. What's important is flexibility that allows you to make changes."

Source: Allan Lynch writes for PROFIT magazine and is author of *Sweat Equity: Atlantic Canada's New Entrepreneurs*.

Why Develop a Business Plan?

Your business plan can accomplish many things for you and your proposed venture. These can largely be categorized into two basic areas:

1. **For the internal evaluation of your business**, both as a checklist to see that you have covered all the important bases and as a timetable for accomplishing your stated objectives

2. **For external use** in attracting resources and obtaining support for your venture

From an internal perspective, developing a plan forces you to seriously consider the important elements of your venture and the steps you feel are necessary to get it off the ground. Your plan can be used to inform employees about the goals and direction of your business. It lets everyone know how they fit into the organization and what you expect of them. Your plan can also help you develop as a manager. It requires you to deal with problems relating to competitive conditions, promotional opportunities, and other situations that will confront your business.

Externally, your business plan can serve as an effective sales document and is considered by many experts to be the heart of the capital-raising process. Any knowledgeable banker or prospective investor will expect you to be professional in your approach, fully prepared, and armed with a thoroughly researched, well-written business plan when seeking their support. Very little money has been raised for business ideas scribbled on the back of envelopes or on restaurant placemats despite considerable folklore to the contrary.

In the course of attracting external support for your venture a number of people may have occasion to read your plan. These include bankers, suppliers, prospective customers, and potential investors. Each of them will be viewing your business from a slightly different perspective. Bankers, for example, are primarily interested in the business' fixed assets and other available collateral. They want to know if you can pay back their loan at prevailing interest rates. Venture capitalists and other private investors, on the other hand, are more interested in their expected return on investment. They tend to like innovative products and services in growth industries that promise significant returns. These differing viewpoints should be taken into account in developing your plan.

Reprinted with permission of King Features Syndicate.

How Long Should Your Business Plan Be?

Business plans can be broadly categorized into three types: the summary business plan, the full business plan, and the operational business plan.

The Summary Business Plan

Summary business plans commonly run about 10 pages or so; considerably shorter than the 40 or so pages traditional for business plans. Summary business plans have become increasingly popular and accepted for use by early-stage businesses in applying for a bank loan, or they may be all that is required for a small, lifestyle businesses such as a convenience store, home-based business, graphic design company, or consulting firm. A summary business plan may also be sufficient to whet the appetite of friends, relatives, and other private investors who might subsequently receive a copy of the full plan if sufficiently interested.

The Full Business Plan

A full business plan similar to the one you would develop by following the samples at the end of this Stage will likely run from 10 to 40 pages. This is the traditional plan. It covers all the key subjects in enough depth to permit a full exploration of the principal issues. The full business plan is most appropriate when you are trying to raise a substantial amount of external financing or if you are looking for a partner or other major private investors.

The Operational Business Plan

The operational business plan will usually exceed 40 pages in length but is used only infrequently, such as when a business is planning to grow very rapidly and must try to anticipate a wide variety of issues. Or it might be part of an annual process where it is necessary to get into great detail about distribution, production, advertising, and other areas where it is essential for everyone involved with the organization to understand clearly everything that is going on. Traditional business plans that grow to this length should be avoided as they reflect a lack of discipline and focus.

Who Should Write Your Business Plan

You should write your business plan. If someone else develops the business plan for you, it becomes *their* plan, not *yours*. If you are part of a management team, each individual should contribute his or her part to the overall project.

Do not under any circumstances hire someone else to write the plan for you. This doesn't mean that you shouldn't get help from others in compiling information, obtaining licences, permits, patents, and other legal considerations, or preparing your pro forma financial statements — only that the final plan should be written by you and your team.

The people who may be assessing your plan want to know that you see the big picture as it relates to your business and understand all the functional requirements of your company, not that you can hire a good consultant. It is very difficult to defend someone else's work. If you put it together yourself, you have a better understanding and feel for the business. Your business plan should be a personal expression written in your own unique style, though of course it should be professionally done.

How Long Does It Take?

Putting together a business plan does not happen overnight; the process can stretch over several months. Table 11.1 outlines the steps that should be taken to prepare a business plan, and the amount of time it may take to complete each step.

TABLE 11.1 SUGGESTED STEPS IN DEVELOPING YOUR BUSINESS PLAN

Step	Description	Completion Date
1	Decide to go into business for yourself.	
2	Analyze your strengths and weaknesses, paying special attention to your business experience, business education, and desires.	Third week
3	Choose the product or service that best fits your strengths and desires.	Fourth week
4	Research the market for your product or service.	Seventh week
5	Forecast your share of market if possible.	Eighth week
6	Choose a site for your business.	Eighth week
7	Develop your production plan.	Tenth week
8	Develop your marketing plan.	Tenth week
9	Develop your personnel plan.	Twelfth week
10	Decide whether to form a sole proprietorship, a partnership, or a corporation.	Twelfth week
11	Explain the kinds of records and reports you plan to have.	Twelfth week
12	Develop your insurance plan.	Twelfth week
13	Develop your financial plan.	Fifteenth week
14	Write a summary overview of your business plan, stressing its purpose and promise.	Sixteenth week

FIGURE 11.2 FLOWCHART OF THE STEPS IN DEVELOPING A BUSINESS PLAN

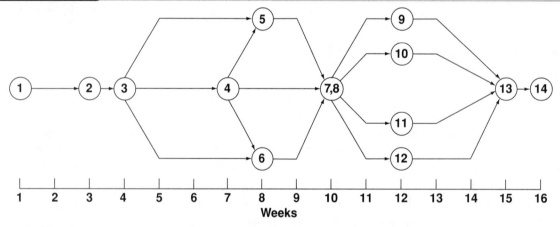

KEY

1. Decide to go into business.
2. Analyze yourself.
3. Pick product or service.
4. Research market.
5. Forecast sales revenues.
6. Pick site.
7. Develop production plan.
8. Develop marketing plan.
9. Develop personnel plan.
10. Decide whether to incorporate.
11. Explain need for records.
12. Develop insurance plan.
13. Develop financial plan.
14. Write summary overview.

Adapted from Nicholas C. Siropolis, *Small Business Management: A Guide to Entrepreneurship*, 2nd ed. (Boston: Houghton Mifflin Co., 1982), pp. 138–141.

The flowchart in Figure 11.2 indicates how all these steps in developing a business plan interrelate. It shows how certain key steps cannot be undertaken until others have been completed. For example, you cannot effectively research the market (step 4) until you have selected a particular product or service idea (step 3). Similarly, until the market has been researched (step 4), a site chosen (step 6), and a revenue forecast prepared (step 5), you can't develop your detailed marketing plan (step 8).

The 16-week time span shown here is only for illustrative purposes — the actual time required to prepare your business plan will vary with the nature of your venture. A plan for a relatively simple, straightforward business might be completed within a few weeks, while a plan for a complex, high-growth new venture could take many months.

What Should Your Plan Contain?

Your business plan is the nuts and bolts of your proposed business venture put down on paper. You will have to decide exactly what information to include, how your plan can be best organized for maximum effectiveness, and what information should be given particular emphasis. All plans, however, require a formal, structured presentation so that they are easy to read and follow and tend to avoid confusion. A number of forms and sample outlines for a business plan are available but virtually all suggest that business plans contain the following components: (1) letter of transmittal, (2) title page, (3) table of contents, (4) executive summary and fact sheet, (5) body, and (6) appendices. The contents of a typical business plan are outlined in figure 11.3. You can use this framework as a guideline to assist you in the development of the plan for your business.

1. Letter of Transmittal

The letter of transmittal officially introduces your business plan to the reader. It explains your reason for writing the plan, gives the title of the plan or the name of your business, and outlines the major features of your plan that may be of interest.

2. Title Page

The title page, or "cover page," of your plan provides identifying information about you and your proposed business. It should include the name, address, and telephone number of the business as well as similar information about yourself. The date the plan was finalized or submitted to the recipient should also be included on the title page.

3. Table of Contents

The table of contents is a list of the major headings and subheadings contained in your plan. It provides the reader with a quick overview of the contents of your plan and allows them to quickly access the particular sections that may be of primary interest to them.

4. Executive Summary and Fact Sheet

The executive summary may be the most important part of your business plan. It must capture the attention of the reader, stimulate interest, and get the reader to keep on reading the rest of your plan. In two or three pages this summary should concisely explain your business' current status; describe its products or services and their benefits to your customers; provide an overview of your venture's objectives, market prospects, and financial forecasts; and, if you are using the plan to raise external financing, indicate the amount of financing needed, how the money is to be used, and the benefits to the prospective lender or investor.

FIGURE 11.3 A TYPICAL BUSINESS PLAN

Business Plan Contents

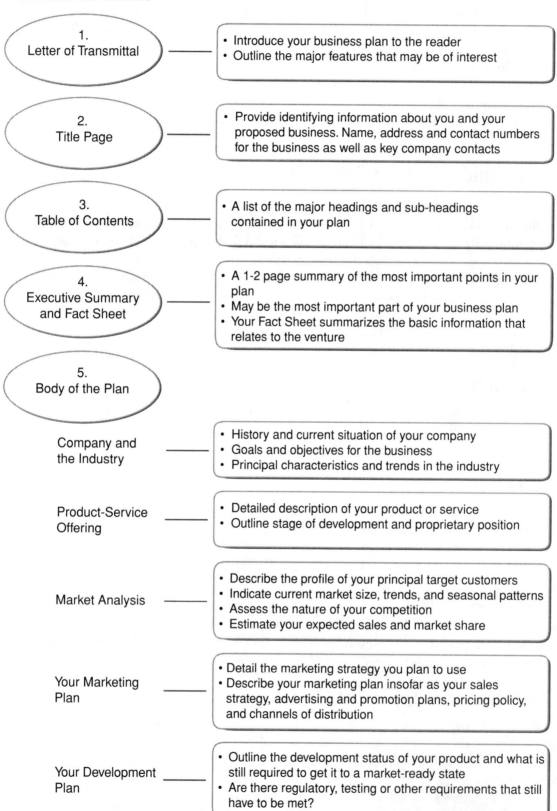

1.
Letter of Transmittal
- Introduce your business plan to the reader
- Outline the major features that may be of interest

2.
Title Page
- Provide identifying information about you and your proposed business. Name, address and contact numbers for the business as well as key company contacts

3.
Table of Contents
- A list of the major headings and sub-headings contained in your plan

4.
Executive Summary and Fact Sheet
- A 1-2 page summary of the most important points in your plan
- May be the most important part of your business plan
- Your Fact Sheet summarizes the basic information that relates to the venture

5.
Body of the Plan

Company and the Industry
- History and current situation of your company
- Goals and objectives for the business
- Principal characteristics and trends in the industry

Product-Service Offering
- Detailed description of your product or service
- Outline stage of development and proprietary position

Market Analysis
- Describe the profile of your principal target customers
- Indicate current market size, trends, and seasonal patterns
- Assess the nature of your competition
- Estimate your expected sales and market share

Your Marketing Plan
- Detail the marketing strategy you plan to use
- Describe your marketing plan insofar as your sales strategy, advertising and promotion plans, pricing policy, and channels of distribution

Your Development Plan
- Outline the development status of your product and what is still required to get it to a market-ready state
- Are there regulatory, testing or other requirements that still have to be met?

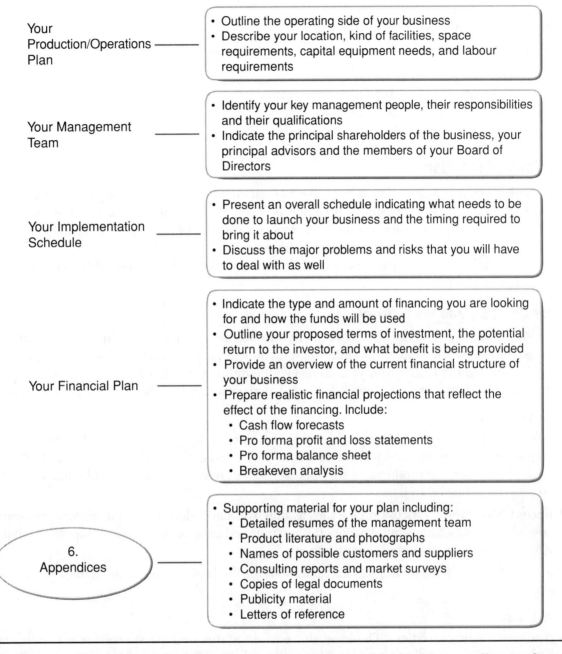

Your Production/Operations Plan
- Outline the operating side of your business
- Describe your location, kind of facilities, space requirements, capital equipment needs, and labour requirements

Your Management Team
- Identify your key management people, their responsibilities and their qualifications
- Indicate the principal shareholders of the business, your principal advisors and the members of your Board of Directors

Your Implementation Schedule
- Present an overall schedule indicating what needs to be done to launch your business and the timing required to bring it about
- Discuss the major problems and risks that you will have to deal with as well

Your Financial Plan
- Indicate the type and amount of financing you are looking for and how the funds will be used
- Outline your proposed terms of investment, the potential return to the investor, and what benefit is being provided
- Provide an overview of the current financial structure of your business
- Prepare realistic financial projections that reflect the effect of the financing. Include:
  - Cash flow forecasts
  - Pro forma profit and loss statements
  - Pro forma balance sheet
  - Breakeven analysis

6. Appendices
- Supporting material for your plan including:
  - Detailed resumes of the management team
  - Product literature and photographs
  - Names of possible customers and suppliers
  - Consulting reports and market surveys
  - Copies of legal documents
  - Publicity material
  - Letters of reference

This summary should give the essence of your plan and highlight its really significant points. In many instances the summary will either sell the reader on continuing to read the rest of the document or convince them to forget the whole thing; the game may be won or lost on the basis of the executive summary.

The fact sheet should appear as a separate page at the back of the executive summary. It summarizes the basic information that relates to your venture:

1. Company name
2. Location and telephone
3. Type of business and industry
4. Form of business organization (proprietorship, partnership, or corporation)
5. Principal product or service line
6. Registered patents or trademarks
7. Number and name of founders/partners/shareholders

8.   Length of time in business
9.   Current and/or projected market share
10.   Funds invested in the business to date and their source
11.   Additional financing required
12.   Proposed terms and payback period
13.   Total value or net worth of the business
14.   Name of business advisors (legal counsel, accountant, others)

5. Body of the Plan

The body of your business plan is by far the longest component, because it presents the detailed story of your business proposition. It should be broken down into major divisions using headings, and each major division divided into sections using subheadings. It is probably better to have too many rather than not enough headings and subheadings.

What follows is a typical overview of the kind of material that should be included in the body of your plan.

Your Company and the Industry

Describe the start-up and background of your business and provide the reader with some context within which to fit all the information you will be providing later in your plan.

Familiarize the reader with your company; the industry within which you will be competing, your understanding of it, and where it is headed; and what opportunities you see for your business.

Your Company

Background   Give the date your business was started, its present form of organization, its location, and pertinent historical information on the firm. Name the founders and other key people, how your key products or services were chosen and developed, and what success the business has achieved to date.

Current Situation   Discuss such issues as how you have identified your market opportunity, assessed the competition, and developed some unique factor or distinctive competence that will make your business stand out from the rest.

Future Plans   Discuss your goals and ambitions for the business and your strategy for achieving them.

The Industry

Principal Characteristics   Describe the current status and prospects for the industry in which your business will operate. How big is the industry? What are its total sales in dollars? In units? What are typical industry standards, gross margins, seasonal patterns, and similar factors?

Major Participants   Identify the major industry participants and describe their role, market share, and other performance measures. What are their principal strengths and weaknesses and how do you feel you will be able to successfully compete in this situation?

Industry Trends   Discuss how you feel the industry will evolve in the future. Is it growing or stable? What do you feel industry sales will be five and ten years from now? What general trends are evident and how is the industry likely to be affected by economic, social, technological, environmental, and regulatory trends?

Your Product/Service Offering

Description   Describe the product or service you plan to sell in detail explaining any unique characteristics or particular advantages. How will features of your product or service give you some advantage over competitors?

Indicate the stage of development your product is at and whether prototypes, working models, or finished production units are available. Include photographs if possible.

Proprietary Position Describe any patents or trademarks you may hold or have applied for, or any licensing agreements or other legal contracts that may provide some protection for your product or service. Are there any regulatory or government-approved standards or requirements your product must meet? How and when do you plan to obtain this certification?

Potential Outline your market opportunity as you see it and explain how you plan to take advantage of it. What are the key success factors in this business and how do you plan to exploit them to your advantage?

Market Analysis

This section of your plan should convince the reader that you thoroughly understand the market for your product or service, that you can deal with the competition and achieve sufficient sales to develop a viable and growing business. You should describe the total market and how you feel it can be broken down into segments. You can then indicate the segment or niche you plan to concentrate on and what share of this business you will be able to obtain.

Your analysis of the market may be based on:

1. Market studies available from private research firms and government departments and agencies

2. Statistics Canada or U.S. Bureau of the Census data

3. Information from trade associations and trade publications

4. Surveys or informal discussions with dealers, distributors, sales representatives, customers, or competitors

This is often one of the most difficult parts of the business plan to prepare, but it is also one of the most important. Almost all other sections of your business plan depend on the sales estimates developed from your market analysis. The outline described in Stage Six can help you in this process.

Target Market and Customers Identify who constitute your primary target markets — individual consumers, companies, health care or educational institutions, government departments, or other groups.

Examine beforehand if these target markets can be segmented or broken down into relatively homogeneous groups having common, identifiable characteristics such as geographic location, age, size, type of industry, or some other factor. Present these facts in the most logical or appropriate format.

Describe the profile of your principal target customers. Who and where are they? What are the principal bases for their purchase decisions? What are their major applications for your product? What principal benefit will they obtain from using your product rather than one of your competitors'?

Identify, if possible, some major buyers who may be prepared to make purchase commitments. If possible, get a purchase order.

Market Size and Trends Estimate the size of the current total market for your product or service in both units and dollars. How are sales distributed among the various segments you identified? Are there any strong weekly, monthly, or seasonal patterns? Ensure you include answers to these questions.

Describe how the market size for each of these segments has changed over the past three to four years in units and dollars. Outline how it is expected to change over the next three to four years.

Include the major factors that have affected past market growth, i.e., socioeconomic trends, industry trends, regulatory changes, government policy, population shifts, etc. What is likely to happen in these areas in the future?

Competition   Identify each of your principal competitors. Make a realistic assessment of each of these firms and their product or service offering. Compare these competing products or services on the basis of price, quality, performance, service support, warranties, and other important features.

Present your evaluation of the market share of each segment by each competitor, their relative profitability, and their sales, marketing, distribution, and production capabilities. How do you see these factors changing in the future?

Estimated Sales and Market Share   Estimate the share of each segment of the market and the sales in units and dollars that you feel you will acquire for each of the next three to five years. This should be developed by month for the next year and annually for each year thereafter. This information can best be presented in tabular form. Indicate on what assumptions you have based these projections.

Your Marketing Plan

Your marketing plan outlines how your sales projections will be achieved. It details the marketing strategy you plan to use to establish your product or service in the marketplace and obtain a profitable share of the overall market. Your marketing plan should describe *what* is to be done, *when* it is to be done, *how* it is to be done, and *who* will do it insofar as your sales strategy, advertising and promotion plans, pricing policy, and channels of distribution are concerned.

Pricing   Summarize the general financial characteristics of your business and the industry at large. What will be typical gross and net margins for each of the products or services you plan to sell? How do these compare with those of other firms in the industry? Provide a detailed breakdown of your estimated fixed, variable, and semivariable costs for each of your various products or services.

Discuss the prices you plan to charge for your product. How do they compare with your major competitors'? Is your gross margin sufficient to cover your transportation costs, selling costs, advertising and promotion costs, rent, depreciation, and similar expenses — and still provide some margin of profit?

Detail the markups your product will provide to the various members of your channel of distribution. How do these compare with those they receive on comparable products? Does your markup provide them with sufficient incentive to handle your product?

Indicate your normal terms of sale. Do these conform to industry norms? Do you plan to offer cash, quantity, or other discounts?

Indicate how long it will take you to break even, basing your opinion on your anticipated cost structure and planned price.

Sales and Distribution   Indicate the methods you will use to sell and distribute your product or service. Do you plan to use your own salaried or commissioned salespeople, rely on manufacturer's agents or other wholesalers and distributors, or utilize a more non-traditional means of distributing your product such as export trading companies, direct mail selling, mail order houses, party plan selling, or other means of selling direct to the final consumer?

If you plan to use your own sales force, describe how large it will be and how it will be structured. Indicate how salespeople will be distributed, who they will call on, how many calls you estimate it will take to get an order, the size of a typical order, how much you estimate a typical salesperson will sell each year, how he or she will be paid, how much he or she is likely to make in a year, and how this compares with the average for the industry.

If you plan to use distributors or wholesalers, indicate how they have been or will be selected, who they are if possible, what areas or territory they will cover, how they will be compensated, credit and collection policies, and any special policies such as exclusive rights, discounts, and cooperative advertising programs.

Indicate any plans for export sales or international marketing arrangements.

Advertising and Promotion Describe the program you plan to use to make consumers aware of your product or service. What consumers are you trying to reach? Do you plan to use the services of an advertising agency? What media do you plan to use — radio, television, newspapers, magazines, billboards, direct mail, coupons, brochures, trade shows, etc. How much do you plan to spend on each medium? When? Which specific vehicles?

Outline any plans to obtain free publicity for your product or company.

Service and Warranty Program Indicate your service arrangements, warranty terms, and method of handling service problems. Describe how you will handle customer complaints and other problems. Will service be handled by the company, dealers and distributors, or independent service centres? How do these arrangements compare with those of your competitors?

Your Development Plan

If your product or service involves some further technical development, the planned extent of this work should be discussed in your business plan. Prospective investors, bankers, and others will want to know the nature and extent of any additional development required, how much it will cost, and how long it will take before your business has a finished, marketable product.

Development Status Describe the current status of your product and outline what still remains to be done in order to make it marketable. Do you presently have only a concept, detailed drawings, a laboratory prototype, a production prototype, or a finished product? Is further engineering work required? Has the necessary tooling to produce the product been adequately developed? Are the services of an industrial designer or other specialist required to refine the product into marketable form?

Costs Indicate how much money has been spent on product development to date and where it has been spent. Present a development budget indicating the additional funds required, how they will be spent, and the timing involved in completing the project.

Proprietary Issues Indicate any patents or trademarks that you own, have, or for which you plan to apply. Are there any regulatory requirements to produce or market the product? Has the product undergone standardized testing through Underwriter's Laboratory, the Canadian Standards Association (CSA), or some other agency? If not, what are your plans? Have you tested the product at all in the marketplace? What was the result?

Your Production/Operations Plan

Your production/operations plan outlines the operating side of your business. It should describe your plant location, the kind of facilities needed, space requirements, capital equipment needed, and your labour requirements.

If your plan is for a manufacturing business, you should also discuss such areas as your purchasing policy, quality control program, inventory control system, production cost breakdown, and whether you plan to manufacture all subcomponents of the product yourself or have some of them produced for you by someone else.

Location Describe the planned location of your business and discuss any advantages or disadvantages of this location in terms of the cost and availability of labour, proximity to customers, access to transportation, energy supplies or other natural resources, and zoning and other legal requirements.

Discuss the characteristics of your location in relation to market size, traffic flows, local and regional growth rates, income levels, and similar market-related factors.

Facilities and Equipment   Describe the property and facilities currently used or that will be required to operate your business. This should include factory and office space, selling space, storage space, property size and location, etc. Will these facilities be leased or purchased? What is the cost and timing of their acquisition?

Detail the machinery and equipment that is required for your manufacturing process. Is this highly specialized or general-purpose equipment? Is it leased or purchased? New or used? What is the cost? What will it cost for equipment setup and facility layout? What is its expected life? Will it have any residual or scrap value?

If possible, provide a drawing of the physical layout of the plant and other facilities.

Manufacturing Plans and Costs   Develop a manufacturing cost outline that shows standard production costs at various levels of operation. Break total costs down into raw material, component parts, labour, and overhead. Indicate your raw material, work-in-process, and finished goods inventory requirements at various sales levels. How will seasonal variations in demand be handled?

Indicate your key suppliers or subcontractors for various raw materials and components. What are the lead times for these materials? Are backup suppliers or other alternatives available?

Outline the quality control procedures you will use to minimize service problems. Do you need any other production control measures?

On the basis of this configuration of facilities and equipment, indicate your production capacity. Where can this be expanded? Do you have any plans to modify existing plant space? What is the timing and cost?

Labour   Describe the number of employees you have or need and their qualifications. Will they be full-time or part-time? Have you developed a job description for each position? What in-house training will be required? How much will each employee be paid? What kinds of pension plan, health insurance plan, profit-sharing plan, and other fringe benefits will be required? Have you registered with the necessary government departments?

Indicate whether your employees will be union or non-union. If employees will be members of a union, describe the principal terms of their contract and when it expires.

Environmental and Other Issues   Indicate any approvals that it may be necessary for you to obtain related to zoning requirements, permits, licences, health and safety requirements, environmental approvals, etc. Are there any laws or regulatory requirements unique to your business? Are there any other legal or contractual matters that should be considered?

Your Management Team

Your management team and your directors are the key to success. You should identify: who your key people are; their qualifications; what they are being paid; who has overall authority; who is responsible for the various functional areas of the business such as sales, marketing, production, research and development, and financial management; and so forth.

In most small businesses there are no more than two or three really key players — including yourself. Concentrate on these individuals, indicating their education, qualifications, and past business achievements. Indicate how they will contribute to the success of the present venture. Don't hire friends, relatives, or other people for key positions who do not have the proper qualifications.

Many external investors are more concerned about the management of the business than the business itself. They invest in the people rather than the project. They will conduct a thorough and exhaustive investigation of each of your key players to determine whether they are the kind of people in which they wish to invest. This portion of your plan should instill confidence in the management of your business in the mind of the reader.

Description of Management Team   Outline the exact duties and responsibilities of each key member of your management team. Prepare a brief résumé of each individual indicating age, marital status, education, professional qualifications, employment experience, and other personal achievements. (You will include a complete, more detailed résumé for each of these individuals in an appendix to your plan.)

Directors Indicate the size and composition of your board of directors. Identify any individuals you are planning to invite to sit on your board. Include a brief statement on each member's background indicating what he or she will bring to the company.

Management and Directors' Compensation List the names of all members of your management team and board of directors and the compensation they will receive in fees or salary. Initially, at least, you and your management team should be prepared to accept modest salaries, perhaps well below what you received in your previous job, if you hope to attract external investors to your business.

Shareholders Indicate the name of each of the individual shareholders (or partners) in your business, the number of shares each owns, the percentage of ownership, and the price paid.

Describe any investors in your business other than your management team and members of your board. How many shares do they have? When were they acquired? What price did they pay?

Summarize any incentive stock option or bonus plans that you have in effect or plan to institute. Also indicate any employment contracts or agreements you may have made with members of your management team.

Professional Advisors Indicate the name and complete address of each of your professional advisors, for example your lawyer, accountant, banker, and management or technical consultants. Disclose any fees or retainers that may have been paid to any of these people.

Implementation Schedule and Risks Associated with the Venture

It is necessary to present an overall schedule indicating the interrelationship among the various events necessary to launch your business and the timing required to bring it about. This is similar to the type of framework in Figure 11.2. A well-prepared schedule demonstrates to external investors that you have given proper thought to where you are going and have the ability to plan. This schedule can be a very effective sales tool.

Your plan should also discuss the major problems and risks you feel you will have to deal with in developing your business.

Milestones Summarize the significant goals that you and your business have already reached and still hope to accomplish in the future. What still needs to be done in order for the business to succeed? Who is going to do these things? When will they be completed?

Schedule Develop a schedule of significant events and their priority for completion. What kind of strategic planning has been done in order to see that things occur as necessary? Have you developed a fallback or contingency position in case things don't come off as you have planned?

Risks and Problems You might start by summarizing the major problems you have already had to deal with and how they were resolved. Were any particularly innovative or creative approaches used in addressing these issues?

Identify the risks your business may be faced with in the future. What are you attempting to do to avoid these? How will you deal with them if they arise? How can their impact on your business be minimized?

Summarize the downside risk. What would happen in the "worst case" scenario? What, if anything, could be salvaged from the business for your investors?

Your Financial Plan

Your financial plan is basic in order to enable a prospective investor or banker to evaluate the investment opportunity you are presenting. The plan should illustrate the current financial status of your business and represent your best estimate of its future operations. The results presented should be both realistic and attainable.

Your financial plan should also describe the type of financing you are seeking, the amount of money you are looking for, how you plan to use these funds in the business, the terms of repayment and desired interest rate, or the dividends, voting rights, and redemption considerations related to the offering of any common or preferred stock.

Funding Requested   Indicate the amount and type (debt or equity) of funding you are looking for. For what do you intend to use the money? How will it be applied in your business — to acquire property, fixtures, equipment, or inventory, or to provide working capital?

Give an overview of the current financial structure of your business. Indicate the level of investment already made in the business and where the funds came from. What effect will the additional capital have on your business in terms of ownership structure, future growth, and profitability?

Outline your proposed terms of investment. What is the payback period and potential return on investment for the lender or investor? What collateral, tax benefit, or other security is being offered?

Current Financial Statements   If your venture is already in operation, you should provide copies of financial statements (profit and loss statement and a balance sheet) for the current year and the previous two years.

Financial Projections   In developing your financial plan, a number of basic projections must be prepared. These should be based on realistic expectations and reflect the effect of the proposed financing. The projections should be developed on a monthly basis for the first year of operation and a quarterly or annual basis for another two to four years. These projections should include the following statements:

1. **Profit and loss forecasts** These pro forma income statements indicate your profit expectations for the next few years of operation of your business. They should be based on realistic estimates of sales and operating costs and represent your best estimate of actual operating results.

2. **Pro forma balance sheets** Your pro forma balance sheet indicates the assets you feel will be required to support your projected level of operations and how you plan to finance these assets.

3. **Projected cash flow statements** Your cash flow forecasts are probably your most important statements, because they indicate the amount and timing of your expected cash inflows and outflows. Typically the operating profits during the start-up of a new venture are not sufficient to finance the business' operating needs. This often means that the inflow of cash will not meet your business' cash requirements, at least on a short-term basis. These conditions must be anticipated in advance so that you can predict cash needs and avoid insolvency.

4. **Breakeven analysis** A breakeven analysis indicates the level of sales and production you will require to cover all your fixed and variable costs. It is useful for you and prospective lenders and investors to know what your breakeven point is and how easy or difficult it will likely be to attain.

An example of each of these statements and a discussion on how to determine the breakeven point for your venture is presented in Stage Seven of this book.

6. Appendices

The appendixes are intended to explain, support, and supplement the material in the body of your business plan. In most cases this material is attached to the back of your plan. Examples of the kind of material that might be included in an appendix are:

1. Product specifications and photographs
2. Detailed résumés of the management team
3. Lists of prospective customers
4. Names of possible suppliers
5. Job descriptions for the management team
6. Consulting reports and market surveys
7. Copies of legal documents such as leases, franchise and licensing agreements, contracts, licences, patent or trademark registrations, and articles of incorporation
8. Letters of reference
9. Relevant magazine, trade journal, and newspaper articles

Conclusion

It is important that your plan make a good first impression. It should demonstrate that you have done a significant amount of thinking and work on your venture. You should ensure your material is presented to prospective investors, lenders, and others in an attractive, readable, and understandable fashion.

To assist you in completing your business plan, Figure 11.4 provides a business plan outline for a retail or service-type business, while Figure 11.5 provides a similar outline for a manufacturing company. There are some differences in the information that should be incorporated into the plan for each type of business, particularly in describing the distribution strategy for the business and detailing the production/operations plan. These need to be specifically taken into account in preparing your plan. These forms are intended for use as a rough draft only. You can then use them as a basis from which to prepare a formal, professional-looking plan on your typewriter or word processor.

Figure 11.6 provides you with an example of a sample business plan for The Darting Lamp Company. This is the business plan for the idea described in Entrepreneurs in Action #8 that enabled Bryce Kumka and Doug Palmer to win the Enterprise Creation Competition at Miami University in Oxford, Ohio in competition with students from universities across North America. It is a good example of a comprehensive and well-written plan.

Figure 11.7 provides a checklist that you can use to assess your plan when it is finished for completeness, clarity and persuasiveness.

The length of your business plan should not exceed 40 double-spaced, typewritten pages, not including appendices. Each section should be broken down into appropriate and clearly identifiable headings and subheadings. Make sure your plan contains no errors in spelling, punctuation, or grammar.

Prepare a number of copies of your plan and number each one individually. Make sure each copy is appropriately bound with a good-quality cover on which the name of your business has been printed or embossed.

FIGURE 11.4   BUSINESS PLAN OUTLINE FOR A RETAIL OR SERVICE FIRM

1. **LETTER OF TRANSMITTAL**
2. **TITLE PAGE**
3. **TABLE OF CONTENTS**
4. **EXECUTIVE SUMMARY**

Fact Sheet

Company name _____

Location and telephone _____

_____

_____

_____

Type of business and industry _____

_____

_____

Form of business organization _____

_____

Principal product or service line _____

_____

_____

Registered patents or trademarks (if any) _____

_____

_____

Names of founders/partners/shareholders _____

_____

_____

Length of time in business (if appropriate) _____

_____

Current and/or projected market share _____

_____

Funds invested in the business to date and their source _____

_____

_____

_____

_____

Additional financing required _____

_____

_____

Proposed terms and payback period _____

_____

_____

_____

Total value or net worth of the business _____

_____

_____

_____

_____

NAMES OF BUSINESS ADVISORS

Legal counsel _____

_____

Accountant _____

_____

Banker _____

_____

Other _____

_____

5. BODY

A. Your Company and the Industry

THE COMPANY

Date business started _____

Location _____

_____

Form of business organization _____

_____

Founders and other key individuals _____

_____

_____

Principal products and services _____

_____

_____

_____

Success the Business Has Achieved to Date

	Estimated Total Annual Market (year)		Company Sales (year)		Market Share (%)
Product/service 1	$_____		$_____		_____
	_____ units		_____ units		_____
Product/service 2	$_____		$_____		_____
(etc.)	_____ units		_____ units		_____

continued

Business Plan Outline (Retail or Service) — continued

Future Goals and Plans

_____

_____

_____

_____

_____

Principal strategy for achieving these goals _____

_____

_____

_____

_____

_____

_____

THE INDUSTRY

Prospects for the Industry

Total Estimated Industry Sales ($)

Product/ Service	Three Years Ago	Two Years Ago	Last Year	This Year	Next Year	In Two Years	In Three Years
1. _____	$_____	$_____	$_____	$_____	$_____	$_____	$_____
2. _____	$_____	$_____	$_____	$_____	$_____	$_____	$_____
3. _____	$_____	$_____	$_____	$_____	$_____	$_____	$_____

(etc.)

General industry standards and performance requirements _____

_____

_____

General trends within the industry and factors likely to affect these trends _____

_____

_____

Major Industry Participants

Name and Location of Competitor	Estimated Sales	Estimated Market Share (%)	Principal Strengths and Weaknesses
_____	$_____	_____	_____
_____			_____
_____	$_____	_____	_____
_____			_____
_____	$_____	_____	_____
_____			_____

Business Plan Outline (Retail or Service) — continued

B. Product/Service Offering

DESCRIPTION OF PRINCIPAL PRODUCTS/SERVICES

Product/Service	Description	Unique Features	Stage Of Development
_____	_____	_____	_____
_____	_____	_____	_____
_____	_____	_____	_____
_____	_____	_____	_____
_____	_____	_____	_____

Patents or trademarks held or applied for _____

_____

Franchise or licensing agreements and regulatory, certification, or other requirements

_____

_____

Discuss key success factors in your business and how you plan to exploit them _____

_____

_____

_____

_____

Outline your time frame and schedule for the implementation of your program _____

_____

_____

C. Market Analysis (repeat for each product/service offered)

TARGET MARKET AND CUSTOMERS

Describe your target market and prospective customers in terms of geography and/or customer type or profile _____

_____

_____

Describe the principal factors these consumers consider in the purchase of products like yours

_____

_____

Outline the principal benefit they will receive from patronizing your firm rather than one of your competitors_____

_____

_____

continued

Business Plan Outline (Retail or Service) — continued

Describe how your target market might be broken down into segments, and outline how these segments have changed over time and how they might be expected to change in the future

_____

_____

_____

Describe any weekly, monthly, seasonal, or other sales patterns _____

_____

_____

_____

_____

COMPARISON WITH COMPETITORS

	Name of Competitor		
Factor	1. _____	2. _____	3. _____
Price	_____	_____	_____
Convenience of location	_____	_____	_____
Availability of parking	_____	_____	_____
Image	_____	_____	_____
Breadth of product/service line	_____	_____	_____
Depth of product/service line	_____	_____	_____
Credit policy	_____	_____	_____
Display and fixtures	_____	_____	_____
Sales training and effectiveness	_____	_____	_____
Sales support	_____	_____	_____
Availability of delivery	_____	_____	_____
Other:	_____	_____	_____
_____	_____	_____	_____
_____	_____	_____	_____

Indicate what, if anything, is really unique about your product/service offering or firm situation

_____

_____

_____

_____

_____

_____

_____

Business Plan Outline (Retail or Service) — continued

SUMMARY OF ESTIMATED SALES BY PRODUCT/SERVICE LINE AND MARKET SEGMENT

Market Segment Description I _____

Product/Service Line	Estimated Sales by Month ($ or units)												
	1	2	3	4	5	6	7	8	9	10	11	12	Total
_____													
_____													
_____													
_____													_____
											Total		_____

Market Segment Description II _____

Product/Service Line	Estimated Sales by Month ($ or units)												
	1	2	3	4	5	6	7	8	9	10	11	12	Total
_____													
_____													
_____													
_____													_____
											Total		_____

Market Segment Description III _____

Product/Service Line	Estimated Sales by Month ($ or units)												
	1	2	3	4	5	6	7	8	9	10	11	12	Total
_____													
_____													
_____													
_____													_____
											Total		_____

(etc.)

D. Marketing Plan

PRICING

Principal Direct-Cost Elements of Your Operation

Material and supplies costs _____

_____

Labour costs _____

_____

Operating expenses and overhead _____

_____

continued

Business Plan Outline (Retail or Service) — continued

Discuss the prices you plan to charge, and typical gross and net margins for each of your product/service lines and how they compare with those of other firms _____

_____
_____

Describe your credit arrangements, returns policy, and other terms of sale _____

_____
_____
_____

PERSONAL SELLING PROGRAM

Outline your personal selling requirements — the number and type of people in your sales force and how they will be paid _____

_____
_____

ADVERTISING AND PROMOTION PROGRAMS

Media	Audience Size	Schedule	Frequency of use	X	Cost of a Single Occasion	=	Estimated Cost
_____	_____	_____	_____		$_____		$_____
_____	_____	_____	_____		$_____		$_____
_____	_____	_____	_____		$_____		$_____
_____	_____	_____	_____		$_____		$_____
_____	_____	_____	_____		$_____		$_____
_____	_____	_____	_____		$_____		$_____

Total Estimated Cost $_____

Describe any plan to obtain free publicity or other sales promotion activity _____

_____
_____

Other services you plan to provide and their anticipated costs:

Service	Estimated Cost
_____	$_____
_____	_____
_____	_____
_____	_____

E. Operations Plan

Describe your location and its pros and cons:

Location _____

_____

Advantages _____

_____

Business Plan Outline (Retail or Service) — continued

Disadvantages _____

_____

Traffic flows and patterns _____

_____

Zoning requirements _____

_____

Access _____

_____

Parking _____

_____

Visibility _____

_____

Cost _____

_____

Condition _____

_____

Other _____

_____

_____

_____

_____

Indicate the major fixtures and equipment you will require:

Type of Fixture or Equipment	Buy or Lease	Number Required	x	Unit Cost	=	Total Cost
				$_____		$_____

Total Cost $_____

Develop a drawing or floor plan of the physical layout of your store or other facilities.

Where do you plan to buy your floor stock for resale?

Name of Item	Name of Supplier	Price	Order Policy	Discounts Offered	Delivery Time	Freight Costs	Back Order Policy
		$_____				$_____	

continued

Business Plan Outline (Retail or Service) — continued

Where do you plan to buy your operating supplies and materials?

Name of Item	Name of Supplier	Price	Order Policy	Discounts Offered	Delivery Time	Freight Costs	Back Order Policy
_____	_____	$_____	_____	_____	_____	$_____	_____
_____	_____	_____	_____	_____	_____	_____	_____
_____	_____	_____	_____	_____	_____	_____	_____
_____	_____	_____	_____	_____	_____	_____	_____
_____	_____	_____	_____	_____	_____	_____	_____
_____	_____	_____	_____	_____	_____	_____	_____

Outline your inventory control procedures

OPENING INVENTORY REQUIREMENTS

Item	Number Required	x	Cost per Unit	=	Total Cost
_____	_____		$_____		$_____
_____	_____		_____		_____
_____	_____		_____		_____
_____	_____		_____		_____
_____	_____		_____		_____
_____	_____		_____		_____

Total Initial Inventory $_____

OUTLINE OF EMPLOYEE REQUIREMENTS

Job	Qualification Required	Full-or Part-time	Job Description (yes or no)	Compensation	Benefits
_____	_____	_____	_____	$_____	_____
_____	_____	_____	_____	_____	_____
_____	_____	_____	_____	_____	_____
_____	_____	_____	_____	_____	_____

PERMITS OR LICENCES REQUIRED AND NECESSARY INSPECTIONS

Permit, Licences, or Necessary Inspection	Date Received or Completed
_____	_____
_____	_____
_____	_____
_____	_____

Business Plan Outline (Retail or Service) — continued

F. Management Team

Develop an organization chart indicating who is responsible for each of the major areas of activity in your business; list each function and indicate the name of the individual who will perform that function and to whom he or she will be responsible:

Function	Performed by:	Responsible to:
Sales	_____	_____
Marketing	_____	_____
Operations management	_____	_____
Bookkeeping and accounting	_____	_____
Personnel management	_____	_____
_____	_____	_____

Present a brief résumé of each of these individuals _____
_____
_____
_____

Outline the size and composition of your board of directors _____
_____
_____
_____

Present a brief résumé of each individual on your board who is not part of your management team
_____
_____
_____
_____

Indicate the compensation received by each member of your management team and board of directors:

Individual	Salary	Fees or Bonuses	Total Compensation
_____	$_____	$_____	$_____
_____	_____	_____	_____
_____	_____	_____	_____
_____	_____	_____	_____
_____	_____	_____	_____
_____	_____	_____	_____

Describe the ownership structure of your business:

Individual	Types of Shares Held	Percentage of Total Issued	Number of Shares Held	x	Price Paid per Share	=	Total
_____	_____	_____	_____		$_____		$_____
_____	_____	_____	_____		_____		_____
_____	_____	_____	_____		_____		_____
_____	_____	_____	_____		_____		_____
_____	_____	_____	_____		_____		_____

Total Capitalization $_____

continued

Business Plan Outline (Retail or Service) — continued

Indicate any options to acquire additional stock that may be held or could be earned by your management team or others _____

_____

_____

Provide complete information regarding your professional advisors:

Advisor	Name	Address	Telephone	Fees or Retainers Paid
Lawyer	_____	_____ _____	_____	$_____
Accountant	_____	_____ _____	_____	$_____
Banker	_____	_____ _____	_____	$_____
Other	_____	_____ _____	_____	$_____

G. Implementation Schedule

Lay out a schedule of milestones or significant events for the implementation of your business and a timetable for completion; indicate who will be responsible for the completion of each task:

Milestone	Tasks Required to Accomplish	Who is Responsible	Scheduled Completion
_____	_____	_____	_____
	_____	_____	_____
	_____	_____	_____
	_____	_____	_____
_____	_____	_____	_____
	_____	_____	_____
	_____	_____	_____
	_____	_____	_____
_____	_____	_____	_____
	_____	_____	_____
	_____	_____	_____

Describe the risks your business may be faced with in implementing your plan, and the risk for any prospective investor _____

_____

_____

_____

Business Plan Outline (Retail or Service) — continued

H. Financial Plan

START-UP COSTS

If yours is a new venture, indicate your estimate of the start-up financial requirements of your business:

ESTIMATED MONTHLY EXPENSES			What to put in column 2 (these figures are typical for one kind of business. You will have to decide how many months to allow for in your business)
Item	Your estimate of monthly expenses based on sales of $ _____ per year	Your estimate of how much cash you need to start your business (see column 3)	
	Column 1	Column 2	Column 3
Salary of owner-manager	$	$	2 times column 1
All other salaries, wages and benefits			3 times column 1
Rent			3 times column 1
Advertising			3 times column 1
Delivery expense			3 times column 1
Supplies			3 times column 1
Telephone			3 times column 1
Other utilities			3 times column 1
Insurance			Payment required by insurance company
Interest			3 times column 1
Maintenance			3 times column 1
Legal and other professional fees			3 times column 1
Miscellaneous			3 times column 1
ONE-TIME FINANCIAL REQUIREMENTS			Leave column 2 blank
Fixtures and equipment			
Decorating and remodelling			
Installation of fixtures and equipment			
Starting inventory			
Deposits with public utilities			
Legal and other professional fees			
Licences and permits			
Advertising and promotion for opening			
Accounts receivable			
Cash			
Other			
TOTAL ESTIMATED CASH YOU NEED TO START WITH	$		Add up all the numbers in column 2

continued

Business Plan Outline (Retail or Service) — continued

PRESENT FINANCIAL STRUCTURE

Provide an overview of the current financial structure of your business and the proportion of your total start-up requirements obtained to date:

Source of Funds	Amount	Debt or Equity	Repayment Schedule
Self	$_____	_____	_____
Friends, neighbours, relatives	_____	_____	_____
Other private investors	_____	_____	_____
Banks, savings and loans, credit unions, and other financial institutions	_____	_____	_____
Mortgage and insurance companies	_____	_____	_____
Credit from suppliers	_____	_____	_____
Government grants and loans	_____	_____	_____
Other sources:	_____	_____	_____
_____	_____	_____	_____
_____	_____	_____	_____
_____	_____	_____	_____
_____	_____	_____	_____
_____	_____	_____	_____

Additional Funds Required

Indicate the additional funds required and the shares, return on investment, collateral, or other security you are prepared to provide to the prospective lender or investor

_____

_____

_____

_____

_____

_____

_____

_____

_____

_____

_____

_____

_____

Business Plan Outline (Retail or Service) — continued

Current Financial Statements

If your business is already in operation, provide an income statement and a balance sheet for the current year to date and the previous two years; the following forms will serve as guidelines indicating the basic information to provide for each year:

INCOME STATEMENT
for the period ending [date]

Gross sales	$_____	
Less: Cash discounts	_____	
Net Sales	$_____	**(A)**
Less: Cost of goods sold:		
Beginning inventory	$_____	
Plus: Net purchases	_____	
Total goods available for sale	_____	
Less: Ending inventory	_____	
Cost of Goods Sold	_____	**(B)**
Gross Margin (or Profit) (C = A – B)	$_____	**(C)**
Less: Operating expenses:		
Owners' salaries	$_____	
Employees' wages and salaries	_____	
Employee benefits	_____	
Rent	_____	
Utilities (heat, light, water, power)	_____	
Telephone	_____	
Supplies and postage	_____	
Repairs and maintenance	_____	
Advertising and promotion	_____	
Vehicle expense	_____	
Delivery expense	_____	
Taxes and licences	_____	
Depreciation or Capital Cost Allowance	_____	
Bad debt allowance	_____	
Interest	_____	
Travel	_____	
Insurance	_____	
Legal and accounting fees	_____	
Other expenses	_____	
Total Operating Expenses	_____	**(D)**
Net Operating Profit (Loss) (E = C – D)	_____	**(E)**
Income Tax (estimated)	_____	**(F)**
Net Profit (Loss) After Income Tax (G = E – F)	_____	**(G)**

continued

Business Plan Outline (Retail or Service) — continued

**BALANCE SHEET FOR
[NAME OF COMPANY]
as of [date]**

ASSETS

   Current Assets

   Cash $_____

   Accounts receivable   _____

   Inventory   _____

   Other current assets   _____

   Total current assets   _____ **(A)**

   Fixed Assets

   Land and buildings $_____

   Furniture and fixtures   _____

   Equipment   _____

   Trucks and automobiles   _____

   Other fixed assets   _____

   Total fixed assets   _____ **(B)**

   Total Assets (C = A + B) $_____ **(C)**

LIABILITIES

   Current Liabilities (debt due within 12 months)

   Accounts payable $_____

   Bank loans/other loans   _____

   Taxes owed   _____

   Total current liabilities   _____ **(D)**

   Long-Term Liabilities

   Notes payable (due after 1 year)   _____

   Total long-term liabilities   _____ **(E)**

   Total Liabilities (F = D + E) $_____ **(F)**

NET WORTH (CAPITAL)

   Total Net Worth (G = C - F)   _____ **(G)**

   Total Liabilities and Net Worth (H = F + G) $_____ **(H)**

FINANCIAL PROJECTIONS

Develop profit and loss forecasts, projected cash flow statements, and pro forma balance sheets for your business. Each of these statements should be presented for the following time frames:

* **Pro forma profit and loss statements** Monthly for the next year of operation and quarterly or annually for another two to four years

* **Cash flow forecasts** Monthly for the next year of operation and annually for another two years

* **Pro forma balance sheets** Annually for each of the next three to five years

The following forms will serve as guidelines to be followed in developing and presenting this information.

Business Plan Outline (Retail or Service) — continued

PRO FORMA INCOME STATEMENT
For the period ending [date]

		Month												
		1	2	3	4	5	6	7	8	9	10	11	12	Total
Gross sales															
Less Cash discounts															
Net Sales	**(A)**														
Cost of goods sold:															
Beginning inventory															
Plus: Net purchases															
Total goods available for sale															
Less: Ending inventory															
Cost of Goods Sold	**(B)**														
Gross Margin (C = A − B)	**(C)**														
Less: Variable expenses															
Owner's salary															
Employees' wages and salaries															
Supplies and postage															
Advertising and promotion															
Delivery expense															
Bad debt expense															
Travel															
Legal and accounting fees															
Vehicle Expenses															
Miscellaneous expenses															
Total Variable Expenses	**(D)**														
Less: Fixed expenses															
Rent															
Utilities (heat, light, water, power)															
Telephone															
Taxes and licences															
Depreciation or Capital Cost Allowance															
Interest															
Insurance															
Other Fixed Expenses															
Total Fixed Expenses	**(E)**														
Total Operating Expenses (F = D + E)	**(F)**														
Net Operating Profit (Loss) (G = C − F)	**(G)**														
Income Taxes (estimated)	**(H)**														
Net Profit (Loss) After Income Tax (I = G − H)	**(I)**														

continued

ESTIMATED CASH FLOW FORECAST

	Month 1	Month 2	Month 3	Month 4	Month 5	Month 6	Month 7	Month 8	Month 9	Month 10	Month 11	Month 12	Year 1 TOTAL	Year 2 TOTAL	Year 3 TOTAL
Cash Flow From Operations (during month)															
1. Cash Sales															
2. Payments for Credit Sales															
3. Investment Income															
4. Other Cash Income															
A. TOTAL CASH FLOW ON HAND	$	$	$	$	$	$	$	$	$	$	$	$	$	$	$
Less Expenses Paid (during month)															
5. Inventory or New Material															
6. Owners' Salaries															
7. Employees' Wages and Salaries															
8. Supplies and Postage															
9. Advertising and Promotion															
10. Delivery Expense															
11. Travel															
12. Legal and Accounting Fees															
13. Vehicle Expense															
14. Maintenance Expense															
15. Rent															
16. Utilities															
17. Telephone															
18. Taxes and Licences															
19. Interest Payments															
20. Insurance															
21. Other Cash Expenses															
B. TOTAL EXPENDITURES	$	$	$	$	$	$	$	$	$	$	$	$	$	$	$
Capital															
Purchase of Fixed Assets															
Sale of Fixed Assets															
C. CHANGE IN CASH FROM PURCHASE OR SALE OF ASSETS	$	$	$	$	$	$	$	$	$	$	$	$	$	$	$
Financing															
Payment of Principal on Loan															
Inflow of Cash From Bank Loan															
Issuance of Equity Positions															
Repurchase of Outstanding Equity															
D. CHANGE IN CASH FROM FINANCING	$	$	$	$	$	$	$	$	$	$	$	$	$	$	$
E. INCREASE (DECREASE) IN CASH	$	$	$	$	$	$	$	$	$	$	$	$	$	$	$
F. CASH AT BEGINNING OF PERIOD	$*	$	$	$	$	$	$	$	$	$	$	$	$*	$**	$**
G. CASH AT END OF PERIOD	$	$	$	$	$	$	$	$	$	$	$	$	$	$	$
MEET MINIMUM CASH BALANCE	Acceptable	Acceptable	Acceptable	Acceptable	Acceptable	Acceptable	Acceptable	Acceptable	Acceptable	Acceptable	Acceptable	Acceptable	Acceptable	Acceptable	Acceptable

* This entry should be the same amount as for month 1 at the beginning of the year. All other rows will be the total for the entire year.

** These entries should be the same as the ending cash balance from the previous period.

Business Plan Outline (Retail or Service) — continued

PRO FORMA BALANCE SHEET
[NAME OF COMPANY]
as of [date]

ASSETS

Current Assets

Cash	$_____	
Accounts receivable	_____	
Inventory	_____	
Other current assets	_____	
Total current assets		_____ (A)

Fixed Assets

Land and Buildings	$_____	
Furniture and fixtures	_____	
Equipment	_____	
Trucks and automobiles	_____	
Other fixed assets	_____	
Total fixed assets		_____ (B)

Total Assets (C = A + B) $_____ (C)

LIABILITIES

Current Liabilities (debt due within 12 months)

Accounts payable	$_____	
Bank loans/other loans	_____	
Taxes owed	_____	
Total current liabilities		_____ (D)

Long-Term Liabilities

Mortgages payable	$_____	
Notes payable (due after 1 year)	_____	
Loans from partners or shareholders	_____	
Total long-term liabilities		_____ (E)

Total Liabilities (F = D + E) $_____ (F)

NET WORTH (CAPITAL)

Total Net Worth (G = C – F) _____ (G)

Total Liabilities and Net Worth (H = F + G) $_____ (H)

Indicate the minimum level of sales you will require to cover all your fixed and variable costs and to break even:

$$\text{Breakeven Point (in Sales Dollars)} = \frac{\text{Total Estimated Operating Expenses (F in Pro Forma Profit and Loss Satement)}}{1 - \dfrac{\text{Gross Margin Percentage}}{100}}$$

6. APPENDICES

FIGURE 11.5 BUSINESS PLAN OUTLINE FOR A MANUFACTURING COMPANY

1. **LETTER OF TRANSMITTAL**

2. **TITLE PAGE**

3. **TABLE OF CONTENTS**

4. **EXECUTIVE SUMMARY**

Fact Sheet

Company name _____

Location and telephone_____

_____

_____

Type of business and industry _____

_____

_____

Form of business organization _____

_____

_____

Principal product or service line _____

_____

_____

Registered patents or trademarks (if any) _____

_____

_____

Names of founders/partners/shareholders _____

_____

_____

_____

Length of time in business (if appropriate) _____

_____

Current and/or projected market share _____

_____

Funds invested in the business to date and their source _____

_____

_____

_____

Additional financing required _____

_____

_____

_____

Business Plan Outline (Manufacturing Company) — continued

Proposed terms and payback period _____

_____

_____

Total value or net worth of the business _____

_____

_____

NAMES OF BUSINESS ADVISORS

Legal counsel _____

_____

Accountant _____

_____

Banker _____

_____

Other _____

_____

5. BODY

A. Your Company and the Industry

THE COMPANY

Date business started _____

Location _____

_____

Form of business organization _____

_____

Founders and other key individuals _____

_____

_____

Principal products and related services _____

_____

_____

Success the Business Has Achieved to Date

	Estimated Total Annual Market (year)		Company Sales (year)		Market Share (%)
Product 1	$_____		$_____		_____
	_____ units		_____ units		_____
Product 2	$_____		$_____		_____
	_____ units		_____ units		_____
(etc.)					

continued

Business Plan Outline (Manufacturing Company) — continued

Future Goals and Plans

_____

_____

_____

_____

_____

Principal strategy for achieving these goals _____

_____

_____

_____

_____

_____

_____

THE INDUSTRY

Prospects for the Industry

Total Estimated Industry Sales ($)

Product/ Service	Three Years Ago	Two Years Ago	Last Year	This Year	Next Year	In Two Years	In Three Years
1. _____	$_____	$_____	$_____	$_____	$_____	$_____	$_____
2. _____	$_____	$_____	$_____	$_____	$_____	$_____	$_____
3. _____	$_____	$_____	$_____	$_____	$_____	$_____	$_____

(etc.)

Describe general trends within the industry and factors likely to affect these trends _____

_____

_____

Describe general industry standards and performance requirements _____

_____

_____

Major Industry Participants

Name and Location of Competitor	Estimated Sales	Estimated Market Share (%)	Principal Strengths and Weaknesses
_____	$_____	_____	_____
_____			_____
			_____
_____	$_____	_____	_____
_____			_____
			_____
_____	$_____	_____	_____
_____			_____
			_____

Business Plan Outline (Manufacturing Company) — continued

B. Product Offering

DESCRIPTION OF PRINCIPAL PRODUCTS

Product	Description	Unique Features	Stage Of Development

Describe patents or trademarks held or applied for _____

_____

Describe franchise or licensing agreements, and regulatory, certification, or other requirements

_____

_____

Discuss key success factors in your business and how you plan to exploit them _____

_____

_____

Outline your time frame and schedule for the implementation of your program _____

_____

_____

C. Market Analysis (repeat for each product or product line offered)

TARGET MARKET AND CUSTOMERS

Describe your target market and prospective customers in terms of geography and/or customer type or profile _____

_____

_____

Describe the principal factors these consumers consider in the purchase of products like yours

_____

_____

Outline the principal benefit they will receive from patronizing your firm rather than one of your competitors_____

_____

_____

continued

Business Plan Outline (Manufacturing Company) — continued

Describe how your target market might be broken down into segments, and outline how these segments have changed over time and how they might be expected to change in the future

_____
_____
_____
_____

Describe any weekly, monthly, seasonal, or other sales patterns _____
_____
_____

COMPARISON WITH COMPETITORS

Factor	Name of Competitor 1. ___	2. ___	3. ___
Price	___	___	___
Breadth of product line	___	___	___
Depth of product line	___	___	___
Performance	___	___	___
Speed and accuracy	___	___	___
Durability	___	___	___
Versatility	___	___	___
Ease of operation or use	___	___	___
Ease of maintenance or repair	___	___	___
Ease or cost of installation	___	___	___
Size or weight	___	___	___
Design or appearance	___	___	___
Other characteristics:	___	___	___
_____	___	___	___
_____	___	___	___

Indicate what, if anything, is really unique about your product offering or firm situation

_____
_____
_____
_____
_____
_____
_____
_____
_____

Business Plan Outline (Manufacturing Company) — continued

SUMMARY OF ESTIMATED SALES BY PRODUCT LINE AND MARKET SEGMENT

Market Segment Description I _____

Product Line	Estimated Sales by Month ($ or units)												
	1	2	3	4	5	6	7	8	9	10	11	12	Total
_____													
_____													
_____													
_____												Total	_____

Market Segment Description II _____

Product Line	Estimated Sales by Month ($ or units)												
	1	2	3	4	5	6	7	8	9	10	11	12	Total
_____													
_____													
_____													
_____												Total	_____

Market Segment Description III _____

Product Line	Estimated Sales by Month ($ or units)												
	1	2	3	4	5	6	7	8	9	10	11	12	Total
_____													
_____													
_____													
_____												Total	_____

(etc.)

D. Marketing Plan

PRICING

Bill of Material List for Principal Products or Product Lines

Raw Material or Component Part	Description	Supplier	Direct Material Costs		
			Landed Cost	x No./or Quantity Reqd. per Unit	= Cost per Unit Prod.
_____	_____	_____	$_____	_____	$_____
_____	_____	_____	_____	_____	_____
_____	_____	_____	_____	_____	_____
_____	_____	_____	_____	_____	_____

Total Material Costs per Unit $_____ **(A)**

continued

Business Plan Outline (Manufacturing Company) — continued

Direct Labour Costs

Assembly or Manufacturing Process	Estimated Labour Time per Unit	x	Hourly Rate	=	Labour Cost per Unit
_____	_____		$_____		$_____
_____	_____		_____		_____
_____	_____		_____		_____

Total Labour Cost per Unit $_____ **(B)**

Total Direct Manufacturing Cost per Unit (C = A + B) $_____ **(C)**

Total Estimated Packaging and Shipping Cost per Unit   _____ **(D)**

Total Direct Cost per Unit (E = C + D) $_____ **(E)**

Discuss the prices you plan to charge distributors and customers for your product, typical gross and net margins for each of your product lines, and how they compare with those of other firms

_____

_____

_____

Describe your schedule for quantity, cash, functional and other discounts, credit arrangements, returns policy, and other terms of sale _____

_____

_____

_____

_____

DISTRIBUTION

Describe the channels of distribution you will use to get your product to the ultimate consumer

_____

_____

_____

Outline your personal selling requirements — the number and type of people and how they will be paid

_____

_____

_____

Business Plan Outline (Manufacturing Company) — continued

List your principal distributors by name and their expected sales:

Distributor	Address	Territory	Terms of Sale	Exclusive or Non-Exclusive	Total Expected Sales ($ or units)
_____	_____	_____	_____	_____	_____
	_____	_____			
_____	_____	_____	_____	_____	_____
	_____	_____			
_____	_____	_____	_____	_____	_____
	_____	_____			

List your principal customers by name and the total amount they are expected to buy from you:

Customer	Product	Total Expected Purchases ($ or units)	Share of Your Sales (%)
_____	1. _____	_____	_____
	2. _____	_____	_____
	3. _____	_____	_____
_____	1. _____	_____	_____
	2. _____	_____	_____
	3. _____	_____	_____
_____	1. _____	_____	_____
	2. _____	_____	_____
	3. _____	_____	_____

ADVERTISING AND PROMOTION PROGRAM

Describe product packaging requirements and estimated costs for development and use

_____

_____

Outline requirements for product brochures and similar descriptive material indicating development costs and expected cost of production _____

_____

_____

Indicate the trade shows you plan to attend to exhibit your product:

Trade Show	Location	Timing	Estimated Cost
_____	_____	_____	$ _____
_____	_____	_____	_____
_____	_____	_____	

Total Estimated Cost $ _____

continued

Business Plan Outline (Manufacturing Company) — continued

Advertising Program

Media	Audience Size	Schedule	Frequency of use	x	Cost of a Single Occasion	=	Estimated Cost
————	————	————	————		$—————		$—————
————	————	————	————		$—————		$—————
————	————	————	————		$—————		$—————
————	————	————	————		$—————		$—————
————	————	————	————		$—————		$—————
————	————	————	————		$—————		$—————

Total Estimated Cost $—————

Describe any plan to obtain free publicity or other sales promotion activity ———————
——————————————————————————————————
——————————————————————————————————

Describe any repair, informational, or other support services you plan to provide and their anticipated costs:

Service	Estimated Cost
————————	$—————————
————————	—————————
————————	—————————
————————	—————————

E. Production/Operating Plan

Describe your location and its pros and cons:

Location ———————————————————————————
——————————————————————————————————

Description———————————————————————————
——————————————————————————————————

Advantages ————————————————————————————
——————————————————————————————————

Disadvantages ————————————————————————
——————————————————————————————————

Accessibility to suppliers ————————————————————
——————————————————————————————————

Availability of transport services ————————————————
——————————————————————————————————

Zoning situation ——————————————————————————
——————————————————————————————————

Cost——————————————————————————————
——————————————————————————————————

Business Plan Outline (Manufacturing Company) — continued

Condition_____

_____

Other factors _____

_____

Describe your basic manufacturing processes and list the basic operations your facility will have to perform_____

_____

_____

Indicate the space required or allocated to each of the following activities:

Activity	Space Required or Allocated (sq. ft.)
Manufacturing:	
Fabrication	_____
Machining	_____
Assembly	_____
Finishing	_____
Inspection	_____
Other_____	_____
_____	_____
Storage	_____
Shipping	_____
Receiving	_____
Office area	_____
Restrooms and employee facilities	_____
Other activities _____	_____
_____	_____
_____	_____
Total Space Required or Allocated (sq. ft.)	_____

Develop a scale drawing or floor plan of the physical layout of your facility.

List the machinery and equipment you will need to perform your manufacturing and other operations:

Type of Machinery or Equipment	Buy or Lease	Number Required	x	Unit Cost	=	Total Cost
_____	_____	_____		$_____		$_____
_____	_____	_____		_____		_____
_____	_____	_____		_____		_____
_____	_____	_____		_____		_____
_____	_____	_____		_____		_____
				Total Cost		$_____

continued

Business Plan Outline (Manufacturing Company) — continued

Indicate where you plan to buy your raw materials and component parts:

Raw Material/ Component	Supplier	Price	Order Policy	Discount Offered	Delivery Time	Freight Costs	Back Order Policy
_____	_____	$_____	_____	_____	_____	$_____	_____
_____	_____	_____	_____	_____	_____	_____	_____
_____	_____	_____	_____	_____	_____	_____	_____
_____	_____	_____	_____	_____	_____	_____	_____
_____	_____	_____	_____	_____	_____	_____	_____
_____	_____	_____	_____	_____	_____	_____	_____

Indicate where you plan to buy your consumable tools and shop supplies:

Tools or Supplies	Supplier	Price	Order Policy	Discounts Offered	Delivery	Freight Costs	Back Order Policy
_____	_____	$_____	_____	_____	_____	$_____	_____
_____	_____	_____	_____	_____	_____	_____	_____
_____	_____	_____	_____	_____	_____	_____	_____
_____	_____	_____	_____	_____	_____	_____	_____
_____	_____	_____	_____	_____	_____	_____	_____
_____	_____	_____	_____	_____	_____	_____	_____

Outline your inventory control procedures _____

_____

_____

_____

OPENING INVENTORY REQUIREMENTS

Raw Materials and Component Parts

Item	Quantity Required	x	Cost per unit	=	Total Cost
_____	_____		$_____		$_____
_____	_____		_____		_____
_____	_____		_____		_____
_____	_____		_____		_____
_____	_____		_____		_____
_____	_____		_____		_____

Total Raw Material Inventory $_____ **(A)**

Business Plan Outline (Manufacturing Company) — continued

Consumable Tools and Supplies

Item	Quantity Required	x	Cost per unit	=	Total Cost
			$_____		$_____
			_____		_____
			_____		_____
			_____		_____
			_____		_____
			_____		_____

Total Tools and Supplies $_____ **(B)**

Total Opening Inventory Requirements (C = A + B) $_____ **(C)**

OUTLINE OF EMPLOYEE REQUIREMENTS

Job	Qualifications Required	Full-or Part-time	Job Description (yes or no)	Compensation	Benefits
				$_____	

Describe permits or licences required and necessary inspections:

Permit, Licences, or Necessary Inspection	Date Received or Completed

F. Management Team

Develop an organization chart indicating who is responsible for each of the major areas of activity in your business; list each function and indicate the name of the individual who will perform that function and to whom they will be responsible:

Function	Performed by:	Responsible to:
Sales		
Marketing		
Operations management		
Bookkeeping and accounting		
Personnel management		
Research and development		

Present a brief résumé of each of these individuals.

Outline the size and composition of your board of directors _____

_____

_____

_____

continued

Business Plan Outline (Manufacturing Company) — continued

Present a brief résumé of each individual on your board who is not part of your management team.

Indicate the compensation received by each member of your management team and board of directors:

Individual	Salary	Fees or Bonuses	Total Compensation
_____	$_____	$_____	$_____
_____	_____	_____	_____
_____	_____	_____	_____
_____	_____	_____	_____
_____	_____	_____	_____
_____	_____	_____	_____

Describe the ownership structure of your business:

Individual	Types of Shares Held	Percentage of Total Issued	Number of Shares Held	x	Price Paid per Share	=	Total
_____	_____	_____	_____		$_____		$_____
_____	_____	_____	_____		_____		_____
_____	_____	_____	_____		_____		_____
_____	_____	_____	_____		_____		_____
_____	_____	_____	_____		_____		_____

Total Capitalization $_____

Indicate any options to acquire additional stock that may be held or could be earned by your management team or others _____
_____
_____

Provide complete information regarding your professional advisors:

Advisor	Name	Address	Telephone	Fees or Retainers Paid
Lawyer	_____	_____	_____	$_____
		_____		
Accountant	_____	_____	_____	$_____
		_____		
Banker	_____	_____	_____	$_____
		_____		
Other	_____	_____	_____	$_____
		_____		

Business Plan Outline (Manufacturing Company) — continued

G. Implementation Schedule

Lay out a schedule of milestones or significant events for the implementation of your business and a timetable for completion; indicate who will be responsible for the completion of each task:

Milestone	Tasks Required to Accomplish	Who is Responsible	Scheduled Completion
_____	_____	_____	_____
	_____	_____	_____
	_____	_____	_____
	_____	_____	_____
_____	_____	_____	_____
	_____	_____	_____
	_____	_____	_____
	_____	_____	_____
_____	_____	_____	_____
	_____	_____	_____
	_____	_____	_____
	_____	_____	_____

Describe the risks your business may be faced with in implementing your plan, and the risk for any prospective investor _____
_____
_____
_____
_____

continued

Business Plan Outline (Manufacturing Company) — continued

H. Financial Plan

START-UP COSTS

If yours is a new venture, indicate your estimate of the start-up financial requirements of your business:

ESTIMATED MONTHLY EXPENSES			
Item	Your estimate of monthly expenses based on sales of $ _____ per year	Your estimate of how much cash you need to start your business (see column 3)	What to put in column 2 (these figures are typical for one kind of business. You will have to decide how many months to allow for in your business)
	Column 1	Column 2	Column 3
Salary of owner-manager	$	$	2 times column 1
All other salaries, wages and benefits			3 times column 1
Rent			3 times column 1
Advertising			3 times column 1
Delivery expense			3 times column 1
Supplies			3 times column 1
Telephone			3 times column 1
Other utilities			3 times column 1
Insurance			Payment required by insurance company
Interest			3 times column 1
Maintenance			3 times column 1
Legal and other professional fees			3 times column 1
Miscellaneous			3 times column 1
ONE-TIME FINANCIAL REQUIREMENTS			Leave column 2 blank
Fixtures and equipment			
Decorating and remodelling			
Installation of fixtures and equipment			
Starting inventory			
Deposits with public utilities			
Legal and other professional fees			
Licences and permits			
Advertising and promotion for opening			
Accounts receivable			
Cash			
Other			
TOTAL ESTIMATED CASH YOU NEED TO START WITH		$	Add up all the numbers in column 2

Business Plan Outline (Manufacturing Company) — continued

PRESENT FINANCIAL STRUCTURE

Provide an overview of the current financial structure of your business and the proportion of your total start-up requirements obtained to date:

Source of Funds	Amount	Debt or Equity	Repayment Schedule
Self	$_____	_____	_____
Friends, neighbours, relatives	_____	_____	_____
Other private investors	_____	_____	_____
Banks, savings and loans, credit unions, and other financial institutions	_____	_____	_____
Mortgage and insurance companies	_____	_____	_____
Credit from suppliers	_____	_____	_____
Government grants and loans	_____	_____	_____
Other:			
_____	_____	_____	_____
_____	_____	_____	_____
_____	_____	_____	_____
_____	_____	_____	_____
_____	_____	_____	_____

Additional Funds Required

Indicate the additional funds required and the shares, return on investment, collateral, or other security you are prepared to provide to the prospective lender or investor

_____

_____

_____

_____

_____

_____

_____

_____

_____

_____

_____

_____

Current Financial Statements

If your business is already in operation, provide an income statement and a balance sheet for the current year to date and the previous two years. The following forms will serve as guidelines indicating the basic information to provide for each year.

continued

Business Plan Outline (Manufacturing Company) — continued

INCOME STATEMENT
for the period ending [date]

Gross sales	$_____	
Less: Cash discounts	_____	
Net Sales		$_____ (A)
Less: Cost of goods sold:		
Beginning inventory	$_____	
Plus: Net purchases	_____	
Total goods available for sale	_____	
Less: Ending inventory	_____	
Cost of Goods Sold		_____ (B)
Gross Margin (or Profit) (C = A – B)		$_____ (C)
Less: Operating expenses:		
Owner's salary	$_____	
Employees' wages and salaries	_____	
Employee benefits	_____	
Rent	_____	
Utilities (heat, light, water, power)	_____	
Telephone	_____	
Supplies and postage	_____	
Repairs and maintenance	_____	
Advertising and promotion	_____	
Vehicle expense	_____	
Delivery expense	_____	
Taxes and licences	_____	
Depreciation or Capital Cost Allowance	_____	
Bad debt allowance	_____	
Interest	_____	
Travel	_____	
Insurance	_____	
Legal and accounting fees	_____	
Other expenses	_____	
Total Operating Expenses		_____ (D)
Net Operating Profit (Loss) (E = C – D)		_____ (E)
Income Tax (estimated)		_____ (F)
Net Profit (Loss) After Income Tax (G = E – F)		$_____ (G)

Business Plan Outline (Manufacturing Company) — continued

BALANCE SHEET FOR
[NAME OF COMPANY]
as of [date]

ASSETS

Current Assets

Cash	$_____	
Accounts receivable	_____	
Inventory	_____	
Other current assets	_____	
Total current assets		_____ **(A)**

Fixed Assets

Land and buildings	$_____	
Furniture and fixtures	_____	
Equipment	_____	
Trucks and automobiles	_____	
Other fixed assets	_____	
Total fixed assets		_____ **(B)**

Total Assets (C = A + B) $_____ **(C)**

LIABILITIES

Current Liabilities (debt due within 12 months)

Accounts payable	$_____	
Bank loans/other loans	_____	
Taxes owed	_____	
Total current liabilities		_____ **(D)**

Long-Term Liabilities

Notes payable (due after 1 year)	_____	
Total long-term liabilities		_____ **(E)**

Total Liabilities (F = D + E) $_____ **(F)**

NET WORTH (CAPITAL)

Total Net Worth (G = C - F) _____ **(G)**

Total Liabilities and Net Worth (H = F + G) $_____ **(H)**

FINANCIAL PROJECTIONS

Develop profit and loss forecasts, projected cash flow statements, and pro forma balance sheets for your business. Each of these statements should be presented for the following time frames:

- **Pro forma profit and loss statements** Monthly for the next year of operation and quarterly or annually for another two to four years
- **Cash flow forecasts** Monthly for the next year of operation and annually for another two years
- **Pro forma balance sheets** Annually for each of the next three to five years

The following forms will serve as guidelines to be followed in developing and presenting this information.

continued

Business Plan Outline (Manufacturing Company) — continued

PRO FORMA INCOME STATEMENT
For the period ending [date]

		1	2	3	4	5	6	7	8	9	10	11	12	Total
Gross sales														
Less Cash discounts														
Net Sales	**(A)**													
Cost of goods sold:														
Beginning inventory														
Plus: Net purchases														
Total goods available for sale														
Less: Ending inventory														
Cost of Goods Sold	**(B)**													
Gross Margin (C = A − B)	**(C)**													
Less: Variable expenses														
Owner's salary														
Employees' wages and salaries														
Supplies and postage														
Advertising and promotion														
Delivery expense														
Bad debt expense														
Travel														
Legal and accounting fees														
Vehicle Expenses														
Miscellaneous expenses														
Total Variable Expenses	**(D)**													
Less: Fixed expenses														
Rent														
Utilities (heat, light, water, power)														
Telephone														
Taxes and licences														
Depreciation or Capital Cost Allowance														
Interest														
Insurance														
Other Fixed Expenses														
Total Fixed Expenses	**(E)**													
Total Operating Expenses (F = D + E)	**(F)**													
Net Operating Profit (Loss) (G = C − F)	**(G)**													
Income Taxes (estimated)	**(H)**													
Net Profit (Loss) After Income Tax (I = G − H)	**(I)**													

ESTIMATED CASH FLOW FORECAST

	Month 1	Month 2	Month 3	Month 4	Month 5	Month 6	Month 7	Month 8	Month 9	Month 10	Month 11	Month 12	Year 1 TOTAL	Year 2 TOTAL	Year 3 TOTAL
Cash Flow From Operations (during month)															
1. Cash Sales															
2. Payments for Credit Sales															
3. Investment Income															
4. Other Cash Income															
A. TOTAL CASH FLOW ON HAND	$	$	$	$	$	$	$	$	$	$	$	$	$	$	$
Less Expenses Paid (during month)															
5. Inventory or New Material															
6. Owners' Salaries															
7. Employees' Wages and Salaries															
8. Supplies and Postage															
9. Advertising and Promotion															
10. Delivery Expense															
11. Travel															
12. Legal and Accounting Fees															
13. Vehicle Expense															
14. Maintenance Expense															
15. Rent															
16. Utilities															
17. Telephone															
18. Taxes and Licences															
19. Interest Payments															
20. Insurance															
21. Other Cash Expenses															
B. TOTAL EXPENDITURES	$	$	$	$	$	$	$	$	$	$	$	$	$	$	$
Capital															
Purchase of Fixed Assets															
Sale of Fixed Assets															
C. CHANGE IN CASH FROM PURCHASE OR SALE OF ASSETS	$	$	$	$	$	$	$	$	$	$	$	$	$	$	$
Financing															
Payment of Principal on Loan															
Inflow of Cash From Bank Loan															
Issuance of Equity Positions															
Repurchase of Outstanding Equity															
D. CHANGE IN CASH FROM FINANCING	$	$	$	$	$	$	$	$	$	$	$	$	$	$	$
E. INCREASE (DECREASE) IN CASH	$	$	$	$	$	$	$	$	$	$	$	$	$	$	$
F. CASH AT BEGINNING OF PERIOD	$*	$	$	$	$	$	$	$	$	$	$	$	$*	$**	$**
G. CASH AT END OF PERIOD	$	$	$	$	$	$	$	$	$	$	$	$	$	$	$
MEET MINIMUM CASH BALANCE	Acceptable	Acceptable	Acceptable	Acceptable	Acceptable	Acceptable	Acceptable	Acceptable	Acceptable	Acceptable	Acceptable	Acceptable	Acceptable	Acceptable	Acceptable

* This entry should be the same amount as for month 1 at the beginning of the year. All other rows will be the total for the entire year.

** These entries should be the same as the ending cash balance from the previous period.

Business Plan Outline (Manufacturing Company) — continued

PRO FORMA BALANCE SHEET
[NAME OF COMPANY]
as of [date]

ASSETS

Current Assets

Cash $_____

Accounts receivable   _____

Inventory   _____

Other current assets   _____

Total current assets   _____ **(A)**

Fixed Assets

Land and buildings $_____

Furniture and fixtures   _____

Equipment   _____

Trucks and automobiles   _____

Other fixed assets   _____

Total fixed assets   _____ **(B)**

Total Assets (C = A + B) $_____ **(C)**

LIABILITIES

Current Liabilities (debt due within 12 months)

Accounts payable $_____

Bank loans/other loans   _____

Taxes owed   _____

Total current liabilities   _____ **(D)**

Long-Term Liabilities

Mortgages payable $_____

Notes payable (due after 1 year)   _____

Loans from partners or shareholders   _____

Total long-term liabilities   _____ **(E)**

Total Liabilities (F = D + E) $_____ **(F)**

NET WORTH (CAPITAL)

Total Net Worth (G = C – F)   _____ **(G)**

Total Liabilities and Net Worth (H = F + G) $_____ **(H)**

Business Plan Outline (Manufacturing Company) — continued

Indicate the minimum level of sales you will require to cover all your fixed and variable costs and to break even:

$$\text{Breakeven Point (in Units)} = \frac{\text{Total Operating Expenses (F in Pro Forma Profit and Loss Statement)}}{\text{Your Average Selling Price per Unit} - \text{Total Direct Cost per Unit}}$$

$$\text{Breakeven Point (in Sales Dollars)} = \frac{\text{Total Operating Expenses (F in Pro Forma Profit and Loss Statement)}}{1 - \dfrac{(\text{Average Selling Price per Unit} - \text{Total Direct Cost per Unit})}{100}}$$

6. APPENDICES

FIGURE 11.6 SAMPLE BUSINESS PLAN

DARTING LAMP COMPANY

Prepared By:
Bryce Kumka
Douglas Palmer

SAMPLE BUSINESS PLAN

Table of Contents

SAMPLE BUSINESS PLAN

1) Executive Summary:

With the constant barrage of speed that is focused into our everyday activities, time-poor consumers are looking to spend their free time in a safe, relaxing environment. Hence, people are "cocooning," spending their free time within the safe and relaxing boundaries of their homes. Darting Lamp Co. has realized an incredible market opportunity to reach out and fulfill the needs of today's time-poor society.

As a result of the increasing cocooning practices of the modern consumer, the sales figures of indoor activity equipment, such as dartboards, is increasing at an expeditious rate. With the consumer's desires in mind, Darting Lamp Co. has crafted a high-quality dartboard floor lamp (Exhibit 9.2).

Spearheaded by Bryce Kumka and Douglas Palmer, Darting Lamp Co. has an experienced and enthusiastic management team. Together they have 13 years combined experience in the service and retail industries. Each member has achieved levels of excellence within their profession, and carries their enthusiasm and work ethic to the Darting Lamp Co. operation.

Based on our market research, and using conservative estimates, Darting Lamp Co. proposes to sell 9300 units resulting in $1.6 million dollars in sales within its first year. That sales figure will rise to 17,000 units and $3.0 million dollars in sales by the end of year five. This impressive growth rate will provide investors with a 64 percent return on investment.

The opportunity to invest in Darting Lamp Co. provides investors with a surefire method of capitalizing on one of the largest trends dominating today's market. Darting Lamp Co.'s radical and exciting dartboard floor lamp will provide for hours of enjoyable indoor activity. No games room will be complete without a Darting Lamp Co. lamp.

1.1) Fact Sheet

Company Name:
>   Darting Lamp Co.

Product Name:
>   The Darting Lamp

Location and Telephone:
>   804 McPhillips Street, Winnipeg, Manitoba, Canada,
>   R2X 2J5. Phone: (204)-555-8441, Fax: (204)-555-3110.

Type of Business and Industry:
>   Production Coordinator/Sales Company

Form of Business Organization:
>   Corporation

Principal Product or Service Line:
>   A stainless steel floor lamp, which has a cabinet dartboard unit attached to the body of
>   the lamp at regulation play height.

Manufacturer:
>   Hanford Marketing, 1444 Sommerville Avenue, Winnipeg, Manitoba, Canada, R3T 1C5.
>   Phone: (204)-555-6775, Fax: (204)-555-6737

Cost of Manufacturing Lamp:
> $113.93. Includes: parts, materials, and labour.

Names of Partners:
>   Bryce Kumka and Douglas Palmer

Projected Market Share:
>   9300 units (<0.1%) of dart throwers in our primary target market of 21,100,000 enthusiasts.

Financing Required:
>   1. Funds Invested in the business by the founders: $150,000 @ $75,000 ea.
>   2. Additional Financing Required: $75,000

Total Value or Net Worth of Business at Day 1 of Operations:
> $225,000

Names of Business Advisors:
>   A. Legal Council: George E. Chapman, QC. Principal partner of Chapman Goddard
>   Kaggan, Attorneys at Law.
>   B. Accountant: Allan Grant of Lazer Grant & Company.
>   C. Insurance Broker: Irwin Kumka of Ryan Gateway Insurance.

2

2) Company Overview:

Darting Lamp Co. is dedicated to providing exceptional quality game products to the consumer of indoor activities, focusing on the home owner. As an energetic new company, our first project involves a revolutionary combination of a cabinet dartboard, combined with a floor lamp. Such innovative products serve as a symbol for the creative intentions of Darting Lamp Co.

Highlighting our product is our supreme standard of quality. This is achieved by the selection of a manufacturer that uses parts that meet the highest standards set for durability by the American Lighting Association. Our company focuses not on the "bazaar fever" of big box stores, but on the constant demand of specialists. By marketing our product through exclusive game stores, we will capture the attention of consumers who are looking for quality and a product which will stand the test of time.

2.1) Darting Lamp Co.'s Consumer

This group of people is represented by the increasing population of time-poor consumers who are "cocooning," and hence building a games room in their home. Our target group of consumers tends to be in the 35-55 age range and are building or renovating their homes. In speaking with homebuilders, the general feeling is that within five years every new home will be built with a games room. Before 1990, few floor plans included a specific area for a games room.

2.2) Mission Statement

> *To provide safe, reliable, leisure game products for the enjoyment of our customers. Through our product we will meet and try to exceed the expectations of our customers. We will achieve our goal through superior workmanship, quality, and aesthetic playability.*

3) Product:

Darting Lamp Co. will sell a floor lamp that is built through a cabinet dartboard (Exhibit 9.2 & 9.3). The cabinet dartboard unit will meet the rules and regulation standards of play, including the correct height of the board off the ground. People will be able to throw a game of darts using our board attached to the floor lamp, rather than a conventional board attached to the wall.

We will have our lamp manufactured by Hanford Marketing. Hanford Marketing has an exceptional record of producing high-quality lamp products. With over sixteen years of experience in the lighting industry, Hanford will produce the lamp to Darting Lamp Co.'s specifications.

3.1) Lamp Specifications

The lamp itself is constructed of steel parts. The base of the floor lamp, finished in a brushed steel finish, has been made oversized, and overweight. A regular base averages 9"x9"x1/2" and approximately 5 pounds. Our Base measures 25" long, 15" wide, and 1" deep, and weighs

SAMPLE BUSINESS PLAN

15 pounds. This oversize base serves two purposes: both in keeping the lamp from being tipsy when throwing a game of darts, and also fitting into the current popular styles found in the lighting industry. Stainless Steel has been the major trend in lighting finishes, and will be the most popular colour choice over the coming years, according to both interior designers, and *Residential Lighting* magazine.

The body of the floor lamp consists of two steel "arms," which run from the base of the lamp to a steel dish housing the socket. The two arms of the lamp are created from four separate rods. These rods must be screwed together to assemble the two arms. Each rod measures 40" in height, and is $^1/_2$" in diameter. The arms are placed 19" apart on the base, leaving an inch on either side to the edge of the base. This spacing allows for the body of the floor lamp to run through the cabinet without interfering with the playing area of the dartboard.

The shade of our floor lamp is constructed of steel, and is in a style commonly referred to as an indirect lighting dish. It is a metal bowl, measuring 20" across and 2" deep. The dish has two $^1/_2$ inch holes drilled through it, 19" apart, allowing it to be easily attached to the body of our floor lamp. As with the base and the rods, the shade is stainless steel. The inside of the shade is painted white, and has an 18-inch reflective aluminum strip attached perpendicular to the holes. The strip is attached by being tucked underneath the small lip of the shade, which runs around the inside of the circumference (Exhibit 9.4).

To attach the dartboard to the floor lamp, four holes are drilled. Two sets of holes parallel to each other on the top and bottom of the cabinet, 19" apart. The cabinet and board are then slipped over the rods, and come to rest on two circular metal washers that have been spot welded to the arms at the 57-inch mark. This will allow for the centre of the dartboard to be sitting at exactly the regulation 5-foot 8-inch mark. The cabinet measures 22 $^1/_2$" high and 20" wide.

The power source for the floor lamp is a 15-foot long piece of black 18/2 lamp cord with a polarized plug end. The polarized plug provides an electrical ground complying with CSA specifications. Approximately 7 feet of the lamp cord is run through the left arm of the floor lamp, where it is attached to the lamp's ballast. This leaves approximately 8 feet of cord, protruding from the bottom of the base, with which to "plug in" the lamp. We attach an on/off foot switch to the lamp cord, approximately 3 feet from where the cord protrudes from the base of the lamp. This particular type of switch allows the lamp to be turned on and off by pressing on the switch, resting on the floor, with your foot. This is the easiest switch to operate, and has a higher durability than a conventional "turn-knob" switch.

3.2) Lamp Aesthetics

The "twin rail" look of our floor lamp also allows for a chameleon effect, which in the lighting industry is the label given to a product with simple lines, able to fit into and look like it belongs in multiple types of home decor.

The dartboard is finished in traditional red and green striping. It is a high-quality 1 $^1/_2$" thick, regulation 18" circumference board, housed inside an oak cabinet. The oak is stained in a medium honey finish. The cabinet offsets the stainless steel finish of our lamp in an extremely fashionable manner. The choice of stain is a neutral finish, appealing to a broad range of consumers. On the inside of each of the doors, a chalkboard has been attached. Directly below the dartboard, there is a channel carved in the bottom of the cabinet as a place to store chalk. Also, along the inside bottom of the door is a protruding strip of wood, with three small holes drilled in it as a place to store your darts.

The cabinet housing the dartboard catches the stray darts. The cabinet is seen as the industry average in terms of the size of adequate backing. The target market is comprised of a majority of people with families. This segment is more tolerant of the inevitable wear and tear on a games room caused by children.

3.3) Light Source

The floor lamp is lit with an 18-watt compact fluorescent bulb. This type of light is ideal for a games room, as it is does not produce the unseemly glare of the industry standard halogen floor lamp, and will add to the atmospherics of a game or recreation room. Also, the bulb is energy efficient, and costs little to run. Using the 18-watt fluorescent bulb gives the same light as a 100-watt incandescent bulb. We have integrated a small ballast and quad-pin fluorescent socket to our dish to be able to provide this type of light. We chose this socket because it has a clear, heat-resistant protective lexan shield. This ensures that our bulb is protected against any stray darts falling into the dish.

The compact fluorescent light is also ideal, because the bulb does not get hot. For example, if a dart was to land in the dish, and come into direct contact with the bulb, the dart is in no danger of melting, let alone catching on fire. You could leave tissue paper sitting on top of the bulb with no danger.

This fact, combined with the environmental benefits of a bulb using less than a quarter of the energy of a regular bulb, ensures speedy approval by the Canadian Standards Association. Our manufacturer has ensured approval inside of one month, based on our lamp schematics and the use of their CSA-approved parts.

3.4) Packaging and Transportation

The cost of the box and packaging material (popcorn) to protect the lamp during shipping is $4 per unit. This is based on a box which measures 48" long, 25" wide, and 6" deep. It also includes the approximate 20 litres of popcorn needed to package the lamp for safe travel.

Darting Lamp Co. will be shipping bi-monthly to both the Dufferin and Sharper Image distribution centres. This will minimize our production costs, because it reduces the inventory holding cost of our supplier. The shipping cost is based on a "nose load," which is the first 20 feet of a semi-trailer. This breaks down to two rows of five pallets, each pallet containing 40 lamps. Trucks will cost $2000 per month. Hence our packaging cost is $5 per lamp.

3.5) International Concerns

Through the new rules prescribed in the NAFTA agreement it is now possible to compete effectively in the United States market. The abolishment of duty and taxes on the exporting of indoor sporting activities and lighting products will allow us to export our unique floor lamp into this lucrative market.

SAMPLE BUSINESS PLAN

4) Market Analysis:

In today's society, many companies are trying to figure out how to serve the "time-poor" consumer faster than before. Darting Lamp Co. did not want to develop a product to help speed up their lives, but rather one to help with the enjoyment of their ever more precious leisure time. Families are spending more time than ever before inside their homes. This trend, known as cocooning, has evolved because people want to spend their small, and valuable, amount of free time with family in a safe place. Hence at the end of the day, more families are staying at home rather than planning extended outings and involved activities. Growth of the time-poor segment is seen in the pre-planning of games rooms in new home development by the consumer. Renovations of existing space into games rooms are on the rise. Several trade companies, including home builders and electricians, estimate they have seen a 50 percent increase in home renovations involving games rooms in the last year.[1]

4.1) The Dart Industry
Looking at the dart industry in particular, we found patterns of growth that will support healthy sales of our product. From 1985 to 1994, the number of people throwing darts in North America increased from 9.4 million to 21.1 million, and it remains one of the fastest-growing categories according to the National Sporting Good Association.[2] In 1996 dart throwers spent almost $223 million on dartboards and related equipment.[3]

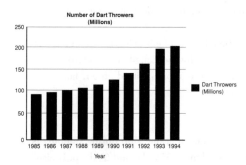

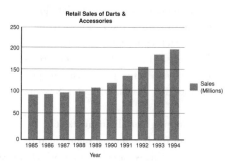

4.2) Darting Lamp Co. and the Consumer
This is where Darting Lamp Co. will satisfy our consumers' needs. Our dart board floor lamp provides a popular indoor activity and lights the games room. It is pertinent to note the environmental friendliness and safety of our product. Using the compact fluorescent bulb technology we will receive Power-Smart designation. This light source is much safer than the current halogen floor lamps, which have come under intense public scrutiny for causing fires. Our lamp provides the consumer with a safe alternative. Even in the extreme situation of having a bulb break, our fluorescent unit implodes safely within the dish. This in comparison to a halogen bulb, which explodes, and due to the great heat it produces is a high safety risk.

---

[1] Spoke with representatives from: ParkHill Homes, Sommerville Homes, C. Gamble Electric, Harry Hoffman Electric, Robinson Lighting, and SuperLite.
[2] *Sporting Goods Business.* Volume 28. Issue 11, November 1995. Page 40-42.
[3] Discount Store News. *Aiming Higher.* Volume 37. Issue 11, July 1998.

4.3) Pricing

Our floor lamp will cost $113.93 to have manufactured for Darting Lamp Co. through Hanford Marketing. (Exhibit 9.1)

In Canada we will sell our lamp to retailers for $160. Suggested retail price of our lamp is $289. When you consider the price of a high-quality dart board and cabinet, approximately $120, and the cost of a high-quality indirect floor lamp, approximately $250, our product is able to combine both elements without pricing itself out of a consumer's consideration set.

In the United States we will sell our lamp to retailers for $123.75 in U.S. dollars. Suggested retail price of our lamp is $249 in U.S. dollars. This converts to a selling price of $187.50 and a retail price of $373.50 in Canadian dollars. As in the Canadian market, the combination price of purchasing a lamp and dartboard separately closely matches the $249 price tag.

4.4) The Target Market

Since our product is at the upper end of the quality spectrum, we decided to use the same target groups as consumers currently purchasing floor lamps and cabinet dartboard units separately. This group of consumers consists of middle to upper class families, who have disposable family incomes in excess of $50,000. Our consumers tend to be 35 to 55 years old, and are most likely homeowners.

We have also identified a secondary target market, referred to as the echo of the Baby Boomers. These individuals are now reaching their early- to mid-twenties, are leaving home, and are looking for rental accommodations. On average they are obtaining well-paying jobs and are looking for just the right accessories for their apartments. An apartment layout will not usually accommodate a designated dartboard area. The Darting Lamp can be placed anywhere you would normally place a floor lamp. It allows these consumers to own a dartboard that will not look out of place and is readily playable.

In the competitive market, we will be competing against the traditional wall-hung dartboard and cabinet dartboard units. By offering a new and unique twist, combining both the game and lighting aspects of the consumer's needs, Darting Lamp Co. will shake up the industry and capture sales from this market. Our product is going to appeal to those consumers who are serious dart throwers, and/or are looking for a lighting product, and want a character piece in their games room.

4.5) Market Research

When considering market acceptance of the project, Darting Lamp Co. contacted the current President of the American Lighting Association, Bruce Robinson. Bruce Robinson is also the co-owner and vice-president of B.A. Robinson Co. Bruce oversees the operations of all the Robinson Lighting showrooms in western Canada. From a lighting perspective, he felt the idea was sound, and that it incorporated the latest high fashion trends of the industry, creating desire on the part of the consumer.

With approval from Bruce Robinson, we took our product to the eye of the public. Over a 4-week period, we were allowed to question customers who shop at Robinson Lighting about what they thought of our floor lamp. This was an excellent place to conduct research because the customers who shop at Robinson Lighting fall into Darting Lamp Co.'s segmented population category. This means we were receiving feedback from the same type of consumer that will be purchasing our floor lamp.

7

SAMPLE BUSINESS PLAN

We presented the customers with both the concept of the floor lamp, the approximate $289 retail price tag, and asked for feed back. Approximately 80 percent of respondents were enthusiastic about the idea, and demonstrated favourable support for the concept. Of that 80 percent, 47 percent indicated they would seriously consider purchasing the floor lamp at the mentioned price.

Number of Customers Questioned	76	Percentage of Positive Responses
Number of Favourable Responses	60	78.95%
Number Who Would Consider Purchasing	28	36.84%

The favourable response from customers shows a preliminary interest in our product, and the idea may have broad appeal to the mass market, rather than just the inventors of the product. Darting Lamp Co. members are confident after testing the market that we have eliminated the risk of marketing myopia, and we will have significant demand to sustain and grow a viable business.

5) The Management Team:

Bryce Kumka (President and Director of Finance)
Bryce Kumka completed his degree in the Bachelor of Commerce Honours Program. He graduated in April 1999 with a double major in Small Business and Marketing. For the past six years he has been employed as a general Insurance Broker with Ryan Gateway Insurance Brokers Inc. He has participated in the sales process as well as tracking and reporting sales results for all six locations of Ryan Gateway Insurance. Through his employment Bryce has learned the teamwork skills necessary to function in a highly competitive market. These skills will be applied throughout Darting Lamp Co. to foster the essential competitive edge required to compete in the North American market.

Doug Palmer (Vice President of Sales, Marketing, and New Product Development)
Doug Palmer completed his degree in the Bachelor of Commerce Honours Program and graduated with a double major in Small Business and Marketing. For the past seven years he has been employed as a sales person with Robinson Lighting. Three years ago Doug earned his designation as a certified Lighting Specialist through the American Lighting Association. His in-depth knowledge of the lighting industry and attention to the current style developments will prove to be a great asset to Darting Lamp Co.

5.1) Board of Directors
In order to compete and be productive in the market, we recognize external sources of information are of great use to our company. We have selected our board based on the attributes that we hope to learn and develop through contact with these people. They represent skills and knowledge of the small business industry and have proven to understand what it takes to run a business successfully. The following board has been established to guide the founders of Darting Lamp Co. in the direction of a successful business of our own. These carefully-selected members include:

Brock Cordes:	President, Seabrook Industries Ltd., Professor of Small Business Management, Small Business Finance, and Sales Management at the University of Manitoba.
Irwin Kumka:	Executive Vice President (Sales & Marketing), Ryan Gateway Insurance Brokers Inc.
Bruce Robinson:	Vice President, B.A. Robinson Co. Ltd., Honorary President, American Lighting Association.
George Chapman QC:	Principal Partner, Chapman Goddard Kaggan, Attorneys at Law.
Allan Grant:	Lazer Grant & Company, Chartered Accountants
James MacDonald:	Vice President, RBC Dominion Securities

6) Operating Strategies:

We will be actively marketing our lamp through the Dufferin Games Room and Sharper Image catalogues, as well as the Sharper Image online store. Our product is constructed in a fashion that the quality will speak for itself. As a consumer gazes upon the lamp for the first time, it will be obvious that it is a product which has received extended craftsmanship and care in being produced.

6.1) Marketing Channels

Our floor lamp's image will be combined with the atmosphere of the stores in which it will be purchased. In Canada we distribute through the 51 Dufferin Games Room stores. Dufferin Games Room is a retail outlet specializing in indoor activities such as billiards and darts. In the United States we distribute through the 105 Sharper Image stores. Sharper Image sells high-end, unique consumer merchandise and electronics. Because of the stores' atmospherics, they add automatic credibility to our product.

This fits into our image and marketing plans for our floor lamp. We will employ a focused differentiation strategy when marketing the lamp in the retail stores. This strategy allows us to maintain our high margin while reaching our target consumer. Our merchandise has a high price, and thus we will be dealing in a lower volume. The major attributes of our product allow for a higher price than would be traditionally found for either a floor lamp or that of a dart board. This is due to the value-added aspects of the combination of the two-in-one product. We also offer the consumer a safe alternative to a halogen floor lamp, while providing an environmentally friendly and aesthetically pleasing light source.

Beginning in year two as a hedge against the possibility of losing the Dufferin or Sharper Image contract, we will investigate wholesaling to smaller regional, traditional specialty stores. This is facilitated by the addition of four full-time sales people, and an increase in our advertising budget. By including these stores in our consideration set of possible buyers, we are not solely relying on sales orders from the larger stores. We will not reduce the attention that we provide to Dufferin Games Room stores or the Sharper Image stores, but continue to visit each location a minimum of two times per year.

6.2) Advertising Budget

We have budgeted an allowance for advertising equal to 5 percent of our gross sales. This allowance will be enough to cover some rudimentary but extremely important methods of advertising. By targeting our advertising through specialty catalogues we are more apt to reach potential customers. By advertising in the Dufferin and Sharper Image specialty catalogues, we will create an immediate awareness with our North American consumer. Another important method that Sharper Image uses to market their products is by placing their catalogues in airline seat back pouches. These consumers are a captive audience and are more apt to read through the entire catalogue.

The cost associated with the Dufferin catalogue is $1500 per issue. The cost per issue with Sharper Image is $5000, adjusted to Canadian dollars. Each of these specialty retailers produces a monthly catalogue, which with our set advertising budget will allow us to advertise in each retailers' catalogue every issue of the year. During the months of August through December, we will increase our advertising expenditures by $500 per month. This will pay for increased cost of additional holiday co-op advertising.

By marketing our product in this fashion, we will gain more credibility in terms of a specialty product designed for the fashion-forward homeowner. The floor lamp is a unique concept, and when seen in the context of the specialty showroom, it will be seen as a serious alternative to a wall-hung dartboard.

6.3) Pre-Launch Marketing Strategy

The pre-launch strategy is based upon our negotiations for the launch of our product through our two major purchasers. The first introduction will be to the Dufferin Games Room store managers at their annual new product introduction meeting at the Whistler Mountain resort over the third weekend in February. This is the annual showcase for all the product that will go on sale for the next sales year that begins in mid-April. We will have full production models at the showcase and the managers of the stores will be able to ask any question of us at that time. Upon request we will also visit individual outlets as the need arises.

The same basic strategy will be maintained for the new product introduction to the Sharper Image stores. The new product introduction for Sharper Image will be held two weeks after that of Dufferin. The Sharper Image meeting will be held in Vail, Colorado on the first weekend of March.

6.4) Product Launch Strategy

The official launch will be the last week of April, the time that both the Sharper Image and Dufferin Games Room Catalogues are mailed to their potential customers and distributed to the airlines. We will place a large prominent advertisement in these publications that will be accompanied by a brief product description and price. The products will be on sale in stores coinciding with the product introduction in the catalogues. This requires us to begin production in mid-March with shipping dates in mid-April, directly following the introduction to store managers.

10

6.5) Manufacturing Process

Darting Lamp Co. has researched and selected a high-quality lamp manufacturer and cabinet dartboard units with which to build our floor lamp. In order to be able to service our international market, Darting Lamp Co. understands each step of the production process. Our manufacturer proceeds through these nine steps:

1. Insert the threaded nipples into the four rods that create the two arms of the lamp.
2. Spot-weld the 1-inch washers into place.
3. Drill out the dartboard and place snugly into position on the upper rods of the lamp.
4. Attach socket and ballast to the shade using universal mounting bars and 2G11 pop rivet screws.
5. Attach foot switch to lamp cord two feet from the polarized plug.
6. Thread the cord through the base, two corresponding rod sections, and into the shade. Ensure that the lock washer and hex nut assemblies are all in correct position.
7. Make electrical connection from the lamp cord to the ballast.
8. Package lamp in cardboard container, using popcorn as the packaging material.
9. Ship lamp to retailer.

6.6) Customer Assembly

When the consumer purchases the lamp, they have six parts to assemble in three steps to have a functioning dartboard lamp. The detailed instructions are as follows:

1. Screw the lower section arms of the floor lamp to the upper arm sections of the floor lamp. (The upper arm sections are the two pieces which have been put through the dartboard cabinet.)
2. Screw the two arms of the floor lamp to the base using the lock washer and hex nut assemblies. (The hex nuts attach to the nipples which have already been affixed to the arms by the manufacturer.)
3. Screw the dish of the lamp to the two arms using the lock washer and hex nut assemblies. (The hex nuts attach to the nipples which have already been affixed to the arms by the manufacturer.)

6.7) Research and Development

Over the life of our product, Darting Lamp Co. will be continuously conducting research and development to improve and diversify our product. Examples of innovations we could assimilate into our lamp design include such options as adding a range of colour schemes to our line up. We could use an iodine metal staining process, because this process is incredibly resistant to scratching. We will also look at introducing different coloured cabinets to the line up.

Darting Lamp Co. will look at the viability of offering a model with an electronic dartboard. This is a fast-growing segment of the dart market, but at this point the boards are still very expensive, and as a result are priced out of most people's budgets. However, as prices begin to drop in the next couple of years, the electronic dartboard could prove to be very popular because it scores games automatically. It will be a market trend that Darting Lamp Co. follows closely, and we will change our product to reinforce our position as an industry leader.

11

SAMPLE BUSINESS PLAN

7) Critical Risks:

We have identified several areas of concern through discussions with our Insurance Broker. He has suggested the below-mentioned coverage to help hedge against unforeseen risks.

7.1) Keyman Insurance

The most prominent internal risk would be the death of one of the partners. This could cause the downfall of the company. As an example, there is the problem that the deceased's shares of the company would be turned over to his next of kin. The next of kin may have absolutely no interest in running the company, or getting along with the other partner. This would cause major havoc for the surviving partner, especially if he was not currently in a financial position where he had the personal income to be able to purchase the shares from the next of kin.

Considering this, Darting Lamp Co. obtained estimates for Keyman insurance. We took the insurance out in the name of the company, which means the policy pays out to the company rather than an individual. In so doing, if one of the partners were to pass away, the money pays out to the company, and the surviving partner uses the money to purchase the shares from the deceased's next of kin. We chose a value of $100,000 to begin with, and selected a rider that will allow us, if we choose, to increase the value of the policy by $100,000-dollar increments every two years.

We also purchased the Keyman policy with a rider that allows us to renew the policy without a medical exam. This is beneficial because at this point the partners of Darting Lamp Co. are both healthy young males. However, this may not always be the case, and if either partner was to develop a disease, we are already locked in at our current and, therefore, much lower rates. Darting Lamp Co. obtained a quote from Zurich Life through Palmer Financial Services that worked out to $365 annually.

7.2) Liability Insurance

Next we considered the possibility of our floor lamp causing an accident in someone's home. Our product involves the use of sharp thrown objects in the form of darts, and it is also an electrical device. The chance someone could have an accident does exist. To guard against such an occurrence we took out a liability insurance policy. Upon discussing our project with Ryan Gateway Insurance,[4] a policy to cover Darting Lamp Co. for our Canadian sales would cost approximately $1000 a year. The cost of the same policy for coverage in the United States of America would cost approximately $5000 a year.

7.3) Blanket Policy

Our company discovered shipping companies are only required, by North American convention, to pay out $2 per pound for damaged goods, regardless of the goods' actual value. Darting Lamp Co. has many shipments both arriving at and leaving from our manufacturer's shipping docks. If we were to lose, for example a $10,000 shipment of dartboards,

---

[4] This quote, and all other insurance quotes, unless otherwise specified were provided by Ryan Gateway Insurance Brokers. Contact: Irwin Kumka.

and only receive $2000 in compensation from the shipping company, it could seriously affect our cash flow for several months.

The policy that works best for Darting Lamp Co. is referred to as a blanket policy. A blanket policy, purchased on a yearly basis, will cover all the goods shipped from and arriving at Darting Lamp Co.'s manufacturer for their actual value. This means we would be paid out on the realized value of any damaged goods, and not the monetary $2 per pound. The quote we obtained on a policy for our company based on its size, and the value of goods being shipped to and from, would cost approximately $200 per year.

7.4) Property Insurance

What would happen if the Darting Lamp Co. building were to burn? Or for that matter, if it were broken into and vandalized? This would result in the loss of our equipment and place of business. We would not want to have to absorb these costs, and hence chose a property insurance package that would cover the losses sustained by Darting Lamp Co. We obtained an estimate for property insurance that worked out to approximately $500 per year.

7.5) Business Interruption Policy

However, this raised the question of what would happen to our business in the interim if there were, for example, a fire? While we would have the cost of our equipment covered, would we be able to get back on our feet quickly enough? For example, if we had a fire near the end of August, which is when we are selling an above-average number of units in preparation for the seasonal demand of our product, could we replace all of our equipment fast enough? Even if we could replace the equipment, would we be able to recover all of the data we lost in the fire in time to ensure all of our orders were placed properly?

We could lose a significant portion of our sales, and it could even result in the company going bankrupt. This is because while we are not making sales, the bills still have to be paid, and the bank will not show sympathy because you have had a fire.

This is why Darting Lamp Co. felt it was essential to purchase a business interruption policy. This policy is set up to cover a business in just such a circumstance, and it pays out to the company based on the gross margin and sales of their product. This ensures that in the event of an unforeseen tragedy, Darting Lamp Co. will have the money to meet their bills and will be able to avoid any uncertainty about having to shut the doors. The quote on this policy for our company was approximately $900 per year.

7.6) External Risks/Possible Competitors

In terms of the external risks, Darting Lamp Co. has to be most concerned with competing companies copying our design. In the lighting industry, it is quite common for designs to be copied within months of a high-end company introducing a new style.

However, following the current trend of the large companies in the lighting industry, we will not do anything to discourage the knock-offs. The companies that do produce the imitation pieces are always companies that cater to the lower end of the quality spectrum. The high-end companies realize it is futile to copy each others' designs, because to uphold

13

their own reputation they would not be able to produce one any cheaper than their immediate competition, which is already established with that product.

So the lower-end retailer takes its design and sells to the big box stores. Because these retailers cater to a different income class, the availability of similar-looking products at different price levels does not affect the high-end retailers' sales. Industry representatives are in agreement that the few sales they lose to a low-end knock-off are recaptured in a sale to a customer who would usually buy from the low-end retailer. Hence it is not worth the expense of patenting every design or pursuing those who do copy their patented designs.

Considering the market, we are going to launch our product without an expensive patents, and we will create our market security by being the first in the industry. This will result in a sustainable competitive advantage for Darting Lamp Co. Darting Lamp Co. will be the original from day one. If a low-price competitor does arise, we do not have to worry about them stealing our sales, because they will not be attracting our profiled customer anyway. In terms of the high-end companies, history has shown they will not undertake building a similar product, because they have missed out on capturing the competitive advantage of being the first on the scene.

7.7) Harvest Strategy

Darting Lamp Co.'s aggressive research and development program will continue to create demand for our product over the span of our business operations. By keeping our product fresh, we will be able to maintain our share of market sales. At the end of year five business operations, it is the intention of the owners to have the company run without their direct involvement.

A formal review of Darting Lamp Co. operations will be conducted at the end of each quarter. This review will be used to examine the company's profitability and the growth trends of the market. This will allow the owners to evaluate the business and determine if it still meets their expectations.

As long as Darting Lamp Co. is still profitable, it will continue to produce and sell its product. In so doing, Darting Lamp Co. will continue to generate income for the owners and employees. Bryce and Doug will use the resultant profit to fund new venture projects.

8) Report on Financial Information (Exhibits 9.5-9.15)

8.1) Cash Control

The basic strategy for Darting Lamp Co. is that of self-financing all of its operation with cash flow. We will expect payment from 25 percent of our customers within 30 days and the remainder within 60 days. Hanford Marketing, our manufacturer, has offered us 30-day credit on our orders.

8.2) Sources of Funding

Darting Lamp Co. will be financed through a combination of personal investments by the owners, and a bank loan or equity investments. The personal commitments by the two owners will amount to $75,000 by each individual. These funds will be raised through friends, family members, and personal finances. The preferred method of raising the remaining financing would be to have minority limited partners. The minimum investment on the part of the minority limited partner would be $25,000 and a maximum of $75,000. This investment would be repaid at 10.5 percent over a 5-year period, thus a bank loan would be an equal substitute. Equity is preferred over debt investment because equity investors tend to be more flexible than chartered banks.

8.3) Taxation Strategy

As you can see from a careful analysis of the pro forma financial statements provided for Darting Lamp Co., we expect to be profitable within the first year. The protection of these profits from taxation is the key to a strong future in Canadian business. We have sought to minimize the amount of tax paid, while maintaining a strong financial position. This will be accomplished through what is referred to as a year-end straddle. We will declare bonuses to the shareholders' holding companies at the year end of February 28. These bonuses will be paid out six months later to take full advantage of the tax shield. These bonuses will then be returned to the company net of the taxes payable in the same manner. Tax will have to be paid by the holding company in the amount of 25 percent before it is returned as a share-holder's loan. The year end of the holding companies will be one month prior to that of Darting Lamp Co. Thus we can defer payment of the tax on the profits of Darting Lamp Co. by 18 months. This only works in amounts less than $200,000. If the bonuses exceed $200,000, then tax is payable at the marginal rate of 50 percent, and thus the tax shield is no longer effective. We do not avoid paying any of the taxes on the profits, but we do gain the use of the money for 18 months within the corporate structure.

Basically what we do is maintain Darting Lamp Co.'s net profit as close to $200,000 as is possible by declaring bonuses to our holding companies. Thus we avoid paying tax at the marginal rate of 50 percent on Darting Lamp Co. profits and defer the payment of the taxes for 18 months on the bonuses. An example would be in year one, when we would have to pay tax in the amount of $140,707.43, and under the tax shelter we pay tax in the amount of $39,103.71 in April 2000, $31,250 in April 2001, and $31,250 in April 2002.

SAMPLE BUSINESS PLAN

Exhibit 9.1

Cost Break Down of Darting Lamp Co.'s Dart Board Floor Lamp

Product Code:	Qty. (Per Lamp):	Item Description:	Supplier:	Price (ea.):
DLCNI-BASE	1	Brushed Nickel Floor Lamp Base	Superior Mnfg.	$7.8700
DLCNI-DISH	1	Brushed Nickel Floor Lamp Shade	Superior Mnfg.	$3.9000
2001-CP	2	1" Brushed Nickel Washers	Classic Parts	$0.0500
1/4-80"U-CP	2	80" Brushed Nickel Floor Lamp Arms	Classic Parts	$3.8400
1182-CP	4	1/4" Lock-Washer	Classic Parts	$0.0025
UB-9-CP	2	Universal Socket Mounting Bar	Classic Parts	$0.0500
2G11-cp	4	Screws to Hold Ballast and Socket	Classic Parts	$0.0025
LC-25-CP	1	Fluorescent Ballast	Classic Parts	$7.9500
13452/000-CP	1	Fluorescent Socket	Classic Parts	$1.2100
18248/601-CP	1	15' Black 18/2 Lamp Cord and Plug	Classic Parts	$1.9800
37679/001-CP	1	Black Foot Switch	Classic Parts	$2.6200
CABINET-1	1	Dart Board and Cabinet	Bobwood Ind.	$43.5000
Labour	1			$28.00
Packaging	1			$4.00
Shipping	1			$5.00
Total Cost Per Lamp:				**$113.93**

SAMPLE BUSINESS PLAN

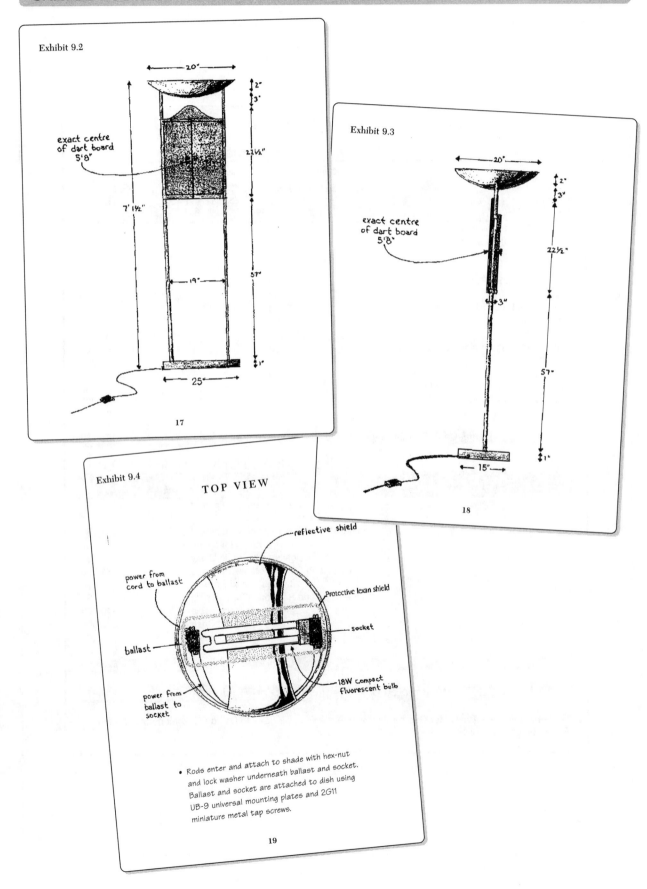

Exhibit 9.2

20"

2"
3"

exact centre
of dart board
5'8"

22½"

7' 1½"

19"

57"

25"

1"

17

Exhibit 9.3

20"

2"
3"

exact centre
of dart board
5'8"

22½"

3"

57"

1"

15"

18

Exhibit 9.4

TOP VIEW

reflective shield

power from
cord to ballast

Protective lexan shield

socket

ballast

18W compact
fluorescent bulb

power from
ballast to
socket

- Rods enter and attach to shade with hex-nut
  and lock washer underneath ballast and socket.
  Ballast and socket are attached to dish using
  UB-9 universal mounting plates and 2G11
  miniature metal tap screws.

19

SAMPLE BUSINESS PLAN

Exhibit 9.5

Required Start-Up Funds for Darting Lamp Co.

Estimated Monthly Expenses

Item	Column 1 Your Estimate of Monthly Expenses Based on Sales of $ 1.6m Per Year	Column 2 Number of Months of Cash Required to Cover Expenses	Column 3 Cash Required To Start Business (Column 1 X Column 2)*
Salary of Owner-Manager	$8,000	8	$64,000
All Other Salaries and Wages	$2,500	8	$20,000
Rent	$500	8	$4,000
Advertising	$6,500	8	$52,000
Delivery Expense/Transportation	$1,000	8	$8,000
Supplies	$50	8	$400
Telephone, Fax, Internet Service	$500	8	$4,000
Other Utilities	$65	8	$520
Insurance	$664	8	$5,312
Taxes Including Employment Insurance	$0	8	$0
Interest	$525	8	$4,200
Maintenance	$0	8	$0
Legal and Other Professional Fees	$0	8	$0
Miscellaneous - Travel	$3,000	8	$24,000
- Lease expense	$500	8	$4,000

Total Cash Requirements for Monthly Recurring Expenses:	**$190,432**

Starting Costs You Only Have to Pay Once

	Cash Required to Start Business
Fixtures and Equipment	$0
Decorating and Remodelling	$0
Installation of Fixtures and Equipment	$0
Starting Inventory	$0
Deposits with Public Utility	$0
Legal and Other Professional Fees	$1,000
Licenses and Permits	$0
Advertising and Promotion for Opening	$0
Accounts Receivable	$10,000
Cash	$15,000
Miscellaneous	$2,000

Total One-Time Cash Requirements:	**$28,000**

Total Estimated Cash Required to Start Business:	**$218,432**

*These Figures Are Typical for One Kind of Business. You Will Have to Decide How Many Months to Allow For Your Business

SAMPLE BUSINESS PLAN

Exhibit 9.6

Darting Lamp Company Ltd.
Pro Forma Monthly Income Statement
Mar 1 1999 to Feb 28 2000

	March	April	May	June	July	August	September	October	November	December	January	February	Total
Income:													
U.S. Sales in Units	-	-	105	105	315	420	525	525	1575	2100	315	315	6300
U.S. Sales in Dollars	$ -	$ -	$ 19,687.50	$ 19,687.50	$ 59,062.50	$ 78,750.00	$ 98,437.50	$ 98,437.50	$ 295,312.50	$ 393,750.00	$ 59,062.50	$ 59,062.50	$1,181,250.00
Canadian Sales in Units	-	-	51	51	153	153	255	255	765	1020	153	153	3009
Canadian Sales in Dollars	$ -	$ -	$ 8,159.49	$ 8,159.49	$ 24,478.47	$ 24,478.47	$ 40,797.45	$ 40,797.45	$ 122,392.35	$ 163,189.80	$ 24,478.47	$ 24,478.47	$481,409.91
Cost of Goods Sold	-	-	17,777.76	17,777.76	53,333.28	65,299.08	88,888.80	88,888.80	266,666.40	355,555.20	53,333.28	53,333.28	1,060,853.64
Gross Margin	$ -	$ -	$ 10,069.23	$ 10,069.23	$ 30,207.69	$ 37,929.39	$ 50,346.15	$ 50,346.15	$ 151,038.45	$ 201,384.60	$ 30,207.69	$ 30,207.69	$ 601,806.27
Expenses:													
Rent	500.00	500.00	500.00	500.00	500.00	500.00	500.00	500.00	500.00	500.00	500.00	500.00	6,000.00
Advertising	6,500.00	6,500.00	6,500.00	6,500.00	6,500.00	7,000.00	7,000.00	7,000.00	7,000.00	7,000.00	6,500.00	6,500.00	80,500.00
Insurance	663.75	663.75	663.75	663.75	663.75	663.75	663.75	663.75	663.75	663.75	663.75	663.75	7,965.00
Utilities	65.00	65.00	65.00	65.00	65.00	65.00	65.00	65.00	65.00	65.00	65.00	65.00	780.00
Telephone	500.00	500.00	500.00	500.00	500.00	500.00	500.00	500.00	500.00	500.00	500.00	500.00	6,000.00
Business License	12.50	12.50	12.50	12.50	12.50	12.50	12.50	12.50	12.50	12.50	12.50	12.50	150.00
Office Supplies	50.00	50.00	50.00	50.00	50.00	50.00	50.00	50.00	50.00	50.00	50.00	50.00	600.00
Travel Expense	3,000.00	3,000.00	3,000.00	3,000.00	3,000.00	3,000.00	3,000.00	3,000.00	3,000.00	3,000.00	3,000.00	3,000.00	36,000.00
Prototype	2,000.00	-	-	-	-	-	-	-	-	-	-	-	2,000.00
Leased equipment	500.00	500.00	500.00	500.00	500.00	500.00	500.00	500.00	500.00	500.00	500.00	500.00	5,892.70
Interest	531.25	524.11	516.93	509.69	502.40	495.06	487.67	480.22	472.72	465.17	457.57	449.91	126,000.00
Salary	10,500.00	10,500.00	10,500.00	10,500.00	10,500.00	10,500.00	10,500.00	10,500.00	10,500.00	10,500.00	10,500.00	10,500.00	125,000.00
Bonuses												125,000.00	
Incorporation Cost	1,000.00												1,000.00
Miscellaneous	200.00	200.00	200.00	200.00	200.00	200.00	200.00	200.00	200.00	200.00	200.00	200.00	2,400.00
Total Expenses	$ 25,822.50	$ 22,815.36	$ 22,808.18	$ 22,800.94	$ 22,793.65	$ 23,286.31	$ 23,278.92	$ 23,271.47	$ 23,263.97	$ 23,256.42	$ 22,748.82	$ 17,593.00	$ 406,287.70
Income Before Tax	$ (25,822.50)	$ (22,815.36)	$ (12,738.95)	$ (12,731.71)	$ 7,414.04	$ 14,643.08	$ 27,067.23	$ 27,074.68	$ 127,774.48	$ 178,128.18	$ 7,458.87	$ 12,614.69	$ 195,518.57
Tax	$ (5,164.50)	$ (4,563.07)	$ (2,547.79)	$ (2,546.34)	$ 1,482.81	$ 2,928.62	$ 5,413.45	$ 5,414.94	$ 25,554.90	$ 35,625.64	$ 1,491.77	$ 2,522.94	$ 39,103.71
Net Income	$ (20,658.00)	$ (18,252.29)	$ (10,191.16)	$ (10,185.37)	$ 5,931.23	$ 11,714.46	$ 21,653.78	$ 21,659.74	$ 102,219.58	$ 142,502.54	$ 5,967.10	$ 10,091.75	$ 156,414.86

21

SAMPLE BUSINESS PLAN

Exhibit 9.7

Darting Lamp Company Ltd.
Pro Forma Quarterly Income Statement
Mar 1 2000 to Feb 28 2001

	Quarter 1	Quarter 2	Quarter 3	Quarter 4	Total
U.S. Sales in Units	1040	1386	1617	4620	8663
U.S. Sales in Dollars	$ 194,906.25	$ 259,875.00	$ 303,187.50	$ 866,250.00	$ 1,624,218.75
Canadian Sales in Units	505	673	785	2244	4208
Canadian Sales in Dollar	$ 80,778.95	$ 107,705.27	$ 125,656.15	$ 359,017.56	$ 673,157.93
Cost of Goods Sold	175,999.82	234,666.43	273,777.50	782,221.44	1,466,665.20
Gross Margin	$ 99,685.38	$ 132,913.84	$ 155,066.14	$ 443,046.12	$ 830,711.48
Expenses:					
Rent	1500.00	1500.00	1500.00	1500.00	$6,000.00
Advertising	28717.21	28717.21	28717.21	28717.21	$114,868.83
Insurance	2031.08	2031.08	2031.08	2031.08	$8,124.30
Utilities	198.90	198.90	198.90	198.90	$795.60
Telephone	1530.00	1530.00	1530.00	1530.00	$6,120.00
Business License	150.00	0.00	0.00	0.00	$150.00
Office Supplies	153.00	153.00	153.00	153.00	$612.00
Travel Expense	10710.00	10710.00	10710.00	10710.00	$42,840.00
Prototype / R&D	5000.00	0.00	0.00	0.00	$5,000.00
Leased equipment	2700.00	2700.00	2700.00	2700.00	$10,800.00
Interest	1303.24	1232.34	1159.92	1085.95	$4,781.45
Salary	73800.00	73800.00	73800.00	73800.00	$295,200.00
Bonuses	0.00	0.00	0.00	135000.00	$135,000.00
Miscellaneous	612.00	612.00	612.00	612.00	$2,448.00
Total Expenses	$ 128,405.42	$ 123,184.52	$ 123,112.10	$ 258,038.13	$ 632,740.18
Income before tax	$ (28,720.05)	$ 9,729.31	$ 31,954.04	$ 185,007.99	$ 197,971.29
Tax	$ (5,744.01)	$ 1,945.86	$ 6,390.81	$ 37,001.60	$ 39,594.26
Net Income	$ (22,976.04)	$ 7,783.45	$ 25,563.23	$ 148,006.39	$ 158,377.03

Darting Lamp Company Ltd.
Pro Forma Quarterly Income Statement
Mar 1 2001 to Feb 28 2002

	Quarter 1	Quarter 2	Quarter 3	Quarter 4	Total
U.S. Sales in Units	1143	1525	1779	5082	9529
U.S. Sales in Dollars	$ 214,396.88	$ 285,862.50	$ 333,506.25	$ 952,875.00	$ 1,786,640.63
Canadian Sales in Units	555	741	864	2468	4628
Canadian Sales in Dollar	$ 88,856.85	$ 118,475.79	$ 138,221.76	$ 394,919.32	$ 740,473.72
Cost of Goods Sold	193,599.81	258,133.08	301,155.25	860,443.58	1,613,331.72
Gross Margin	$ 109,653.91	$ 146,205.22	$ 170,572.76	$ 487,350.73	$ 913,782.62
Expenses:					
Rent	1500.00	1500.00	1500.00	1500.00	6000.00
Advertising	31588.93	31588.93	31588.93	31588.93	126355.72
Insurance	2071.70	2071.70	2071.70	2071.70	8286.79
Utilities	202.88	202.88	202.88	202.88	811.51
Telephone	1560.60	1560.60	1560.60	1560.60	6242.40
Business License	150.00	0.00	0.00	0.00	150.00
Office Supplies	156.06	156.06	156.06	156.06	624.24
Travel Expense	10924.20	10924.20	10924.20	10924.20	43696.80
Prototype / R&D	5100.00	0.00	0.00	0.00	5100.00
Leased equipment	2700.00	2700.00	2700.00	2700.00	10800.00
Interest	1010.40	933.23	854.40	773.91	3571.94
Salary	87516.00	87516.00	87516.00	87516.00	350064.00
Bonuses	0.00	0.00	0.00	150000.00	150000.00
Miscellaneous	624.24	624.24	624.24	624.24	2496.96
Total Expenses	$ 145,105.00	$ 139,777.83	$ 139,699.00	$ 289,618.51	$ 714,200.36
Income before tax	$ (35,451.09)	$ 6,427.39	$ 30,873.75	$ 197,732.22	$ 199,582.27
Tax	$ (7,090.22)	$ 1,285.48	$ 6,174.75	$ 39,546.44	$ 39,916.45
Net Income	$ (28,360.87)	$ 5,141.91	$ 24,699.00	$ 158,185.77	$ 159,665.81

22

SAMPLE BUSINESS PLAN

Exhibit 9.8

Darting Lamp Company Ltd.
Pro Forma Yearly Income Statement
For the Year Ended

	Feb 28 2000	Feb 28 2001	Feb 28 2002	Feb 28 2003	Feb 28 2004
U.S. Sales in Units	6300	8662	9528	10482	11530
U.S. Sales in Dollars	$ 1,181,250.00	1,624,218.75	$ 1,786,640.63	1,965,304.69	$ 2,161,835.16
Canadian Sales in Units	3,009.00	4,207.50	4,628.25	5091	5600
Canadian Sales in Dollars	$ 481,409.91	673,157.93	$ 740,473.72	814,521.09	$ 895,973.20
Cost of Goods Sold	$ 1,060,853.64	1,466,665.20	$ 1,613,331.72	1,774,664.89	$ 1,952,131.38
Gross Margin	$ 601,806.27	830,711.48	$ 913,782.62	1,005,160.88	$ 1,105,676.97
Expenses:					
Rent	6,000.00	6,000.00	6,000.00	6000.00	6000.00
Advertising	80,500.00	114,868.83	126,355.72	138991.29	152890.42
Insurance	7,965.00	8,124.30	8,286.79	9115.46	10027.01
Utilities	780.00	795.60	811.51	892.66	981.93
Telephone	6,000.00	6,120.00	6,242.40	6866.64	7553.30
Business License	150.00	150.00	150.00	150.00	150.00
Office Supplies	600.00	612.00	624.24	686.66	755.33
Travel Expense	36,000.00	42,840.00	43,696.80	48066.48	52873.13
Prototype	2,000.00	5,000.00	5,100.00	5610.00	6171.00
Leased equipment	6,000.00	10,800.00	10,800.00	10800.00	10800.00
Interest	5,892.70	4,781.45	3,571.94	2255.54	822.78
Salary	126,000.00	295,200.00	350,064.00	385070.40	423577.44
Bonuses	125,000.00	135,000.00	150,000.00	190000.00	231000.00
Incorporation Costs	1,000.00	-	-	0.00	0.00
Miscellaneous	2,400.00	2,448.00	2,496.96	2746.66	3021.32
Total Expenses	$ 406,287.70	632,740.18	$ 714,200.36	807,251.80	$ 906,623.66
Income before tax	$ 195,518.57	197,971.29	$ 199,582.27	197,909.09	$ 199,053.31
Tax	$ 39,103.71	39,594.26	$ 39,916.45	39,581.82	$ 39,810.66
Net Income	$ 156,414.86	158,377.03	$ 159,665.81	158,327.27	$ 159,242.65

23

SAMPLE BUSINESS PLAN

Exhibit 9.9

Darting Lamp Company Ltd.
Pro Forma Cash Flow Projections(Pessimistic)
Mar 1 1999 to Feb 28 2000

	March	April	May	June	July	August	September	October	November	December	January	February
Beginning Cash Balance	225,000.00	197,832.51	173,815.02	149,797.53	114,964.03	101,015.77	64,935.48	63,581.76	62,405.56	88,234.22	5,902.75	78,843.65
Operating Cash Flows												
Sales	-	-	27,846.99	27,846.99	83,540.97	103,228.47	139,234.95	139,234.95	417,704.85	556,939.80	83,540.97	83,540.97
Collection from sales 30 Days	-	-	-	6,961.75	6,961.75	20,885.24	25,807.12	34,808.74	34,808.74	104,426.21	139,234.95	20,885.24
Collection from sales 60 Days	-	-	-	-	20,885.24	20,885.24	62,655.73	77,421.35	104,426.21	104,426.21	313,278.64	417,704.85
Total Cash Inflows	-	-	-	6,961.75	27,846.99	41,770.49	88,462.85	112,230.09	139,234.95	208,852.43	452,513.59	438,590.09
Purchases												
Payments to Manufacturer	-	-	-	(17,777.76)	(17,777.76)	(53,333.28)	(65,299.08)	(88,888.80)	(88,888.80)	(266,666.40)	(355,555.20)	(53,333.28)
Cash Outflows												
Rent	(500.00)	(500.00)	(500.00)	(500.00)	(500.00)	(500.00)	(500.00)	(500.00)	(500.00)	(500.00)	(500.00)	(500.00)
Advertising	(6,500.00)	(6,500.00)	(6,500.00)	(6,500.00)	(6,500.00)	(7,000.00)	(7,000.00)	(7,000.00)	(7,000.00)	(7,000.00)	(6,500.00)	(6,500.00)
Insurance	(663.75)	(663.75)	(663.75)	(663.75)	(663.75)	(663.75)	(663.75)	(663.75)	(663.75)	(663.75)	(663.75)	(663.75)
Utilities	(65.00)	(65.00)	(65.00)	(65.00)	(65.00)	(65.00)	(65.00)	(65.00)	(65.00)	(65.00)	(65.00)	(65.00)
Telephone	(500.00)	(500.00)	(500.00)	(500.00)	(500.00)	(500.00)	(500.00)	(500.00)	(500.00)	(500.00)	(500.00)	(500.00)
Business License	(150.00)											
Office Supplies	(50.00)	(50.00)	(50.00)	(50.00)	(50.00)	(50.00)	(50.00)	(50.00)	(50.00)	(50.00)	(50.00)	(50.00)
Travel Expense	(3,000.00)	(3,000.00)	(3,000.00)	(3,000.00)	(3,000.00)	(3,000.00)	(3,000.00)	(3,000.00)	(3,000.00)	(3,000.00)	(3,000.00)	(3,000.00)
Prototype	(2,000.00)											
Leased equipment	(500.00)	(500.00)	(500.00)	(500.00)	(500.00)	(500.00)	(500.00)	(500.00)	(500.00)	(500.00)	(500.00)	(500.00)
Interest	(531.25)	(524.11)	(516.93)	(509.69)	(502.40)	(495.06)	(487.67)	(480.22)	(472.72)	(465.17)	(457.57)	(449.91)
Repayment of Principal	(1,007.49)	(1,014.63)	(1,021.81)	(1,029.05)	(1,036.34)	(1,043.68)	(1,051.07)	(1,058.52)	(1,066.02)	(1,073.57)	(1,081.17)	(1,088.83)
Salary	(10,500.00)	(10,500.00)	(10,500.00)	(10,500.00)	(10,500.00)	(10,500.00)	(10,500.00)	(10,500.00)	(10,500.00)	(10,500.00)	(10,500.00)	(10,500.00)
Incorporation Cost	(1,000.00)											
Miscellaneous	(200.00)	(200.00)	(200.00)	(200.00)	(200.00)	(200.00)	(200.00)	(200.00)	(200.00)	(200.00)	(200.00)	(200.00)
Total Cash Outflow	(27,167.49)	(24,017.49)	(24,017.49)	(41,795.25)	(41,795.25)	(77,850.77)	(89,816.57)	(113,406.29)	(113,406.29)	(291,183.89)	(379,572.69)	(77,350.77)
Net Operating Cash Flow	(27,167.49)	(24,017.49)	(24,017.49)	(34,833.50)	(13,948.26)	(36,080.29)	(1,353.73)	(1,176.20)	25,828.66	(82,331.47)	72,940.90	361,239.32
Ending Cash Flow	$ 197,832.51	$ 173,815.02	$ 149,797.53	$ 114,964.03	$ 101,015.77	$ 64,935.48	$ 63,581.76	$ 62,405.56	$ 88,234.22	$ 5,902.75	$ 78,843.65	$ 440,082.97

SAMPLE BUSINESS PLAN

Exhibit 9.10

Darting Lamp Company
Pro Forma Balance Sheet

Assets	Beginning of Year		End of Year 1
Current:			
Cash	225,000.00		440,082.97
Accounts Receivable	-		146,196.70
Total Current Assets	$ 225,000.00		$ 586,279.67
Total Assets	$ 225,000.00		$ 586,279.67
Liabilities and Owners Equity			
Current liabilities:			
Accounts Payable	-		53,333.28
Taxes Payable	-		39,103.71
Bonuses Payable	-		125,000.00
Total Current liabilities	$ -		$ 217,436.99
Long-term liabilities			
Loan Payable	75,000.00		62,427.82
Total Long-term liabilities	75,000.00		62,427.82
Total Liabilities	$ 75,000.00		$ 279,864.81
Owners' Equity			
Capital	150,000.00		150,000.00
Shareholders' Loans	-		-
Retained Earnings	-		156,414.86
Total Shareholders' Equity	$ 150,000.00		$ 306,414.86
Total liabilities & Owners' Equity	$ 225,000.00		$ 586,279.67

25

SAMPLE BUSINESS PLAN

Exhibit 9.11

Break-even Point for the First year

Operating Expenses	
Owners' Salaries	$96,000
Employees' Wages	$30,000
Supplies and Postage	$600
Advert. and Promotion	$80,500
Delivery Expense	$12,000
Bad Debt Allowance	$0
Travel	$36,000
Professional Fees	$0
Vehicle Expense	$0
Maintenance Expense	$0
Other Variable Expenses	$0
Rent	$6,000
Utilities	$780
Telephone	$6,000
Taxes & Licenses	$0
Depreciation	$0
Interest	$6,300
Insurance	$8,000
Other Fixed Expenses	$6,000
TOTAL OPERATING EXPENSES	**$288,180**

CONTRIBUTION MARGIN = $\dfrac{\text{Gross Margin}}{\text{Net Sales}}$ = 0.36

BREAKEVEN POINT ($Sales) = $\dfrac{\text{Total Operating Expenses}}{\text{Contribution Margin}}$

$800,500

Exhibit 9.12

Financial Ratios for
Darting Lamp Company

				End of Year 1
1. Gross Margin/Sales	=	Gross Profit / Net Sales	=	$601,806 / $1,662,659 → 0.36
2. Current Ratio	=	Current Assets / Current Liabilities	=	$586,280 / $217,437 → 2.70
3. Debt/Equity	=	Total Debt / Total Equity	=	$62,428 / $306,415 → 0.20
4. Net Profit/Net Worth	=	Net Profit / Net Worth	=	$156,415 / $306,415 → 0.51
5. Sales/Net Worth	=	Net Sales / Net Worth	=	$1,662,659 / $306,415 → 5.43
6. Current Liabilities/Net Worth	=	Current Liabilities / Net Worth	=	$217,437 / $306,415 → 0.71
7. Total Liabilities/Net Worth	=	Total Liabilities / Net Worth	=	$279,865 / $306,415 → 0.91
8. Debt/Net Worth	=	Total Outstanding Debt / Net Worth	=	$62,428 / $306,415 → 0.20
9. Return On Assets	=	Net Income (After Tax) / Total Assets	=	$156,415 / $586,280 → 0.25

27

SAMPLE BUSINESS PLAN

Exhibit 9.13

Darting Lamp Company Ltd.
Pro Forma Monthly Income Statement (Pessimistic)
Mar 1 1999 to Feb 28 2000

	March	April	May	June	July	August	September	October	November	December	January	February	Total
Income:													
U.S. Sales in Units	-	-	84	84	252	336	420	420	1260	1680	252	252	5040
U.S. Sales in Dollars	$ -	$ -	$ 15,750.00	$ 15,750.00	$ 47,250.00	$ 63,000.00	$ 78,750.00	$ 78,750.00	$ 236,250.00	$ 315,000.00	$ 47,250.00	$ 47,250.00	$ 945,000.00
Canadian Sales in Units	-	-	41	41	122	122	204	204	612	816	122	122	2407
Canadian Sales in Dollars	$ -	$ -	$ 6,527.59	$ 6,527.59	$ 19,582.78	$ 19,582.78	$ 32,637.96	$ 32,637.96	$ 97,913.88	$ 130,551.84	$ 19,582.78	$ 19,582.78	$ 385,127.93
Cost of Goods Sold	-	-	14,222.21	14,222.21	42,666.62	52,239.26	71,111.04	71,111.04	213,333.12	284,444.16	42,666.62	42,666.62	848,682.91
Gross Margin	$ -	$ -	$ 8,055.38	$ 8,055.38	$ 24,166.15	$ 30,343.51	$ 40,276.92	$ 40,276.92	$ 120,830.76	$ 161,107.68	$ 24,166.15	$ 24,166.15	$ 481,445.02
Expenses:													
Rent	500.00	500.00	500.00	500.00	500.00	500.00	500.00	500.00	500.00	500.00	500.00	500.00	6,000.00
Advertising	6,500.00	6,500.00	6,500.00	6,500.00	6,500.00	7,000.00	7,000.00	7,000.00	7,000.00	7,000.00	6,500.00	6,500.00	80,500.00
Insurance	663.75	663.75	663.75	663.75	663.75	663.75	663.75	663.75	663.75	663.75	663.75	663.75	7,965.00
Utilities	65.00	65.00	65.00	65.00	65.00	65.00	65.00	65.00	65.00	65.00	65.00	65.00	780.00
Telephone	500.00	500.00	500.00	500.00	500.00	500.00	500.00	500.00	500.00	500.00	500.00	500.00	6,000.00
Business License	12.50	12.50	12.50	12.50	12.50	12.50	12.50	12.50	12.50	12.50	12.50	12.50	150.00
Office Supplies	50.00	50.00	50.00	50.00	50.00	50.00	50.00	50.00	50.00	50.00	50.00	50.00	600.00
Travel Expense	3,000.00	3,000.00	3,000.00	3,000.00	3,000.00	3,000.00	3,000.00	3,000.00	3,000.00	3,000.00	3,000.00	3,000.00	36,000.00
Prototype	2,000.00	-	-	-	-	-	-	-	-	-	-	-	2,000.00
Leased equipment	500.00	500.00	500.00	500.00	500.00	500.00	500.00	500.00	500.00	500.00	500.00	500.00	6,000.00
Interest	531.25	524.11	516.93	509.69	502.40	495.06	487.67	480.22	472.72	465.17	457.57	449.91	5,892.70
Salary	10,500.00	10,500.00	10,500.00	10,500.00	10,500.00	10,500.00	10,500.00	10,500.00	10,500.00	10,500.00	10,500.00	10,500.00	126,000.00
Bonuses	-	-	-	-	-	-	-	-	-	-	-	5,000.00	5,000.00
Incorporation Cost	1,000.00	-	-	-	-	-	-	-	-	-	-	-	1,000.00
Miscellaneous	200.00	200.00	200.00	200.00	200.00	200.00	200.00	200.00	200.00	200.00	200.00	200.00	2,400.00
Total Expenses	$ 25,822.50	$ 22,815.36	$ 22,808.18	$ 22,800.94	$ 22,793.65	$ 23,286.31	$ 23,278.92	$ 23,271.47	$ 23,263.97	$ 23,256.42	$ 22,748.82	$ 17,593.00	$ 286,287.70
Income Before Tax	$ (25,822.50)	$ (22,815.36)	$ (14,752.80)	$ (14,745.56)	$ 1,372.50	$ 7,057.20	$ 16,998.00	$ 17,005.45	$ 97,566.79	$ 137,851.26	$ 1,417.33	$ 6,573.15	$ 195,157.32
Tax	$ (5,164.50)	$ (4,563.07)	$ (2,950.56)	$ (2,949.11)	$ 274.50	$ 1,411.44	$ 3,399.60	$ 3,401.09	$ 19,513.36	$ 27,570.25	$ 283.47	$ 1,314.63	$ 39,031.46
Net Income	$ (20,658.00)	$ (18,252.29)	$ (11,802.24)	$ (11,796.44)	$ 1,098.00	$ 5,645.76	$ 13,598.40	$ 13,604.36	$ 78,053.43	$ 110,281.01	$ 1,133.87	$ 5,258.52	$ 156,125.85

SAMPLE BUSINESS PLAN

Exhibit 9.14

Darting Lamp Company Ltd.
Pro Forma Quarterly Income Statement (Pessimistic)
Mar 1 2000 to Feb 28 2001

	Quarter 1	Quarter 2	Quarter 3	Quarter 4	Total
U.S. Sales in Units	832	1109	1294	3696	6930
U.S. Sales in Dollars	$ 155,925.00	$ 207,900.00	$ 242,550.00	$ 693,000.00	$ 1,299,375.00
Canadian Sales in Units	404	539	628	1795	3366
Canadian Sales in Dollars	$ 64,623.16	$ 86,164.21	$ 100,524.92	$ 287,214.05	$ 538,526.34
Cost of Goods Sold	140,799.86	187,733.15	219,022.00	625,777.15	1,173,332.16
Gross Margin	$ 79,748.30	$ 106,331.07	$ 124,052.91	$ 354,436.90	$ 664,569.18
Expenses:					
Rent	1500.00	1500.00	1500.00	1500.00	$6,000.00
Advertising	22973.77	22973.77	22973.77	22973.77	$91,895.07
Insurance	2031.08	2031.08	2031.08	2031.08	$8,124.30
Utilities	198.90	198.90	198.90	198.90	$795.60
Telephone	1530.00	1530.00	1530.00	1530.00	$6,120.00
Business License	150.00	0.00	0.00	0.00	$150.00
Office Supplies	153.00	153.00	153.00	153.00	$612.00
Travel Expense	10710.00	10710.00	10710.00	10710.00	$42,840.00
Prototype / R&D	5000.00	0.00	0.00	0.00	$5,000.00
Leased equipment	2700.00	2700.00	2700.00	2700.00	$10,800.00
Interest	1303.24	1232.34	1159.92	1085.95	$4,781.45
Salary	66675.00	66675.00	66675.00	66675.00	$266,700.00
Bonuses	0.00	0.00	0.00	20000.00	$20,000.00
Miscellaneous	612.00	612.00	612.00	612.00	$2,448.00
Total Expenses	$ 115,536.98	$ 110,316.08	$ 110,243.66	$ 130,169.69	$ 466,266.42
Income before tax	$ (35,788.68)	$ (3,985.01)	$ 13,809.25	$ 224,267.20	$ 198,302.76
Tax	$ (7,157.74)	$ (797.00)	$ 2,761.85	$ 100,920.24	$ 39,660.55
Net Income	$ (28,630.94)	$ (3,188.01)	$ 11,047.40	$ 123,346.96	$ 158,642.21

Darting Lamp Company Ltd.
Pro Forma Quarterly Income Statement (Pessimistic)
Mar 1 2001 to Feb 28 2002

	Quarter 1	Quarter 2	Quarter 3	Quarter 4	Total
U.S. Sales in Units	915	1220	1423	4066	7623
U.S. Sales in Dollars	$ 171,517.50	$ 228,690.00	$ 266,805.00	$ 762,300.00	$ 1,429,312.50
Canadian Sales in Units	444	592	691	1975	3703
Canadian Sales in Dollars	$ 71,085.48	$ 94,780.64	$ 110,577.41	$ 315,935.45	$ 592,378.97
Cost of Goods Sold	154,879.85	206,506.46	240,924.20	688,354.87	1,290,665.38
Gross Margin	$ 87,723.13	$ 116,964.18	$ 136,458.20	$ 389,880.59	$ 731,026.10
Expenses:					
Rent	1500.00	1500.00	1500.00	1500.00	6000.00
Advertising	25271.14	25271.14	25271.14	25271.14	101084.57
Insurance	2071.70	2071.70	2071.70	2071.70	8286.79
Utilities	202.88	202.88	202.88	202.88	811.51
Telephone	1560.60	1560.60	1560.60	1560.60	6242.40
Business License	150.00	0.00	0.00	0.00	150.00
Office Supplies	156.06	156.06	156.06	156.06	624.24
Travel Expense	10924.20	10924.20	10924.20	10924.20	43696.80
Prototype / R&D	5100.00	0.00	0.00	0.00	5100.00
Leased equipment	2700.00	2700.00	2700.00	2700.00	10800.00
Interest	1010.40	933.23	854.40	773.91	3571.94
Salary	73950.00	73950.00	73950.00	73950.00	295800.00
Bonuses	0.00	0.00	0.00	50000.00	50000.00
Miscellaneous	624.24	624.24	624.24	624.24	2496.96
Total Expenses	$ 125,221.22	$ 119,894.05	$ 119,815.22	$ 169,734.73	$ 534,665.21
Income before tax	$ (37,498.09)	$ (2,929.87)	$ 16,642.99	$ 220,145.86	$ 196,360.89
Tax	$ (7,499.62)	$ (585.97)	$ 3,328.60	$ 99,065.64	$ 39,272.18
Net Income	$ (29,998.47)	$ (2,343.90)	$ 13,314.39	$ 121,080.22	$ 157,088.71

29

SAMPLE BUSINESS PLAN

Exhibit 9.15

Darting Lamp Company Ltd.
Pro Forma Yearly Income Statement (Pessimistic)
For the Year Ended

	Feb 28 2000	Feb 28 2001	Feb 28 2002	Feb 28 2003	Feb 28 2004
U.S. Sales in Units	5,040.00	6,930.00	7,623.00	8385	9224
U.S. Sales in Dollars	$ 945,000.00	1,299,375.00	1,429,312.50	1,572,243.75	1,729,468.13
Canadian Sales in Units	2,407.20	3,366.00	3,702.60	5091	5600
Canadian Sales in Dollars	$ 385,127.93	538,526.34	592,378.97	814,521.09	895,973.20
Cost of Goods Sold	$ 848,682.91	1,173,332.16	1,290,665.38	1,535,767.70	1,689,344.46
Gross Margin	$ 481,445.02	664,569.18	731,026.10	850,997.14	936,096.86
Expenses:					
Rent	6,000.00	6,000.00	6,000.00	6,000.00	6,000.00
Advertising	80,500.00	91,895.07	101,084.57	119,338.24	131,272.07
Insurance	7,965.00	8,124.30	8,286.79	9,115.46	10,027.01
Utilities	780.00	795.60	811.51	892.66	981.93
Telephone	6,000.00	6,120.00	6,242.40	6,866.64	7,553.30
Business License	150.00	150.00	150.00	150.00	150.00
Office Supplies	600.00	612.00	624.24	686.66	755.33
Travel Expense	36,000.00	42,840.00	43,696.80	48,066.48	52,873.13
Prototype	2,000.00	5,000.00	5,100.00	5,610.00	6,171.00
Leased equipment	6,000.00	10,800.00	10,800.00	10,800.00	10,800.00
Interest	5,892.70	4,781.45	3,571.94	2,255.54	822.78
Salary	126,000.00	266,700.00	295,800.00	325,380.00	354,000.00
Bonuses	5,000	20,000.00	50,000.00	115,000.00	155,000.00
Incorporation Costs	1,000		-	-	-
Miscellaneous	2,400	2,448.00	2,496.96	2,746.66	3,021.32
Total Expenses	$ 286,287.70	466,266.42	534,665.21	652,908.35	739,427.87
Income before tax	$ 195,157.32	198,302.76	196,360.89	198,088.79	196,668.99
Tax	$ 39,031.46	39,660.55	39,272.18	39,617.76	39,333.80
Net Income	$ 156,125.85	158,642.21	157,088.71	158,471.04	157,335.19

30

SAMPLE BUSINESS PLAN

Exhibit 9.16

Darting Lamp Company Ltd.
Pro Forma Cash Flow Projections(Pessimistic)
Mar 1 1999 to Feb 28 2000

	March	April	May	June	July	August	September	October	November	December	January	February
Beginning Cash Balance	225,000.00	197,832.51	173,815.02	149,797.53	117,127.23	101,165.12	67,397.40	61,410.92	55,566.46	71,325.89	557.22	54,106.44
Operating Cash Flows												
Sales	-	-	22,277.59	22,277.59	66,832.78	82,582.78	111,387.96	111,387.96	334,163.88	445,551.84	66,832.78	66,832.78
Collection from sales 30 Days	-	-	-	5,569.40	5,569.40	16,708.19	20,645.69	27,846.99	27,846.99	83,540.97	111,387.96	16,708.19
Collection from sales 60 Days	-	-	-	-	16,708.19	16,708.19	50,124.58	61,937.08	83,540.97	83,540.97	250,622.91	334,163.88
Total Cash Inflows	-	-	-	5,569.40	22,277.59	33,416.39	70,770.28	89,784.07	111,387.96	167,081.94	362,010.87	350,872.07
Purchases												
Payments to Manufacturer	-	-	-	(14,222.21)	(14,222.21)	(42,666.62)	(52,239.26)	(71,111.04)	(71,111.04)	(213,333.12)	(284,444.16)	(42,666.62)
Cash Out flows												
Rent	(500.00)	(500.00)	(500.00)	(500.00)	(500.00)	(500.00)	(500.00)	(500.00)	(500.00)	(500.00)	(500.00)	(500.00)
Advertising	(6,500.00)	(6,500.00)	(6,500.00)	(6,500.00)	(6,500.00)	(7,000.00)	(7,000.00)	(7,000.00)	(7,000.00)	(7,000.00)	(6,500.00)	(6,500.00)
Insurance	(663.75)	(663.75)	(663.75)	(663.75)	(663.75)	(663.75)	(663.75)	(663.75)	(663.75)	(663.75)	(663.75)	(663.75)
Utilities	(65.00)	(65.00)	(65.00)	(65.00)	(65.00)	(65.00)	(65.00)	(65.00)	(65.00)	(65.00)	(65.00)	(65.00)
Telephone	(500.00)	(500.00)	(500.00)	(500.00)	(500.00)	(500.00)	(500.00)	(500.00)	(500.00)	(500.00)	(500.00)	(500.00)
Business License	(150.00)											
Office Supplies	(50.00)	(50.00)	(50.00)	(50.00)	(50.00)	(50.00)	(50.00)	(50.00)	(50.00)	(50.00)	(50.00)	(50.00)
Travel Expense	(3,000.00)	(3,000.00)	(3,000.00)	(3,000.00)	(3,000.00)	(3,000.00)	(3,000.00)	(3,000.00)	(3,000.00)	(3,000.00)	(3,000.00)	(3,000.00)
Prototype	(2,000.00)											
Leased equipment	(500.00)	(500.00)	(500.00)	(500.00)	(500.00)	(500.00)	(500.00)	(500.00)	(500.00)	(500.00)	(500.00)	(500.00)
Interest	(531.25)	(524.11)	(516.93)	(509.69)	(502.40)	(495.06)	(487.67)	(480.22)	(472.72)	(465.17)	(457.57)	(449.91)
Repayment of Principle	(1,007.49)	(1,014.63)	(1,021.81)	(1,029.05)	(1,036.34)	(1,043.68)	(1,051.07)	(1,058.52)	(1,066.02)	(1,073.57)	(1,081.17)	(1,088.83)
Salary	(10,500.00)	(10,500.00)	(10,500.00)	(10,500.00)	(10,500.00)	(10,500.00)	(10,500.00)	(10,500.00)	(10,500.00)	(10,500.00)	(10,500.00)	(10,500.00)
Incorporation Cost	(1,000.00)											
Miscellaneous	(200.00)	(200.00)	(200.00)	(200.00)	(200.00)	(200.00)	(200.00)	(200.00)	(200.00)	(200.00)	(200.00)	(200.00)
Total Cash out flow	(27,167.49)	(24,017.49)	(24,017.49)	(38,239.70)	(38,239.70)	(67,184.11)	(76,756.75)	(95,628.53)	(95,628.53)	(237,850.61)	(308,461.65)	(66,684.11)
Net Operating Cash flow	(27,167.49)	(24,017.49)	(24,017.49)	(32,670.30)	(15,962.11)	(33,767.73)	(5,986.48)	(5,844.46)	15,759.43	(70,768.67)	53,549.22	284,187.96
Ending Cash Flow	$ 197,832.51	$ 173,815.02	$ 149,797.53	$ 117,127.23	$ 101,165.12	$ 67,397.40	$ 61,410.92	$ 55,566.46	$ 71,325.89	$ 557.22	$ 54,106.44	$ 338,294.40

Exhibit 9.17

Darting Lamp Company Ltd.
Pro Forma Balance Sheet(Pessimistic)

Assets	Beginning of Year		End of Year 1
Current:			
Cash	225,000.00		338,294.40
Accounts Receivable	-		116,957.36
Total Current assets	$ 225,000.00		$ 455,251.76
Total Assets	$ 225,000.00		$ 455,251.76
Liabilities and Owners Equity			
Current liabilities:			
Accounts Payable	-		42,666.62
Taxes Payable	-		39,031.46
Bonuses Payable	-		5,000.00
Total Current liabilities	$ -		$ 86,898.09
Long-term liabilities			
Loan Payable	75,000.00		62,427.82
Total Long-term liabilities	75,000.00		62,427.82
Total Liabilities	$ 75,000.00		$ 149,325.91
Owners' Equity			
Capital	150,000.00		150,000.00
Shareholders' Loans	-		-
Retained Earnings	-		156,125.85
Total Shareholders' Equity	$ 150,000.00		$ 306,125.85
Total liabilities & Owners' Equity	$ 225,000.00		$ 455,451.76

Further Information

Further Reading

Banks

Royal Bank of Canada (www.royalbank.com)

- Starting Out right
- Borrowing Money
- Managing Your Cash Flow
- Disk: The Big Idea
- Definitive Guides to …
  - Small Business Financing in Canada
  - Exporting for Small Business In Canada
  - Personal Financial Management
  - Managing Human Resources
  - Understanding Business Cycles for Growing Companies
- The 10 Minute Guides to …
  - The Year 2000
  - Business on the Internet
  - The Euro
  - Managing Foreign Exchange Risk
  - Winning Business from Big Business

Bank of Montreal (www.bankofmontreal.com) or (www.bmo.com)

Small Business Problem Solver Series

- The Cycles of Your Business
- Using Other People's Help
- Sources of Capital
- Developing Your Business Plan
- Making Sense of Terms and Jargon
- Cash Flow Planning
- Measuring Performance
- Managing Your Cash Flow
- The Financial Proposal
- Dealing With Your Banker
- Are You an Entrepreneur
- Marketing Your Business
- Becoming a People Manager
- Computers for Your Business
- Doing Business Internationally

Other Publications
- Business: Export Financing. New Financing Options for Small- and Medium-Sized Canadian Exporters
- Financing Your Business: Small Business Loan Application Guide
- Planning Your Success: Outline for a Business Plan

Scotiabank (www.scotiabank.ca)
- Scotiabusiness PlanWriter software
- Business Loan Answer Book

CIBC (www.cibc.com)
- Business Focus software

Toronto Dominion Bank (www.tdbank.ca)
- Business Banking Services
- Small Business Loans
- Commercial Mortgage
- Cash Flow Budgeting Brochure
- Business Planner
- Business Terms Loans and Leases

Business Development Bank of Canada (www.bdc.ca)
- Analyzing Financial Statements
- Arranging Financing
- Credit and Collection Tips
- Evaluating the Purchase of a Small Business
- Forecasting and Cash Flow Budgeting

Accounting Firms
BDO Dunwoody (www.bdo.ca)
- Self-Employment: Is It for You?

Ernst & Young (www.ey.com/industry/entrepreneur/default.asp)
- Business Now Online Magazine
- Outline For a Business Plan – A Proven Approach for Entrepreneurs Only (download from www.ey.com/publicate/entrepreneur/default.asp)

Federal Government
Industry Canada (www.ic.gc.ca)
- A Guide to Patents
- A Guide to Trademarks
- A Guide to Copyright
- A Guide to Industrial Designs
- Small Business Guide to Federal Incorporation
- Bankruptcy
- Consumer Protection
- Sector Competitiveness Frameworks
- Small Business Quarterly
- Loans for Small Business

Foreign Affairs and International Trade Canada (www.infoexport.gc.ca)

- Export Information Kit
- Directory of Canadian Foreign Trade Representatives and Canadian Consulates Abroad (online at http://198.103.104.20/tcs/main.asp)
- Guide for Canadian Exporters Series (www.infoexport.gc.ca/menu-e.asp)
- CanadExport Trade Newsletter (www.dfait-maeci.gc.ca/english/news/newsletr/canex/menu.htm)

Revenue Canada – Customs and Excise (www.rc.gc.ca)

- Revenue Canada Initiative for Small- and Medium-Sized Enterprises
- Guide to Importing Commercial Goods
- Revenue Canada Small Business Page (www.rc.gc.ca/menu/EmenuNBA.html)

Public Works and Government Services Canada (www.pwgsc.gc.ca)

- Subcontracting Opportunities Contacts for Major Crown Projects
- The Supply Manual

Provincial Governments

Prince Edward Island Economic Development and Tourism (www.pe.ca/enterprisepei and www.peibusinessdevelopment.com)

- Starting a Business
- Industrial Parks
- Running a Business

New Brunswick Department of Economic Development and Tourism (www.gov.nb.ca)

- Marketing a Small Business
- Key Steps to Business Improvement
- Corporate Directories
- Going Public

Québec Ministre de l'Industrie, du Commerce, de la Science et de la Technologie (www.gouv.qc.ca/affaires/indexa.htm)

- L'entrepreneurship féminin: en tête de nos affaires
- Corporate Directories
- PME: entrepreneurship et croissance
- Starting Up Right
- Partnership Guide
- Starting a Business

The following can be downloaded from www.mic.gouv.qc.ca/entreprisesentrepreneurship.html

- Entreprendre au féminin
- Fonder une enterprise
- Le démarrage d'entreprise et le plan d'affaires
- Profils des petites entreprises

Ontario Ministry of Economic Development and Trade (www.gov.on.ca)

- Business Plan Preparation Series
- Manufacturing
- Service
- Retail
- Professional Service
- Guide: Starting a Small Business in Ontario

- Record Keeping Made Easy
- How to Prepare a Business Plan
- Marketing for a Small Business

Manitoba Department of Industry, Trade, and Tourism (www.gov.mb.ca/itt/index.html)
Information Pamphlets
- Starting a Small Business in Manitoba
- Monter une petite entreprise au Manitoba

Small Business Management Systems
- Retail Business Plan
- Service Business Plan
- Construction Business Plan
- Manufacturing Business Plan
- Small Business Finance Plan
- Marketing
- Bookkeeping

Entrepreneur's Handbooks
- Importing
- Forms of Business Organization
- Starting a Retail Clothing Outlet
- Starting a Bookstore
- Starting a Convenience Food Store
- Starting a Sporting Goods Store
- Starting a Service Station
- Starting a Mail Order Business
- Starting a Hardware Store
- Starting a Restaurant

Self-Evaluation Guides to Starting a Business on Your Own
- Stage 1: Assessing Your Potential for an Entrepreneurial Career
- Stage 2: Finding and Evaluating a Product or Service Idea
- Stage 3: Should You Start a New Business or Buy an Existing One?

Saskatchewan Department of Economic and Co-operative Development (www.gov.sk.ca/govt/econdev)
- See the C/SBSC listing for information

Alberta Economic Development and Trade (www.edt.gov.ab.ca and www.gov.ab.ca/edt/map.htm)
- Financing a Small Business
- Marketing for a Small Business
- Starting a Small Service Firm
- Buying a Franchise
- Franchising Checklist
- Buying a Business
- Accounting and Bookkeeping in a Small Business

The Following can be downloaded from www.gov.ab.ca/edt/guides/index.html
- Starting a Small Business
- Starting a Home Based Business
- Marketing a Small Business
- Managing a Small Business

- Record Keeping for Small Business
- Financial Planning for a Small Business

British Columbia Ministry of Small Business, Tourism, and Culture (www.sbtc.gov.bc.ca)
- Small Business Start-up Kit

Solutions for Small Business (Download from www.tbc.gov.bc.ca/gasbc/publications/index.html)
- Exploring Business Opportunities: An Innovative Guide for BC Entrepreneurs
- Resource Guide for British Columbia Businesses: Guidelines and Requirements for Business
- Home-based Business Manual: Starting Your Home-based Business
- Business Planning and Cash Flow Forecasting for Business
- Resource Guide for BC Businesses (English, Punjabi, Chinese)
- BC Business Co-operatives
- Employee Share Ownership Program
- Equity Capital Program
- Overview of Government Assistance Programs
- Profile of Small and Medium Exporters
- RU Y2K BC?
- An Overview of Mentoring and Existing Mentoring Programs
- Starting Your Own Business: A Resource Guide for Women
- Starting a Business in Canada: A Guide for New Canadians

The following can be accessed at www.tbc.gov.bc.ca/gasbc/publications/solutions.html
- Interactive Business Planner

Associations and Other Organizations
Canadian Franchise Association (www.cfa.ca)

The following can be ordered from www.cfa.ca/pub.html
- The CFA "Guide to Buying a Franchise Business" Information Kit
  - Guide to Buying a Franchise Business
  - CFA's Membership Directory
  - The Pros and Cons of Franchising in Canada
  - The latest issue of Canadian Business Franchise Magazine
  - CFA Code of Ethics and Disclosure Document Guide
  - Checklist for Franchisees
- So You Want to Buy a Franchise (Douglas Gray and Norman Friend)
- How to Make Your Numbers Talk (Jason C. Orr)
- Where to Go When the Bank Says No (Gary Fitchet with Kathleen Aldridge)
- Franchising Your Business (the law firm of Siskind, Cramery, Ivey, and Dowler)
- So You Think You Need a Lawyer (Maureen F. Fitzgerald)
- What to Say When Your Customers Won't Pay (Judy Smith, Michael Shulman)
- 1999 Franchise Annual
- Canadian Business Franchise Magazine
- Franchising: So You Want to Be on the Leading Edge (Dennis Epstein, Horwath Orenstein, Chartered Accountants)
- Legal Considerations of Franchising in Canada
- Starting a Successful Business in Canada
- Protecting Trade Secrets

The following can be accessed at www.francon.com/canadian_facts.htm
- Franchise Statistics (Canada)

The following can be accessed at www.cfa.ca/members/affil.html
- Affiliate Member List

Dun and Bradstreet (www.dnb.ca/reference/cdnref.htm)
- Canadian Key Business Directory
- Canadian Regional Business Directory
- Guide to Canadian Manufacturers

Some Useful Contacts

Federal Government

Industry Canada (www.ic.gc.ca)
235 Queen St.
Ottawa, ON K1A 0H5
Phone: 613.954.2788
Fax: 613.954.1894

Foreign Affairs and International Trade Canada (www.dfait-maeci.gc.ca)
125 Sussex Drive
Ottawa, ON K1A 0G2
Phone: 613.996.9134 or 800.267.8376
Email: enqserv@dfait-maeci.gc.ca

Statistics Canada (www.statcan.ca)
Customer Inquiries
Tunney's Pasture
Ottawa, ON K1A 0T6
Phone: 613.951.8116 or 800.263.1136
Email: infostats@statcan.ca

Canadian Intellectual Property Office (www.ic.gc.ca)
Industry Canada
Place du Portage, Phase 1
50 Vicoria St., 2nd Floor
Hull, QC K1A 0C9
Phone: 819.997.1936
Fax: 819.953.7620
Email: cipo.contact@ic.gc.ca

Canada Business Service Centres (www.cbsc.org/main.html)

Canada/British Columbia Service Centre (www.sb.gov.bc.ca/smallbus/sbhome.html)
601 West Cordova St.
Vancouver, BC V6B 1G1
Phone: 604.775.5525 or 800.667.2272 (within BC)
Fax: 604.775.5520
InfoFax: 604.775.5515 or 800.667.2272
Email: olson.dave@cbsc.ic.gc.ca
- Small business planner
- Online workshop
- Top 40 questions
- Links

The Business Link (www.cbsc.org/alberta/index.html)
Business Service Centre
100 – 10237 104th St. NW
Edmonton, AB T5J 1B1
Phone: 780.422.7722 or 800.272.9675
Fax: 780.422.0055
InfoFax: 780.427.7971 or 800.563.9926
Email: buslink@cbsc.ic.gc.ca

Canada/Saskatchewan Business Service Centre (www.cbsc.org/sask/main-pages/main-menu.cfm)
122 3rd Ave. N.
Saskatoon, SK S7K 2H6
Phone: 306.956.2323 or 800.667.4374
Fax: 306.956.2328
InfoFax: 306.956.2310 or 800.667.9433
Email: saskatooncsbsc@cbsc.ic.gc.ca

Canada/Manitoba Business Service Centre (www.cbsc.org/manitoba/index.html)
PO Box 2609
250 – 240 Graham Ave.
Winnipeg, MB R3C 4B3
Phone: 204.984.2272 or 800.665.2019
Fax: 204.983.3852
InfoFax: 204.984.5527 or 800.665.9386
Email: manitoba@cbsc.ic.gc.ca

Canada/Nova Scotia Business Service Centre (www.cbsc.org/ns/index.html)
1575 Brunswick St.
Halifax, NS B3J 2G1
Phone: 902.426.8604 or 800.668.1010
Fax: 902.426.6530
TTY: 902.426.4188 or 800.797.4188
InfoFax: 902.426.3201 or 800.401.3201
Email: halifax@cbsc.ic.gc.ca

Canada Business Service Centre (www.cbsc.org/nf/index.html)
PO Box 8687, Station A
90 O'Leary Ave.
St. John's, NF A1B 3T1
Phone: 709.772.6022 or 800.668.1010
Fax: 709.772.6090
InfoFax: 709.772.6030
Email: st.johns@cbsc.ic.gc.ca

Canada/Ontario Business Service Centre (cbsc.org/ontario)
Toronto, ON M5C 2W7
Phone: 416.954.4636 or 800.567.2345
Fax: 416.954.8597
InfoFax: 416.954.8555 or 800.240.4192
Email: info@cobsc.org
Aboriginal Business Service Network
Phone: 877.668.2272
Fax: 416.973.2272

Team Canada Trade Enquiries
Phone: 888.811.1119

Info entrepreneurs (www.infoentrepreneurs.org/eng/index.html)
5 Place Ville Marie
Plaza Level, Suite 12500
Montreal, QC H3B 4Y2
Phone: 514.496.4636 or 800.322.4636
Fax: 514.496.5934
InfoFax: 514.496.4010 or 800.322.4010
Email: infoentrepreneurs@cbsc.ic.gc.ca

Canada/New Brunswick Business Service Centre (www.cbsc.org/nb/index.html)
570 Queen St.
Fredericton, NB E3B 6Z6
Phone: 506.444.6140 or 800.668.1010
TTY: 506.444.6166 or 800.887.6550
Fax: 506.444.6172
InfoFax: 506.444.6169 or 800.401.3201
Email: cbscnb@cbsc.ic.gc.ca

Canada/Prince Edward Island Business Service Centre (www.cbsc.org/pe/index.html)
PO Box 40
75 Fitzroy St.
Charlottetown, PE C1A 7K2
Phone: 902.368.0771 or 800.668.1010
Fax: 902.566.7377
TTY: 902.368.0724
InfoFax: 902.368.0776 or 800.401.3201
Email: pei@cbsc.ic.gc.ca

Canada/Yukon Business Service Centre (www.cbsc.org/yukon/index.html)
201 – 208 Main St.
Whitehorse, YT Y1A 2A9
Phone: 867.633.6257 or 800.661.0543
Fax: 867.667.2001
InfoFax: 867.633.2533 or 800.841.4320
Email: perry.debbie@cbsc.ic.gc.ca

Canada NWT Business Service Centre (www.cbsc.org/nwt/index.html)
PO Box 1320
8th Floor Scotia Centre
Yellowknife, NT X1A 2L9
Phone: 867.873.7958 or 800.661.0599
Fax: 867.873.0101
InfoFax: 867.873.0575 or 800.661.0825
Email: yel@cbsc.ic.gc.ca

Canada/Nunavut Business Service Centre (www.cbsc.org/nunavut/index.html)
   • In production at time of printing

Provincial Governments

British Columbia
Ministry of Small Business, Tourism, and Culture
6th Floor, 1405 Douglas St.
Victoria, BC V8W 9W1
Phone: 250.387.2065
Fax: 250.387.6055
Email: mike.cowley@gems4.gov.bc.ca
Web: www.sbtc.gov.bc.ca/index.html

Alberta
Alberta Economic Development
Industry Development Division
5th Floor, Commerce Place
10155 102nd St.
Edmonton, AB T5J 4L6
Phone: 780.427.6987
Fax: 780.422.0626
Email: adrienne.brown@gov.ab.ca
Web: www.edt.gov.ab.ca

Saskatchewan
Department of Economic Development
Head Office
1919 Saskatchewan Dr.
Regina, SK S4P 3V7
Phone: 306.787.2232
Fax: 306.787.2159
Email: bryon.burnett@ecd.gov.sk.ca
Web: www.gov.sk.ca/govt/econdev

Manitoba
Department of Industry, Trade, and Tourism
Small Business & Co-operative Development Branch
PO Box 2609
250 – 240 Graham Ave.
Winnipeg, MB R3C 4B3
Phone: 204.984.2272 or 800.665.2019
Email: manitoba@cbsc.ic.gc.ca
Web: www.gov.mb.ca/itt/index.html

Ontario
Ministry of Economic Development, Trade, and Tourism
900 Bay St.
Hearst Block
Toronto, ON M7A 2E1
Phone: 416.325.6666
TTY: 416.325.6707
Fax: 416.325.6688
Email: mcdtt-general@gov.on.ca
Web: www.ontario-canada.com

Quebec
Ministère de l'Industrie du Commerce
710, Place d'Youville
Québec, QC G1R 4Y4
téléphone: (418) 691-5950
télécopieur: (418) 644-0118
Email: info@mic.gouv.qc.ca
Web: www.mic.gouv.qc.ca/index.html
Or

770 rue Sherbrooke Ouest
Montréal, QC H3A 1G1
téléphone: 514.982.3010
télécopieur: 514.873.6279

New Brunswick
Department of Economic Development, Tourism, and Culture
PO Box 6000
5th Floor, Centennial Building
Fredericton, NB E3B 5H1
Phone: 506.453.3984
Fax: 506.444.4586
Email: wwwedt@gov.nb.ca
Web: www.gov.nb.ca/edt/index.htm

Nova Scotia
Department of Economic Development and Tourism
PO Box 519
World Trade Centre, Floors 5, 6 and 7,
1800 Argyle St.
Halifax, NS B3J 2R7
Phone: 902.424.8920
Email: econ.edt@gov.ns.ca
Web: www.gov.ns.ca/ecor/infocent/startbus.htm

Prince Edward Island
Department of Development
Shaw Building, 5th Floor
PO Box 2000
105 Rochford St.
Charlottetown, PE C1A 7N8
Telephone: 902.368.4240
Facsimile: 902.368.4224
Or

Enterprise PEI
PO Box 910
Charlottetown, PE C1A 7L9
Phone: 902.368.6300 or 800.563.3734
Fax: 902.368.6301
Email: invest@gov.pe.ca
Web: www.peibusinessdevelopment.com

Newfoundland
Department of Industry, Trade, and Technology
PO Box 8700
Confederation Annex
4th Floor
St. John's, NF A1B 4J6
Phone: 709.729.5600
Fax: 709.729.5936
Email: ittinfo@mail.gov.nf.ca
Web: www.success.nfld.net

Northwest Territories
Department of Resources, Wildlife, and Economic Development
PO Box 1320
Yellowknife, NT X1A 2L9
Phone: 867.669.2301
Fax: 867.873.0169
Email: Paul_Jones@gov.nt.ca
Web: www.gov.nt.ca

Yukon Territory
Yukon Economic Development
400 – 211 Main St.
Whitehorse, YT Y1A 2C6
Phone: 867.667.5466
Fax: 867.668.8601
Web: www.economicdevelopmt.yk.ca

Nunavut
Web: www.icon.gov.nu.ca
Email: icon@nunanet.com

Others

Canadian Franchise Association
Building 9, Suite 401
5045 Orbitor Dr.
Mississauga, ON L4W 4Y4
Phone: 905.625.2896 or 800.665.4232
Fax: 905.625.9076
Email: info@cfa.ca
Web: www.cfa.ca

International Franchise Association
900 – 1350 New York Ave. NW
Washington, DC 20005
USA
Phone: 202.628.8000
Fax: 202.628.0812
Web: www.franchise.org
Email: ifa@franchise.org

Canadian Venture Capital Association
301 – 234 Eglinton Avenue East
Toronto, ON M4P1K5
Phone: 416.487.0519
Fax: 416.487.5899
Email: kryan@cvca.ca
Web: www.cvca.ca

A Selection Of Canadian Venture Capital Companies

AGRI-FOOD EQUITY FUND
Regina (306) 787-0818
Focus: Agribusiness
(www.agr.giv.sk.ca/afef/index.html)

AGRIVEST CAPITAL CORPORATION
Calgary (403) 215-7720
Focus: Science & Technology
(www.agrivestcapital.com)

BUSINESS DEVELOPMENT BANK OF CANADA (BDC) VENTURE CAPITAL
Offices in Montreal (514) 283-8030, Quebec (514) 283-7542, Vancouver (604) 666-7814,
Toronto (416) 973-0034, Halifax (902) 426-7867 and Ottawa (613) 995-8835.
Focus: Most sectors
(www.bdc.ca)

CROCUS INVESTMENT FUND
Winnipeg (204) 925-2401
Focus: Manitoba

ELNOS
Elliot Lake, Ont. (705) 848-0229
Focus: Northern Ontario

FONDS DE SOLIDARITÉ DES TRAVAILLEURS DU QUÉBEC (FTQ)
Montreal (514) 383-8383
Focus: Small- & Medium-sized business
(www.fondsftq.com)

HELIX INVESTMENTS (CANADA) INC.
Toronto (416) 367-1290
Focus: Technology

McLEAN WATSON CAPITAL INC.
Toronto (416) 363-2000
Focus: Software and information technology
(www.McLeanWatson.com)

ROYAL BANK CAPITAL CORPORATION
Offices in Toronto (416) 974-5088, Montreal (514) 874-5081 and Vancouver (604) 665-0460
Focus: Knowledge-based industries
(www.royalbank.com/english/kbi/rbcc.html)

SASKATCHEWAN OPPORTUNITIES CORPORATION
Offices in Regina (306) 787-8597
Focus: Export-oriented and import replacement businesses
(www.gov.sk.ca/soco/)

SOFINOV
Montreal (514) 847-2613
Focus: Innovative technologies
(www.sofinov.lacaisse.com)

TD CAPITAL
Toronto (416) 982-6235
Focus: All sectors

TRIAX GROWTH FUND
Toronto (416) 362-2929
Focus: All sectors
(www.triaxcapital.com)

VENTURES WEST MANAGEMENT INC.
Offices in Vancouver (604) 688-9495, Saskatoon (306) 653-8887 and Toronto (416) 861-0700
Focus: Technology

WORKING OPPORTUNITY FUND
Vancouver (604) 688-9631
Focus: British Columbia
(www.wofund.com/wof)

WORKING VENTURES CANADIAN FUND
Offices in Saskatoon (306) 242-1023, Saint John (506) 652-5704, Halifax (902) 492-2292 and
Ottawa (613) 225-4775
Focus: All sectors

Helpful Web Sites

General Information

The Globe and Mail's Report on Business Magazine (www.robmagazine.com)
- Updated monthly
- Good general information for people trying to keep track of the Canadian economy and news as well as get some insight into different sectors

Profit guide (www.profitguide.com/profitguide/guide.asp)
- Rated links to sites that help you determine the best way to start your own business

Welcome to Alberta: Industry Alberta's Master Page (www.infostream.ab.ca/alberta/)
- Access and links to all Alberta's web sites for business, marketing, and alliances
- Lists of associations for prospecting
- Alberta Business Index

Western Economic Diversification Canada (www.wd.gc.ca/eng/content/advisor/index.html)
- Information on starting and planning a business
- General information of use to any small business owner

Human Resources Development Canada – Small Business Site (www.hrdc-drhc.gc.ca/common/employr.shtml#market)
- On-line Business Week Magazine
- Market and industry information
- Human resources planning
- Additional business links

Canadian Association of Family Enterprise (www.cafeuc.org)
- Find the chapter nearest you at www.cafeuc.org/about/chapters.html
- Personal advisory groups, mentoring, family councils – CAFÉ tries to look out for the family in family business
- Associate members welcome (those who would be of service to members)

CanadaOne (www.canadaone.com)
- Online magazine, business and resource directory, links to other great sites

Wall Street Journal Online (www.wsj.com)
- Mainly American information, but a comprehensive site, easy to move around
- WSJ Small Business Site (bd.dowjones.com/category.asp?CatID=9&gif=smallb&CatName=Small+Business)
  - Covers everything from e-commerce, starting a small business, women and minorities, and franchising.
- Entrepreneurial information links can be found at http://bd.dowjones.com/category.asp?CatID=131&TTop=9&gif=smallb&CatName=Entrepreneurs+%26+Start%2DUps
- Access small business reference information at http://bd.dowjones.com/category.asp?CatID=134&TTop=9&gif=smallb&CatName=Small+Business+Reference
  - Many of the links contain excellent information from starting a small business, to setting up a home office and making links in the business world.

The Canadian Industrial Innovation Centre (www.innovationcentre.ca)
- A site dedicated to helping inventors and innovators with information and resources related to market research, product and process engineering, international promotion, licensing and similar topics.

CNN Small Business Website (www.cnnfn.com/smbusiness/)
- American site
- General background information on business news
- Links to the CNN main site if you want to see what the headlines of the day are

Fortune Magazine (cgi.pathfinder.com/fortune/)
- American site
- Excellent for background business information and to get ideas
- Try the small business site at http://cgi.pathfinder.com/yourco/ to get some up-to-date information on the environment affecting your business

The Small Business Journal (www.tsbj.com/)
- American site
- Covers areas of interest to all small business owners
- Management, sales and marketing, financial, tax and legal, etc.
- Updated consistently

CCH Canadian Limited (www.ca.cch.com/frsub2a.html)
- This URL takes you right to the site map
- Information on taxes affecting Canadian companies
- Links to accounting and law firms

Khera Communications, Inc. (www.morebusiness.com/)
- An American site with good updated links and daily news about building a business, starting a business, getting more profit from your business, and business planning.

Globenet: The Globe & Mail Homepage (www.globeandmail.ca)
- Report on Business (www.globeandmail.ca/hubs/rob.html)
  - All kinds of general information on business and industry in Canada
  - Updated continuously

Home Biz Network (www.homebiznetwork.net/)
- Radio call-in show for home office entrepreneurs
- E-commerce
- Resource links

Strategis (strategis.ic.gc.ca/engdoc/main.html)
- Huge site contains information on everything you would ever want to know about business and markets. A must see, but don't get lost in the site.
- To get directly to the sitemap go to http://strategis.ic.gc.ca/engdoc/sitemap.html
- Main areas of interest are:
  - Company Directories
  - Trade and Investment
  - Business Information by Sector
  - Economic Analysis and Statistics
  - Research Technology and Innovation
  - Business Support and Financing
  - Licences, Legislation, and Regulation
  - Employment and Learning Resources
  - Consumer Information

CIBC Small Business Information Exchange (www.cibc.com/SmallBusiness/sbie.html)
- Links to other sites based on industry and geographic location

Entrepreneur of the Year Magazine (www.ey.com/industry/entrepreneur/eoy/magazine/default.asp)
- Excellent site for all kinds of information (e-commerce, succession plans, entrepreneur interviews)

Ernst & Young General Site (www.ey.com)
- Must view. Excellent site for everything from industry to specific interests
- Always changing

Quicken Small Business Centre (www.quicken.ca/eng/soho/index.html)
- Free software, marketing hints, developing a home office, online advice about small business and taxation
- Small Business Café
- The Quicken.ca Consultant
- Links to financing
- Easy to read and browse – appealing

Costco Online: Your Business (www.costco.com/frameset.asp?trg=Info/costconews/costconews.htm)
- General interest small business site
- New articles all the time. Covers areas of theft, women in business, franchising, mission statements, etc.

Assessing Your Personal Potential

Western Economic Diversification Canada (www.wd.gc.ca/eng/content/index.html)
- "Am I an entrepreneur?": Self-assessment quiz
- Links to the C/BCBSC OnLine Small Business Workshop

Business Development Bank of Canada Entrepreneurial Self-Assessment (www.bdc.ca/bdc/home/Default.asp)
- Online self-assessment test, gives immediate feedback and insight.

Atlantic Canada Opportunities Agency – Is Entrepreneurship for Me? (www.acoa.ca/english/frameset_main.html)
- A list of traits entrepreneurs have as well as links to CBSC and the Canadian Youth Business Council
- Financial Help
- Small Business Profiles
- Management Practices Questionnaire (www.acoa.ca/english/frameset_main.html)

Canada Business Service Centres (www.cbsc.org/main.html)
- Links to all the CBSCs, covering all areas of business
- Interactive Business Planners
- Online small business workshop
- Electronic commerce info-guide
- Local information
- Canada/British Columbia Service Centre (www.sb.gov.bc.ca/smallbus/sbhome.html)
- The Business Link (www.cbsc.org/alberta/index.html)
- Canada/Saskatchewan Business Service Centre (www.cbsc.org/sask/main-pages/main-menu.cfm)
- Canada/Manitoba Business Service Centre (www.cbsc.org/manitoba/index.html)
- Canada/Nova Scotia Business Service Centre (www.cbsc.org/ns/index.html)
- Canada Business Service Centre – Newfoundland (www.cbsc.org/nf/index.html)
- Canada/Ontario Business Service Centre (cbsc.org/ontario)
- Info entrepreneurs (www.infoentrepreneurs.org/eng/index.html)
- Canada/New Brunswick Business Service Centre (www.cbsc.org/nb/index.html)
- Canada/Prince Edward Island Business Service Centre (www.cbsc.org/pe/index.html)
- Canada/Yukon Business Service Centre (www.cbsc.org/yukon/index.html)
- Canada NWT Business Service Centre (www.cbsc.org/nwt/index.html)
- Canada/Nunavut Business Service Centre (www.cbsc.org/nunavut/index.html)

New Business Opportunities

Western Economic Diversification Canada – Selling to Government (www.wd.gc.ca/eng/content/selgv/index.html)
- Becoming a supplier
- Should you be selling to government? What does it take to win a government contract?

Canadian Company Capabilities (strategis.ic.gc.ca/sc_coinf/ccc/engdoc/homepage.html)
- Connecting buyers and sellers
- Links to other online directories
- Search for companies
- Register your company
- Update your company information

Business Opportunities Handbook (www.busop1.com)
- Links, opportunities, listings, articles, shows
- Excellent links, although most in U.S.

Franchising

Profit guide (www.profitguide.com/profitguide/guide.asp)
- Rated links to franchise sites – helps you determine best sites to hit and saves time.

Canadian Franchise Association (www.cfa.ca)
- Excellent list of publications, access to associates, member lists

Wall Street Journal Franchising Page (bd.dowjones.com/category.asp?CatID=169&TTop= 9&gif= smallb&CatName=Franchisers)
- Links to companies that provide franchise opportunities
- The franchising reference page is much better suited to people looking into franchising and can be accessed at http://bd.dowjones.com/category.asp?CatID=168&TTop= 9&gif=smallb&CatName=Franchising+Reference

The Franchise Handbook On-Line (www.franchise1.com/franchise.html)
- Franchise information
- Directory of franchise opportunities
- News from the franchise industry
- Expert advice
- Business opportunities

Be the Boss (www.betheboss.com)
- Provides detailed profiles of the franchises mentioned
- Reference to an extensive archive of articles on franchising

FranNet: The Franchise Connection (www.frannet.com)
- Has an extensive on-line reference library on franchising
- A U.S. company but you can connect with their Canadian offices as well

Protection of Intellectual Property

Canadian Intellectual Property Office (strategis.ic.gc.ca/sc_mrksv/cipo/welcome/welcom-e.html)
- Search patents on-line
- Trade marks
- Copyrights
- Industrial designs
- News
- Canadian and international links
- Events
- Frequently asked questions, background on intellectual property
- An excellent site for anyone considering the possibility of protecting their intellectual property

Financing

Profit guide (www.profitguide.com/profitguide/guide.asp)
- Rated links to small business banking sites
- Rated links to small business finance sites

Western Economic Diversification Canada – Accessing Capital (www.wd.gc.ca/eng/content/funds/index.html)
- Links to different lenders and the Small Business Loans Act

Business Development Bank of Canada (www.bdc.ca)
- Links to location nearest you, entrepreneur awards, student business loans, Profit$ e-zine
- Descriptions and links to Young Entrepreneur financing and Youth Business programs (www.bdc.ca/scripts/site/function-get-challenge.asp?&chk=1&language=eng &challenge=sec_head_youthbiz.gifqk248kq16)

Aboriginal Business Canada (abc.gc.ca)
- A list of Aboriginal Capital Corporations by region (strategis.ic.gc.ca/SSG/ab00011e.html)
- Entrepreneurship Development, financial and business development, strategic business development (strategis.ic.gc.ca/SSG/ab00009e.html)

Atlantic Canada Opportunities Agency – Venture Capital (www.acoa.ca/english/frameset_main.html)
- What Is It?
- Do You Have the Commitment?
- Is it for You?
- Are You Prepared?
- Links to Sources (many are national)

Canadian Venture Capital Association (www.cvca.ca/opportunities/index.html)
- Address and contact information is on the site

CIBC's Small Business Site (www.cibc.com/needs/business/) or (www.pcbanking.cibc.com/retail.html? SmallBusiness)
- Covers the areas of PC Banking, E-commerce, Internet Banking, Small Business Services, and Information Exchange.

Quicken Small Business Centre (www.quicken.ca/eng/soho/index.html)
- Free software, marketing hints, developing a home office, online advice about small business and taxation
- Small Business Café
- The Quicken.ca Consultant
- Links to financing
- Easy to read and browse – appealing

Strategis (Industry Canada) (strategis.ic.gc.ca/sc_mangb/sources/engdoc/homepage.html)
- An extensive database of links to financial providers for small and medium-sized business

Developing a Business Plan

Ottawa-Carlton Entrepreneurship Centre Business Plan Outline (www.entrepreneurship.com/bspl_eng.htm)
- A good business plan template indicating what should be included in each section

Moneyhunter Business Plan Template (www.moneyhunter.com/htm/btemp_dload.htm)
- A U.S. site reputed to have the best business plan outline on the Web

Canada/British Columbia Business Service Centre Business Plan Outline (www.sb.gov.bc.ca/smallbus/workshop/sample.html)
- Has a well-developed business plan outline plus a sample plan for a fictitious manufacturing company

Palo Alto Software (www.bplans.com/samples/index.cfm?affiliate=pas)
- Site contains sample business plans for a variety of businesses such as a consulting firm, flower importer, furniture manufacturer, golf pro shop, a coffee shop, a medical equipment company and a number of others

Profit guide (www.profitguide.com/profitguide/guide.asp)
- Links to business plan generators. All rated.

Business Development Bank of Canada Business Plan (www.bdc.ca/bdc/home/Default.asp)
- What is a business plan?
- Why do you need a business plan?
- Template
- Good especially if you are approaching BDC – they will want a well thought out business plan. You can make a business plan in literally thousands of different ways, so giving a plan to them in a format that they want is half the battle

Entrepreneurship Institute of Canada - Business Start-up Guides and Resource Books (www.entinst.ca/prod01.html)
- A list of guides and paperback books covering everything from starting and financing your business to business plans for particular industries
- Books must be purchased

Nova Scotia Economic Development and Tourism (www.gov.ns.ca/ecor/ced/busplan/)
- How to prepare a business plan. A sample business plan with text explaining the purpose of each section of the plan

Deloitte and Touche LLP: Developing an Effective Business Plan (www.dtonline.com/writing/wrcover.htm)

Canada Business Service Centres (www.cbsc.org/main.html)
- Links to all the CBSCs, covering all areas of business
- Interactive Business Planners
- Online small business workshop
- Electronic commerce info-guide
- Local information
- Canada/British Columbia Service Centre (www.sb.gov.bc.ca/smallbus/sbhome.html)
- The Business Link (www.cbsc.org/alberta/index.html)
- Canada/Saskatchewan Business Service Centre (www.cbsc.org/sask/main-pages/main-menu.cfm)
- Canada/Manitoba Business Service Centre (www.cbsc.org/manitoba/index.html)
- Canada/Nova Scotia Business Service Centre (www.cbsc.org/ns/index.html)

- Canada Business Service Centre – Newfoundland (www.cbsc.org/nf/index.html)
- Canada/Ontario Business Service Centre (cbsc.org/ontario)
- Info entrepreneurs (www.infoentrepreneurs.org/eng/index.html)
- Canada/New Brunswick Business Service Centre (www.cbsc.org/nb/index.html)
- Canada/Prince Edward Island Business Service Centre (www.cbsc.org/pe/index.html)
- Canada/Yukon Business Service Centre (www.cbsc.org/yukon/index.html)
- Canada NWT Business Service Centre (www.cbsc.org/nwt/index.html)
- Canada/Nunavut Business Service Centre (www.cbsc.org/nunavut/index.html)

Khera Communications, Inc. (www.morebusiness.com/templates_worksheets/bplans/)
- An American site with good updated links and daily news about building a business, starting a business, getting more profit from your business, and business planning

BizPlanit (www.bizplanit.com/vplan.htm)
- Provides a complete guide to creating a business plan

CIBC Business Focus (www.cibc.com/SmallBusiness/EN307.html)
- A comprehensive business planning software package that can be previewed and/or ordered via this web site

The Royal Bank's Big Idea for Small Business (www.royalbank.com/business/tools/bigidea.html)
- A free, downloadable, interactive software program designed to help you create a rudimentary business plan

TD Business Planner (www.tdbank.ca/tdbank/Small_Business/BUSPLANLIC.HTML)
- A free, downloadable business planning software template

Scotiabusiness Plan Writer (www.scotiabank.ca/Software.html)
- A user-friendly business planning tool that can be downloaded for free

Youth Entrepreneurs

Business Development Bank of Canada – Youth Business Site (www.bdc.ca/scripts/site/function-get-challenge.asp?&chk=1&language=eng&challenge=sec_head_youthbiz.gifqk248kq16)
- Descriptions and links to Young Entrepreneur financing and Youth Business programs

Atlantic Canada Opportunities Agency – Young Entrepreneur's Info Guide (www.acoa.ca/english/frameset_main.html)
- Market trends and opportunities in Atlantic Canada
- Financial Help
- Small Business Profiles

L'Association des Services d'aide aux jeunes entrepreneurs du Québec (SAJE) (www.saje.qc.ca)
- The site describes the association and what they do. If you are a resident of QC, between the ages of 18 and 35, and an entrepreneur or small business owner, you might want to contact them and see how they can help you with your business
- Site is in English and French

Canadian Federation of Independent Business – Links (www.cfib.ca/youth/links/Default_e.asp)
- Links to such sites as the Marketing Resource Centre, Entrepreneurship Centre

Aboriginal Youth Business Council (www.aybc.org)
- Business profiles
- Directories
- Networking email directory

Association of Collegiate Entrepreneurs (www.acecanada.ca)
- Site is dedicated to providing students with skills, resources and contacts to make sure their ventures are successful
- Links to other excellent sites for business start-ups and small business owners

Youth Business On-line Intervision Extra! Newsletter (www.cybf.ca/station/extra/extra.htm)
- Updated weekly, covers all areas for today's entrepreneur

Canadian Youth Business Foundation (www.cybf.ca)
- Includes the Intervision Extra! Newsletter
- Nicely laid out site dedicated to those considering starting a new business or young entrepreneurs with questions about improving their current business

Young Entrepreneur's Association (www.yea.ca)
- Simply describes the association and the benefits such as newsletter, networking, lower ticket prices for events

Women Entrepreneurial Business Owners

Business Development Bank's Step Up Training and Mentoring for Women Entrepreneurs (www.bdc.ca/scripts/site/function-get-challenge.asp?&chk=1&language=eng&challenge= sec_head_ecom.gifqk1173kq156)
- Outlines the program to help women develop and expand their companies

Centre for Women in Business (serf.msvu.ca/cwb/)
- Designed to help women start their own business
- Virtual women's business bureau, business counselling
- Centred in Atlantic Canada, a lot of good on-line information and guidance as well

Wall Street Journal Woman and Minorities Links Page (bd.dowjones.com/category.asp?CatID= 138&TTop=9&gif=smallb&CatName=Women+%26+Minorities)
- This site provides links to many other sites dealing with women and minorities in business. Concepts range from the Women's Internet Directory to Minority Enterprise Development

Beyond Borders: Canadian Businesswomen in International Trade (www.infoexport.gc.ca/business-women/beyond_borders/menu-e.asp)
- 7.6MB downloadable document in PDF format. Looks at the unique challenges faced by women involved in international trade
- Advice from successful women exporters
- Summary of findings

Women Business Owners of Canada Inc. (www.wboc.ca/)
- A not-for-profit business association representing the interests and concerns of women entrepreneurs across Canada
- Newsletter, on-line networking forum, database of women owned businesses and resources available to those women, and cost saving programs and services
- Links to other women business owner sites

Aboriginal Entrepreneurs

Aboriginal Business Canada (abc.gc.ca)
- Entrepreneurship Development, financial and business development, strategic business development (strategis.ic.gc.ca/SSG/ab00009e.html)

CIBC's Aboriginal Banking Site (www.cibc.com/aboriginal/home.html)
- CIBC's holistic approach to banking with the aboriginal peoples of Canada

Aboriginal Youth Business Council (www.aybc.org)
- Business profiles
- Directories
- Networking email directory

Business Development Bank of Canada (www.bdc.ca/scripts/site/function-get-challenge.asp? &chk=1&language=eng&challenge=sec_head_aborigbiz.gifqk249kq17)
- Aboriginal finance programs
- Links to other financial institution aboriginal finance programs

E-Commerce

Doing business on-line (www.canbus.com/dbo/cbnews.htm)
- Information and resources about how to approach your on-line presence
- Links to other e-commerce sites

Wall Street Journal E-Commerce (bd.dowjones.com/category.asp?CatID=165&TTop= 9&gif= smallb&CatName=Electronic+Commerce)
- The site includes links to other sites specializing in e-commerce

CIBC Small Business Internet Commerce Solutions (www.cibc.com/SmallBusiness/InternetCommerce/)
- Tools and links to IBM's HomePage Creator

Ernst & Young eCommerce (www.ey.com/ecommerce/default.asp)
- Case studies, alliances, solutions and descriptions of e-commerce.

Home Biz Network (www.homebiznetwork.net/ecommerce/mainecommerce.html)
- Radio call-in show for home office entrepreneurs
- E-commerce
- Resources links

Market Information

Strategis Business Information by Sector (strategis.ic.gc.ca/sc_indps/engdoc/homepage.html)
- Another section of the Strategis web site, contains information on business sectors, strategic information guides, guides to Canadian industries, changing articles.

Human Resources Development Canada – Market and Industry Information (www.hrdc-drhc.gc.ca/ common/employr.shtml#market)
- Links to other sites where you can gather information

Export Development Corporation (www.edc.ca)
- Export risk profiler
- Links to other sites
- Foreign market information

Atlantic Canada Opportunities Agency (www.acoa.ca)
- Market trends and opportunities in Atlantic Canada
- Financial Help
- Small Business Profiles

Canadian Federation of Independent Business Research (www.cfib.ca/youth/links/Default_e.asp)
- Provincial outlooks, publications, research reports

Canadian Chamber of Commerce — Library (www.chamber.ca/english/library/index.htm)
- The library contains information on the chamber's activities as well as publications of interest to someone looking into developing their business

PR Newswire (www.prnewswire.com)
- Excellent site to gather up-to-the-minute news when doing market or industry research
- Canadian News can be found at www.newswire.ca
- Want to export to Latin America? Check the markets at www.prnewswire.com

CIBC Economics Online (www.cibc.com/products/economics/)
- A look at economic indicators in the provinces
- Provincial forecasts
- Industry reviews

Export Source Foreign Market Research (exportsource.gc.ca/expkit_3F/navxx.html)
- From government and other sources
- Country Information
- Trade Statistics and Leads
- List of potential exporting partners.

Strategis (strategis.ic.gc.ca/engdoc/main.html)
- Huge site contains information on everything you would ever want to know

Southam Online – Business (www.southam.com/)
- This site provides links and search capabilities to look for past articles that may help you in the development of your business plan or market expansion

Exporting

Profit guide (www.profitguide.com/profitguide/guide.asp)
- Rated links to helpful export sites

Western Economic Diversification Canada – Going International (www.wd.gc.ca/eng/content/inter/index.html)
- Information on the International Trade Personnel Program, export readiness, and frequently asked questions.

Export Development Corporation (www.edc.ca)
- Export risk profiler
- Links to other sites
- Foreign market information

Business Development Bank of Canada Consulting Services – Exporting (www.bdc.ca/scripts/site/function-get-challenge.asp?&chk=1&language=eng&challenge=sec_head_exporting.gifqk245kq13)
- Initiatives and links to other export oriented sites.

Department of Foreign Affairs and International Trade's Info Export Site (www.infoexport.gc.ca/menu-e.asp)
- Everything you need to know about exporting from general questions to contacts and rules
- Links to other pertinent sites

Shedding Light on Exporting Services (exportsource.gc.ca/expkit_3F/navxx.html)
- Information from determining whether you have the skills to creating the plan and implementing it

PR Newswire Latin America Page (www.prnewswire.com)
- Excellent site to gather up-to-the-minute news when doing market or industry research
- Want to export to Latin America? Check the markets at www.prnewswire.com

Asia Week Online (www.pathfinder.com/@@M9oCjRGyMAMAQLOR/asiaweek/)
- A good site if you are looking at getting into business in Asia or exporting to Asia and want to get some background info. on the marketplace, politics, and general news.

ExportCanada.com (www.ExportCanada.com)
- A database of Canadian companies looking to expand into foreign markets

Glossary of Financial Terms

Accounts payable Money owed by a firm to its suppliers for goods and services purchased for the operation of the business. A current liability.

Accounts receivable Money owed to a firm by its customers for goods or services they have purchased from it. A current asset.

Amortization To pay off a debt over a stated time, setting aside fixed sums for interest and principal at regular intervals, like a mortgage.

Angels Private individuals with capital to invest in business ventures.

Assets The resources or property rights owned by an individual or business enterprise. Tangible assets include cash, inventory, land and buildings, and intangible assets including patents and goodwill.

Bad debts Money owed to you that you no longer expect to collect.

Balance sheet An itemized statement which lists the total assets and total liabilities of a given business, to portray its net worth at a given moment in time.

Bankruptcy The financial and legal position of a person or corporation unable to pay its debts.

Capital asset A possession, such as a machine, which can be used to make money and has a reasonably long life, usually more than a year.

Capital costs The cost involved in the acquisition of capital assets. They are "capitalized," showing up on the balance sheet and depreciated (expensed) over their useful life.

Capital requirement The amount of money needed to establish a business.

Capital stock The money invested in a business through founders' equity and shares bought by stockholders.

Cash discount An incentive provided by vendors of merchandise and services to speed up the collection of accounts receivable.

Cash flow The movement of cash in and out of a company. Its timing is usually projected month by month to show the net cash requirement during each period.

Cash flow forecast A schedule of expected cash receipts and disbursements (payments) highlighting expected shortages and surpluses.

Collateral Assets placed by a borrower as security on a loan.

Cost of goods sold The direct costs of acquiring and/or producing an item for sale. Usually excludes any overhead or other indirect expenses.

Current assets Cash or other items that will normally be turned into cash within one year (accounts receivable, inventory and short-term notes), and assets that will be used up in the operation of a firm within one year.

Current liabilities Amounts owed that will ordinarily be paid by a firm within one year. Such items include accounts payable, wages payable, taxes payable, the current portion of a long-term debt and interest, and dividends payable.

Current ratio Current assets divided by current liabilities. Used as an indication of liquidity showing how easily a business can meet its current debts.

Debt Money that must be paid back to someone else, usually with interest.

Debt capital Capital invested in a company which does not belong to the company's owners. Usually consists of long-term loans and preferred shares.

Debt-to-equity ratio The ratio of long-term debt to owner's equity. Measures overall profitability.

Demand loan A loan that must be repaid in full, on demand.

Depreciation A method of writing off the costs to a firm of using a fixed asset, such as machinery, buildings, trucks, and equipment over time.

Equity The difference between the assets and liabilities of a company, often referred to as net worth.

Equity capital The capital invested in a firm by its owners. The owners of the equity share capital in the firm are entitled to all the assets and income of the firm after all the claims of creditors have been paid.

Financial statements Documents that show your financial situation.

Fiscal year An accounting cycle of 12 months that could start at any point during a calendar year.

Fixed assets Those things that a firm owns and uses in its business and that it keeps for more than one year (including machinery, land, buildings, vehicles, etc.).

Fixed costs or expenses Those costs that don't vary from one period to the next and usually are not affected by the volume of business (e.g., rent, salaries, telephone, etc.).

Franchise The right to sell products or services under a corporate name or trade mark, usually purchased for a fee plus a royalty on sales.

Goodwill The value of customer lists, trade reputation, etc., which is assumed to go with a company and its name, particularly when trying to arrive at the sale price for the company. In accounting terms it is the amount a purchaser pays over the book value.

Gross margin or gross profit margin The difference between the volume of sales your business generates and the costs you pay out for the goods that are sold.

Income statement The financial statement that looks at a business' revenue, less expenses, to determine net income for a certain period of time. Also called profit-and-loss statement.

Industry ratios Financial ratios established by many companies in an industry, in an attempt to establish a norm against which to measure and compare the effectiveness of a company's management.

Intangible asset Assets such as trade names or patent rights which are not physical objects or sums of money.

Interest A charge for the use of money supplied by a lender.

Inventory The supply of goods, whether raw materials, parts, or finished products, owned by a firm at any one time, and its total value.

Inventory turnover The number of times the value of inventory at cost divides into the cost of goods sold in a year.

Investment capital The money set aside for starting a business. Usually this would cover such costs as inventory, equipment, pre-opening expenses, and leasehold improvements.

Lease An agreement to rent for a period of time at an agreed price.

Liabilities All the debts of a business. Liabilities include short-term or current liabilities such as accounts payable, income taxes due, the amount of long-term debt that must be paid within 12 months; and long-term liabilities such as long-term debts and deferred income taxes. On a balance sheet, liabilities are subtracted from assets; what remains is the shareholder's equity.

Line of credit An agreement negotiated between a borrower and a lender establishing the maximum amount of money against which the borrower may draw.

Liquid assets Cash on hand and anything that can easily and quickly be turned into cash.

Liquidation value The estimated value of a business after its operations are stopped and the assets sold and the liabilities paid off.

Liquidity A term that describes how readily a firm's assets can be converted into cash.

Long-term liabilities Debts that will not be paid off within one year.

Markup The amount a vendor adds to the purchase price of a product to take into account their expenses plus profit.

Net worth The value of a business represented by the excess of the total assets over the total amounts owing to outside creditors (total liabilities) at a given moment in time. Also referred to as book value.

Operating costs Expenditures arising out of current business activities. What it costs to do business — the salaries, electricity, rental, deliveries, etc., that are involved in performing the operations of a business.

Operating loan A loan intended for short-term financing, supplying cash flow support or to cover day-to-day operating expenses.

Overhead Expenses such as rent, heat, property tax, etc. (e.g., monthly, fixed, or variable) incurred to keep a business open.

Pro forma A projection or estimate. A pro forma financial statement is one that shows how the actual operations of the business will turn out if certain assumptions are realized.

Profit The excess of the selling price over all costs and expenses incurred in making the sale. Gross profit is the profit before corporate income taxes. Net profit is the final profit of the firm after all deductions have been made.

Profit-and-loss statement A financial statement listing revenue and expenses and showing the profit (or loss) for a certain period of time. Also called an income statement.

Profit margin The ratio of profits (generally pre-tax) to sales.

Quick ratio Current cash and "near" cash assets (e.g., government bonds, current receivables, but excluding inventory) compared to current liabilities (bank loans, accounts payable). The quick ratio shows how much and how quickly cash can be found if a company gets into trouble. Sometimes called acid test ratio.

Retained earnings The profits that are not spent or divided among the owners but kept in the business.

Return on investment (ROI) The determination of the profit to be accrued from a capital investment.

Term loan A loan intended for medium-term or long-term financing to supply cash to purchase fixed assets such as land or buildings, machinery and equipment or to renovate business premises.

Terms of sale The conditions concerning payment for a purchase.

Trade credit The credit terms offered by a manufacturer or supplier to other businesses.

Turnover The number of times a year that a product is sold and reordered.

Variable expenses Costs of doing business that vary with the volume of business such as manufacturing cost and delivery expenses.

Venture capital Funds that are invested in a business by a third party either as equity or some form of subordinated debt.

Working capital The funds available for carrying on the day-to-day operation of a business. Working capital is the excess after deduction of the current liabilities from the current assets of a firm, and indicates a company's ability to pay its short-term debts.

Step-by-Step Guide to the Spreadsheet-Based Financial Schedules (Diskette) for Building a Dream

This supplement is a spreadsheet-based tool to help you analyze the financial aspects of your new business idea. It will also facilitate preparation of the financial statements contained in Stage Seven to assess the feasibility of your idea or those in Stage Eleven that you will require for your comprehensive business plan.

The schedules contained in the spreadsheet model are based on the comparable figures in the book. However, they have been incorporated into a computer framework to simplify their completion for you. You do not have to be an accountant or understand much financial accounting to use these schedules. In fact, just the opposite is true. The principal idea behind the development of the model is to enable you to fill in some of the simple financial information and prepare a professional-looking set of statements to incorporate into your feasibility study or business plan.

Computer System Requirements

Before starting the program make sure you have the following computer hardware and software:

- An Industry Standard Architecture (ISA) computer such as an IBM PC or compatible or an Apple® computer capable of running on a Windows® based platform
- A graphics card compatible with Microsoft® Windows 95® or Windows 98®, such as an IBM VGA, EGA or Hercules graphics card
- At least a 486 33 megahertz processor; a Pentium 75 megahertz processor is recommended
- At least 4 megabytes of random access memory (RAM)
- Both a printer and a mouse are recommended
- Windows 95® or Windows 98® operating system
- Microsoft® Excel® Version 5.0 or Version 7.0 for Windows®

Setting Up the Program

While many parts of the model have been automated to save you time, a basic knowledge of the spreadsheets will be assumed. When commands are given for a spreadsheet operation the Microsoft® Excel® command sequence will be indicated.

Loading, Starting, and Running the Program

The following list can be followed when opening, starting, and running this program:

1. Open Microsoft® Excel® for Windows®.

2. Go to the **File Menu** and Choose **Open**.

3. A "Dialog Box" will appear. First, select the appropriate drive to access the model. When you have completed this, on the left hand side of the dialog box a list of all of the .xls files on that drive will appear. Click on **Main.xls** and then click on **OK**.

4. It will take a few seconds for the file to open, but you will notice at the bottom of the screen the words "opening Main.xls" and the blue squares moving to the right indicating how much longer it will take the file to open.

5. When the file is open, the main screen of the model will appear, with a list of all of the schedules available to you.

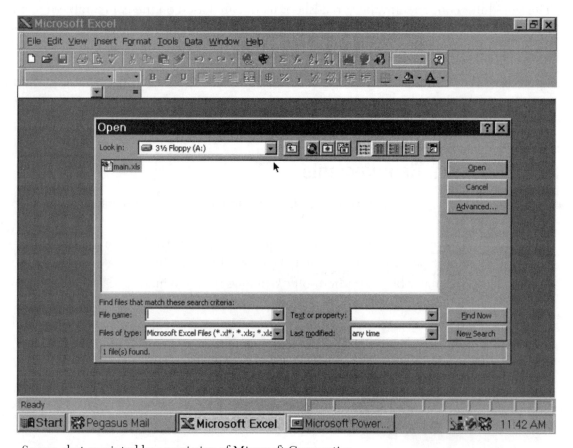

Screen shot reprinted by permission of Microsoft Corporation.

Using the Program

The following schedules are included in your spreadsheet model business plan:

- Required Start-up Funds
- Pro-Forma Income Statements
  - Most Likely
  - Optimistic
  - Pessimistic
- Pro-Forma 5-Year Income Statement
- Pro-Forma Cash Flow Forecast
- Pro-Forma Balance Sheet
- Financial Ratio Analysis
- Break-Even Analysis
- Return On Investment

It is probably best if you familiarize yourself with how this program operates before you begin filling in any information on the various schedules. At the bottom of the screen you will notice various tables with different file names, such as Main Menu and Cash Required for Start-Up. By clicking on any of these file names you can switch to that schedule and enter the necessary information. To view more of the files observe the arrows to the left of the file names. By clicking on these arrows you can scroll through the names of the various schedules (right or left depending on which arrow you press) and easily access any schedule you require.

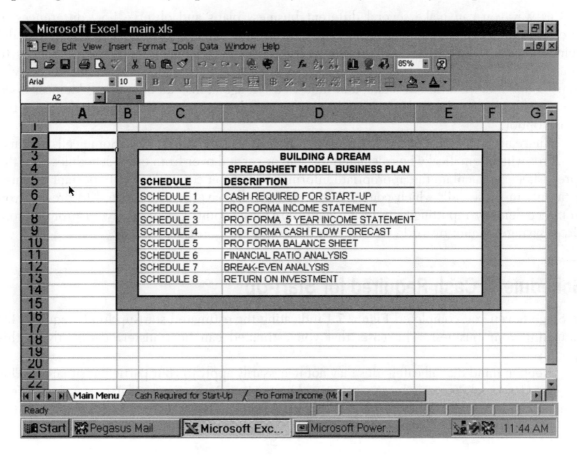

At any time it is possible to print any of the schedules individually or all of the schedules at once. Microsoft® Excel® utilizes the print to fit capability, which makes for an appealing presentation. To print any one schedule, first, go to that schedule. Second, press the icon which looks like a printer **OR** go to the **File** menu and choose **Print**. You will be presented with a dialog box asking if you wish to print the current sheet (which is one schedule) or the entire Workbook (which is all of the schedules and the main menu). Pick the circle of your choice by clicking on it, then click on **OK**.

If you are preparing the financial information for a complete business plan it is suggested that you start with Schedule 1. You should always complete one schedule before proceeding to the next, as some of the information needed in later schedules must be transferred from a previous one.

When preparing your business plan you may want to use a number of different forecasts, such as an optimistic, most likely, and pessimistic forecast. To do this, after entering any data and leaving the model, save the file under a different name. It is good practice to save the file under a different name anyway even if you only plan on creating one business plan, so that you always have one "clear" set of templates to come back to if you have made any mistakes.

To save the file simply:

1. Go to the **File** menu and select the **Save As** option.
2. A dialog box similar to the one used to open the model will appear. Click on the box containing the current model name in the top left corner and type in whatever you want the new model to be called (i.e., Main2.xls).
3. Select the drive to which you want to save your model. This is done the same way as when you opened your original model.
4. Click on **OK**.

In this way you can make several different business plans and observe how differences in forecasts can affect the performance outcome of your business. If you forget to save the model before you exit the file you will receive a prompt upon exiting asking "Save Changes to Main.xls?". Click on **Cancel**, and go back and follow steps 1 through 4. When you have saved your model under a different name, and want to use it again, instead of opening Main.xls open the new file name, Main2.xls. To exit the model, simply go to the **File** menu and choose the **Close** option.

There are blue zeros on the schedules indicating where to input data. Some cells containing zeros will automatically be calculated for you, or carried over from other schedules. For the spreadsheet to calculate the appropriate information for you correctly, it is important to enter data only in those cells which contain zeros. Some cells have been protected to prevent you from accidentally inputting data in an inappropriate location. If you receive a prompt from Excel saying "Cannot override protected cell," simply click on **OK**.

Schedule 1: Cash Required for Start-Up

In Stage Seven you completed Figure 7.1 indicating the estimated start-up funds required for launching your business. The costs that you estimated can be transferred directly to this spreadsheet.

Keep in mind that all categories may not necessarily apply to your particular situation. This is a generic model. You may have very general cost categories or you may have developed very specific requirements. You will have to do your best to assign your expected costs to the categories provided on the spreadsheet.

Schedule 1 — Required Start-Up Funds

Estimated Monthly Expenses

Item	Column 1 Your Estimate of Monthly Expenses Based on Sales of $_____ Per Year	Column 2 Number of Months of Cash Required to Cover Expenses	Column 3 Cash Required To Start Business (Column 1 X Column 2)*
Salary of Owner-Manager	$0	2	$0
All Other Salaries and Wages	$0	3	$0
Rent	$0	3	$0
Advertising	$0	3	$0
Delivery Expense/Transportation	$0	3	$0
Supplies	$0	3	$0
Telephone, Fax, Internet Service	$0	3	$0
Other Utilities	$0	3	$0
Insurance	$0	3	$0
Taxes Including Employment Insurance	$0	4	$0
Interest	$0	3	$0
Maintenance	$0	3	$0
Legal and Other Professional Fees	$0	3	$0
Miscellaneous - Travel	$0	3	$0

Total Cash Requirements for Monthly Recurring Expenses: **$0**

Starting Costs You Only Have to Pay Once

	Cash Required to Start Business
Fixtures and Equipment	$0
Decorating and Remodelling	$0
Installation of Fixtures and Equipment	$0
Starting Inventory	$0
Deposits with Public Utility	$0
Legal and Other Professional Fees	$0
Licenses and Permits	$0
Advertising and Promotion for Opening	$0
Accounts Receivable	$0
Cash	$0
Miscellaneous	$0

Total One-Time Cash Requirements: **$0**

Total Estimated Cash Required to Start Business: **$0**

*These Figures Are Typical for One Kind of Business. You Will Have to Decide How Many Months to Allow For Your Business

This schedule determines the funds that will be necessary to start your business. The first section of this schedule calculates the necessary cash you will need to have on hand to cover the monthly cash outflows of your business over the first few months of operations. The second section of this schedule calculates the one-time cash requirements that are necessary to begin operations.

Section 1

The cash outflows in section one are monthly expenses that will occur naturally as a result of operating your business. Over the first few months of operation the inflow of cash into your business will likely be insufficient to cover these expenses. Therefore, it will be necessary to ensure that you have enough funds on hand to cover these expenses over the first few months of operations. Some of these expenses will be the same from month to month and are known as fixed expenses. Fixed expenses do not vary with the level of sales or production of your business. Other expenses are variable, and may change from month to month depending on your projection of sales or production. Other expenses may actually be annual expenses, such as insurance, and will have to be divided by 12 before being entered into the sheet.

You should indicate your estimate of each monthly expense and enter it in column 1 of this schedule. For items such as "owner's salary" be sure to calculate a personal expense budget on the basis of the absolute minimum amount you will require to get by as the business will likely not be in a position to provide much cash to cover your own personal expenses. In estimating expenses it is always better to over-estimate and be pleasantly surprised at year-end than to underestimate and run the possibility of not having enough funds to continue operating your business. You may want to look at a few scenarios (pessimistic, most-likely, optimistic) to see how sensitive your need for start-up funds is to changes in the assumptions you have used to calculate your expenses.

In column 2 you can enter the number of months of cash you believe you will require to cover these monthly expenses. Default values for a generic small business have been inputted for you but you should consider whether these values are appropriate for your business. You should consider how soon cash will flow into your business (cash flows are developed further in schedule 4) and the type of payment arrangements you can negotiate. The schedule will multiply column 1 by column 2 for you to calculate the total funds you will require to cover initial monthly expenses.

Section 2

The second section of this schedule calculates the one-time cash requirements you will need to begin operations. These may be down payments that are required on furniture or fixtures or investments in accounts-receivables that will be necessary until collections from sales begin to flow in. Keep in mind that all categories may not apply to your specific business.

The sum of the requirements from section 1 and section 2 will give you a good approximation of the total funds that you will require to start up your business. These funds may be in the form of your own invested capital, long-term debt financing such as a bank loan, or short-term debt financing such as a line of credit. Some combination of the above financial instruments will likely be the most appropriate; the exact mixture again depends upon the specific requirements of your business.

Schedules 2 and 3: Pro Forma Income Statements

In your spreadsheet package there are three types of monthly income statements provided — Most likely, optimistic, and pessimistic. While it is not necessary to complete all three statements it is recommended and very useful. The most likely monthly income statement is provided in the model as Schedule 3. The optimistic and pessimistic monthly income statements can be found at the end of the model following the Return on Investment calculation. When completing the pessimistic forecast it may be useful to overestimate expenses or underestimate revenues or both. A pessimistic income statement will provide you with an understanding of the type of risk involved with your new venture. It is necessary to complete the most-likely monthly income statement to continue with future schedules.

The first row reflects your expected level of gross sales. Using the information generated from Figure 6.3 in Stage Six you will have to estimate your total market size and determine what you feel is an accurate estimate of your expected annual gross sales. You must also schedule when those sales will be realized throughout your initial year of operation.

- Your estimate of **Gross Sales** is an important figure since a number of other decisions are based on it. Your sales may fluctuate during the course of the year. You must decide when sales will rise and fall and reflect this seasonality in your monthly sales forecasts. Your forecasted sales from months 1 through 12 must add up to what you estimated as your total expected annual sales.
- Total expected **Cash Discounts** should be estimated.
- **Beginning Inventory** can be found on Schedule 1 as "Starting Inventory."
- **Purchases** can be a difficult figure for you to estimate. You should enter what you feel is an appropriate and reasonable amount. One method you can use is to purchase enough stock so that you can cover one-half or more of your next month's expected sales. An alternative method that can be employed is to schedule purchases to replace the stock you have sold. That is, if your sales equal 100%, and the expected Cost of Goods Sold in your retail business is 60%, then purchases equivalent to 60% of your sales would be required to maintain your inventory at a constant level. This method is simple and also allows you to readily determine the value of your Ending Inventory; it must always be the same as your starting inventory. This method, however, does not take into account expected seasonal sales fluctuations. Your estimated purchases are based on previous sales, not what you expect to sell in subsequent months. This may leave you short of inventory if sales are projected to increase dramatically.
- **Total** is the total of your Beginning Inventory plus Purchases. This calculation is performed for you.
- **Ending Inventory:** However you determine your expected purchases, you will need to know what is left in ending inventory.
- **Cost of Goods Sold** is simply the difference between the total available stock less your ending inventory. This calculation is performed for you automatically.
- **Gross Profit Margin:** Again this calculation is performed automatically for you.
- **Monthly Expenses** fall largely into two broad categories, "**Fixed**" and "**Variable**." It is suggested that you first fill in the initial month of the fixed expenses such as rent, telephone, and insurance. These expenses will automatically be transferred to the following months; however, you can change the expenses in the following months if you wish to do so.

Owner's Salary is an estimate of the monthly salary you feel you need to withdraw from the business in order to live.

Employees' Wages and Salaries vary, based in part on sales. In determining your expected employee costs, keep in mind minimum wage laws, holiday pay requirements, and deductions such as CPP and Employment Insurance, to which the employer must also contribute.

Delivery Expense is an expense that is dependent on your volume of purchases, and the number of times you order from your suppliers. If you order once a month, the delivery charge will likely remain reasonably constant from month to month. However, if you order more than once a month, or from different suppliers at different times, this will be constantly changing and needs to be projected.

SCHEDULE 2

Pro Forma Income Statement for (Company) for the Year Ending (Date)

	Month 1	Month 2	Month 3	Month 4	Month 5	Month 6	Month 7	Month 8	Month 9	Month 10	Month 11	Month 12	TOTAL
1. Gross Sales	0	0	0	0	0	0	0	0	0	0	0	0	0
2. Less: Cash Discounts	0	0	0	0	0	0	0	0	0	0	0	0	0
A. NET SALES	$0	$0	$0	$0	$0	$0	$0	$0	$0	$0	$0	$0	$0
Cost of Goods Sold:													
3. Beginning Inventory	0	0	0	0	0	0	0	0	0	0	0	0	0
4. Plus: Net Purchases	0	0	0	0	0	0	0	0	0	0	0	0	0
5. Total Available for Sale	0	0	0	0	0	0	0	0	0	0	0	0	0
6. Less: Ending Inventory	0	0	0	0	0	0	0	0	0	0	0	0	0
B. COST OF GOODS SOLD	$0	$0	$0	$0	$0	$0	$0	$0	$0	$0	$0	$0	$0
C. GROSS MARGIN	$0	$0	$0	$0	$0	$0	$0	$0	$0	$0	$0	$0	$0
Less: Variable Expenses													
7. Owner's Salary	0	0	0	0	0	0	0	0	0	0	0	0	0
8. Employee's Wages and Salaries	0	0	0	0	0	0	0	0	0	0	0	0	0
9. Supplies and Postage	0	0	0	0	0	0	0	0	0	0	0	0	0
10. Advertising and Promotion	0	0	0	0	0	0	0	0	0	0	0	0	0
11. Delivery Expense	0	0	0	0	0	0	0	0	0	0	0	0	0
12. Bad Debt Expense	0	0	0	0	0	0	0	0	0	0	0	0	0
13. Travel	0	0	0	0	0	0	0	0	0	0	0	0	0
14. Legal and Accounting Fees	0	0	0	0	0	0	0	0	0	0	0	0	0
15. Vehicle Expense	0	0	0	0	0	0	0	0	0	0	0	0	0
16. Maintenance Expense	0	0	0	0	0	0	0	0	0	0	0	0	0
17. Miscellaneous Expenses	0	0	0	0	0	0	0	0	0	0	0	0	0
D. TOTAL VARIABLE EXPENSES	$0	$0	$0	$0	$0	$0	$0	$0	$0	$0	$0	$0	$0
Less: Fixed Expenses													
18. Rent	0	0	0	0	0	0	0	0	0	0	0	0	0
19. Utilities (Heat, Light, Power)	0	0	0	0	0	0	0	0	0	0	0	0	0
20. Telephone	0	0	0	0	0	0	0	0	0	0	0	0	0
21. Taxes and Licenses	0	0	0	0	0	0	0	0	0	0	0	0	0
22. Depreciation	0	0	0	0	0	0	0	0	0	0	0	0	0
23. Interest	0	0	0	0	0	0	0	0	0	0	0	0	0
24. Insurance	0	0	0	0	0	0	0	0	0	0	0	0	0
25. Other Fixed Expenses	0	0	0	0	0	0	0	0	0	0	0	0	0
E. TOTAL FIXED EXPENSES	$0	$0	$0	$0	$0	$0	$0	$0	$0	$0	$0	$0	$0
F. TOTAL OPERATING EXPENSES	$0	$0	$0	$0	$0	$0	$0	$0	$0	$0	$0	$0	$0
G. NET OPERATING PROFIT (LOSS)	$0	$0	$0	$0	$0	$0	$0	$0	$0	$0	$0	$0	$0
H. INCOME TAXES (estimated)													$0
I. NET PROFIT (LOSS) AFTER INCOME TAX													$0

SCHEDULE 2
OPTIMISTIC

Pro Forma Income Statement for (Company) for the Year Ending (Date)

	Month 1	Month 2	Month 3	Month 4	Month 5	Month 6	Month 7	Month 8	Month 9	Month 10	Month 11	Month 12	TOTAL
1. Gross Sales	0	0	0	0	0	0	0	0	0	0	0	0	0
2. Less: Cash Discounts	0	0	0	0	0	0	0	0	0	0	0	0	0
A. NET SALES	$0	$0	$0	$0	$0	$0	$0	$0	$0	$0	$0	$0	$0
Cost of Goods Sold:													
3. Beginning Inventory	0	0	0	0	0	0	0	0	0	0	0	0	0
4. Plus: Net Purchases	0	0	0	0	0	0	0	0	0	0	0	0	0
5. Total Available for Sale	0	0	0	0	0	0	0	0	0	0	0	0	0
6. Less: Ending Inventory	0	0	0	0	0	0	0	0	0	0	0	0	0
B. COST OF GOODS SOLD	$0	$0	$0	$0	$0	$0	$0	$0	$0	$0	$0	$0	$0
C. GROSS MARGIN	$0	$0	$0	$0	$0	$0	$0	$0	$0	$0	$0	$0	$0
Less: Variable Expenses													
7. Owner's Salary	0	0	0	0	0	0	0	0	0	0	0	0	0
8. Employee's Wages and Salaries	0	0	0	0	0	0	0	0	0	0	0	0	0
9. Supplies and Postage	0	0	0	0	0	0	0	0	0	0	0	0	0
10. Advertising and Promotion	0	0	0	0	0	0	0	0	0	0	0	0	0
11. Delivery Expense	0	0	0	0	0	0	0	0	0	0	0	0	0
12. Bad Debt Expense	0	0	0	0	0	0	0	0	0	0	0	0	0
13. Travel	0	0	0	0	0	0	0	0	0	0	0	0	0
14. Legal and Accounting Fees	0	0	0	0	0	0	0	0	0	0	0	0	0
15. Vehicle Expense	0	0	0	0	0	0	0	0	0	0	0	0	0
16. Maintenance Expense	0	0	0	0	0	0	0	0	0	0	0	0	0
17. Miscellaneous Expenses	0	0	0	0	0	0	0	0	0	0	0	0	0
D. TOTAL VARIABLE EXPENSES	$0	$0	$0	$0	$0	$0	$0	$0	$0	$0	$0	$0	$0
Less: Fixed Expenses													
18. Rent	0	0	0	0	0	0	0	0	0	0	0	0	0
19. Utilities (Heat, Light, Power)	0	0	0	0	0	0	0	0	0	0	0	0	0
20. Telephone	0	0	0	0	0	0	0	0	0	0	0	0	0
21. Taxes and Licenses	0	0	0	0	0	0	0	0	0	0	0	0	0
22. Depreciation	0	0	0	0	0	0	0	0	0	0	0	0	0
23. Interest	0	0	0	0	0	0	0	0	0	0	0	0	0
24. Insurance	0	0	0	0	0	0	0	0	0	0	0	0	0
25. Other Fixed Expenses	0	0	0	0	0	0	0	0	0	0	0	0	0
E. TOTAL FIXED EXPENSES	$0	$0	$0	$0	$0	$0	$0	$0	$0	$0	$0	$0	$0
F. TOTAL OPERATING EXPENSES	$0	$0	$0	$0	$0	$0	$0	$0	$0	$0	$0	$0	$0
G. NET OPERATING PROFIT (LOSS)	$0	$0	$0	$0	$0	$0	$0	$0	$0	$0	$0	$0	$0
H. INCOME TAXES (estimated)													
I. NET PROFIT (LOSS) AFTER INCOME TAX													$0

SCHEDULE 2
PESSIMISTIC

Pro Forma Income Statement for (Company) for the Year Ending (Date)

	Month 1	Month 2	Month 3	Month 4	Month 5	Month 6	Month 7	Month 8	Month 9	Month 10	Month 11	Month 12	TOTAL
1. Gross Sales	0	0	0	0	0	0	0	0	0	0	0	0	0
2. Less: Cash Discounts	0	0	0	0	0	0	0	0	0	0	0	0	0
A. NET SALES	$0	$0	$0	$0	$0	$0	$0	$0	$0	$0	$0	$0	$0
Cost of Goods Sold:													
3. Beginning Inventory	0	0	0	0	0	0	0	0	0	0	0	0	0
4. Plus: Net Purchases	0	0	0	0	0	0	0	0	0	0	0	0	0
5. Total Available for Sale	0	0	0	0	0	0	0	0	0	0	0	0	0
6. Less: Ending Inventory	0	0	0	0	0	0	0	0	0	0	0	0	0
B. COST OF GOODS SOLD	$0	$0	$0	$0	$0	$0	$0	$0	$0	$0	$0	$0	$0
C. GROSS MARGIN	$0	$0	$0	$0	$0	$0	$0	$0	$0	$0	$0	$0	$0
Less: Variable Expenses													
7. Owner's Salary	0	0	0	0	0	0	0	0	0	0	0	0	0
8. Employee's Wages and Salaries	0	0	0	0	0	0	0	0	0	0	0	0	0
9. Supplies and Postage	0	0	0	0	0	0	0	0	0	0	0	0	0
10. Advertising and Promotion	0	0	0	0	0	0	0	0	0	0	0	0	0
11. Delivery Expense	0	0	0	0	0	0	0	0	0	0	0	0	0
12. Bad Debt Expense	0	0	0	0	0	0	0	0	0	0	0	0	0
13. Travel	0	0	0	0	0	0	0	0	0	0	0	0	0
14. Legal and Accounting Fees	0	0	0	0	0	0	0	0	0	0	0	0	0
15. Vehicle Expense	0	0	0	0	0	0	0	0	0	0	0	0	0
16. Maintenance Expense	0	0	0	0	0	0	0	0	0	0	0	0	0
17. Miscellaneous Expenses	0	0	0	0	0	0	0	0	0	0	0	0	0
D. TOTAL VARIABLE EXPENSES	$0	$0	$0	$0	$0	$0	$0	$0	$0	$0	$0	$0	$0
Less: Fixed Expenses													
18. Rent	0	0	0	0	0	0	0	0	0	0	0	0	0
19. Utilities (Heat, Light, Power)	0	0	0	0	0	0	0	0	0	0	0	0	0
20. Telephone	0	0	0	0	0	0	0	0	0	0	0	0	0
21. Taxes and Licenses	0	0	0	0	0	0	0	0	0	0	0	0	0
22. Depreciation	0	0	0	0	0	0	0	0	0	0	0	0	0
23. Interest	0	0	0	0	0	0	0	0	0	0	0	0	0
24. Insurance	0	0	0	0	0	0	0	0	0	0	0	0	0
25. Other Fixed Expenses	0	0	0	0	0	0	0	0	0	0	0	0	0
E. TOTAL FIXED EXPENSES	$0	$0	$0	$0	$0	$0	$0	$0	$0	$0	$0	$0	$0
F. TOTAL OPERATING EXPENSES	$0	$0	$0	$0	$0	$0	$0	$0	$0	$0	$0	$0	$0
G. NET OPERATING PROFIT (LOSS)	$0	$0	$0	$0	$0	$0	$0	$0	$0	$0	$0	$0	$0
H. INCOME TAXES (estimated)													$0
I. NET PROFIT (LOSS) AFTER INCOME TAX													$0

SCHEDULE 3

Pro Forma Income Statement for (Company) for the Year Ending (Date)

	End of Year 1	End of Year 2	End of Year 3	End of Year 4	End of Year 5
1. Gross Sales	0	0	0	0	0
2. Less: Cash Discounts	0	0	0	0	0
A. NET SALES	$0	$0	$0	$0	$0
Cost of Goods Sold:					
3. Beginning Inventory	0	0	0	0	0
4. Plus: Net Purchases	0	0	0	0	0
5. Total Available for Sale	0	0	0	0	0
6. Less: Ending Inventory	0	0	0	0	0
B. COST OF GOODS SOLD	$0	$0	$0	$0	$0
C. GROSS MARGIN	$0	$0	$0	$0	$0
Less: Variable Expenses					
7. Owner's Salary	0	0	0	0	0
8. Employee's Wages and Salaries	0	0	0	0	0
9. Supplies and Postage	0	0	0	0	0
10. Advertising and Promotion	0	0	0	0	0
11. Delivery Expense	0	0	0	0	0
12. Bad Debt Expense	0	0	0	0	0
13. Travel	0	0	0	0	0
14. Legal and Accounting Fees	0	0	0	0	0
15. Vehicle Expense	0	0	0	0	0
16. Maintenance Expense	0	0	0	0	0
17. Miscellaneous Expenses	0	0	0	0	0
D. TOTAL VARIABLE EXPENSES	$0	$0	$0	$0	$0
Less: Fixed Expenses					
18. Rent	0	0	0	0	0
19. Utilities (Heat, Light, Power)	0	0	0	0	0
20. Telephone	0	0	0	0	0
21. Taxes and Licenses	0	0	0	0	0
22. Depreciation	0	0	0	0	0
23. Interest	0	0	0	0	0
24. Insurance	0	0	0	0	0
25. Other Fixed Expeses	0	0	0	0	0
E. TOTAL FIXED EXPENSES	$0	$0	$0	$0	$0
F. TOTAL OPERATING EXPENSES	$0	$0	$0	$0	$0
G. NET OPERATING PROFIT (LOSS) (G = C - F)	$0	$0	$0	$0	$0
H. INCOME TAXES (estimated)	$0	$0	$0	$0	$0
I. NET PROFIT (LOSS) AFTER INCOME TAX	$0	$0	$0	$0	$0

Bad Debt Allowance will depend on your volume of credit sales and how liberal you are with your credit policies. The larger your credit sales, typically, the higher the required allowance for bad debts.

Legal and Accounting Fees are usually incurred at the beginning or the end of the year. These expenses must be entered at the appropriate time of the year. Taxes and Licences are also a once-a-year expense which must be accounted for at the appropriate time.

Telephone: You can usually expect your telephone expense to be fairly constant from month to month. However, there is one thing worth mentioning. Most utilities require an initial deposit. After some period this deposit is refunded to you, not all at once but as a reduction in your bill until the deposit is used up.

Depreciation is the notion of expending an asset over time. The equipment to be depreciated should have been reflected on Schedule 1. Depreciation is not an allowed expense under Revenue Canada regulations. It commonly must be added back to Net Income and the Capital Cost Allowance (CCA) taken. To save time and simplify the calculations we suggest that CCA be taken in lieu of Depreciation right from the start. For this purpose examples of the CCA allowance for different types of common assets are included in the Appendix on page 371 of this book.

- **Total Fixed Expenses** are totalled for you.
- **Total Operating Expenses** is the sum of Total Variable Expenses and Total Fixed Expenses.
- **Net Operating Profit (Loss)** will be the difference between your Gross Profit Margin and Total Operating Expenses.
- **Income Taxes** have been automatically calculated at 22% of Net Income. This is the general tax rate which applies to most small businesses in Canada. The formula also takes into account whether your expected Net Income is positive or negative. What the formula does not consider is that losses can be carried forward for a number of years and deducted from your future income. If this is the case, remember to deduct prior losses from future years' profits before determining Income Tax. If your Net Income is over $200,000 for one fiscal year the corporate tax rate is calculated at 48%.

The totals for year 1 financial projections should be carried over to Schedule 3, which is the Income statement for the first 5 years of operation of your business. You will need to go through these same steps for the subsequent years 2 through 5.

Supplement: Cash Budget Input Table

In order to schedule when Payments will come into your business and when you will have to make payments you need to estimate your collection and disbursement patterns. This will assist you in projecting the flow of cash through your business.

Your desired *Minimum Cash Balance* should be indicated and maintained constant throughout the planning period either from cash generated by the business or through borrowing. Your *Beginning Cash Balance* can be found on Schedule 1 as "Cash for Unexpected Expenses."

The *Collection Pattern* is an estimate of what percentage of your sales will be for cash, what percentage will be credit sales paid within 30 days, and the percentage which will be paid between 30 and 60 days.

The terms of credit that you extend will be an issue between you and your customers. In general, failure to extend credit can cost you sales that otherwise could have been realized. It is also true that the credit you extend becomes a risk to your business. Should you extend credit to your customers, your collection pattern may reflect this risk by not adding up to 100%. The percentage of your credit sales that may be uncollectible is referred to as a "bad debt allowance."

For your *Payment Pattern* the total of all percentages should add up to 100% and reflect the credit terms you are able to obtain from your suppliers. Your cash payments and payments within 30 days should be made to take advantage of any discounts your suppliers may offer. Any remaining payments are typically made within 30 to 60 days.

CASH BUDGET INPUT TABLE

**Minimum Required
Balance** _____

**Beginning Cash
Balance** _____

Collection Pattern		Payment Pattern	
% Cash Sales		% Cash Payment	
% Within 30 Days		% Within 30 days	
% 30-60 Days		% 30-60 Days	

Schedule 4: Cash Flow Forecast

The purpose of this statement is to help keep your business solvent. The business cycle depends on cash coming in from your customers and going out to pay your bad debts.

Your opening cash balance can be found on the above Cash Budget Input Table. For subsequent months after the first, your opening Cash Balance should be the greater of: the minimum required cash balance you indicated in the above table, or the balance remaining at the end of the previous month. Any deficiency should be made up by borrowing. Your minimum required cash balance should also be indicated at the top of Schedule 4.

Investment income and other cash income you expect to receive should be filled in as well.[1] One suggestion to keep in mind is, if your actual cash balance at the end of each month is greater than your minimum cash balance, the difference should either be used to pay down your outstanding debt or invested.

Expenses paid must be inputted manually. The remaining rows will be automatically calculated for you. At the bottom of this schedule is a line which reads "Meet Minimum Cash Balance." If the projections which you have made meet your indicated minimum cash balance the word "Acceptable" will appear. However, if your projections have left you with an ending period cash balance below your indicated minimum cash balance the word "Finance" will appear. In this scenario it is necessary to further finance your venture or find other sources of cash inflows.

---

[1] Cash received should be entered on the Schedule as a (+) number. Cash disbursments should be as a (−) number.

SCHEDULE 4

Pro Forma Cash Flow Forecast for (Company)
12 - Month Cash Flow Projections

Minimum Cash Balance Required = _____

	Month 1	Month 2	Month 3	Month 4	Month 5	Month 6	Month 7	Month 8	Month 9	Month 10	Month 11	Month 12	YEAR 1 TOTAL	YEAR 2 TOTAL	YEAR 3 TOTAL
Cash Flow From Operations (during month)															
1. Cash Sales	0	0	0	0	0	0	0	0	0	0	0	0	0	0	0
2. Payments for Credit Sales	0	0	0	0	0	0	0	0	0	0	0	0	0	0	0
3. Investment Income	0	0	0	0	0	0	0	0	0	0	0	0	0	0	0
4. Other Cash Income	0	0	0	0	0	0	0	0	0	0	0	0	0	0	0
A. TOTAL CASH FLOW ON HAND	$0	$0	$0	$0	$0	$0	$0	$0	$0	$0	$0	$0	$0	$0	$0
Less Expenses Paid (during month)															
5. Inventory or New Material	0	0	0	0	0	0	0	0	0	0	0	0	0	0	0
6. Owner's Salary	0	0	0	0	0	0	0	0	0	0	0	0	0	0	0
7. Employee's Wages and Salaries	0	0	0	0	0	0	0	0	0	0	0	0	0	0	0
8. Supplies and Postage	0	0	0	0	0	0	0	0	0	0	0	0	0	0	0
9. Advertising and Promotion	0	0	0	0	0	0	0	0	0	0	0	0	0	0	0
10. Delivery Expense	0	0	0	0	0	0	0	0	0	0	0	0	0	0	0
11. Travel	0	0	0	0	0	0	0	0	0	0	0	0	0	0	0
12. Legal and Accounting Fees	0	0	0	0	0	0	0	0	0	0	0	0	0	0	0
13. Vehicle Expense	0	0	0	0	0	0	0	0	0	0	0	0	0	0	0
14. Maintenance Expense	0	0	0	0	0	0	0	0	0	0	0	0	0	0	0
15. Rent	0	0	0	0	0	0	0	0	0	0	0	0	0	0	0
16. Utilities	0	0	0	0	0	0	0	0	0	0	0	0	0	0	0
17. Telephone	0	0	0	0	0	0	0	0	0	0	0	0	0	0	0
18. Taxes and Licenses	0	0	0	0	0	0	0	0	0	0	0	0	0	0	0
19. Interest Payments	0	0	0	0	0	0	0	0	0	0	0	0	0	0	0
20. Insurance	0	0	0	0	0	0	0	0	0	0	0	0	0	0	0
21. Other Cash Expenses	0	0	0	0	0	0	0	0	0	0	0	0	0	0	0
B. TOTAL EXPENDITURES	$0	$0	$0	$0	$0	$0	$0	$0	$0	$0	$0	$0	$0	$0	$0
Capital															
Purchase of Fixed Assets	0	0	0	0	0	0	0	0	0	0	0	0	0	0	0
Sale of Fixed Assets	0	0	0	0	0	0	0	0	0	0	0	0	0	0	0
C. CHANGE IN CASH FROM PURCHASE OR SALE OF ASSETS	$0	$0	$0	$0	$0	$0	$0	$0	$0	$0	$0	$0	$0	$0	$0
Financing															
Payment of Principal of Loan	0	0	0	0	0	0	0	0	0	0	0	0	0	0	0
Inflow of Cash From Bank Loan	0	0	0	0	0	0	0	0	0	0	0	0	0	0	0
Issuance of Equity Positions	0	0	0	0	0	0	0	0	0	0	0	0	0	0	0
Repurchase of Outstanding Equity	0	0	0	0	0	0	0	0	0	0	0	0	0	0	0
D. CHANGE IN CASH FROM FINANCING	$0	$0	$0	$0	$0	$0	$0	$0	$0	$0	$0	$0	$0	$0	$0
E. INCREASE (DECREASE) IN CASH	$0	$0	$0	$0	$0	$0	$0	$0	$0	$0	$0	$0	$0	$0	$0
F. CASH AT BEGINNING OF PERIOD	$0	$0	$0	$0	$0	$0	$0	$0	$0	$0	$0	$0	$0	$0	$0
G. CASH AT END OF PERIOD	$0	$0	$0	$0	$0	$0	$0	$0	$0	$0	$0	$0	$0	$0	$0
MEET MINIMUM CASH BALANCE	ACCEPTABLE	ACCEPTABLE	ACCEPTABLE	ACCEPTABLE	ACCEPTABLE	ACCEPTABLE	ACCEPTABLE	ACCEPTABLE	ACCEPTABLE	ACCEPTABLE	ACCEPTABLE	ACCEPTABLE	ACCEPTABLE	ACCEPTABLE	ACCEPTABLE

Schedule 5: Pro Forma Balance Sheet

A number of sections of the Opening Balance Sheet can be filled in as a result of decisions you have made in completing earlier schedules. There is no depreciation taken on assets for the first year. In subsequent years, all Fixed Assets except land and buildings should be depreciated by the appropriate Capital Cost Allowance. No depreciation should be taken on land.

Other Current Assets includes either marketable securities, bonds, term deposits, or guaranteed income certificates that are held in the company's name. You must fill in these values, if any.

Bank loans, notes payable, and long term liabilities will also be filled in by you. Keep in mind the portion of all outstanding loans to be repaid within the next 12 months is a current liability, and the portion that is to be repaid after 12 months is long term.

Capital structure will also have to be completed by you, reflecting the manner in which your business is legally organized.

Many of the figures involved in compiling the balance sheet for subsequent years will depend on your actions and the performance of your business. You will need to consolidate your statements at the end of each time period to develop the proper numbers that are needed to complete your Pro Forma Balance Sheet for the years 1, 2, and 3.

Schedule 6: Financial Ratio Analysis

In ratio analysis there are no right or wrong ratios. There are some ratios that serve as caution flags, and trends that can be analyzed. Many bankers will look at these numbers in assessing your financial capacity, so it is a good idea to know what goes into each of the formulas and how it may be affected by a change in your income statement or balance sheet.

The value of each ratio will be automatically calculated for each of your first three years of operation. Observe what happens to each ratio over time. This is more important than determining the absolute level of any one single ratio.

Schedule 7: Break-Even Analysis

This break-even spreadsheet will carry forward many of the expenses from your income statement in order to perform the break-even calculation. Break-even is a determination of the approximate number of units you will have to produce or sell in your first year of operation before you can start to make any money. If this figure is too high you may never make a profit. On the other hand, a low break-even point may indicate your business idea represents a significant profit opportunity.

Schedule 8: Return on Investment

This last schedule calculates your first year return on the capital you have invested in your business. This computation is performed for you automatically. ROI measures the earning power of your firm. Initially, you might expect this percentage to be low until your business gets established and off the ground. If, however, when you compute the expected ROI for subsequent years and the trend continues to be low, you need to ask yourself whether the expected return is sufficient to make the investment worthwhile.

SCHEDULE 5

Pro Forma Balance Sheet for (Company)

	Opening	End of Year 1	End of Year 2	End of Year 3
ASSETS				
Current Assets:				
1. Cash	0	0	0	0
2. Accounts Receivable	0	0	0	0
3. Inventory	0	0	0	0
4. Other Current Assets	0	0	0	0
A. TOTAL CURRENT ASSETS	$0	$0	$0	$0
Fixed Assets:				
5. Land and Buildings	0	0	0	0
less depreciation	0	0	0	0
6. Furniture and Fixtures	0	0	0	0
less depreciation	0	0	0	0
7. Equipment	0	0	0	0
less depreciation	0	0	0	0
8. Trucks and Automobiles	0	0	0	0
less depreciation	0	0	0	0
9. Other Fixed Assets	0	0	0	0
less depreciation	0	0	0	0
B. TOTAL FIXED ASSETS	$0	$0	$0	$0
C. TOTAL ASSETS	$0	$0	$0	$0
LIABILITIES				
Current Liabilities (due within 12 months)				
10. Accounts Payable	0	0	0	0
11. Bank Loans / Other Loans	0	0	0	0
12. Taxes Owed	0	0	0	0
D. TOTAL CURRENT LIABILITIES	$0	$0	$0	$0
Long-term Liabilities				
13. Notes Payable (due after one year)	0	0	0	0
14. Other Long-term Liabilities	0	0	0	0
E. TOTAL LONG-TERM LIABILITIES	$0	$0	$0	$0
F. TOTAL LIABILITIES	$0	$0	$0	$0
NET WORTH (Capital)				
SHARE CAPITAL				
Common Shares	0	0	0	0
Preferred Shares	0	0	0	0
RETAINED EARNINGS	0	0	0	0
G. TOTAL NET WORTH	$0	$0	$0	$0
H. TOTAL LIABILITIES AND NET WORTH	$0 BALANCED	$0 BALANCED	$0 BALANCED	$0 BALANCED

SCHEDULE 6

Financial Ratios for (Company)

			End of Year 1	End of Year 2	End of Year 3
1. Gross Margin/Sales	$\dfrac{\text{Gross Profit}}{\text{Net Sales}}$	=	$0 / $0 → #DIV/0!	$0 / $0 → #DIV/0!	$0 / $0 → #DIV/0!
2. Current Ratio	$\dfrac{\text{Current Assets}}{\text{Current Liabilities}}$	=	$0 / $0 → #DIV/0!	$0 / $0 → #DIV/0!	$0 / $0 → #DIV/0!
3. Quick Ratio	$\dfrac{\text{Current Assets - Inventories}}{\text{Current Liabilities}}$	=	$0 / $0 → #DIV/0!	$0 / $0 → #DIV/0!	$0 / $0 → #DIV/0!
4. Net Profit/Sales	$\dfrac{\text{Net Income (After Tax)}}{\text{Net Sales}}$	=	$0 / $0 → #DIV/0!	$0 / $0 → #DIV/0!	$0 / $0 → #DIV/0!
5. Net Profit/Net Worth	$\dfrac{\text{Net Profit}}{\text{Net worth}}$	=	$0 / $0 → #DIV/0!	$0 / $0 → #DIV/0!	$0 / $0 → #DIV/0!
6. Sales/Net worth	$\dfrac{\text{Net Sales}}{\text{Net Worth}}$	=	$0 / $0 → #DIV/0!	$0 / $0 → #DIV/0!	$0 / $0 → #DIV/0!
7. Fixed Assets/Net Worth	$\dfrac{\text{Fixed Assets}}{\text{Net Worth}}$	=	$0 / $0 → #DIV/0!	$0 / $0 → #DIV/0!	$0 / $0 → #DIV/0!
8. Current Liabilities/ Net Worth	$\dfrac{\text{Current Liabilities}}{\text{Net Worth}}$	=	$0 / $0 → #DIV/0!	$0 / $0 → #DIV/0!	$0 / $0 → #DIV/0!
9. Total Liabilities/Net Worth	$\dfrac{\text{Total Liabilities}}{\text{Net Worth}}$	=	$0 / $0 → #DIV/0!	$0 / $0 → #DIV/0!	$0 / $0 → #DIV/0!
10. Debt/Net Worth	$\dfrac{\text{Total Outstanding Debt}}{\text{Net Worth}}$	=	$0 / $0 → #DIV/0!	$0 / $0 → #DIV/0!	$0 / $0 → #DIV/0!
11. Return On Assets	$\dfrac{\text{Net Income (After Tax)}}{\text{Total Assets}}$	=	$0 / $0 → #DIV/0!	$0 / $0 → #DIV/0!	$0 / $0 → #DIV/0!

SCHEDULE 7   Break-even Point for First Year

Operating Expenses

Owner's Salary	0
Employee's Wages	0
Supplies and Postage	0
Advert. and Promotion	0
Delivery Expense	0
Bad Debt Allowance	0
Travel	0
Professional Fees	0
Vehicle Expense	0
Maintenance Expense	0
Other Variable Expenses	0
Rent	0
Utilities	0
Telephone	0
Taxes & Licenses	0
Depreciation	0
Interest	0
Insurance	0
Other Fixed Expenses	0

TOTAL OPERATING EXPENSES $0

$$\textbf{CONTRIBUTION MARGIN} = \frac{\text{Gross Margin}}{\text{Net Sales}} \qquad \#DIV/0!$$

$$\textbf{BREAKEVEN POINT (\$Sales)} = \frac{\text{Total Operating Expenses}}{\text{Contribution Margin}}$$

#DIV/0!

SCHEDULE 8   Return on Investment

Net Income (before Taxes)   [from Schedule 4]   = $0

Net Worth   [from Schedule 6]   = $0

$$\text{R.O.I.} = \frac{\text{Net Income (before taxes)}}{\text{Net Worth}}$$

=   #DIV/0!   %

Capital Cost Allowance Rates

Capital Cost Allowance (CCA) for a number of the more common types of business assets are listed below. These are only a few examples of the classes of asset to which CCA applies for tax purposes. For a more comprehensive listing of CCA classes, consult Chapter IV of the 1995 *Canadian Master Tax Guide*, published by CCH Canadian Ltd., or contact your local office of Revenue Canada.

ALPHABETICAL TABLE OF RATES

Item	Rate	Class
Aircraft	25%	9
Automobiles	30%	10
Buildings:		
Brick, stone, cement, etc.	4%	1
Frame, log, stucco on frame, galvanized, or corrugated iron	10%	6
Computer hardware and systems software	30%	10
Computer software	100%	12
Contractors' movable equipment:		
Normal	30%	10
Heavy	30%	38
Display fixtures (window)	20%	8
Electrical advertising signs	20%	8
Furniture	20%	8
Manufacturing and processing machinery and equipment	25%	39
Parking area	8%	17
Photocopy machines	20%	8
Telephone system	20%	8
Tools (under $200)	100%	12
Tools (over $200)	20%	8

Note: If using CCA rates, only 1/2 may be claimed in the first year.